Closing the Loop

Benchmarks for Sustainable Buildings

Susan Roaf, with Andrew Horsley and Rajat Gupta

Generously supported by

Chapter 39 'Post Occupancy Evaluation' © Adrian Leaman 2004

Published by
RIBA Enterprises Ltd
15 Bonhill Street
London EC2P 2EA

ISBN 1 85946 118 2
Product code: 33068

British Library Cataloguing in Publications Data.
A catalogue record for this book is available from the British Library.

Publisher: Steven Cross
Editor: Melanie Thompson
Commissioning Editor: Matthew Thompson
Project Editor: Anna Walters
Design and typesetting: Ben Millbank
Printed and bound by MPG Books, Cornwall

Contents

Section 4: Solutions

Section 5: Tools and techniques

Section 6: Appendices

Preface

It is appropriate that much of this book was written during the long hot summer of 2003. Temperatures during August soared to record levels, hitting a UK high of 38.1°C (100.6F) on Sunday 10 August in Gravesend, Kent. In France, the heat-wave is thought to have been to blame for some 15,000 additional deaths (largely among the elderly), while in England and Wales deaths rose by around 900 during the week ending 15 August.

Despite the headline-grabbing temperatures, most people are now aware that there is a link between human activity and the environment. The science of climate change is taught in schools, and sustainability and related environmental issues even feature in TV and radio soap operas. So it is fair to say that "environmental issues" have come of age. Indeed, it is 16 years since the international community signed the Montreal Protocol to eliminate the use of ozone-depleting substances, and in 2004 we will reach the 16th anniversary of the founding of the Intergovernmental Panel on Climate Change, which has provided robust scientific evidence of the global situation.

At the same time we have reached a point where academic research on the nature and extent of the damage we are causing to the planet has reached a critical mass – there is enough cumulative knowledge for us to have some certainty about what must be achieved and how to get there – and we are about to enter a period of change, where theory moves into practice. This book aims to bridge the gap between the two worlds; to set practitioners and their clients on the right route to making sustainable choices for all their projects and constituent communities alike.

But that does not mean the research will stop. In fact, it should increase. As more projects adopt the principles of sustainable construction, so there are more projects to analyse, and more data to gather to feedback into future projects, if we are to steer development in a genuinely more sustainable direction. Post-occupancy evaluation of our buildings is the link that will close the loop and guide us forward.

This book would not have been written without the inspiration and assistance of so many of my colleagues. Particular thanks are due to Rajat Gupta and Andrew Horsley for their chapters and their support; to my research and teaching col-

1

leagues at Oxford Brookes University – Fergus Nicol, David Hyams, Riki Therivel, and Julia Bennet; and thanks to Adrian Leaman, Bill Bordass, Sandi Halliday, Jim Ure and Dave Hampton. Thanks also to my editor, Melanie Thompson, and to the commissioning editor, Matthew Thompson.

On becoming a local councillor I realised how much I needed to know to make the best decisions for today and tomorrow. I dedicate this book to the people of Oxford – citizens, Council Officers and Councillors. I hope that it will provide a common understanding of where we should go together to future-proof our cities and settlements against the enormous challenges we face in the 21st Century, and in so doing, perhaps it will help to make a little more sustainable the lifestyles of our fellow men and women in all the settlements of the world.

Professor Susan Roaf
Oxford Brookes University
June 2004

section 1
Introduction

Introduction

A revolution is occurring within the building industry around the world. At last, people are actually asking to live and work in sustainable, comfortable, healthy buildings!

What has brought about this change?

The most important factor is the public's awareness of climate change. I think that the summer of 2003 will be seen as turning point in the *Zeitgeist*. In August 2003, climate change was first described as a "weapon of mass destruction"[1] and the World Meteorological Office issued its first ever global weather warning.[2] This was the year when heatwaves killed significant numbers in the developed world (some 15,000 excess deaths in France alone), and the sophisticated energy network – on which so many Western cities have become totally dependent – spectacularly failed in New York. It is also the year when former Environment Minister Michael Meacher MP made public the link between war, terrorism and the environment, in a blistering attack on the wars in Iraq and Afghanistan,[3] saying: "The overriding motivation for this political smokescreen is that the US and the UK are beginning to run out of secure hydrocarbon energy supplies."

We are now well aware of the strong link between people, buildings and climate:

- Buildings use so much energy – causing 50 per cent of all carbon dioxide emissions globally[4] – that existing systems can no longer reliably provide it.
- Buildings fail to provide conditions in which we can survive when the energy supply fails.
- Buildings cannot provide affordable survival conditions in many places, even when adequate power is available.
- Worst of all, buildings are using more and more energy, resulting in ever more emissions of greenhouse gases – in a vicious circle that drives climate change and makes it necessary to use more and more energy that we can't supply!

We are increasingly aware that human activity is responsible for numerous subtle changes in the environment over time, from the bleaching of coral reefs and the polluting of oceans by regular oil spills, to the damage to human health caused by harmful processes, materials and buildings. Such impacts are certainly

Figure 1.1 The three-way interaction between climate, people and buildings that dictates our energy needs

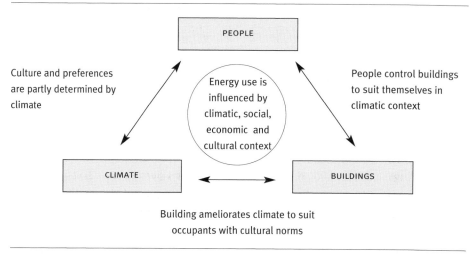

PEOPLE

Culture and preferences are partly determined by climate

Energy use is influenced by climatic, social, economic and cultural context

People control buildings to suit themselves in climatic context

CLIMATE

BUILDINGS

Building ameliorates climate to suit occupants with cultural norms

Source: Fergus Nicol

influencing the rising desire for change around the world.

And there is also a growing realisation that many modern cities and buildings are part of the problem instead of being part of the solution. For a long time we have known that there are major difficulties with much of 20th century architecture – with its often "modern", "minimal" and "brutal" designs.[5] Such buildings are often expensive to maintain,[6] too reliant on fossil fuels at a time when renewable energy technologies could provide a decent proportion of their energy,[7] driven by developers and clients who are obsessed with first cost issues,[8] and all too often poorly conceived and managed, thus never realising their full potential value.[9] The essays in this book's introductory section (Chapters 2 and 3) explore these issues further, first looking at the challenges from the architect's perspective, then considering the client's view.

The second factor is legislation. Of course, without public concern there would be no legislation, but the speed with which international law has been brought to bear on this matter is indicative of the size of the problem we face. In less than 20 years we have seen the introduction and ratification of international treaties – principally the Montreal Protocol, Kyoto Protocol and Agenda 21 – designed to limit the impacts of climate change and embrace sustainability. As we discuss in Chapter 4, the emphasis has now shifted from a predominantly top-down action programme to a more bottom-up process, with a developing range of implementation strategies, including a large number of related laws, taxes, tools and timetables developed since that first Earth Summit at Rio de Janeiro in 1992. We can only hope that it is not too little, too late.

In the UK there are two main drivers for change, and these have emerged as much from international and European legislation as from the domestic political agenda.

The European Buildings Directive (2002/91/EC) was formally adopted by the Council of Ministers on 16 December 2002, and published in the *EU Official Journal* on 4 January 2003. One aim of the Directive is to cut buildings-related carbon dioxide emissions by some 45 million tonnes by 2010. Under the Directive, member states will be required to introduce a general framework for calculating the energy performance of buildings (the methodology of which must be reviewed at least once every two years) and to enforce minimum standards of performance for all new buildings, plus renovations of existing buildings over 1000m². There will also be a requirement to ensure that boilers, heating systems and air-conditioning are inspected regularly; and that when new occupants take responsibility for a building, an energy performance certificate is made available (and displayed in all public buildings plus those visited by the public). Under the Directive every larger project will also be required to have a Strategic Environmental Assesment or Sustainability Appraisal done before planning consent is given for it.[10]

Member states have a maximum of three years in which to implement the provisions, by 4 January 2006, with a further three years allowed for the introduction of full certification and inspection of existing buildings, to allow time for the training of accredited experts to carry out the work.

I believe that the Buildings Directive will herald a paradigm shift – from the lightweight, tight-skinned, highly glazed and highly serviced buildings of the post-1950s era to a new sustainable architecture for the 2050s. Given the life expectancy of most buildings, those on the drawing board today (the buildings of 2005–2015) should be very interesting, as the new 21st Century building prototypes begin to make a mark.

The second significant driver will be the requirement for a Home Condition Report (HCR) to be produced when we sell our homes. Although the Buildings Directive will affect all of us in our homes, the HCR will be the more visible and political tool to drive through change.

A recent government consultation paper[11] invites views on a proposed information pack that home sellers and their agents will be required to have available when homes are marketed for sale. This "seller's pack" is an attempt to simplify and speed up the tortuous English housing market. But it will include an HCR, to be prepared by a qualified home inspector, and thus will provide home sellers, buyers and lenders with an objective report on the condition and energy efficiency of the home. An underlying aim of the report is to increase the marketability of more energy-efficient homes, or at least to further raise the public's awareness of domestic energy usage, but it will also fulfil the government's obligation (under Directive 2002/91/EC) to introduce energy performance certificates for dwellings. And not a moment too soon! Gas and electricity prices are begining to rise – by 10–20 per cent in 2003.

In the light of such developments we hope that this book is timely, and that it will help readers to deal with the changes that are undoubtedly on their way. However, it has another purpose.

A common language

We need to ensure that the aims, strategies and outputs required by governments are directly linked to the needs and aspirations of those at the bottom of the process: the people and communities who occupy buildings and cities – the people who will provide the machinery of change.

People are paramount in the process of sustainable development. A single person can change the mind-set of a whole community, local authority or government. This book contains many examples of what is already being achieved. But to truly succeed, we need a common language.

Our top priority is to ensure that we all clearly understand the issues at hand, how to measure and monitor them, how to report building progress against authoritative benchmarks, and how to use the results to plan our common future. This book aims to provide a common text that all the stakeholders can relate to, from government agencies, planners, architects, engineers and surveyors to estate agents, facilities managers, building owners, occupants and the communities around them. Sections 2 and 3 list indicators for social and environmental issues respectively and these, used wisely, should form the basis of a common language for, and understanding of, the issues of sustainable construction.

The book is all the more timely because we have now reached a certain degree of sophistication, where enlightened professionals and their clients are actively seeking and developing their own benchmarks. The trouble is that many existing benchmarks do not demonstrate "joined-up thinking". The scale of potential confusion is aptly demonstrated by the benchmarks for the single most important indicator of the 21st Century – carbon dioxide emissions. Not only is there no apparent vertical connection between the macro-indicators for global, national and metropolitan emissions, the meso-indicators at the level of individual building, and the micro-indicators at the level of a person or a product, but there is often no horizontal agreement about what benchmarks and target figures exist or should be attained! In the UK alone, we have targets set under the Kyoto Protocol, by the government and by the Royal Commission on Environmental Pollution; while a range of bodies gather and analyse data to calculate emissions and how we are progressing towards these various targets (see Table 10.1 for full details).

In addition, there are often significant differences between the predicted, modelled performance of many new buildings during the design phase, and their actual consumption in use, introducing a third dimension to the discrepancies that exist in the benchmarking process. We now know that predicted performance can be over three times better than that achieved in reality,[12] and what is interesting is that developers often continue to describe the building's performance using the predicted figures rather than upgrade them with the actual measured figures.

The question we all really need to answer is: "How green is this building?"

A number of environmentally conscious designers we have spoken to have expressed real frustration that they are losing out on design projects where the brief requires a "deep green building" to architects who claim to have designed "green" buildings in the past. Many of these claims go unchecked. This is reinforced by Rab Bennetts of Bennetts Associates...

"I would hope that, in this country, we're past the stage on environmental thinking where you can just call something green because you believe it's green. We actually have to find some way of quantifying it or rely on some scientific background to say: 'Yes, it really does help.'" [13]

...and Peter Clegg of Feilden Clegg Bradley.

"In terms of sustainability, well, how do you judge sustainability? It's very difficult to judge it visibly, isn't it? You need opinions, you need appreciation, and you need data. So it's an interesting question, isn't it? Sustainability is not something you normally think you see. Or if it is – if it [the architecture] did something you could see, then one has to be perhaps a little bit suspicious of it, because maybe it's not!" [14]

Something has gone very wrong here. Modern buildings appear to be actually getting less green year on year. Is it a problem of poor communications, or a lack of understanding? Or do people simply not care?

I think three factors contribute to this problem:

- problems with the planning system
- public–private partnerships
- RIBA plan of work.

Planning for sustainability

One significant factor behind the worrying drift to less sustainable buildings is the current planning process. At present there are no checks on the energy performance of a proposed building before it is granted planning permission. So the local council members who decide whether the building will get permission may do so simply because they feel the building is in character with a neighbourhood, or is of an exceptional "design" standard. But they will have no idea of the potential impact of the building in terms of, say, its greenhouse gas emissions, air pollution generated by traffic, health of the occupants, or the quality of life for those in the building. Elected councillors can give approval for buildings with huge environmental problems both internally and externally, and remain blissfully ignorant of the almost impossible task they have passed on to the Building Control Officer, who will need to try to make it conform (or appear to conform) to UK Building Regulations.

All this is changing fast, however. Pioneering steps have been taken by, for example, the London Boroughs of Brent, Ealing and Merton, which require that a "sustainability appraisal" be submitted with the original planning proposal. The appraisal describes how the building has been designed to reduce its environmental impacts over its lifetime. It is possible that soon all local authorities will be required to process such sustainability appraisals in all larger projects, where the technical evaluation of the performance and impacts of the building are given before the building gets planning permission.

Public–private partnerships

The term "public–private partnership" (PPP) describes any private-sector involvement in public services including the transfer of council homes to housing associations using private loans, and the contracting out of services such as rubbish collection or hospital cleaning to private companies. The Private Finance Initiative (PFI), the most popular form of PPP, refers to a strictly defined legal contract for involving private companies in the provision of public services, particularly public buildings.[15]

PPP schemes were introduced under the Conservative government in 1992 but did not take off until Labour took office. For example, according to the NHS plan,[16] more than 100 new hospitals will be provided using the PFI by 2010. In 2001–02 the PFI accounted for 9 per cent of public investment.[17]

Under a PFI scheme, a capital project such as a school, hospital or housing estate has to be designed, built, financed and managed by a private-sector consortium, under a contract that typically lasts for 30 years. The attraction of PFI for the government is that it avoids making expensive one-off payments to build large-scale projects that would involve unpopular tax rises.

However, the contracting consortium in PFI projects is responsible for almost all aspects of the performance of the building, from changing light bulbs to dealing with user concerns and complaints. It is clear that, in order to fulfil their obligations, the building's operators will need to gather in-use performance data, both from the building and from its occupants. With significant numbers of PFI schemes already in operation, and even more schemes in the planning and construction stages, such information is essential to provide invaluable feedback, to both designers and government departments, with which to guide future design and investment decisions, to assess performance over time and to provide legally substantial proof of that performance and, related quality of management. Current practice, however, shows that this important feedback loop – post-occupancy evaluation – is poorly developed, if it exists at all. This is obviously an area in which the construction industry needs to get its house in order, preferably before the first major PFI performance lawsuits are filed.

RIBA Plan of Work

In 1963 the Royal Institute of British Architects (RIBA) published its Plan of Work for Design Team Operation, in which architects' work was broken down into a sequence of tasks ranging from briefing/programming, through design, specification and tendering, to construction, completion and use. A final stage, M, was included to cover "feedback" – at which stage the architect would examine the overall results of the project.

In 1972 the RIBA removed Stage M from its publication on the Architect's Appointment, reportedly because clients were not prepared to pay for feedback as an additional service, and the RIBA did not wish to give the impression that feedback would be given as a matter of course. In 2003 – 40 years after Stage M first appeared – the RIBA Practice Committee has decided to re-introduce it into its published documents.[18] In future, as clients increasingly call for the highest standards of sustainable design, project teams will have to be able to demonstrate the performance of their past building projects. The inclusion of systematic feedback in projects will not only provide an invaluable learning tool for designers, but will be an effective marketing tool for practices – although it may not be welcomed by practices whose buildings have a track record of poor environmental performance.

The way forward

The only way we can intelligently face the huge challenges ahead is to employ an evaluation, monitoring and impact-reduction process, in effect a "sustainable building process", that will enable us to act in time – immediately, if necessary –

to make the changes we need to survive. As Bill Dunster notes:

"There isn't yet this understanding that the problems facing us are so severe, and so urgent, they require immediate action..."[19]

Sections 4 and 5 of this book describe a range of sustainable design options, and the various tools and techniques that can be used to investigate their success. Suffice to say here that there are two main issues that must be addressed by the construction community: closing the loop; and capacity building.

Closing the loop

Feedback and post-occupancy evaluation (POE) must now become central to the process of adapting to the changing climate. POE is discussed in some detail in Chapter 39.

If we do not "close the loop" between design and performance-in-use, we have no hope of steering the built environment towards a more sustainable future. Every building project should now incorporate a sustainability appraisal (SA), explaining the aims of the well-informed and well-developed design brief (B) that can be refined until clients, planners, building control officers and elected councillors are satisfied that they constitute an acceptable level of building performance for that building, community or location. These agreed criteria and benchmarks will form the basis for the design and construction phases of the building project and for the future feedback processes adopted by the building's managers.

A similar process is already common practice with good designers and clients,[20] but what is new would be the routine requirement to go back to the building, once complete, and measure whether the building has actually performed well, or badly, against the original criteria of the SA and the B. The results of this POE will then, by law, be reported in the building certificate or the home condition report, both of which will be periodically updated, either in an annual Environmental Auditing Process or at the point of resale.

Figure 1.2 shows how we might "close the loop". It is based on a diagram used in a presentation on risk, uncertainty and decision-making given by Richenda Connell of the UK Climate Impacts Programme (UKCIP).[21] Connell and her co-author identify risk analysis and feedback as being at the heart of the solution. They also point out that there is much uncertainty about the exact nature of future impacts on society, the environment, businesses and the economy, because our knowledge of the impact of climate is based largely on studies of the past, and this knowledge is, in itself, imperfect.[22]

For large businesses, it is important to have a very clear structure into which to fit the monitoring and management process. This is reflected in the huge success

Figure 1.2 The "framework to support good desision making" was developed by the UK Climate Impacts Programme (UKCIP)

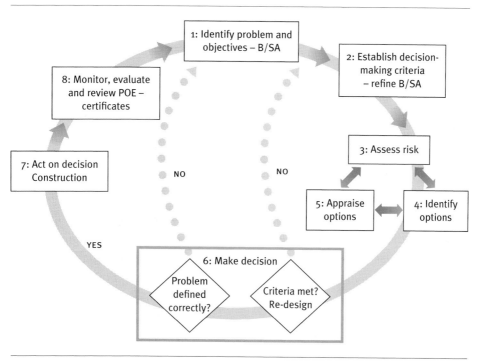

Source: *Climate Adaptation: Risk, uncertainty and decision-making*, Robert Willows & Richenda Connell (eds), UKCIP 2003

of the International Standards Organization's ISO14000, for environmental management schemes (Chapter 26). The success of this Standard really rests on the common sense of the process, which is a "virtuous circle": improve the environmental efficiency of your business, lower energy use and carbon dioxide emissions, and you will make your staff more satisfied at work and improve the community around you; then the business costs less to run, worker productivity improves, punitive landfill, energy and carbon taxes and tariffs are avoided, product prices lower or stabilise and profits rise. It also gives businesses a "green premium", because customers like to feel they are benefiting the environment through their purchases, and they like to know this is happening. In addition, many organisations, particularly government bodies, are now committed to "green purchasing policies" and will only sanction the buying of goods and services from demonstrably environmentally aware suppliers.

Capacity building

Each and every one of us is a stakeholder in the future. It will not be possible for many people, already stretched in their busy working lives, to become sustainability experts. However, we must all make the effort to understand the most important issues that directly affect our own lives. If the house uses too much energy, why? And how can improvements be made? If office workers are reporting high levels of sick building syndrome, what are the likely causes and what are the possible cures?

There is, however, a very strong case to be made for the routine use of "sustainability experts" in communities, buildings and businesses. Many local authorities already have an energy efficiency and renewable energy expert available at the end of a telephone line to help the public. (In Oxford City Council, for example, we have a Home Energy Efficiency information hotline that is now also associated with our Oxford Solar Initiative project.) Such advice should be universally available and more widely publicised, to give maximum access to expert information on how to improve the performance of buildings, as well as to advise on how to make the most of the many schemes that support energy efficiency and renewable energy measures.

Many large businesses already have a sustainability expert, either as a specialist or as part of their facilities management operations. Andrew Horsley, one of this book's authors, played just such a role in Carillion plc, and has first-hand experience to demonstrate that including an intelligent environmental design strategy within a project proposal can make the difference between winning a new contract or not. Julia Bennett, one of our contributors, played a similar role for WS Atkins. In addition to his research work, Rajat Gupta, a co-author of this book, is a building performance consultant to local practices and local authorities, currently looking at the performance of the homes in Poundbury, in the Duchy of Cornwall. And there are many other such specialist consultants in the field.

For large organisations, the expense of employing an expert is justified by the savings in running costs and projects won. For those who need advice only occasionally, the UK government runs a Design Advice Scheme,[23] which funds an initial consultation and a proportion of the costs for subsequent assistance.

In his book *Building Ecology*[24] the Australian Peter Graham proposes such a player in the building process. He calls sustainability experts "BEEs" – Building professionals who are Ecologically literate and Environmentally aware. His book is an exposition of what the problems in the built environment are and how the BEE can act to mitigate them. He would like all building professionals to be at least part-BEE at a time when so many people need rapid and robust advice.

The new breed of building performance experts will be very important to making the necessary changes happen in time, be it in the form of trained Home Energy Report or Building Certificate evaluators, designers or managers for the built environment. New training programmes for such professionals should be a real priority for the current government. And we need more postgraduate courses around the country, like the MSc on Sustainable Design and Energy Efficiency we run at Oxford Brookes University. Such courses are an essential part of the capacity building we need for the New Architecture of the 21st Century.

Conclusion

Sustainable buildings are not about fashion or style; they are about performance, resilience and adaptability.

What follows in this book is a palette of issues, indicators and benchmarks, techniques, methods, and tools – assembled from practices in the UK and around the world to give you an overview and an understanding of the complex challenges we must face if we are indeed to stabilise climate change, while maintaining an adequate quality of life for all, and survive. Because such processes, understanding and benchmarks, set in a "closed loop" are, quite simply, our planet's life-line.

References

1   Houghton Sir John (2003), "Global warming is a weapon of mass destruction", *The Guardian*, 28 July 2003, p 14
2   WMO (2003), "Extreme weather events might increase", Press release issued by World Meteorological Organization, Geneva, 2 July 2003
3   Meacher M (2003), "This war on terrorism is bogus", *The Guardian*, 6 September 2003, p 21
4   Adalberth K (1996), "Energy demand during the life cycle of a building", *CIB Symposium on Energy and Mass Flow in the Life Cycles of Building*, Vienna
5   Hackney R (1990), *The Good, the Bad and the Ugly*, Frederick Muller, London
6   Brand S (1997), *How Buildings Learn*, Weidenfeld & Nicolson, London
7   Rostvik H (1992), *The Sunshine Revolution*, Sun-Lab Publishers, Stavanger, Norway
8   Markus T, Maver T et al (1972), *Building Performance*, Building Performance Research Unit, London
9   Bordass B (2001), *Flying Blind: Everything you wanted to know about energy in commercial buildings but were afraid to ask*, Association for the Conservation of Energy and Energy Efficiency Advice Services for Oxfordshire, London
10 For the full text of the Directive see *http://europa.eu.int* and for a consise introduction to the process of Sustainability Appraisal see: Harridge C A, Mcallister I and Nicholson S (2002), *Guide to Sustainable Appraisal*, Town and Country

Planning Assosiation, London. Available from the TCRA, 17 Carlton House Terrace, London SW1Y SAS.

11 ODPM (2003), *Contents of the Home Information Pack: a consultation paper* Office of The Deputy Prime Minister, London

12 See "System boundaries: joining up actual energy consumption and modelled estimates", a presentation given by Bill Bordass of William Bordass Associates and the Save-EuroProsper team in March 2003 at *www.usablebuildings.co.uk*

13 Rab Bennetts of Bennetts Associates; research interview with Julia Bennett on 8 January 2003

14 Peter Clegg of Fielden Clegg Bradley; research interview with Julia Bennett on 9 January 2003

15 Weaver Matt (2003), "PFI: the issue explained", *The Guardian*, 15 January 2003

16 Ibid.

17 Ibid.

18 Bordass W and Leaman A (in press), "Making feedback and post-occupancy evaluation routine", in Preiser W and Vischer J (eds), *Assessing Building Performance*, Butterworth Heinemann, Oxford

19 Bill Dunster of Bill Dunster Architects; research interview with Julia Bennett on 7 January 2003.

20 Halliday S (2000), *Green Guide to the Architect's Job Book*, RIBA Enterprises, London; Hyams D (2001), *Briefing*, RIBA Enterprises, London

21 Willows R and Connell R (2003), *Climate Adaptation, Risk, Uncertainly and Decision-making*, UKCIP Technical report, UKCIP, Oxford. Available at *www.ukcip.uk*

22 Ibid.

23 See *www.actionenergy.org.uk*

24 Graham P (2003), *Building Ecology: First principles for a sustainable built environment*, Blackwell Science, Oxford

On-line resources

For an excellent discussion site on the implication of the Directive for UK buildings see: *www.europrosper.org*

For a comprehensive directory of related publications see: *www.sustainable-development.gov.uk/sdig/improving/partg/suscon/3.htm*

Further reading

Campbell C J (2003), "The peak of oil: an economic and political turning point for the world", in Low N and Gleeson B (eds), *Making Urban Transport Sustainable*, Palgrave McMillan, Basingstoke, pp 42–67

ICE (2003), *The State of the Nation 2003*, Report published by the Institution of Civil Engineers, London. See: *www.ice.org.uk*

IPCC (2001), "Climate change 2001: Synthesis report", a contribution of Working Groups I, II and III to Watson RT and the Core Writing Team (eds), *Third Assessment Report of the Intergovemmental Panel on Climate Change*, Cambridge University Press, Cambridge

IPCC (2001), "Climate change 2001: Impacts, adaptation, and vulnerability", Contribution of Working Group II to McCarthy JJ et al (eds), *Third Assessment Report of the Intergovemmental Panel on Climate Change*, Cambridge University Press, Cambridge

Rees P (2003), *Urban Environments and Wild Life Law: A manual for sustainable development*, Blackwell Scientific Publishers, Oxford

Royal Commission on Environmental Pollution (2000), *Energy – The Changing Climate: Summary of the RCEP Report*, The Stationery Office, London

Szokolay S (2003), *Introduction to Architectural Science: The basis for sustainable design*, Architectural Press, Oxford

The architect's perspective – briefing for sustainability

by David Hyams

Introduction

In order to discuss briefing in a meaningful way, it is useful to start by being very clear as to where value lies in a building. People are used to thinking of "value" as the market value of the building, but one could argue that this view is rather limited. For instance, value falls if the activities that the building was designed to support no longer exist: there are currently millions of square metres of floor area in England that have virtually no value because no one has activities to perform in them.

> "It is the way a building fulfils its function, and the efficiency with which it does it, that gives it value … The bricks and mortar are simply a means to an end; they do not provide any value in themselves … Although buildings are usually valued in accounting terms as assets, their value is generally not inherent; it is derived from their function … If the need that a building was built to fulfil disappears, then the building's value will derive from its ability to be adapted to an alternative use." [1]

To be a little blunt and perhaps obvious buildings are not put up in order to be sustainable or to reduce energy consumption, they are built and have value if they support activities that people want and need to carry out. This is equally true if they are built as an investment or as a product for sale or rent. It's the demand for an environment to support activities in a particular location that creates value. Briefing consists largely of identifying those activities and specifying the environment necessary to support them.

This chapter investigates the relationship between briefing and sustainability. It is written by David Hyams, an architect who specialises in briefing and strategic space planning. In 1993 David received an ARCUK award for research into briefing, and as well as running his own consultancy, he gives workshops at Oxford Brookes School of Architecture and elsewhere.

The briefing process

The information that drives a brief starts with a role statement. Any organisation larger than a family will usually have a business plan or some equivalent document containing a role or mission statement. This will state the purpose of the organisation and its aims and objectives. In order to fulfil its role, the organisation undertakes certain activities which can be observed or defined and recorded. The person writing the brief simply creates a description of the requirements for serviced, accessible, equipped space that will support those activities and allow for some future growth and change. Put into a practical framework, the logic of briefing can be summarised as:[2]

- Scope: what is the briefing problem?
- Role: what is the user organisation for?
- Activities: what do they *do* to fulfil their role?
- Draft requirements : what do they need to support what they do?
- Testing: is the draft brief feasible?
- Approval: does the amended brief go forward to design?

In this way of working, briefing is "defining the problem to which the design will be a solution". This implies a very real separation between defining the problem on the one hand, and solving it on the other: between briefing and design.

This may appear obvious, but how many architects still reach for their soft pencils to solve problems that have never been clearly defined and documented?

Alongside briefing there are a number of issues or constraints that tend to arise at the same time and which affect the brief but are not part of it. The constraints can be introduced at the feasibility testing stage. Some of these non-briefing areas are:

- winning the project
- fee negotiation
- budget
- programme
- site or building surveys
- feasibility studies
- procurement route
- selection of consultants and contractors
- planning consent
- a predilection for particular technical solutions, even environmentally friendly ones.

They are not brought in at the start of briefing because defining the brief against the constraints of the situation prevents the discovery of what is really needed to support the activities. At the same time, they need not be completely forgotten.

Guidelines and objectives

If the brief defines the problem, what should it consist of? Primarily it should describe the requirements that the building will fulfil. These requirements are of two sorts: quantified and guideline.

Guidelines are those objectives which it would be desirable to come as close to meeting as is feasible. For instance, the brief might state that a space should provide excitement and have a young feeling, or that public access should be maximised. The brief rightly avoids instructing the designer exactly how to achieve these objectives. Then there are quantified requirements, where specific measurable values must be met or at least targeted: these are the benchmarks, and they may cover many other areas in addition to environmental and sustainable.

Both quantified and guideline requirements have their place in the brief. Generally, if it is feasible to quantify a requirement, it should be done.

Looking at energy-efficient, sustainable design, there is a further distinction to be drawn between what space is needed and how it is to be provided. For example, a school building may be needed for educating children: that's the role of the school as an organisation. The building will be required to support classroom, library, sport, theatre, eating, play and other activities. The activities can be described, and spaces to support them can be defined and quantified. Moving into the detail, the brief may require that flooring is non-slip because that meets the needs of children. It might meet the objectives of the client to require that the building meets certain benchmarks for carbon emissions, but this requirement is rather different from requirements related specifically to activities. It is concerned with how the building is to be provided, rather than what it should consist of to support educational activities. The requirement is perfectly valid as a benchmark for performance, but suppose the brief stated that the benchmark for carbon emission should be met by, say, a heat sink, or by super-insulation. This crosses the line mentioned earlier between defining the problem and creating the solution. In most cases, the preference is to leave solutions to the design team and confine the brief to problem definition.

There are of course exceptions. Where a large client has a continuous building programme and certain solutions have been found to work in past projects, it makes sense to build on that experience, by specifying solutions in the brief for similar repeat projects. There are building types where the brief has been standardised. If role and activities are very similar, a standard brief has been produced. Hotel chains, supermarkets, petrol service stations, fast food restaurants all have standard briefs and often standard design elements. There is no reason why benchmarks for sustainable building should not be included in these. The domestic house has of course the most standardised of standard briefs.

There are few challenges to the standard brief, though standards of construction, services and equipment have evolved. There is not necessarily much to be gained by following this rigorous briefing procedure for housing, though benchmarks for environmental performance can of course be included. The process should in any case be tailored to the needs of each project.

Understanding the client's needs

Clearly, the best place to start ensuring that a building incorporates sustainable values is with the brief, and there it is linked with the "role statement". Unless there is a clear commitment to sustainability endorsed at the highest level in the user organisation, there will be no effective follow-through in the detail. Not only that but, for effectiveness, a sustainable building requires ongoing management in use, which can only come from commitment.

While checklists can be drawn up for smaller projects and more detailed design stages, here are some issues to explore with a client while looking at policy related to "role" in a larger project:

1. What is the client's policy on sustainable development?

- Does the client have a written policy on sustainable development?
- If so, how is the policy to be translated into action? Which of the following approaches most closely describes the client's position:

  - Conform to legal requirements and regulations
  - As above, but adopt sustainable solutions where savings can be shown in initial costs
  - As above, but adopt solutions where cost savings can be shown in initial and operating costs over two years, five years, ten years, or long term
  - The new construction and the operations it accommodates will be exemplary in terms of sustainable development, at an additional initial cost of two, five, ten, or more percent over the cost of conventional development.

2. Managing sustainability

- What strategy and plans are there for sustainability?
- Who is in charge of developing environmental policies?
- Who is in charge of setting targets, implementing, and monitoring them?
- What monitoring is being done in relation to existing buildings and operations?
- What targets have been set for energy use, waste water reduction or recycling, air-borne emissions, internal environmental standards, building user satisfaction, solid waste reduction, and so on?

3. Location and site

- What are the implications of location and site development for sustainability?
- Has a site been selected for the new construction? If not, have the following options been considered:

- redesigning operations so that additional space is not required (e.g through redefining the concept of the service or product provided, changing operational method, contracting out certain functions, or adopting new technologies)
- extending an existing building
- leasing additional space
- renovating a newly purchased building
- using a brown-field as opposed to green-field site

- Is it the client's policy to develop the proposed site so as to improve, and at least not degrade:

- the visual quality of the surroundings, by respecting the context
- local traffic pollution and congestion
- the quality of local water resources and watershed systems
- local and on-site wildlife habitat and planting
- minimisation of waste and pollution, air-borne, water-borne, liquid and solid
- cultural, amenity and employment opportunities for the local community (in larger projects)
- health, safety and environmental quality for staff, visitors and the local community
- respect for landscape features and local landmarks, both manmade and natural?

- In the case of large projects, will the local community be involved in comment and discussion early and during briefing and design, beyond the statutory minimum?

23

- Can development of the site be used to benefit the local economy?
- Is it the client's policy to involve local community organisations at an early stage?
- Will steps be taken to control noise, waste generation, traffic, water, and other pollution during construction? [3]

Of course, there are costs attached to decisions in the areas listed above, and there are limits to the control that developers have over some of the issues raised, especially on smaller projects. However, an initial commitment and determination to tackle some of these issues, when carried through into detailed briefing and design, will make a great difference to the final outcome.

Once these policy issues have been agreed, benchmarks can be set at each more detailed stage: for, clearly, briefing is not an event that occurs once at the start of the project. Rather it is a process conducted at least twice, and more in larger projects, of defining requirements in the necessary level of detail to inform each stage in the design.

Finally, the brief, and the benchmarks it contains are essential tools for evaluating the success of a building, post-occupancy. Benchmarks provide the essential tool against which to assess performance in use and user satisfaction.

References

1 Walker P and Greenwood D (2002), *Construction Companion, Risk and Value Management*, RIBA Enterprises, London
2 Hyams D (2001), *Construction Companion, Briefing*, RIBA Enterprises, London
3 Based on D Hyams, ibid.

The client's perspective – corporate social responsibility

by Dave Hampton of ABS Consulting

"We have no doubt that our attention to environmental and social sustainability contributes to the success of our business"

Tony Pidgley
Managing Director, Berkeley Group plc
(74th most profitable quoted company, 2001)

Introduction

As a client you might think: "Why do I need to worry whether or not my projects are sustainable developments? It's not my problem. I'm paying someone to worry about these things for me."

Well, that's fine if you are confident that the people in your employ will always aim to save you money!

Think, for a moment, about the buildings in your company's portfolio, or about the buildings you pass each day on your way to work. How many of them are fuel hungry 'gas-guzzlers', too hot in summer and too cold in winter, unsuitable for changing business needs, or worse – concealing future legislative burdens such as obsolete refrigerants, old plant, or poor fabric?

Now ask yourself: "How much would we be prepared to invest in a building if we could be confident that it would:

- provide capital growth significantly over and above the market in general
- be in the right place, not subject to flooding, and with firm foundations, and within a stable and established, healthy, diverse economy and community
- cost minimal amounts to run and, more important, produce a saleable export – energy
- be flexible and robust to change of use, with surface finishes that are all maintenance free
- be a landmark building loved by those who use it and by those who pass by?

25

Does this sound like an impossible dream?

In fact, there are a growing number of clients who are demanding buildings like this. These clients have embraced sustainability, and with it "corporate social responsibility" (CSR) – a business philosophy that not only brings them better buildings, but improves their businesses too.

Often, such clients start by investigating their use of resources – water, fuel, raw materials – and quickly identify opportunities to save money. The savings have an immediate impact on profitability but, more significantly, improving resource management has many knock-on benefits. For example:

- Management gets easier. It is generally easier to explain that you want people to do things the right way. (Getting people to do what they don't want to do can be as hard as "herding cats".) In turn, this means the company can attract, recruit and retain the best people into the business.
- Supply-side relationships improve. As suppliers become better acquainted with their clients' requirements and aspirations they join the "bandwagon", because they know that their own CSR performance could be used as a differentiator in the tendering and purchasing process.
- Marketing gets a new "edge". Promoting the results of your efforts to "go green" can win new clients, and help retain existing ones.

Gradually, the benefits of CSR will touch all aspects of the business and spread far beyond.

This chapter explores the link between sustainability and CSR, and outlines the core values and key mechanisms that underpin the CSR philosophy. It is based on a briefing paper by Dave Hampton of ABS Consulting which was presented to the CIEF Conference on Corporate Social Responsibility and UK Construction in London on 9 October 2002, and on material extracted from *The Construction Industry Council Client's Guide to Sustainable Construction*,[1] which he co-authored.

Sustainability for businesses

The Brundtland definition of sustainability[2] is:

"Development that meets the needs of today without compromising the ability of future generations to meet their own needs".

Sir Michael Latham[3] referred to sustainability as:

"Basic honour and common sense – for all of us and for the millions yet to be born."

For clients, and for the rest of us too, sustainability is actually about:

- sustained economic growth
- environmental protection
- social equity.

Traditionally, the performance of a business was judged on its financial results (the "bottom line"), which were, of course, crucial for survival. In the future, organisations will increasingly be judged according to whether they are in credit or deficit not just on the financial balance sheet, but also on the two other factors: the "triple bottom line".

What has brought about this change?

With a few notable exceptions (philanthropists such as Cadbury's, Barclays or Rowntree) the history of industrialisation is a story of squeezing the most out of natural resources – including people – to produce as much profit as possible. But by the second half of the 20th Century, many businesses were beginning to pay greater attention to their interaction with the world at large. The oil crisis of the 1970s, for example, highlighted the need for secure power supplies; a number of major industrial accidents prompted some businesses to clean up their act; and a greater awareness of industrial diseases brought others into the court room to fight claims from former employees made sick by their work. Society's reaction was to introduce legislation to force companies to change their dirty or dangerous practices, and the globalisation of trade has made international co-operation a necessity. Today the growth in the number of codes and standards seems relentless.

More recently, attention has turned to what might happen in the future. Scientific research has given us a much greater understanding of the impact we are having on the environment, and of the long-term damage that our activities can cause. We have also seen the development of well-organised pressure groups that raise the public's awareness of the various impacts of businesses. For example, in 2002 the UK government's own survey[4] found that the majority of people – consumers – were concerned about the environment. Of those surveyed, 66 per cent were "very worried" about the disposal of hazardous waste and 50 per cent were also very worried about the loss of plants and animals in the UK. Moreover, people have discovered that they can sometimes change corporate behaviour simply by boycotting products.

These days, any business that has its eye on the bottom line can't afford to ignore environmental or social issues because, although self-regulation is laudable, the need for change is so great that legislation is essential to ensure that even the most ostrich-like managing directors have to look to their "triple bottom line".

Some "eco-taxes" have already been introduced, and more will surely follow.

- In 2002 the UK government raised the cost per tonne of dumping waste in landfill sites, and will probably raise the level again in the near future.
- The Climate Change Levy – a tax on fuel – was introduced in April 2001 as an attempt to make businesses pay more attention to their fuel usage, encourage savings, and thereby reduce emissions.
- Future taxes may affect the consumption of water and raw materials, pollution and energy use.
- Company accounts may have to incorporate reports on environmental and social considerations; and pension funds and other investors may demand reporting of diverse business "impacts".

But there is a way to minimise the effect of yet more regulation, restriction and taxation – put your house in order now, before legislation dictates the route you must choose.

Corporate social responsibility (CSR) is a concept developed to encourage companies to combine profitability and sustainability. Its battle cry is:

"Do well by doing good."

CSR begins at home

The word "eco" comes from the Greek work "oikos", which means home. As individuals we live in homes. As a species we live on "Spaceship Earth". How well are we taking care of our spaceship? Are we "fouling the nest we live in"? Do we have a spare, if we foul up?

"Sustainability" can appear daunting and complex, but it can be summarised simply. All that is required for us all to enjoy our journey on "Spaceship Earth' is that we aim to observe Ray Anderson's four "home truths":[5]

- Put back what we take.
- Only make and use products that are non-toxic and can be broken down.
- Preserve the basis of the eco-systems and natural cycles that make the planet work.
- Uphold open and fair competition.

It seems obvious that "not fouling the nest we live in" is important to our long-term survival, but over what timescale? How radical a stance we choose to take, in this decade, is our collective decision – but how should we decide? This is where CSR becomes important. Stakeholders have views; it pays business to listen to them.

Ultimately, we are all stakeholders, but in business terms, stakeholders might include:

- shareholders
- employees
- suppliers
- customers
- the local community
- the Managing Director's children!

CSR has at least three streams:

- *Philanthropy and community involvement* has evolved from straightforward "good works" to sophisticated partnership projects, awards and indices such as those championed by organisations such as Business in the Community. The common theme is that "the community" is the central stakeholder.
- *Socially responsible investment* (SRI) is about investing funds according to ethical, social or environmental criteria. From a mainstream corporate perspective, SRI has always seemed a sideshow. Nevertheless today in the USA over $2,000 billion are invested in SRI funds. In the UK about half of the £800 billion in pension funds are run by managers who say they do take social, environmental and ethical considerations into account when making investment decisions.
- *Social auditing* was first introduced by George Goyder in his book *The Responsible Company*.[6] In the 1970s this came to mean something that was done to a company by an outside organisation – perhaps a hostile union or an environmental campaigning group. But by the mid-1990s the term had come to mean a systematic appraisal of a company's impact on its stakeholders made by the company and with assurance provided by an independent third party.

CSR was put firmly on the map when, in 1999, Kofi Annan, Secretary-General of the United Nations, called on the world's leading businessmen to initiate a "global compact" of shared values and principles that would give a human face to the global market.[7] His aim was that businesses should determine and embrace a set of core values that cover human rights, labour standards and environmental practices.

His speech resulted in the creation of the "Global Compact", sponsored by the World Economic Forum.[8] The Global Compact involves all relevant social actors: governments, who define the principles on which the initiative is based; companies, whose actions it seeks to influence; labour, in whose hands the process of global production takes place; civil society organisations, representing the wider community of stakeholders; and the United Nations as an authoritative convener and facilitator.

CSR Europe[9] emerged from this platform, and now has over 30 members and access to more than 1000 European businesses through 15 national partner organisations. These businesses, and others outside Europe, are proof that it is possible to care about and respond to *all* stakeholders . . . including shareholders. They have realised that, while conventional economic models and approaches have served us well in the past, it is important to retain an open mind to the idea that new economic systems are emerging – and they might serve us better.

CSR and construction

Another useful way of looking at sustainability is that we should aim to "live off our (planetary) income and not dig into our capital". In other words, we must learn to "live on the planet as if we intend to stay here" . And funnily enough, designing, constructing and operating buildings in this same way is a good start. We should ask: "How would we go about building a home if we knew it was to be the family home for generations to come?"[10] At the same time, we should be aware that, if there is waste anywhere, someone is paying for it. In other words:

"A zero waste objective is a zero loss game."

Think about it like this: in very general terms, for every "unit" spent on designing buildings, we spend five units on construction, and 20–50 units on operating that building over its lifetime. (Compare this with the 200–500 units spent on the occupants' salaries.) If we can design a building that costs, say, half as much to run (saving 10–25 units) and which makes the occupants, say, 10 per cent more productive (saving 20–50 units), then in theory it is possible to justify spending not double, but ten times the amount on the design stage.

Unfortunately, it's not that simple. Capital budgets and operating budgets are not the same "type" of money, and those who pay the running costs are frequently not the owners. However, lower running costs will make the building more rentable and saleable in the future, because good businesses will avoid occupying a building that's going to cost them more money to run than the one next door that looks exactly the same.

Our aim should always be to create "fit buildings":

- fit for purpose
- fit for the planet
- fit for people.

Fit for purpose

Fit buildings are ones that take all the considerations into account without compromise, not just for the immediate future, but for the whole life cycle including final decommissioning. This requires a multidisciplinary approach and teamwork. Some clients are already asking for "environmental co-ordinator" to be appointed to their design teams to add value by providing an "over-arching" sustainability framework.[11]

Bear in mind that at present the best features of a building are too often crossed off the "wish list" at the design stage, purely because of the initial cost. Remember too that final occupiers/end users of the building are not often involved in the design process, but their needs must be met.

Fit for the planet

As the Environment section of this book demonstrates, there are many ways that a building can interact with the environment. At the very least, clients should pay particular attention to the energy use of a building. Half of all *electricity* generated in the UK is used to power and maintain buildings. This figure could be halved for individual buildings if clients put energy efficiency (and the use of electricity from renewable sources) at the top of their "wish list" at the briefing stage for architects and building services engineers. This will not only cut fuel bills; it will also make the building easier to sell because it is likely that in future all buildings – not only houses – will be given energy efficiency ratings, as is already done for domestic appliances.

Refurbishment projects are a good opportunity to make existing buildings more energy efficient. Clients must ensure that designers routinely consider introducing energy-saving improvements such as eliminating the need for air-conditioning, optimising lighting or making the most of daylight, or even introducing combined heat and power (CHP) systems. This is also a chance to make a flagship statement such as installing solar panels. The initial cost of any of these features might be a little more than a conventional choice, but life cycle cost analysis will quickly prove how much it will save over time (see Chapter 29). Again, this information will make the building easier to rent out or sell, and make your company look good in the process.

Above all, give the designers a "performance benchmark" to work from – this book will help you to choose the indicators more appropriate to your project – but make sure that you stress that the benchmarks you give are the minimum performance you will accept.

Fit for people

CSR is about concern for people, their health and safety, and our shared wider environment. Respect for the welfare of all people – whether staff, customers, the local community, or society at large – is a tall order and a long journey, but all journeys start with one step.

If the occupants like their working environment, their performance will improve; and that will increase customer satisfaction too. Although there is still much to learn about the way buildings affect staff, a good starting point is to thoroughly assess requirements before a project begins. Keeping the dialogue going during the project is essential too; but do not stop talking once the staff have moved in. Post-occupancy evaluation, perhaps using the "overall liking score" technique described in Chapter 34, is an excellent way to find out whether design strategies have worked, whether improvements are needed, and whether methods can be taken forward to subsequent projects.

And what about the neighbours? The social sustainability aspect of CSR is about acknowledging the needs of all the stakeholders in a project throughout the process, from inception to demolition. In general the stakeholders will be you (the client), the workforce, suppliers and the immediate community. By recognising the needs of all these groups you are more likely to achieve a high standard of customer satisfaction.

There is no compromise

If you still doubt whether all this applies to you then consider reading Ray Anderson's book.[12] Ray is Founder Chairman and former CEO of Interface, a leading interior furnishing company. The book recounts his awakening to a new way of conducting business – a way that not only halts any damage being done, and

---

Fitness testing

Use these key mechanisms to incorporate your sustainability concerns into the building process:
- project risk analysis
- briefing – design, function and requirement
- legislative and planning requirements
- costs – life cycle costing; running costs
- value engineering
- building performance evaluation – before, during and after construction.

is benign, but which positively "puts something back". In just six years the company cut its emissions by more than a quarter.

Amory Lovins, CEO of the Rocky Mountain Institute, and named by the *Wall Street Journal* as one of 28 people worldwide "most likely to change the course of business in the 90s", has suggested that buildings should:

> ". . . *create delight when entered, harmony when occupied, regret when departed.*"[13]

Do we have examples of buildings that match up to this tall order? They are not that easy to find, but they do exist.

Generally, buildings are a compromise. The whole building industry has developed around the requirements of compromise (as has the man-made world in general). The exciting prospect ahead is that if we are careful enough about how we define every aspect of what we actually want and need from a new construction project, and we also consult stakeholders widely, there is often no need for compromise. Whole communities can want the same thing.

References

1   *The Construction Industry Council Client's Guide to Sustainable Construction*, written by Dave Hampton (ABS Consulting), Bridget Fidler (CIC), Jocelyn Herridge (CIOB) and Christopher Harris (CIRIA), and funded by the DTI, is available from the Construction Industry Council (CIC).

2   World Commission on Environment and Development (1987), *Our Common Future*, Oxford University Press, Oxford. This report, the "Brundtland Report", was written by Dr Gro Harlen Brundtland, former Prime Minister of Norway, in 1987. The report helped to trigger a range of actions, including the United Nations Earth Summits (in 1992 and 2002), the International Climate Change Convention, and worldwide "Agenda 21" programmes. See Chapter 4 for more details.

3   Lathan, Sir M (1994), *Constructing the team,* HMSO DEFRA. For full report see *www.carillionplc.com*

4   DEFRA (2002), *Achieving a Better Quality of Life: Review of progress towards sustainable development*, Department for Environment, Food and Rural Affairs, London, available on-line at *www.defra.gov.uk*

5   Anderson R (1998), *Mid-Course Correction: Towards a Sustainable Enterprise: the Interface Model*, Chelsea Green Pub Co., New York

6   Goyder G (1961), *The Responsible Company*, Blackwell, Oxford

7   World Economic Forum meeting in Davos, Switzerland. See reference 8.

CHAPTER 3

8   See *www.unglobalcompact.org*

9   The European Declaration of Businesses Against Social Exclusion, approved in 1995 by the then President of the European Commission, Jacques Delors, was a precursor of CSR Europe.

10 Although, of course, there will be times when short-duration buildings, with re-usable components, will be appropriate too.

11 See: *www.theFBnet.com*

12 Anderson R (1998), op cit.

13 Lovins, A (1996), The foreward to *Sustainable Design Guide of the Japan Institute of Architects*. The full text can be found on *www.rmi-org*

On-line resources

www.natcap.org
www.forumforthefuture.org.uk
www.neweconomics.org
www.interfacesustainability.com
www.tomorrowscompany.com
www.sustainable-development.gov.uk
www.absconsulting.uk.com

Further reading

It is useful to familiarise yourself with the changes in legislation and regulations. A good place to start is the Environment Agency's website at *www.environment-agency.gov.uk*. Look under the business and industry section to find the latest information on legislation and regulations.

Batty S, Davoudi S and Layard A (eds)(2001), *Planning for a Sustainable Future*, Spon Press, London

Covey S (1999), *The Seven Habits of Highly Effective People*, Simon & Schuster, London

Hawken P (1993), *The Ecology of Commerce*, Harper Business Publishers, New York

Hawken P, Lovins A and Lovins L (2000), *Natural Capitalism*, Earthscan Books, London

Weizsacker E von, Lovins A and Lovins L (1998), *Factor Four*, Earthscan Books, London

Benchmarks in context

Introduction

The European Environment Agency (EEA) defines an indicator as:

"A parameter, or a value derived from parameters, that describe the state of the environment and its impact on human beings, ecosystems and materials, the pressures on the environment, the driving forces and the responses steering that system. An indicator has gone through a selection and/or aggregation process to enable it to steer action." [1]

To put it more simply, an indicator is a "yardstick". In the context of the built environment, for any attribute of a building (e.g. its energy use, noisiness, comfortableness) there is a corresponding yardstick to measure how the building performs in relation to that attribute or issue. However, to be able to read a value off the yardstick there must first be agreement on what length the yardstick is. At one end of the yardstick the measurements represent bad performance and at the other it is judged to be good. By establishing a generally agreed scale it is possible to minimise personal, moral or ethical influences on the procedure of benchmarking.

You may not actually need units along the yardstick to see roughly how a building performs in relation to its comparators. Is it bigger or smaller; more or less? Simply identifying a position of a building on a the yardstick would be adequate for some judgements.

As we build up more and more comparative examples of the performance of different buildings against individual indicators, it is possible to say not only how well a building performs on a yardstick, but also how well it performs in detail in relation to other comparable buildings. It is by comparing performance in this way that performance "benchmarks" evolve on which standards and targets can be set. In other words, a benchmark is nothing more than a point on a yardstick; a notch on the bench, a point on a scale.

At its simplest, the benchmark may represent the one-off performance of one building against one indicator scale – a unique benchmark. But benchmarking has now become an established science, with well-defined methods for deriving different types of benchmark. A compounded benchmark, for example, may be represented by a point on the scale that represents the averaged performance of a group of unique benchmarks that forms a "reference" figure, and can be:[2]

- an absolute benchmark – a benchmark measure that represents a statistically derived national or regional average for the performance of buildings in general, or particular building types, such as offices, against that indicator
- a relative benchmark – a benchmark that provides a more closely related, comparative measure for a similar, more clearly defined or "reference" building types, such as a standard office, or a prestige air-conditioned office
- a tailored benchmark – a benchmark derived from reference buildings that are "tailored" to optimise the usefulness of the diagnostic potential that can be gained from the comparison, for example to provide similar, usefully comparable, circumstances, such as in offices, similar occupation densities, hours of use, levels of equipment and so on.

In summary, a benchmark is:

"A measurable variable used as a baseline or reference in evaluating the performance of an organisation [or environmental indicator]. Benchmarks may be drawn from internal experience or that of other organisations or from legal requirements and are often used to gauge changes in performance over time."[3]

By establishing a set of indicators and choosing appropriate benchmarks for them, and by applying these to a few simple questions, it is possible to reduce our chances of "flying blind"[4] in the processes of developing sustainable buildings and cities. The questions are:

- How is this building, community, city or country working?
- Is that what was intended?
- How can it be improved?
- How can future buildings, communities, cities, countries be improved?
- What are the real social, economic, environmental impacts of implementing /not implementing the proposed changes?

The origins of environmental indicators

The United Nations Conference on the Human Environment in Stockholm,

Sweden, in 1972 was the first major global diplomatic gathering to address human activities in relation to the environment. The Human Environment Conference produced a set of principles known as the Stockholm Declaration, and led to the founding of the United Nations Environment Programme (UNEP). Twenty years later in 1992 the United Nations Conference on Environment and Development (UNCED) met in Rio de Janeiro, Brazil, and kick-started the most significant global environmental action plan ever witnessed, culminating in five major agreements on global environmental issues. Two of these, the Framework Convention on Climate Change and the Convention on Biological Diversity, were formal treaties whose provisions are binding on the parties. The other three UNCED agreements (Agenda 21, the Rio Declaration, and the Statement on Forest Principles) were non-binding, and concerned the relationship between sustainable environmental practices and the pursuit of social and socio-economic development.[5]

What happened during the intervening 20 years to generate such unprecedented international activity?

Probably the first alarm bell to awake us from our 20th Century dreams of "free energy, intergalactic travel and space-age homes for all" was the energy crisis of the mid-1970s. With it came the realisation that oil – the magic energy source where every barrel can do the same "work" as 540 man-hours of effort – would one day run out (see Chapter 11). At that time, futurologists claimed we only had 30 years' worth of oil left, which has proved to be only about half right. But around the world people started counting the barrels, and comparing them to the available reserves, and investing in renewable energy programmes.

The second alarm bell was rung when scientists recognised, and began to monitor, the hole in the ozone layer over the Antarctic (see Chapter 10 for more details). In fact, ground-based measurements of ozone date back to 1956, at Halley Bay, Antarctica. Satellite measurements of ozone started in the early 1970s, but the first comprehensive worldwide measurements started in 1978 with the *Nimbus-7* satellite. By the early 1980s the scale of the ozone depletion problem was recognised, and the United Nations was spurred to sponsor a resolution called the Montreal Protocol, signed in 1987. This Protocol was based on negotiations started in 1983 between European-Scandinavian countries and the US over CFCs (chlorofluorocarbons) that "capture" atmospheric ozone in aerosol sprays.

The Montreal Protocol has gone through a series of revisions, including one agreed in Copenhagen in November 1992, where the most stringent phase-out schedule for CFCs for the world to date was signed by over 100 nations representing 95 per cent of the world's current CFC consumption.

The third alarm sounded in the mid-1980s, when fears began to grow over the potential scale and impacts of climate change, as scientists reported the results of modelling the relationship between the emissions of man-made greenhouse gases and the warming of the global climate (see Chapter 10).

Global response to environmental issues

In 1988, the UNEP and the World Meteorological Organization established the Intergovernmental Panel on Climate Change (IPCC), consisting of hundreds of leading scientists and experts on global warming.[6] The panel was asked to assess the state of scientific knowledge concerning climate change, and to formulate strategies to deal with the problem.

At the Rio Earth Summit in 1992, 172 participating nations (including the UK) agreed to adopt a voluntary target to reduce their greenhouse gas emissions to 1990 levels by the year 2000 – the United Nations Framework Convention on Climate Change (UNFCCC).[7] However, these voluntary measures have not been effective, and many nations, including the United States, are emitting significantly more greenhouse gases than ever before.

The Summit's message spurred many governments into action, and there are now many national and international programmes looking at everything from patterns of production to raising awareness of and concern over the growing scarcity of water. Much of this activity is being achieved under the auspices of Agenda 21 – a wide-ranging blueprint for action to achieve sustainable development worldwide. Although Agenda 21 has been weakened by compromise and negotiation, it is still the most comprehensive effective programme of action ever sanctioned by the international community (see box opposite).

Since the Rio Earth Summit there have been eight follow-up "Conference of Parties" (COP) meetings to try to establish agreements on exactly how emissions and impacts are going to be measured and what the targets and tools for negotiations are.[10]

Most recently, by August 2003, 84 Parties had signed the Convention and 113 Parties have ratified or acceded to the Kyoto Protocol.[11] COP 9, in December 2003, tackled the tricky issue of carbon sinks and emissions trading, and how to incorporate them in the global targets for the Kyoto Protocol.

The impact of Agenda 21

Today, efforts to ensure its proper implementation continue, in many corners of the globe, from the work of local authority Agenda 21 Officers to the signing of treaties by international governments.

Agenda 21

Agenda 21 is nothing if not ambitious. It urges governments to adopt a national strategy for sustainable development, the aim being to harmonise the nation's economic, social and environmental policies and plans. The goal is to ensure sustainable economic development – protecting the resource base and the environment for the benefit of future generations. In addition, it calls for the national strategy to be developed through the widest possible participation, and that it should be based on a thorough assessment of the current situation and initiatives.

It's a cliché, but it's true: you cannot manage what you cannot measure; and thus Agenda 21 also urges nations to develop systems for monitoring and evaluating progress towards achieving sustainable development – indicators and benchmarks.

With "participation" a key goal, local authorities are viewed as the main drivers for action under Agenda 21.

Local authorities construct, operate and maintain economic, social and environmental infrastructure, oversee planning processes, establish local environmental policies and regulations, and assist in implementing national and sub-national environmental policies. So Agenda 21 set specific objectives for local authorities:[8]

- By 1993, the international community should have initiated a consultative process aimed at increasing co-operation between local authorities.
- By 1994, representatives of local authorities and other bodies should have increased levels of co-operation and co-ordination, with the goal of enhancing the exchange of information and know-how.
- By 1996, most local authorities in each country should have undertaken a consultative process with their populations and achieved a consensus on "a local Agenda 21" for the community.

Most significant is the requirement for each local authority to enter into a dialogue with its citizens and stakeholders and adopt a "local Agenda 21".[9] The consultation involved in this process is intended to increase household awareness of sustainable development issues, while at the same time ensuring that local needs are co-ordinated into the "matrix" of local, national, regional and international activities – a "top-down, bottom-up" approach.

Much of the success of Agenda 21 has been derived from the ability to properly monitor change, using agreed units, carefully developed indicators, benchmarks and programmes to "capacity-build" organisations and communities (i.e. by teaching them how to apply and understand these measures and their impacts).

Agenda 21 has many current action programmes, including:

- changing consumption patterns
- protection and promotion of human health
- promoting sustainable human settlement development
- integrating environment and development into decision-making
- protecting the atmosphere, oceans and seas
- combating deforestation
- managing fragile ecosystems and conserving biodiversity
- promoting sustainable agriculture and rural development
- environmentally sound management of biotechnology
- protecting the quality and supply of fresh water resources
- environmentally sound management of wastes (including hazardous wastes)
- recognising and strengthening the role of indigenous people and their communities
- strengthening the role of workers and their trade unions; and of business and industry
- promoting education, public awareness and training.[12]

Benchmarks in action

Today we have reached a point where there is frenetic monitoring of the environment on an unprecedented scale. This is partly because we have developed:

- the technology and communications systems to monitor
- the will to act, fired by the growing realisation of the need to act to survive
- the realisation of the importance of applying indicators and benchmarks in order to survive.

However, one lesson learned from the Kyoto Protocol is that is it is extremely difficult to get people to agree to reduce their perceived standard of living today, even if it is they themselves who will suffer most when the levelling impacts of climate change strike home. The Kyoto process of benchmarking and providing targets for national greenhouse gas emissions is actually now leading to the demonisation of major environmental abusers. For instance, many now question why the United States of America, which so overtly boasts of being a God-fearing nation, continues to pollute the global atmosphere with impunity, issuing 25 per cent of all global emissions yet having only 4 per cent of the world's population. There is an impression that the majority of the population live air-conditioned lives, drive gas-guzzling vehicles and have no concern at all for the well-being of others – not just of other nations of the world, but also its own poor in climatically exposed regions of its continental heartlands. But we should not be too hasty to condemn everyone because the average performance of the nation, as a whole, is so very poor: there are many passionate environmental activists in the USA. In this situation, the benchmarks have become sticks.

No one is going to voluntarily adopt a benchmarking system if it shows them up in a bad light. Benchmarks must be used carefully for what they are best at – as effective aids for improving building performance. The sooner an organisation (or a nation) understands the importance of environmental benchmarking and begins to use it effectively to promote change, the quicker they will reap the rewards of their efforts.

Having decided to opt for change, it is essential to choose the right indicators and benchmarks for the issue in hand. The remainder of this chapter offers brief guidance on how to make this crucial decision.

Understand the source

In making a choice about indicators and benchmarks we must exercise due caution. During the development of this book, we have read through the hundreds of benchmarks and indicators out there in cyberspace, and it is difficult not to become wary of some websites and published sources that offer so-called "authoritative indicators". There are a surprising number of apparently top-drawer, international organisations that appear to be promoting useful information, but on closer inspection their advice seems to be a little skewed in a direction that tends to favour the interests of their sponsors (seldom well advertised, and often an international corporation or industry).

In addition, some indicator sets present confused agendas. For example, in the UK in 1997 the Construction Task Force, chaired by Sir John Egan, was commissioned to advise the Deputy Prime Minister, from the clients' perspective, on the opportunities to improve the efficiency and quality of delivery of UK construction, to reinforce the impetus for change, and to make the industry more responsive to customer needs. The Construction Task Force published its report, *Rethinking Construction*,[13] in 1998. It contained the clear message that the industry would not improve significantly unless it embarked upon radical change. This would involve a totally new approach to the delivery of the construction product.

The report proposed the creation of a "movement for change", which would be a dynamic, inspirational, non-institutional body that would truly believe in the need for radical improvement within the construction industry.[14] The resultant "Movement for Innovation" went on to produce a *Sustainability Working Group Report*,[15] which incorporated a system of "Environmental Roses" for reporting on environmental performance. The Roses were based on indicator sets for energy, water, waste, transport, biodiversity and embodied energy. A range of different Roses were developed for different building types, and an impressive list of developers and clients have indeed signed up and provided case study buildings listed on the website.[16]

However, it is difficult to unpick where many of the indicators and benchmarks incorporated into these Roses relate to the challenge of improving the financial and environmental efficiency of the construction processes and the buildings occupied by businesses. Do these indicators refer to predicted performance? And if so, how do they relate to the actual performance as built, rather than having a key aim of improving the quality of life of those who occupy them? Are these indicators more about product validation for an industry and its larger corporations, or are they about improving the quality of life for the people in and around them?

A good rule of thumb for key benchmarks and indicator sets is to stick to sources with a clear rationale, such as those listed in the box below and throughout this book.

Where an issue is one of life and death, environmental degradation associated with severe impacts, or the limitation of the freedom of people to enjoy a minimum standard of living, then the underlying benchmarks will come from international, European or national laws (see box).

Legal resources

Use the following websites to research international, European and UK law pertaining to sustainability.

- United Nations Treaties – *http://untreaty.un.org*
- European law – *http://europa.eu.int/comm/environment/legis_en.htm*; try also *www.eltis.org* for clearly explained policy papers
- UK law – *www.hmso.gov.uk/acts.htm* and *www.hmso.gov.uk/legislation/about_legislation.htm*; there is also a user-friendly interpretation site at *www.environment-agency.gov.uk/netregs*

Aggregated indicators

Indicators quantify and simplify phenomena to help us understand complex situations. Although indicators may be aggregates of raw and processed data, they can also be further aggregated themselves to form complex indices such as the one in Figure 4.1. The problem with some compound, or "black box" indicator

---

Authoritative indicator sites

Global

- World Health Organisation – *www.who.int/en*
- United Nations Programme for the Environment – *www.unep.org*
- United Nations Sustainability Indicators – *www.un.org/esa/sustdev/natlinfo/indicators/isd.htm*
- The International Standards Organisation – *www.iso.ch*

European
- European Environment Agency – *www.eea.eu.int*
- European Union Environment and Sustainable Development treaty – *http://europa.eu.int/comm/enterprise/environment/index.htm*
- Sustainable Cities – *www.sustainable-cities.org*

UK
In the UK today there four levels of related to government (described at *www.sustainable-development.gov.uk*):

- Headline Indicators – 15 indicators used to raise public awareness about sustainable development, and to provide an overview of progress
- National Indicators – a core set of 147 indicators of sustainable development published by the UK government in 1999
- Regional Indicators – the headline indicators reproduced at the regional level for 9 regions of England, and for Wales
- Local Indicators – a set of 29 indicators (some derived from the headline and national indicators, others developed locally), some or all of which can be used as a basis for reporting on sustainable development progress at the local level.

For an excellent site on the UK Indicators see *www.audit-commission.gov .uk/reports*

Figure 4.1 The 'Dashboard of Sustainability Indicators' for nations baed on the United Nations' sustainability indicator set

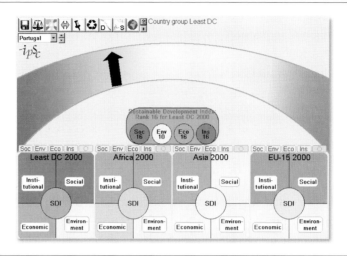

Source: The Consultative Group on Sustainable Development Indicators (CGSDI), Dashboard of Sustainability.
IISD: *http://www.iisd.org/cgsdi/intro_dashboard.htm* and *http://esl.jrc.it/envind/dashboards.htm*

sets, regardless of how attractive they are, is that it is difficult to see clearly what agendas are driving them.

High-level decision-makers dealing with sustainable development issues routinely call for a manageable number of indices that are easy to understand and use in decision-making. They would often prefer a single index to compete with the broad appeal and enormous political power of the "gross domestic product" (GDP), a commonly used index of economic growth. But most indicator experts believe that searching for a single index of sustainable development is something akin to the quest for the unicorn. It is a myth to think that a single number – even one that vastly improved upon the GDP as a proxy for overall national well-being – could have any real functional value as a policy tool.

Many governments have developed their own indices of sustainable development indicators, and throughout this book you will find references to the governments of Japan, Australia or New Zealand, which each having a core set of national indicators of sustainable development. The UK, for instance, uses 15 headline indicators.[17]

Unfortunately, many such national sets are arrived at using different indicators, measurement units and techniques, which makes it difficult to cross-reference performance between nations (see Chapter 13 for a classic example). Indeed, every country or building may have its own idiosyncratic indicator set, as no two countries or buildings are alike. Take for example the Maori indicator in the New

44

Zealand. This is a "cultural" indicator, and the New Zealand government, in conjunction with the Maori people, will have had to decide what are the significant performance characteristics for the sub-indicators, what units to measure them in, how and when to measure them, and what ultimately represents good or bad on the "Maori yardstick".

Similarly, consumption habits are very different, so it is not really sensible to compare the energy consumption of a traditional Maori family lifestyle in Auckland New Zealand, to that of an American family living in Tucson, Arizona. They may be different by a factor of 100 or more! Clearly, indicator sets have to be adaptable, as the length or scale of the indicator yardstick will be different according to the characteristics of the group under investigation, and will change over time.

The International Institute for Sustainable Development in Canada has attempted to create a sustainable development index (SDI) at the national level, and they claim it will prove useful even if it fails because it might force a disciplined effort to present the complexity of sustainable development in a simplified form.[18]

Even a modestly successful effort to produce a small set of indices in an organisation could have the effect of introducing policy – and decision – makers to the goal of sustainable development.

Where possible, it is preferable to use "transparent "indicators associated with clear and rigorous methodologies (see for example Chapter 39, where we discuss the excellent PROBE method).[19] Many groups will prefer to develop their own, tailored and well-understood indicator sets to monitor progress. What is important is that the aims of the process are clear, and that a robust set of indicators is adopted and agreed to test that those aims are being implemented, in a closed loop that can continue to be developed and used over the lifetime of the building.

Compare like with like

Care has to be taken that like is being compared with like, and it is essential to have a clear definition for an indicator. A lack of comparability in the definition of what constitutes an indicator can be used to mask poor performance. One example we recently came across was that of a construction materials industry that wants to hide the poor embodied energy performance of its product. It kept the same length of the yardstick, and uses the same name – embodied energy – for that yardstick, but it turns out that it, in effect, it is an entirely different indicator. The generally accepted meaning of embodied energy is "energy used in production, transport and construction on site". But this, arguably canny, industry has changed this to "energy used over the whole life of the product". So the graphs they show in public labelled "embodied energy", demonstrating the rather average performance of the material are, in fact, figures for total energy used over the lifetime of the building. When using the generally accepted definition of embodied energy the material in question performs much more poorly in relation to competitor materials.

As indicator systems become more sophisticated, agree the definition of the attribute being measured, the length of the yardstick, and measurement units and methods to be used when measuring.

Choose the right scale

The perception of the relative performance of a building for a particular indicator can be packaged very differently according to the scale used on its yardstick. If the yardstick is divided into three categories: good (66–100 per cent), medium (33–66 per cent) or bad (0–33 per cent), then a building can be labelled as good that actually is only 67 per cent good on a percentage scale and would register as OK on a seven point scale. So the grain of the scale (coarse, medium or fine) can have a significant impact on the perceived performance of the product against an indicator yardstick

Think about the user as well as the source

Always think about who the indicator is aimed at, as well as where it has come from.

There are a number of indicator sets currently in use by architectural and engineering design practices to describe the sustainability of their buildings. For instance, Arup, the well-known engineers, have developed their SPeAR® method (Sustainable Project Appraisal Routine) of describing the sustainability performance of buildings.[20]

The reasons given by Arup for why this method works well are:

- simple visual output to express a complex concept
- ability to demonstrate improvement in ESD performance
- applicable across numerous sectors
- applied at various levels of detail
- backed by a concise summary report of all key ESD issues
- identifies strengths and weaknesses to allow informed decision-making
- illustrates the interaction of indicators
- all assessments are fully audit traceable.

SPeAR® is a sustainability tool, not an environmental reporting tool like the Movement for Innovation tool and many others, and is used for a range of functions:

- As a design tool it brings sustainability into the decision-making process with its focus on the key elements of environmental protection, social

Figure 4.2 The SPeAR® diagram developed by Arup

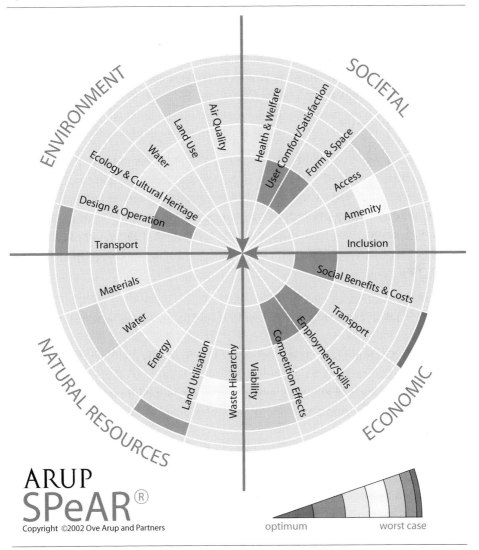

ARUP
SPeAR ®
Copyright ©2002 Ove Arup and Partners

optimum   worst case

Source: © Ove Arup & Partners, 2002

equity, economic viability and efficient use of natural resources. As such the information generated by the appraisal prompts innovative thinking and informs decision-making at all stages of design and development. This allows continual improvement in sustainability performance and objectives.

- As a means of informing, and educating clients, designers and members of the board, succinctly, about the predicted or actual performance of the building against chosen indicators, at a more general level of resolution to provide a general impression of relative sustainability of performance of a building project, set against other projects of its type.

- It provides benchmarks against which the building can be evaluated at the point of post-occupancy evaluations. The SPeAR® diagram (see Figure 4.3) is accompanied by a more detailed report describing the predicted performance of the design against each of the indicators, addressing the way in which the process has been used to optimise the building performance against the range of indicators that can be used later to evaluate performance in use.

While the diagram (Figure 4.2) is a useful visualisation tool for the clients or the design team – particularly when a number of diagrams are produced over time, and where comparisons of design changes and developments are very graphically shown – the report provides a useful second dial of analysis that can be used to refine elements of the detailed performance of schemes using the SPeAR® process.

Learn from experience

Last year I heard a lecture from a leading architect in which he explained carefully the system used by his team to analyse the sustainability aspects of a project he had designed – a fully glazed west-facing glass wall that performed badly against the indicators. He claimed that he was in the dark as to why that should be! Another leading designer claimed that because they had built in a sustainable transport system it was not necessary to have such an energy-efficient building as well.

It seems these loops have a couple of missing links:

- Designers were not being educated, in practice, on how to apply the lessons of the indicator sets to improve their designs.
- Designers might be using the indicators as a trade-off system, as tools for "green-washing" their projects – a front for the business-as-usual practices that are so prevalent in the construction industry today.

A key role for indicators and benchmarks is to enable everyone involved in the building process to learn from experience and use those lessons to improve building performance and reduce related impacts over time.

Conclusions

We can have all the indicators, benchmarks and tools imaginable, but if those who are responsible for making buildings work better do not use them properly, then they simply become part of a "green-washing" process, promoted through indifference or self-interest (ignorance is no longer a valid excuse) that will result in a generation not only of white elephant buildings but of white elephant designers too.

Benchmarking is here to stay, and all stakeholders in the built environment should, if they are not doing so already, embark on:

- Closing the loop – designing the process that will fit into a design or management schedule, making sure it is in the form of a closed loop operating monitored either annually or over a building cycle. This process should include a clear method for continually checking that the performance aims of the building have been, and continue to be, met.
- Choosing the right indicator set – after understanding the relevant range of issues and the context of the project, and selecting appropriate indicators for the job.
- Developing the benchmarks and targets – measuring the existing, or predicted building performance against the chosen indicators to provide the current benchmarks of performance for that building, and compare these to related sets, establish realistic targets and timescales against which the improvements in performance can be achieved over time.

The following chapters are designed to help you make the right decisions for your projects, and to measure, design and demonstrate that you are getting them right.

References

1 Source: *http://glossary.eea.eu.int/EEAGlossary*
2 An excellent site, with extensive related publication lists on types of benchmarks and their applications, is at *www.usablebuildings.co.uk*
3 Source: Sustainability Northwest website at *www.snw.org.uk*
4 See: Bordass W (2001), *Flying Blind: Everything you always wanted to know about energy in commercial buildings but were afraid to ask*, Association for the Conservation of Energy and Energy Efficiency Advice Services for Oxfordshire, London (available at *www.ukace.org*); and Bordass W and Leaman A (not yet published), "Making feedback and post-occupancy evaluation routine", in Preiser W and Vischer J (eds), *Assessing Building Performance*, Butterworth-Heinemann, Oxford
5 Source: Columbia Earth Institute, Columbia University, USA. See *www.ciesin.org*
6 All IPCC reports can be found at *www.ipcc.ch*
7 Source: *www.un.org/geninfo/bp/enviro.html*
8 United Nations (1992), *Earth Summit: Agenda 21*, UN Department of Economic and Social Affairs, Chapter 28; view on-line at *www.un.org/esa*

9   Ibid; para 28.3
10 Source: United Nations Framework Convention on Climate Change at *http://unfccc.int/index.html*
11 For a full list see: *http://unfccc.int/resource/convkp.html*
12 Source: UN Environment Programme, Environment and Development Agenda at *www.unep.org*
13 See: *www.rethinkingconstruction.org*
14 Source: KPIs and benchmarks page on Movement for Innovation website at *www.m4i.org.uk*
15 M4I (2001), *Sustainability Working Group Report*, Movement for Innovation, Watford (download from *www.m4i.org.uk*)
16 Ibid
17 See: *www.sustainable-development.gov.uk/indicators*
18 Source: International Institute for Sustainable Development, *www.iisd.org*
19 See also the Sustainable Cities Ten Indicators we refer to in a number of the following chapters (*www.sustainable-cities.org/aal_uk.html*)
20 See *www.arup.com/sustainability/services/SPeAR.cfm*

Further reading

DETR (2000), *Climate change: the UK programme*, The Stationery Office, Norwich
Preiser W and Vischer J (eds) (in press), *Assessing Building Performance*, Butterworth-Heinemann, Oxford
Preiser W (1997), "Building performance evaluation", in Watson et al, *Time-Saver Standards for Architectural Design Data*, McGraw-Hill, New York, Chapter 20
Roaf S (not yet published), *Adapting Buildings and Cities for Climate Change*, Architectural Press, Oxford
Turco R (2002), *Earth Under Siege*, Oxford University Press, Oxford

Social indicators

Quality of life

Definition

Quality of life (QOL) means different things to different people. The United Nations[1] links QOL to sustainable development, saying: "Development is a multidimensional undertaking to achieve a higher quality of life for all people." Although it does not directly define QOL, this UN report alludes to what this might mean, listing a wide range of factors, including: the eradication of poverty, hunger, disease and illiteracy; the provision of adequate shelter and secure employment for all; respect for all human rights and fundamental freedoms, including the right to development; transparent and accountable governance and administration in all sectors of society; effective participation by civil society; and the empowerment of women and their full participation on a basis of equality in all spheres of society.

Related indicators

Community; Health; Land use; Noise; Pollution; Thermal comfort.

Related tools

Ecological footprints; Sociological survey techniques.

Background

Quality of life (QOL) is at the heart of the "social dimension" of sustainable development. The interconnectedness of human society means that the well-being of each individual depends on the well-being of every member of our communities, our countries and our world. The concept of "equity" will drive development on every continent in the 21st Century.

For any species – from humans to ants – lifestyle, QOL and behaviour patterns are influenced by the size of the population. Researchers who study population have found that, as populations grow, behaviour changes to introduce efficiencies to ensure survival of that species. The term "carrying capacity" is sometimes used to relate the size of the population to the sustainability of the species.

The world's population has risen from 1.65 billion in 1900 to 6.08 billion in 2000. The growth is largely due to plunging death rates, with average life expectancy more than doubling since 1900, from 30 to 63 years. The United Nations Population Division reports[3] that, even though the fertility level is falling and some populations are facing an increase in mortality risk (e.g. from HIV/AIDS), the population of the world is expected to increase by 2.6 billion during the next 47 years, from 6.3 billion in 2002 to 8.9 billion in 2050. In fact, if measures to combat the spread of the HIV/AIDS epidemic are successful and fertility remains at current levels, the total population of the globe could more than double by 2050, reaching 12.8 billion.

In *Sharing Nature's Interest*[4] Nicky Chambers and Craig Simmons have an excellent section on QOL, and they clearly link population to impacts through the simple equation:

$$Impact = Population \times Consumption$$

Their book includes a useful discussion of how to estimate the carrying capacity of the Earth, and suggests that the global population has crossed over the "warning zone" – the point where humans began to exceed the carrying capacity of the Earth. They estimate that this point was reached in the mid-1980s.

The Optimum Population Trust[5] has estimated the carrying capacities of various regions of the world in relation to its own vision of QOL and sustainability. It sug-

---

Carrying capacity

Population factors were recognised as significant to the sustainability debate at the United Nations Conference on Environment and Development, held at Rio de Janeiro in 1992. Agenda 21, which was adopted at this conference, suggested that "population-carrying capacity" could be a useful measurement in the search for sustainability. The "land-carrying capacity" is the maximum population that can be sustainably supported in a given country or area by agricultural activities. Logically, the carrying capacity depends on the prevailing land and climatic characteristics, and on the agricultural technologies used.

In 1982 the Food and Agriculture Organization of the United Nations (FAO) and the International Institute for Applied Systems Analysis (IIASA) assessed potential population-carrying capacity, and there have been a number of studies since (some of which are described in this chapter). The results of the FAO/IIASA research indicated that by the year 2000, more than half of the 117 countries studied would be unable to meet their food needs using low-technology methods.[2]

gests that the optimum population of a country is that which is most likely to produce a good and sustainable quality of life for its inhabitants without adversely
affecting the quality of life of people in other countries. It uses a range of criteria
to calculate carrying capacity, including:

- maintenance of biodiversity
- availability of fresh water
- availability of land.

When calculating the carrying capacity for Britain, the Trust includes indicators
such as food, energy, transport, space, environment, countryside, recreation,
tourism. After taking all these into consideration, together with pinches of salt,
they conclude that the optimum population for a good QOL in the UK cannot be
more than 30 million and is probably far less – around 20 million. Compare this
with Table 5.1, the UK census data for the past 200 years!

QOL in the "global village"

The extraordinary power of the global communications industry now links us
with even the remotest outposts of human society; and this at a time when the
global population is increasing by almost 80 million people per year – about 10
times the average annual increment in the 19th Century.

Figure 5.1 Historical estimates of carrying capacity set against population growth

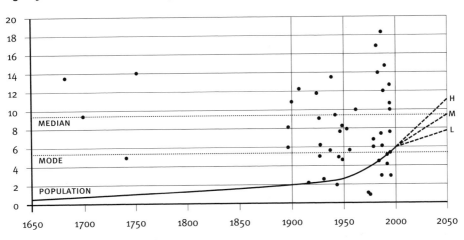

• = Estimates of carrying capacity
Population projections: H = high (11.2 million), M = medium (9.3 million), L = low (7.7 million)
Median estimate is 9.5 billion; modal estimate is 5.5 billion

Source: Chambers et al, 2000

The ease of communication between centres of population is a driving force that fuels envy, crime, terrorism, and the mass migration of people. Such migrations have happened throughout history; people move away from regions stricken by drought, flood, poverty, political instability and lack of education and amenities. There is a biological imperative at the root of these migrations, but it is more than just an urge to survive – it is a quest to find an acceptable QOL for people and, importantly, progeny. (In "developed" countries, QOL may be more strongly related to the difference in income between rich and poor.)

If you think that such geo-political issues are a little remote it is worth noting that, even in the UK, local authorities already include issues of racial mixing (resulting from such migrations) in QOL benchmarks.

QOL indicators vary enormously according to the population concerned and the institution doing the measuring, but for many issues it is possible to define and develop meaningful benchmarks, and these can be used for individual projects so that we can get an idea of how well or how badly a scheme performs.

There is no doubt that the widespread introduction of systematic surveying for QOL, as is recommended in this book, will ensure that those who are powerful in our society do not achieve higher and higher QOL at the expense of those who are weaker.

As we exceed the carrying capacity of our lands, placing ever-growing demands on our ecosystems, the introduction of the social dimension into the design

Table 5.1 Population of England and Wales from UK Census data

YEAR	TOTAL POPULATION FOR ENGLAND AND WALES
1801	8,893,000
1811	10,164,000
1821	12,000,000
1831	13,897,000
1841	15,914,000
1851	17,928,000
1861	20,066,000
1871	22,712,000
1881	25,794,000
1891	29,003,000
1901	32,528,000
1911	36,070,000
2001	58,789,194

Source: www.statistics.gov.uk © Crown copyright

process becomes increasingly important. If there was plenty for all, this would not be a problem.

Global indicators

The need to relate our own well-being to that of the larger "family" around the world is brought home well by the simple and thought-provoking indicators developed to protect the children of the world by UNICEF:[6]

- Eradicate extreme poverty and hunger.
- Achieve universal primary education.
- Promote gender equality and empower women.
- Reduce child mortality.
- Improve maternal health.
- Ensure environmental sustainability.
- Develop a global partnership for development, including fair trade.
- Put an end to war.

These laudable aims seems so sensible in our irrational in a world. It beggars belief that we continue to divert billions of dollars away from these aims, only to spend the money not on the prevention, but on the prosecution of war.

European indicators

In Europe, QOL is related to the economy, but accessibility is an all-important theme. "Quality of Life and Management of Living Resources" is one of the four thematic research programmes developed under the EU's Fifth Framework Programme (1998–2002).[7] Research into QOL issues covers:

- food, nutrition and health
- control of infectious diseases
- environment and health
- sustainable agriculture, fisheries and forestry
- integrated development of rural areas (including mountain areas)
- the ageing population, and disabilities.

QOL is referred to in the 11 EU "common indicators for sustainable cities",[8] in that there is an indicator for "community" and one for "availability of local public open areas and services".

Access to public open areas and basic services is essential for QOL and for the viability and sustainability of the local economy. Having basic services close to home also reduces the need to travel. If basic requirements of food and health are not met, there is a failure to satisfy social needs. The absence of shops selling fresh fruit and vegetables is an indicator of social exclusion (e.g. in the UK) and is a threat to health. Exclusion also occurs if there is a lack of transport for those who rely on it. The EU expects local authorities to play an important role in facilitating access to open areas and basic services. It is interesting to see how these concepts are incorporated into the local authority indicators (see below).

At the heart of this indicator lies the question: "What share of the inhabitants in the municipality live close to public open areas and other basic services?" The unit of measurement used by the EU is:

accessibility (%) = the number of inhabitants living within 300 m of open areas or services total number of inhabitants

The EU authorities use "within 15 minutes' walk" as a rule of thumb to define "accessibility", and has published a fully developed methodology for measuring this indicator.[9]

Basic services are defined as:

- primary public health services (general practitioner, hospitals, first-aid posts, family advice bureaux or other public centres supplying medical services, such as diagnosis or specialist examinations)
- collective transport lines that, at least for part of a common business day, have a minimum frequency (half-hourly service)
- public schools (compulsory attendance schools)
- food shops
- recycling facilities or services for solid waste (including recycling bins).

And open areas[10] are defined as:

- public parks, gardens or open spaces, for the exclusive use of pedestrians and cyclists, except green traffic islands or dividers, graveyards (unless the local authority recognises their recreational function or natural, historical or cultural importance)
- open-air sports facilities, accessible to the public free of charge
- private areas (agricultural areas, private parks), accessible to the public free of charge.

When studying QOL under this programme, researchers are not required to take the quality of the open area or service into account. In other words, it is assumed that the open areas or services perform – all in the same way – the functions for which they are intended. Naturally, this is not always the reality: there are open areas that are more attractive and popular than others, and the same goes for services. This weakness is, however, considered acceptable because the quality of amenities and services is monitored via the "quality of community" indicator.

UK government and local authority indicators

In comfortable Britain, key QOL issues and impacts for social sustainability, as developed by the UK government, are much wider and relate to the social aspirations of a robustly middle class nation where, for instance, quality of education is considered very important.[11]

The importance of improving the life of the citizens (voters) of the UK means that QOL issues are very high on the list of political priorities,[12] and include:

- education and training
- human rights
- equal opportunities
- fair and open dealing between peoples
- building local communities
- participation and local democracy
- eradication of poverty
- reducing crime and fear of crime
- social inclusion
- regeneration
- health and safety at work
- health
- personal safety
- access to decent housing
- local environmental quality
- consumer rights and interests
- access to services, infrastructure and landscape.

The government's most recent report on the UK's progress towards sustainable development[13] summarises the progress on these issues in a "quality of life barometer" (see Table 5.2).

In addition, the Audit Commission has developed a very comprehensive set of QOL indicators[14] that are now driving the agenda in the country's local authorities. They cover the authority's "behaviour" towards its stakeholders (e.g. how accessible are its buildings), and its performance in other areas that it manages e.g.

Table 5.2 Headline indicators for QOL in the UK

INDICATOR	OVERALL SINCE 1990	SINCE 1999
Economic output	B	B
Investment	S	S
Employment	S	B
Poverty	S	B
Education	B	B
Health	S	S
Housing	B	B
Robbery	W	W
Car crime/burglary	B	B
Climate change	B	B
Air quality	B	S
Road traffic	W	W
River water quality	B	B
Wildlife/farmland birds	W	S
Woodland birds	W	B
Land use	B	B
Waste management (recycling)	W	W

Key:
B = getting better
W = getting worse
S = no significant change

leisure, education, and the environment.

These indicators include:

- average weekly costs per dwelling
- percentage of relevant housing repairs completed within government time limits
- net expenditure per head of population
- number of swims and other visits per 1,000 population
- number of playgrounds and play areas provided by the council, per 1,000 children under 12
- number of visits/usages to museums per 1,000 population
- percentage of highways that are of a high standard of cleanliness
- number of public conveniences providing access for disabled people and/or baby-changing facilities
- net spending per head of population on environmental health and consumer protection
- children under five in local authority-maintained schools as a percentage of all three and four year-olds
- percentage of all four-year-olds in nursery places provided by the council
- number of nights of respite care provided or funded by the authority per

A survey conducted by *Country Life* magazine offers a sideways view of the "traditional British quality of life".

Country Life is an up-market glossy magazine that is a very British institution. In an attempt to find the place with the highest QOL the magazine devised a list of desirable criteria, then awarded points to locations throughout England, Scotland and Wales adding up to a possible 10,015. The results surprised even the magazine, and identified ten places – all towns – with the highest QOL.

The *Country Life* QOL indicators are:

- local identity – *Country Life* thought this was a most important factor, and allocated up to 15 points – including distinctive vernacular architecture, or links with celebrated artists or writers
- quality of landscape (also worth up to 15 points)
- the "five Ps" – pub, public transport, parish church, primary school and post office
- a pleasant climate
- affordable housing (cost of housing in each place was measured against the average for the respective county; if the cost of housing is beyond the reach of local people the town or village will become a commuter dormitory)
- ambience – cultural life, or local important historic buildings
- bonus points for good local fresh food, farmers' markets, and food shops stocking local produce
- exceptional sporting opportunities locally (e.g. salmon fishing or a sporting centre)
- good rail and road links to cities
- low crime levels and low traffic levels in streets.

First place was given to Alnwick in Northumberland, which scored well in all categories except climate.

1,000 adults
- number of items issued by the authority's libraries per head of population
- percentage of pedestrian crossings with facilities for disabled people.

Building-level indicators

The move to larger buildings led to the creation of the "facilities management" (FM) profession. These days, FM has a much wider remit than simply managing energy use. Facilities managers now play an important role in the health and sustainability of businesses because people have become increasingly aware that good indoor environments lead to higher worker satisfaction and productivity.

Energy costs in the 20th Century were so low compared with other business costs that improving the productivity of the workforce was a far more urgent consideration. A one or two percent change in productivity could have enormous cost implications for a well-paid workforce. In the 1990s, personnel costs – for salaries, employers costs (e.g. National Insurance) and benefits – were around 80–87 per cent of the running costs of an office building, whereas energy costs could be as low as 0.2–2.2 per cent[16] Today, with energy costs on the increase, and with diminishing fossil fuel sources, the gap between those two percentages is destined to shrink. Happily, there is plenty of evidence to show that energy-efficient buildings are also pleasant places to work, so clients can have the best of both worlds. Indicators for energy usage are described in Chapter 11, but indicators for occupant satisfaction are more difficult to come by, as we shall discuss in detail in Chapters 34 and 39.

Every building, location and workplace is different, so there is no impetus to develop a single methodology to measure how happy people are in their buildings. Indeed, there is even disagreement among building professionals. Building services engineers, for example, seek operational "satisfaction"; while the architect Liza Hershong[17] describes her search for "thermal delight" in buildings – which may possibly be much more fun. However, the PROBE studies described in Chapter 39 found that the perceived QOL factors in buildings are very positively associated with the design of a building, and survey results[18] showed that people are happier with buildings in which:

- people are tied to jobs in one place
- people work in small groups
- the depth of the building is shallow, and, in particular there is a high proportion of window seats
- occupancy is low – not too crowded
- individuals feel they have good levels of control
- there is high management responsiveness to problems when they are reported
- and which are naturally ventilated and maximise daylight.

Personal indicators

Because we are all kings of the home, and homes typically belong to one person or a family, issues of control are not so pressing, but here, behind locked doors, personal preferences are paramount.

Each and every one of us can draw up our own idea of what, for us, constitutes quality of life in our home, as well as our workplace. Some of us like big or small houses, rural or urban locations, brick or wood, and modern or old. It is important that every building occupier and designer should think hard about what constitutes "quality" in the invisible or visible environment in which they spend most of their lives. So often in post-1960s buildings designers appear to be intent on following fashion and adhering to stereotypes – for instance, "minimalism" or "modernity" – that they produce buildings that are hard, sterile and inhuman. So often the designers themselves live in comfortable historic homes and would never dream of buying one of their own "modern micro-lofts strung along a street in the sky".

So we as designers have a responsibility to understand QOL in buildings and to provide for other people what we would expect for ourselves. My own list, for instance, for a home with a high QOL would include:

- quiet
- safe
- healthy
- warm in winter; cool in summer; and at a cost I can afford
- offering protection from the elements in winter, not exposed to them
- sunny in spring, autumn and winter; shaded in summer (shaded all year in a hot climate)
- incorporating nurturing spaces; with rooms that are rooms not corridors
- rich, warm colours and textures
- good natural light
- low maintenance and energy bills
- no overheating or cold sources
- contact with the outside/garden/green
- nice road, area and community.

References

1   United Nations (1997), *Agenda for Development*, a report of the 103rd plenary meeting on 20 June 1997, can be viewed at *www.un.org/esa*
2   Further information can be found in the UN document, *Review of Population*

Trends, Policies and Programmes: Monitoring of world population trends and policies, a report of the 28th session of the UN Population Commission, 21 February – 2 March 1995, (document reference no. E/CN.9/1995/2), which can be viewed at *www.un.org/esa*

3   UN Population Division (26 February 2003), *World Population Prospects*, the 2002 Revision Highlights (document reference no. ESA/P/WP.180), which can be viewed at *www.un.org/esa*

4   Chambers N, Simmons C and Wackernagel M (2000), *Sharing Nature's Interest: Ecological footprints as an indicator of sustainability*, Earthscan Publications Ltd, London

5   Visit *www.optimumpopulation.org*

6   UNICEF (July 2002), *A World Fit for Children*, United Nations Childrens Fund, New York, which can be downloaded from *www.www.unicef.org/publications*

7   Visit *www.cordis.lu/life/home.html*

8   Expert Group on the Urban Environment (March 1996), *European Sustainable Cities: Report*, European Commission DGXI Environment, Nuclear Safety and Civil Protection, Brussels. This report can be downloaded from *www.europa.eu.int/comm/environment/pubs/studies.htm*

9   *Towards a Local Sustainability Profile: European Common Indicators (Methodology sheets)*, published by the European Commission, can be down-loaded from *www.sustainable-cities.org/indicators/index2.htm* (go to "Documents" page.)

10 A complete data analysis of accessibility to "open areas" can only be achieved if the indicator is calculated twice: first, relating to areas greater than 5,000m^2, and second for all areas used by the public for leisure and open air activities, regardless of their dimension.

11 This indicator is probably much less significant in Guinea Bissau in West Africa, one of the poorest nations in the world.

12 DETR (May 1999), *A Better Quality of Life: A strategy for sustainable development for the UK*, Department of the Environment, Transport and the Regions, The Stationery Office, Norwich. Download a copy from *www.sustainable-development.gov.uk/uk_strategy/content.htm*

13 DEFRA (March 2002), *Achieving a Better Quality of Life: Review of progress towards sustainable development*, Department for Environment, Food and Rural Affairs, The Stationery Office, Norwich. Download the document from *www.sustainable-development.gov.uk/ar2002/index.htm*

14 See *www.audit-commission.gov.uk/pis/quality-of-life-indicators.shtml*

15 Mitchell S (2002), "We go in search of Quality of Life", in: *Country Life,* October 31, pp 56–63

16 Robertson G (1992), "A case study for atria", in: *Energy Efficient Buildings,* Roaf S and Hancock M (eds), Blackwell Scientific Publishers, Oxford, pp 129–144

17 Hershong L (1979), *Thermal Delight in Architecture,* MIT Press, Cambridge, MA

18 Bordass W (1998), "Factors for success or how to compensate for things you take away", *Workplace Comfort Forum,* London, 3 December.

On-line resources

International Society for Quality of Life Studies: *www.cob.vt.edu/market/isqols*

Planning policy guidance – related documents (see Appendix 1 for details)

1	2	3	4	5	6	7	8	9	10	11	12	13
x	x	x				x				x	x	

14	15	16	17	18	19	20	21	22	23	24	25	
	x	x	x							x	x	

Community

Background

Well-being is an important part of a "sustainable society"; and well-being is, of course, intimately linked with Quality of Life (QOL) (Chapter 5), decent work and, importantly, having real opportunities to participate in local planning and decision-making processes. Having a sense of "community" – human relationships, and personal, social, and spiritual QOL – is an indicator that is every bit as important as more practical physical attributes such as whether there is a school, a hospital or a post office.

Creating a sense of place, and a sense of being part of that place and its people, lies at the heart of the design and development of a real "community". There was no need to tell the village builders of history what ingredients they needed to build a community, because they knew already. They would have known, and possibly been related to, many people in their village or neighbourhood and would have been able to build on decades or centuries of trial and error in moulding that place to its own occupants' aspirations and lifestyles. They also had land, and with it nature, all around them.

It was with the development of the large industrial conurbations from the 19th Century onwards that caused the dislocation of communities, as people went in search of work. In the early days the relatively small scale of new developments precluded too large a social impact being imposed on cities and villages, because suburbs were built up street by street. By the 20th Century new visions, new magnitudes of impact, increased mobility of populations and the growing power of manufacturing and industry meant that the pace of change began to accelerate. The Garden Suburb and City movements created vast areas of new housing, which before the Second World War were typically well resourced with amenities.

By the 1960s the growing social and political ambitions to provide decent housing tempted planners to abandon any sense of caution, and resulted in cities and towns engulfed in a tide of concrete, prefabrication, tower blocks and dwelling "units". Many mistakes were made; architects appeared to be unaware of their own limitations in the field of urban and community design, particularly as change was on a scale of development never attempted before in the cities of Britain.

The mistakes were often recognised too late, condemning residents to a life of misery in high-rise ghettos. Eventually the tide turned, and many of the largest of these developments have now been demolished, un-mourned by their residents, who could not wait to abandon areas such as Hulme in Manchester, where astronomic heating bills, discomfort and exhausting access routes were coupled with very high levels of crime, poor local facilities and services and an almost complete lack of a sense of community. (See Chapter 8 – Health.)

From such ruins arose the "Community Architecture" movement[1] among others, which has provided new techniques and methods to understand the communal aspirations of local populations and to record if and how they are being achieved.[2] Such methods are now widely used by architects, urban designers and planners to question communities and to inform their briefs and designs for new developments.

Many different bodies are now involved in developing and applying methods to evaluate and benchmark "community qualities", but this is not a straightforward activity. Who can be sure that the results are reliable indicators, when they are produced by a survey of public perception about an argument so variable and influenced by many external factors, including political opinions?

Global indicators

Indicators of the "health" of the global community must reflect the way in which peoples across the world are working together to create a sustainable future for all future generations. Therefore, indicators might include:

- numbers of countries that sign up to major international environmental treaties such as the United Nations Climate Change Convention (1992) or the Kyoto Protocol (1997)
- amount spent each year by each country on overseas development
- number of countries engaged in Fair Trade activities
- number of countries at war.

European indicators

Delegates to the European Conference on Sustainable Cities & Towns signed the Charter of European Cities & Towns Towards Sustainability in Aalborg, Denmark on 27 May 1994 (the Aalborg Charter).[3] Under this Charter, citizen satisfaction with the local community is one of ten sustainability indicators.

Key questions are:

- How satisfied, in general, are the citizens with the municipality, community or neighbourhood as a place to live and work?
- How satisfied are citizens with various features in the municipality, community or neighbourhood?
- How do citizens evaluate various features in the municipality, and which of these features are considered as the most important for their quality of life?

Aalborg-based surveys[4] measure overall levels of satisfaction, or link satisfaction to particular features of the municipality. For example:

Do you feel very satisfied, fairly dissatisfied, neither satisfied nor dissatisfied, fairly dissatisfied, very dissatisfied with:

- *quality/strength of social relationships in your local community?*
- *availability of formal/informal associations offering support, social opportunities and services?*
- *standards, availability, affordability of housing in your local community?*
- *employment opportunities in your local community?*

- *quality and amount of natural environment in your local community?*
- *quality of the built environment (streets, open spaces or the appearance/cleanliness of buildings) in your local community?*
- *level of health services in your local community?*
- *level of cultural, leisure, recreational facilities in your local community?*
- *standard of schools in your local community?*
- *level of public transport in your local community?*
- *opportunities to particulate in local planning and decision-making processes in your local community?*
- *level of personal safety in your local community?*

Such questions include a number of other issues and overlap strongly with the QOL indicators. In addition, an important part of any such survey is an open question at the end of the survey sheet where interviewees are asked to indicate other features of the community they consider significant. (Sociological survey techniques are discussed in more detail in Chapter 34.)

UK government indicators

Housing is seen as a key part of the UK government's wider drive to raise the quality of life for the less privileged in society through actions on increasing prosperity, reducing inequalities, providing more employment, better public services, better health, better education, tackling crime and anti-social behaviour, and much more.

These objectives are being carried forward by the Office of the Deputy Prime Minister (ODPM), which has placed these matters at the heart of its housing policies for local authorities. A major fund has been established to:

- improve housing and communities, especially in deprived areas
- implement a regional approach to housing policy
- provide more affordable homes, particularly for key workers
- support people who wish to move into home ownership
- refurbish empty properties.

The initiative includes: £2.8 billion to bring council homes up to a decent standard; £260 million to tackle homelessness; action to tackle bad landlords; and action to protect green belt and improve the local environment (parks and public spaces).

The ODPM's document *Sustainable Communities*[5] asks: What makes a sustainable community? It suggests that the key requirements of sustainable communities are:

- a flourishing local economy to provide jobs and wealth
- strong leadership to respond positively to change
- effective engagement and participation by local people, groups and businesses, especially in the planning, design and long-term stewardship of their community, and an active voluntary and community sector
- a safe and healthy local environment with well-designed public and green space
- sufficient size, scale and density, and the right layout to support basic amenities in the neighbourhood and minimise use of resources (including land)
- good public transport and other transport infrastructure, both within the community and linking it to urban, rural and regional centres
- buildings – both individually and collectively – that can meet different needs over time, and that minimise the use of resources
- a well-integrated mix of decent homes of different types and tenures to support a range of household sizes, ages and incomes
- good-quality local public services, including education and training opportunities, health care and community facilities, especially for leisure
- a diverse, vibrant and creative local culture, encouraging pride in the community and cohesion within it
- a "sense of place"
- the right links with the wider regional, national and international community.

There is no single group of indicators or targets for community, because conditions between regions vary so enormously. The indicators listed in Table 6.1 recognise that the feelings of well-being of people within communities are important elements of sustainability.[6]

Local authority indicators

A number of UK local authorities are now actively benchmarking their own performance and that of local politicians, and this includes work on "community" issues.[8]

Each local authority now has a statutory responsibility to put into action a plan to strengthen its own local community, and in order to measure how well the communities are going the Audit Commission has developed a range of 29 performance indicators.[9] These generally explore:

Table 6.1 A selection of themes concerned with sustainable communities; indicators are in parentheses

THEME	ISSUE/OBJECTIVE *(KEY INDICATOR)*
Promoting economic vitality and employment	Improve economic performance and enhance regional competitiveness *(regional variations in GDP)*
	Close the gap between the poorest communities and the rest *(index of local deprivation)*
	Local business diversity *(new business start-ups and failures)*
	Reduce disproportionate unemployment among ethnic minorities *(ethnic minority unemployment)*
Better health for all	Improve the health of the population overall *(expected years of healthy life)*
	Deliver key health targets *(death rates for heart disease and strokes, cancer, accidents etc)*
	Environmental factors affecting health *(respiratory illness)*
	Access to effective healthcare, based on patients' needs, and not on where they live or their ability to pay *(hospital waiting lists)*
Less travel, better access	Reduce the need to travel, improve choice in transport and improve access to education, jobs, leisure and services *(road traffic, passenger travel by mode, average journey length by purpose etc)*
	Break the link between rising prosperity and increased travel *(distance travelled relative to income)*
Access to services	Improve access to services *(access for urban and rural services; access for people with disabilities)*
Access to housing	Reduce the proportion of unfit housing stock *(homes judged unfit to live in)*
	Ensure that everyone has the opportunity of a decent home *(temporary accommodation/rough sleepers)*
	Improve significantly the energy efficiency of all residential accommodation *(fuel poverty)*
Better planning and design	Re-use previously developed land, in order to protect the countryside and encourage urban regeneration *(new homes built on previously developed land)*
	Bring empty homes back into use and convert buildings to new uses *(vacant land and properties and derelict land)*
	Shopping and other key town centre uses should, wherever possible, be located within existing centres *(retail floor space in town centres and out of town)*
	Ensure that development takes account of history, and look for opportunities to conserve local heritage *(buildings of Grade I and II* at risk of decay)*
Local environmental quality	Attractive streets and buildings, with low levels of traffic, noise and pollution, and green spaces *(quality of surroundings, access to local green space, noise levels etc)*

Source: *Quality of Life Counts*, DETR, London 1999. © Crown copyright

- the involvement of local people in decision-making
- participation of local citizens in community activities
- activities to build "community capacity" (i.e. strength)
- the extent of local democracy
- how well informed the community is
- accessibility of the local authority to its citizens
- community spirit (e.g. percentage of people who know their neighbours and have done them a favour!)
- satisfaction with the local area.

Leicester City Council measures its citizens' overall satisfaction with their neighbourhoods using local surveys.[10] For Leicester the following results were recorded in 2001:[11]

- Satisfaction with the neighbourhood as a place to live has declined over a long period with net satisfaction declining from 67 per cent in 1998 to 63 per cent in 2001, but still remains fairly high (77 per cent of respondents very or fairly satisfied).
- Satisfaction with arts and entertainments is 82 per cent compared with 72 per cent in 1998.
- Satisfaction with museums is 85 per cent compared with 84 per cent in 1998.
- Satisfaction with libraries is 81 per cent compared with 87 per cent in 1998. (The decrease can be explained by the proposed library closures in 2000, subsequently withdrawn.)
- Satisfaction with sports facilities is 62 per cent compared with 75 per cent in 1998. (The decrease can be explained by the closure of two central sports centres. A new sports centre is under development.)

Personal indicators

Thus far we have looked at "top-down" indicators – how institutions measure "community" issues. To these indicators, we should add indicators developed at the sharp end – by the communities themselves.

The Hockerton Housing Project has compiled a list of "bottom-up" indicators – issues of concern to people keen to build their own community in which they will feel that they, and the people around them, really do matter and can achieve a high QOL. We could almost define this as "eQOLity" – the idea that a person's well-being depends on the well-being of those around them; a fundamentally sustainable philosophy.

Hockerton Housing Project's indicators[12] include:

- a community to share resources (eg. child rearing, food production, comsumption)
- social interaction and fun
- mutual support
- a common philosophy – sharing ideas
- sharing knowledge/skills
- benefits of scale (strength in numbers/greater effectiveness/economy of scale)
- reduced environmental impact/saving resources
- security
- improved level of community responsibility and morality
- extended family
- sense of belonging
- personal and shared responsibility
- spiritual benefits
- a sense of place.

The disadvantages of close communities are also mentioned, such as:

- lack of personal space
- potential for strained relationships
- excessive dependence.

All of the indicators discussed in this chapter may be used to measure the health and effectiveness of local communities, but they are of little use as working tools for designers who want to build, or rebuild all or part of a community. For a textbook on how to create "inclusive" design, in which everyone is welcomed to take part, we need to turn to a designer like Christopher Day. As he points out, our current concern with community may be largely due to the fact that there are so many "non-communities" in our towns and cities, and skill is needed to reintegrate ordinary people back into their social surrounds. The process of "community design" can act as a powerful tool to achieve this.

"Of course, in a lot of places, people may live and work near each other, but these people aren't really communities. Neighbourhoods in modern times may have scant 'social glue'. Often their only layer of bond is proximity. People work, shop and holiday elsewhere. They don't work together or for each other; share childcare, hardships, resentments against employers or bus services; nor worship, culture, festivals or very much of anything else.

"Shaping the future together, however, is bond forming. When it involves

struggle against opposition (as when defending land from a new road) or against invisible, but witheringly potent forces like urban blight, it is especially so. While planning together can bond community, it also can drive it into bitterly opposing camps. Small-townism is rife – and not only in small towns. Common as this is, it's not inevitable. It can easily be avoided through the consensus approach."[13]

I recommend that anyone who is embarking on building, or changing their own communities, should read both of the books by Christopher Day that are mentioned in this chapter.

References

1 Wates N and Knevitt C (1987), *Community Architecture: How people are creating their own environment*, Penguin Books, London

2 Wates N (2000), *The community planning handbook*, Earthscan Books, London

3 Over 200 cities have signed the Aalborg Charter, and more are joining every year. Members of the "Sustainable Cities group" range from large cities such as Bristol, Birmingham, Oslo and Stockholm to medium-sized and smaller cities such as Oxford and Campolietto in Italy. Visit *www.sustainable-cities.org/aal_uk.html*

4 The sample should include representatives from the resident population over 16. It could also include tourists and commuters, but this data should be collected, and reported, separately. In large cities, between 0.25 per cent and 1.0 per cent of the population can be considered representative. If the sampling method relies on "reference families" rather than individuals, then a cross-section of family types should be surveyed forming at least 1 per cent of the population. But in both cases at least 1,000 interviews should be collected. For smaller communities then the total number of respondents will be less but the percentage of the population will be higher.

5 See ODPM (30 July 2003), *Creating sustainable communities; Making it happen* at *www.odpm.gov.uk/stellent/groups/odpm_communities/documents/sectionhomepage/odpm_communities_page.hcsp*

6 For more information on UK government sustainability targets, see DEFRA (2002), Building Sustainable Communities at *www.sustainable-development.gov.uk*

7 For the full list of indicators, see DETR (1999), Quality of life counts, DETR, London or visit *www.sustainable-development.gov.uk/sustainable/quality99/annexa.htm*

8 Key performance indicators for local authorities can be found at *www.local-pi-*

library.gov.uk/index.shtml

9 Visit *www.audit-commission.gov.uk/pis/quality-of-life-indicators.shtml*

10 The indicator is reported in the form of a "net value", i.e. the percentage of respondents that answer either "very satisfied" or "fairly satisfied", minus the percentage that answer either "very dissatisfied" or "fairly dissatisfied". Where a neither/nor answer is recorded it does not contribute to the net value calculation.

11 For a full report see: *www.leicester.gov.uk/departments/page.asp?pgid=3229*

12 Hockerton Housing Project (2001), *The sustainable community: A practical guide*, published by Hockerton Housing Project, Southwell, Notts. View extracts of the guide at *www.hockerton.demon.co.uk*

13 Day C (2003), *Consensus Design*, Architectural Press, Oxford, p 13

Further reading

Day C (2002), *Spirit and Place*, Architectural Press, Oxford

On-line resources

International Society for Quality of Life Studies: *www.cob.vt.edu/market/ isqols*
"Our Future; Our Choice" at: *www.europa.eu.int/comm/environment/index_en.htm*
Sustainable Measures of North Andover, USA: *www.sustainablemeasures.com*
Global Ecovillage Network: *http://gen.ecovillage.org*
UK government sites: *www.sustainable-development.gov.uk/ar2002/index. htm*
and *www.sustainable-development.gov.uk/uk_strategy/content. htm*

Planning policy guidance – related documents (see Appendix 1 for details)

1	2	3	4	5	6	7	8	9	10	11	12	13
x	x	x				x				x	x	

14	15	16	17	18	19	20	21	22	23	24	25
	x	x	x							x	x

Building Regulations – related Approved Documents (see Appendix 2 for details)

A	B	C	D	E	F	G	H	I	J	K	L1	L2	M	N
													x	

Human rights

Definition

The UN Convention on Human Rights[1] lists 29 Articles that describe human rights, from the right to life to the right to own property. The Human Rights Act 1998 brought the European Convention on Human Rights (ECHR) into English law. This Act has many implications for the planning system, but Article 8 (Right to Respect for Private and Family Life) is most significant. Under Article 8, everyone has the right to respect for their private and family life, their home and their correspondence, except in special circumstances e.g. in the interests of national security. Article 1 of the First Protocol of the ECHR[2] also gives every natural or legal person a right to peaceful enjoyment of their possessions, with exceptions.

Related indicators

Quality of life, Community, Health.

About this chapter

This chapter is based on text supplied by Michael Crofton Briggs, the Planning Services Business Manager of Oxford City Council. It presents a limited discussion of the implications that the Human Rights Act 1998 has on planning applications from the perspective of residents in local communities. It also explains that a key role of the planning system is to balance the demands for the provision of buildings against the principles of sustainable development. It focuses on Article 8 – the right to respect for privacy and private life, and explains how this right is "qualified" and, therefore, not absolute.

Background

The current planning system in England owes its origins to the post-war Town and Country Planning Act (1948). The legislators knew that planning would be, by its very nature, controversial.

The basis of the planning system is that private proposals must be considered against the wider public interests. This gives a mechanism by which competing interests and views can be assessed in a balanced, open and transparent way. The system includes specific means by which decisions can be scrutinised, most notably the ability for applicants to appeal to an independent planning inspectorate.

The role of planning officers

Every planning application report to a committee of elected members includes two paragraphs relating to the Human Rights Act 1998. These paragraphs explain that officers have considered the Act in reaching their recommendation. They will have considered the potential interference with the rights of the applicant on the one hand in relation to the rights of owners, or occupiers of surrounding properties, on the other. Their statements generally conclude that any interference with such rights is considered to be "proportionate".[3]

If a planning officer receives a letter of objection to a planning application from a neighbour, it is not unreasonable to expect the officer to infer that the author of the letter believes that the application, if permitted by the Council, will interfere with their rights under Article 8. But, in fact, whether Article 8 is relevant depends on the reasons expressed for the objection.

It is important to appreciate that the planning applicant has rights too, as does the public at large. Put simply this means that the Act requires all relevant interests to be balanced before a local authority makes a decision.

Often, council members and members of the public seek to employ the Human Rights Act to inform their decisions of planning matters, particularly as seen from the point of view of the resident. There are many cases where genuine concern exists that an area, long enjoyed, will now be changing. The question for planning officers is: "What weight is it reasonable for us to put on the expectations of such residents to go on enjoying their own home and surroundings?"

Qualified rights

Article 8 is "qualified". This means that it does not confer an absolute right for individuals, as some of the Articles do. It states that a public authority should not interfere with the exercise of this right:

"*except such as:*
- *is in accordance with the law, and*
- *is necessary in a democratic society in the interests of . . . the economic well-being of the country . . . or for the protection of the rights and freedoms of others.*"

Guidance on planning questions

The best source of up-to-date UK government guidance on the planning system is in *Planning Policy Guidance Note 1 (PPG1): General Policy and Principles*.[4] Its opening sentence recognises that planning is all about finding the best balance between competing demands.

It has always been a basic principle of the planning system that the presumption is in favour of development. Planning permission should be granted unless there are good reasons to refuse permission. Thus the onus is upon the planning authority to substantiate why permission should be refused; it is not beholden on the applicant to prove why permission should be granted.

There is one main exception to this, and that is in the Green Belt, where the presumption is reversed. This principle is best explained by reference to paragraph 40 of PPG1:

"The Government is committed to a plan-led system of development control. This is given statutory force by section 54A of the 1990 Act. Where an adopted or approved development plan contains relevant policies, section 54A requires that an application for planning permission, or an appeal, shall be determined in accordance with the plan, unless material considerations indicate otherwise. Conversely, applications which are not in accordance with the relevant policies in the plan should not be allowed unless material considerations justify granting a planning permission. Those deciding such planning applications or appeals should always take into account whether a proposed development would cause demonstrable harm to interests of acknowledged importance."

It should be mentioned that the adopted plan policies are not always categorical about whether a particular development is acceptable or not. Most of the policies consist of a series of criteria or tests against which an individual application must be assessed on its own merits, e.g. by assessing the degree to which the proposal is over-development or poorly designed. There may also be policies that, on an initial inspection, appear to conflict with each other as each seeks to achieve something different. So, again there is the need to make a balanced judgement, weighing up a number of competing factors.

PPG1 also devotes a section to the place of private interests in the planning system. Put simply, the guidance explains that the planning system does not exist to protect the private interests of one person against the activities of another. Paragraph 64 states:

"The basic question is not whether owners and occupiers of neighbouring

properties would experience financial or other loss from a particular development, but whether the proposal would unacceptably affect the amenities and the existing use of land and buildings which ought to be protected in the public interest."

The local plan

The "local plan" establishes what is in the public interest by providing a framework within which a whole range of competing public interests can be balanced. Creating such a balance is not easy and is often controversial, which is why the process includes rounds of consultation and a public inquiry.

Once the local plan is adopted by an authority, it carries a lot of weight because it represents an expression of what is in the overall public interest.

Housing issues

There have been recent changes in government policy, most notably introduced by Planning Policy Guidance Note 3 (PPG3) on housing.

Government policy now requires increased densities of development within urban areas. Such development is described as "sustainable" in that it is to be located alongside existing facilities and enables less reliance on the car for movement.

In Oxford, for example, higher densities of housing and lower car parking standards are needed to meet the considerable demands for housing. These demands flow from the way that local people are now choosing to live in ever smaller households, rather than any significant influx of new people. Therefore, in broad terms it is both government policy and in the public interest that a greater density of use is accommodated within existing urban areas.

In many areas greater densities are being achieved through small planning applications for the conversion or replacement of houses with flats, while larger applications on redevelopment sites are for higher densities of development that currently prevail in a local area. Understandably, this is being perceived as bringing too much change to a particular area and having an adverse impact on local residents who have lived there for many years.

The key question is whether this change infringes the Human Rights under Article 8 of individuals, especially those who have lived in the area for many years.

In a general sense, some interference with the perceived rights of local residents is necessary in a democratic society in the interests of the economic well-being of the country. After all, these developments are in accordance with the policies of the national government and Oxford's City Council – both of which are democratic institutions, elected by the people.

A balanced judgement has been made in the overall public interest, and this level of interference is acknowledged as permitted and proportionate by the specific qualification to the original Article 8.

For example, a planning officer's report on the redevelopment of the Oxford Bus Depot acknowledged that there would be noise and disturbance as a result of the new housing; but it also carefully identified the impact of a number of the proposed housing blocks on adjacent developments, and assessed whether there will be an adverse impact or if the new development will be overbearing. The report expressed the officer's view that reasonable privacy will be ensured. Local residents had also questioned parking implications, and the report considered the proposed levels of parking against local and national parking standards and against the local circumstances. In the officer's view the level of parking proposed was reasonable.

Everyday cases like this one represent deliberations that lie at the very heart of the planning process which considers private proposals against the wider public interests. The planning process and the Human Rights Act are both mechanisms by which competing interests and views, including those of sustainable development, are assessed in a balanced, open and transparent way.

References

1   Universal Declaration of Human Rights, signed by the General Assembly of the United Nations, 10 December 1948. See *www.un.org/overview/rights.html*

2   European Convention on Human Rights, *First Protocol* (Paris, 20 March 1952), Article 1. See *www.hri.org/docs/ECHR50.html*

3   The term "proportionate" is often used in the context of assessing whether there is an interference with a right conferred by the Act, and it refers to whether the interference with a right in the Act is no more than necessary when balancing all of the victim(s) and whether, on balance, it is fair and supported by good reasons.

4   *Planning Policy Guidance 1: General policy and principles*, Office of the Deputy Prime Minister, London, Download the document (odpm_plan_pdf_ 606895.pdf) from *www.odpm.gov.uk*

Planning policy guidance – related documents (see Appendix 1 for details)

1	2	3	4	5	6	7	8	9	10	11	12	13
x		x										

14	15	16	17	18	19	20	21	22	23	24	25	

Health

Background

The history of the human race is inextricably linked with the search for better homes. We are all well aware of the power that buildings have on our health and well-being. For centuries, the wealthy have endeavoured to improve their living conditions – the Roman invaders understood the benefits of "central heating" in a damp and miserable British climate; the Elizabethans began to link poor town planning and inadequate sewage with the spread of diseases such as bubonic plague and cholera. But it wasn't until the 19th Century that those in power began to make serious attempts to improve the lot of the poor.

By the end of the 19th Century much of the effort to improve the lot of working families was centred on the provision of a healthier environment in the cities, and concentrated on the installation of proper sewage and freshwater systems to alleviate the appalling conditions in cities summed up, for example, in an 1889 map of Manchester's "Nests of fatal diarrhoea".[1]

The visionary movements of the 20th Century – the social housing schemes and garden suburb movements – achieved much to improve health. Nevertheless, it is extraordinary to learn that, in the 21st Century, "fuel poverty" is still a major cause of ill health and death in the UK.

The ready availability of clean drinking water and sophisticated sewage systems was not a panacea for all our buildings-related health problems, however. We are only just beginning to understand the health impacts that our "modern" way of life can have. While our ancestors lived amid smog, coal dust, and toxins such as lead in paints, we are now battling against the effects of asbestos, exhaust fumes, nylon carpet fibres, poor ventilation and the constant "background" hum of computers.

To make matters worse, we are also facing an era of climate change, where changing weather patterns – more flooding, wetter winters and hotter summers – will have a very significant effect on the safety and comfort of our buildings.

The "health" of a building is often given scant consideration by clients, planners, designers and even the general public, but this is an issue that can no longer be ignored. In the 1980s "sick building syndrome" was added to a list of "recognised conditions" by the World Health Organization, and numerous studies (see, for example, the PROBE studies described in Chapter 39) have highlighted the links between productivity and the built environment, so the question of "health" is now becoming one of economics – "healthy" buildings will be "profitable" buildings.

Climate change will introduce three additional ways that buildings can affect health:

- direct impacts – a greater risk of death and injury from damage caused by storms, floods and drought
- indirect impacts – the increase of diseases that are exacerbated by changing weather conditions, e.g. respiratory diseases, hypothermia, or more frequent outbreaks of diseases related to climate events such as floods, such as typhoid and cholera
- migratory impacts – caused by the movement of sources of infection because of changes in weather conditions (warmer, wetter), e.g. malaria and trypanosomiasis (sleeping sickness).

Buildings-related illnesses

A number of diseases are specifically linked to buildings. Legionnaire's disease, for example, is caused by the bacteria *Legionella pneumophila,* which can build up in water-storage tanks. The UK Building Regulations make specific provision for measures to mitigate the risk of this disease (e.g. by setting minimum boiler temperatures to kill the bacteria). Others buildings-related diseases include "humidifier fever", asbestosis, carbon monoxide poisoning, and numerous allergies that are often related to the materials used in finishes (e.g. the volatile organic compounds described in Chapter 17). Mould growth in buildings – also linked to allergies and respiratory diseases – is also on the increase.[2]

Sick building syndrome

Sick building syndrome (SBS) is a condition in which the occupants of a building experience adverse health effects, ranging from mild to acute symptoms which seem to be linked to time spent in a building. SBS reduces occupant productivity and may also increase absenteeism. Symptoms include:

- headaches
- eye, nose and throat irritation
- a dry cough
- dry or itchy skin
- dizziness and nausea
- difficulty in concentrating
- fatigue
- sensitivity to odours
- skin rashes
- chills
- fevers
- muscle aches
- allergic reactions.

The complaints may be localised in a particular room or zone, or may be widespread throughout the building.

One significant factor in the rise of SBS over the last two decades is the increased use of air-conditioning systems.[3] These systems can harbour potentially killer chemicals, bugs such as Legionella, moulds and particulates that are released back into the ducts from the filter, particularly when the weather changes, for instance when it becomes warmer and wetter because of a warm front.[4] In fact, the dirty filters, ducts and plant of air-conditioning systems often introduce air that is dirtier than if you simply opened the window, even in the city![5]

Many internal air-conditioning ducts are seldom cleaned, but to make matters worse they are often impossible to get at, and there is the chance that toxic fumes can be emitted from the plant, seals and ductwork itself. This already dirty duct air is then mixed with a cocktail of volatile organic compounds (VOCs), formaldehydes, moulds, fungi, dust mites and potentially toxic cleaning materials already inside rooms – which all adds up to ideal conditions to create SBS. This may explain why many more people in air-conditioned buildings succumb to SBS.[6] Air-conditioning and ventilation systems that incorporate filters and inaccessible duct runs should be avoided at all costs, and of course furnishings and finishes in buildings should be made of natural materials where possible.

SBS has also been linked with chemical contaminants from indoor sources such as adhesives, upholstery, carpeting, photocopying machines, manufactured wood products such as medium-density fibreboard (MDF), cleaning agents and pesticides, pollen, bacteria, viruses, and moulds.

Legionnaires' disease is not one of the sicknesses associated with SBS.[7] (This is logical, because little is known about the causes of SBS, and we certainly do know what causes Legionnaires' disease.)

Figure 8.1 Total number of UK households in fuel poverty

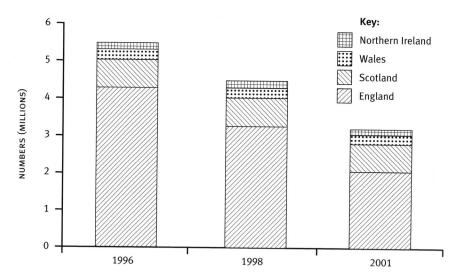

Note: full details of the methodology used to calculate this data can be found in "Linkages between outdoor and indoor air quality issues: pollutants and research problems crossing the threshold" in Proceedings of the 9th International Conference on Indoor Air Quality and Climate, J Mawdely, Vol 1 (2002), pp 12–13

Source: from *'Fuel Poverty Monitoring – Indicators'* at www.dti.gov.uk © Crown copyright

Fuel poverty

The UK government's definition of fuel poverty is:

"[a household]...that cannot afford to keep adequately warm at reasonable cost. The most widely accepted definition of a fuel poor household is one that needs to spend more than 10% of its income on all fuel use and to heat its home to an adequate standard of warmth (generally defined as 21°C in the living room and 18°C in the other occupied rooms)."[8]

The sheer number of households – millions – that are exposed to poor housing conditions and resulting ill-health is surprising, as Figure 8.1 shows. The most recent data (see Figure 8.2) suggests that around 40% of UK dwellings still do not meet the minimum heating regime standard.

Fuel poverty is, of course, not just about the ability to pay to heat a dwelling to a comfortable level. There are obvious health implications if vulnerable people (the elderly, young children, the sick) live in cold buildings during the winter; prolonged exposure to near-freezing temperatures puts an added strain on weak hearts, for instance. But inadequate heating has a long-term effect on the health of the building too, which, in turn, can cause chronic conditions such as asthma, bronchitis and allergies in its occupants.

Figure 8.2 Percentage of households in England that meet the standard and minimum heating regimes

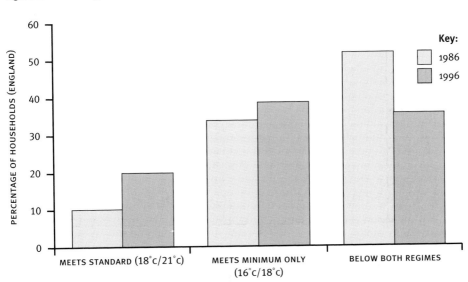

Note: full details of the methodology used to calculate this data can be found at (4).

Source: from *'Fuel Poverty Monitoring – Indicators'* at www.dti.gov.uk © Crown copyright

Moisture generated by the everyday activities of occupants – breathing, cooking, washing – always travels around buildings and will condense on cold surfaces such as corners of rooms, behind furniture, or around windows. The condensation seeps into the wallpaper or plastered surfaces of the building fabric and is an ideal breeding-ground for mould. Mould is not only unsightly, it is directly linked with respiratory infections.

In homes where people are worried that they can't afford to pay their fuel bills, there is a tendency to heat only one or two rooms adequately, and to keep doors and windows tightly closed to avoid losing the expensive warmth. As soon as someone opens a door, however, the warm air escapes into a cold, frequently damp environment, and condensation often results.

Recent "health by postcode" studies have shown that hospital visits can be linked to housing types and areas, demonstrating the impacts of house design on human well-being.[9]

Global indicators

In the 2002 major report by the World Health Organization (WHO),[10] the top 10 health risk factors to the world's population were listed (from 1 to 10) as:

- underweight
- unsafe sex
- high blood pressure
- tobacco consumption
- alcohol consumption
- unsafe water
- sanitation and hygiene
- iron deficiency
- indoor smoke from solid fuel fires
- high cholesterol.

It shows that the problems of the developing nations in not having enough to eat are matched by many in the world suffering health problems from eating too much. Again, the mechanisms for introducing "eQOLity" for all are obviously missing (see Chapters 5 and 6). Collectively, we should look again at the indicators for our global community.

UK government indicators

Health, as it relates to sustainable development and to buildings, is covered by several government departments.

In the UK Sustainable Development Indicators from the Department of the Environment and Rural Affairs (DEFRA), indicator number 6 is health.[11]

The objective for this indicator is to "improve the health of the population overall" and it is measured in "expected years of healthy life". In other words, the indicator makes a distinction between "life" and "healthy/active life". Data gathered for the "healthy life" indicator is based on people's assessment of their own general health – information that correlates with other separate measures of health and is a good predictor of mortality.

The indicator says that improving people's health, especially the health of the worst-off in society, is a key sustainability objective, and that men and women in unskilled occupations generally have lower total life expectancy than those in professional occupations.

DEFRA states that:

"Between 1981 and 1999 average life expectancy in Great Britain increased from 70.9 to 75.1 years for men and from 76.8 to 80.0 years for women. Over the same period healthy life expectancy increased from 64.4 to 66.6 years for men and from 66.7 to 68.9 for women. Between 1995 and 1999 healthy life expectancy increased only slightly from 66.4 years to 66.6 for men and from 68.7 years to 68.9 for women." [11]

The Department of Health publishes statistical data about the nation's health, including housing-related factors;[12] while it is the responsibility of the Department of Trade and Industry to publish indicators relating to fuel poverty,[13] including "excess winter deaths", which can be linked to inadequate heating.

Local authority indicators

The various national indicators are interpreted by local authorities in relation to their own aims and strategies to improve the health of a local population. Most publish details on their websites. Here are two contrasting examples.

Suffolk County Council, a local authority that has been awarded "beacon status" for its work on health strategies, has developed and implemented an action plan[14] that covers the following:

- reducing accidents
- improving community safety
- tackling smoking, promoting exercise and diet
- reducing teenage pregnancy
- helping to reduce suicide.

These actions have performance indicators and link the authority's "Policy and performance plan" to its "Health improvement programme". Examples of key actions include training early years staff in children's diet and exercise, investigating underage sales of cigarettes, supporting victims of racial harassment, reducing the number of fires, and engineering schemes to reduce road accidents.

Devon County Council, on the other hand, has chosen a different range of indicators based on their policy statement that:

"A sustainable community would be one in which health is protected by the creation of safe, clean and pleasant environments and of services which emphasise prevention of illness as well as care for the sick."[15]

Devon's indicators are:

- deaths from suicide per 1,000 population
- deaths from accidents per 1,000 population in persons aged 65 and over
- deaths from all cancers per 1,000 population in persons aged under 75
- deaths from all circulatory diseases per 1,000 population in persons under 75.

Building-level indicators

The US Environmental Protection Agency's fact sheet on SBS[16] reports that there have been concerns about indoor air quality since at least 1984, when a World Health Organization committee report suggested that up to 30 per cent of new and remodelled buildings worldwide may be the subject of excessive complaints related to indoor air quality.

Often indoor air quality problems are temporary, but some buildings have long-term problems. These can arise when a building is operated or maintained in a manner that is inconsistent with its original design or recommended operating procedures. Sometimes indoor air problems are a result of poor building design, or of occupant activities such as drying wet clothes in the house.

How do you know if the building you occupy has SBS?

Any building in which occupants experience acute health and comfort effects that appear to be linked to time spent in a building, but not to a specific illness or cause, may have SBS. The complaints may be localised in a particular room or zone, or may be widespread throughout the building. Indicators of SBS include:

- Building occupant complaints of symptoms associated with acute discomfort e.g. headache; eye, nose, or throat irritation; dry cough; dry or itchy skin; dizziness and nausea; difficulty in concentrating; fatigue; and

sensitivity to odours.
- The cause of the symptoms is not known.
- Most of the complainants report relief soon after leaving the building.

In contrast, the term "building-related illness" (BRI) is used when symptoms of diagnosable illness are identified and can be attributed directly to airborne building contaminants, such as SARS or Legionnaires' disease. Indicators of BRI include:

- Building occupants complain of symptoms such as: cough; chest tightness; fever, chills; and muscle aches.
- The symptoms can be clinically defined and have clearly identifiable causes.
- Complainants may require prolonged recovery times after leaving the building.

In the case of BRI it would be wise to see a doctor. In the case of SBS you need a "building doctor" who can identify where the problem lies: dirty ducts and filters; toxic room finishes; an outbreak of mould; poor ventilation or levels of room dirt or infestations. A good local first port of call would be to contact the local authority's environmental health department.

There is a simple design-driven solution to SBS: choose well-insulated, shallow plan, well-daylit, naturally ventilated buildings with good opening windows and natural finishes to the internal surfaces; and steer clear of the over-glazed or under-glazed, highly serviced buildings with windows that can't be opened. The latter are much more likely to lead to health problems than the good old-fashioned British buildings (providing they meet the higher 21st Century standards, of course).

References

1   The 1889 map of Manchester can still be viewed in the city's Central Library.
2   Roaf S, Fuentes M and Thomas S (2003), *Ecohouse 2: A design guide*, Architectural Press, Oxford, pp 155–159
3   Raw GJ (1992), *Sick Building Syndrome; A review of the evidence on causes and solutions*, HSE Books, London
4   Mauderly J (2002), "Linkages between outdoor and indoor air quality issues: pollutants and research problems crossing the threshold" in: *Proceedings of the 9th International Conference on Indoor Air Quality and Climate*, Monterey, vol. 1, pp 12–13
5   Clausen G, Olm O and Fanger PO (2002), The impact of air pollution from used ventilation filters on human comfort and health, ibid., pp 338–343
6   Bjorkroth M, Asikainen V, Seppanen O and Sateri J (2002), "Cleanliness crite-

ria and test procedures for cleanliness labelling of HVAC components", ibid., pp 670–674

7 Information on how to reduce SBS can be found at *http://www.nsc.org/ ehc/indoor/sbs.htm* and *www.hse.gov.uk/hthdir/noframes/hdsbs.htm*. See also HSE (1995), *How to Deal with Sick Building Syndrome. Guidance for employers, building owners and building managers*, HSE Books, London See *www.dti.gov.uk/energy/consumers/fuel_poverty/index.shtml*

9 Rudge J and Nicol F (2000), *Cutting the Cost of Cold,* E&FN Spon, London

10 WHO (2002), *World Health Report 2002: Reducing risks, promoting healthy life,* World Health Organization, Geneva

11 See *www.sustainable-development.gov.uk/indicators/headline/index.htm*

12 See the Health Survey for England published on-line by the Department of Health at *http://www.doh.gov.uk/public*

13 See *www.dti.gov.uk/energy/consumers/fuel_poverty/monitoringindicators. shtml*

14 See *www.suffolkcc.gov.uk/policy/Key_Policies_and_Strategies/Health_ Strategy.html*, where you can download the document *Health strategy 2001* published by Suffolk County Council – Policy in June 2001.

15 See *http://www.devon.gov.uk/sustain/health/home.html*

16 US EPA (1991), *Indoor Air Facts No 4 (revised): Sick Building Syndrome (SBS),* US Environmental Protection Agency. View the factsheet at *http://www.epa .gov/iaq/pubs/sbs.html*

Further reading

Crowther D (1994), Health considerations in buildings, PhD thesis, Martin Centre, Department of Architecture, University of Cambridge

For information on fuel poverty studies, see *Predicting Fuel Poverty at the Local Level (2003)*, Final Report on the Development of the Fuel Poverty Indicator by William Baker and Graham Starling, CSE, and David Gordon, University of Bristol; and *Rural Fuel Poverty: Defining a Research Agenda* (2002), prepared by CSE for Eaga Charitable Trust. Download these reports from *http://www.cse.org.uk/ cgi- bin/publications.cgi?publications*

Planning policy guidance – related documents (see Appendix 1 for details)

1	2	3	4	5	6	7	8	9	10	11	12	13
		x	x	x	x						x	x

14	15	16	17	18	19	20	21	22	23	24	25

Building Regulations – related Approved Documents (see Appendix 2 for details)

A	B	C	D	E	F	G	H	I	J	K	L1	L2	M	N
		x	x		x	x	x		x	x	x	x		

Thermal comfort

Definition

In research terms, "thermal comfort" is the study of the relationship between a person's sensation of warmth or cold and the thermal conditions that create the sensation (i.e. the ambient temperature). In layman's terms, "thermal comfort" is a feeling that we usually notice more by its absence; we are much more likely to notice "thermal discomfort" i.e. feeling too hot or too cold.

Related indicators

Quality of life; Health; Climate change; Energy.

Related solutions

The building envelope.

Related tools

Climate data tools; Sociological survey techniques; Post-occupancy evaluation.

About this chapter

This chapter is based on text supplied by Professor Fergus Nicol, a lecturer at Oxford Brookes University, and the co-creator (with Professor Michael Humphreys) of the "adaptive model" of thermal comfort.

Building design is not a precise science; buildings operate in the "real world". No matter how sophisticated the management systems that designers incorporate, there will always be an element of unpredictability caused by "external" forces – the weather, the surroundings and the occupants. Designers can only create a truly low-energy building if they understand and allow for the behaviour of occupants.

This chapter gives an overview of thermal comfort as it relates to building design. It describes the various methods of predicting comfort temperatures, and explains the inherent flaws in the acceptable models. It also discusses the implications of these methods for designers of naturally ventilated buildings.

Background

Traditionally, builders used knowledge passed from generation to generation to ensure that their buildings could modify the impact of a hostile outdoor environment. For example, they understood that thermal mass could successfully moderate indoor temperatures across the seasons. However, people's expectations of their buildings were significantly lower than they are today. Inhabitants of northern regions accepted the need to shroud their beds in drapery to reduce draughts, or to wear many layers of clothing in winter; while those in the south accepted that the best way to deal with the heat of the day was to take off their clothes and have a siesta.

In our post-industrial society, people typically accept unnatural working patterns, have become accustomed to more sedentary lifestyles, and have come to expect buildings themselves to regulate indoor temperatures, largely through the power of machines. People have increasingly abandoned their ability to modify indoor climates, and fail to take advantage of "adaptive opportunities" (i.e. change their working practices or clothing).

Personal comfort has always been related to the occupants' ability to control their conditions, but today "control" is typically interpreted as having air-conditioning, and the concept of "thermal comfort" is a product of a relatively new phenomenon – the heating, ventilation and air-conditioning (HVAC) industry.

Designing for comfort and efficiency

In Europe approximately one quarter of all energy consumed is used for heating or, increasingly, cooling buildings: i.e. to provide thermal comfort for the occupants. There are three essential mechanisms by which energy can be saved:

- Construct naturally ventilated (NV) buildings, which typically use less than half the energy consumed by air-conditioned buildings. However, it is important to note that comfort in an NV building can only be achieved if (i) the conditions for comfort are properly specified and (ii) the building is correctly designed to deliver those conditions. (Avoiding deep plan buildings is a good way to start a low-energy design.)
- Where air-conditioning is used, we should encourage the use of variable indoor set-point temperatures. This can typically save about 20 per cent of the energy used for heating and cooling. Again, it is essential that designers carefully specify the set-point temperature and its rate of change with outdoor conditions.
- Design for occupant control – designers should be aware that, if occupants

are uncomfortable, they will take action to restore their comfort. Such actions can save energy (for instance opening a window to achieve comfort rather than resorting to air-conditioning) but they can also increase energy use (for instance the opening of a window in an over-heated building).

Clearly, controlling comfort is no longer the exclusive responsibility of "building services engineers". The overall form of the building, its orientation, fenestration, structure and materials play an important part in achieving a comfortable indoor environment, so successful, comfortable buildings are most likely to be created by multidisciplinary design teams, where building services are considered from the outset.

Buildings services engineers need to specify conditions that people will find comfortable, in terms of temperature, humidity and air movement. They generally do this in two ways:

- by scientific analysis of the heat exchanges between the body and the environment
- by using surveys of comfort in the field and relating this to the physical environment using statistical analysis.

The science of comfort

The starting point for scientists studying "comfort" was to understand the physical process of heat exchange between the body and the environment. However, it soon became apparent that there are many other factors at play, so they developed indices to predict "thermal sensation" based on the known physical variables plus two "personal" variables such as clothing insulation and metabolic rate. The best known of these is the "predicted mean vote" (PMV) index,[1] a methodology which is the basis of most international standards for indoor comfort conditions (e.g. ISO 7730[2]).

However, there is a real problem with the PMV index approach. Increasingly, researchers are recognising that the conditions predicted as being comfortable using the PMV index are, in many cases, different from those found to be comfortable in user surveys of thermal comfort. This is particularly so in buildings where indoor conditions are variable, as is likely to be the case in naturally ventilated buildings (see Figure 9.1).

This also has the effect that conditions which really are comfortable will be predicted to be uncomfortable. The PMV index also has an underlying assumption that constant conditions will be more comfortable than variable conditions.

The inadequacies of the PMV index method mean that existing standards tend to encourage:

Figure 9.1 The 'comfort temperature' (vertical axis) predicted using the PMV heat balance formula (solid line) compared with comfort temperatures reported by subjects during field surveys

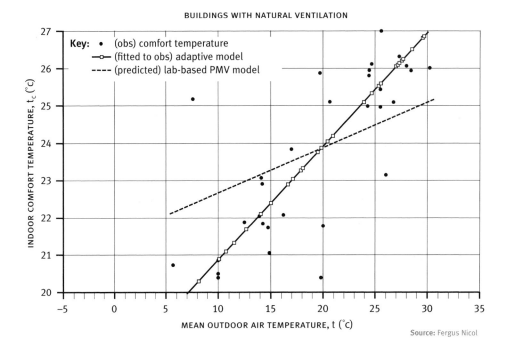

Source: Fergus Nicol

- the use of air-conditioning in circumstances where it may not be necessary
- where air-conditioning is necessary the notion that a narrow range of temperatures is superior to a wider range.

Both these consequences encourage the use of high-energy solutions and, as is shown in Chapter 39 (Post-occupancy evaluation), many high-end prestige buildings often suffer from poor levels of occupant satisfaction.

To overcome the inherent problems of the PMV index, Humphreys and Nicol have developed the "adaptive approach" to thermal comfort.[3]

Understanding occupants' behaviour

Building occupants will either:

- change themselves to suit the conditions in the building (e.g. by adjusting clothing or activity) – the cultural development of appropriate clothing in different climates is an important factor here – or
- change conditions in the building to suit their needs (by opening windows, turning on fans or heaters or closing blinds).

These behaviour patterns need to be taken into account when designing comfort control systems for buildings.

The controls should be:

- effective (i.e. work in the way expected of them)
- appropriate to the occupants' needs
- free from constraints (e.g. outside noise constraining window opening).

Glossary – common terms used in the study of thermal comfort

Adaptive model (adaptive approach): The study of thermal comfort which starts from the observation that there are a range of actions that people can take to achieve thermal comfort, and that discomfort is caused by constraints imposed on the range of actions by social, physical or other factors.

Adaptive processes: The range of actions that people take to achieve thermal comfort.

Air-conditioning: Though strictly defined as control over the internal environment of a building by means of controlling the thermal characteristics of the air supplied to it by the ventilation system, air-conditioning is usually taken to mean "cooling".

ASHRAE scale: A set of seven (or nine) descriptors of subjective response from (Very) Hot to (Very) Cold.

ASHRAE Standard 55: A temperature standard proposed by the American Society of Heating, Refrigeration and Air-conditioning Engineers based on the Gagge's Standard Effective Temperature.

Bedford scale: A set of seven descriptors of subjective response from Much Too Warm to Much Too Cool, differing from the ASHRAE scale in defining the central three categories as Comfortable.

Climate chamber: A laboratory in which the environmental conditions can be changed by the experimenter; widely used to investigate the effects of the thermal environment on subjects.

Clothing insulation: The effective insulation of clothing worn characterised as a single layer covering the whole body surface; measured in clo units (= $0.155 \text{ m}^2/\text{W}$)

Comfort temperature (neutral temperature): The temperature (or environment) judged by a population to be neutral on the ASHRAE scale, or Comfortable, Neither Warm Nor Cool on the Bedford scale: assumed by most workers in the field to be the desired temperature.

Comfort vote: The subjective response given by a subject on a comfort scale

---

such as the ASHRAE or Bedford scales.

Comfort zone: The range of temperature within which a subject will feel comfortable, though not necessarily neutral.

Constraints: Factors in the physical or social environment which prevent people from taking actions to achieve thermal comfort.

Descriptive scale: A subjective scale in which the subject is asked to choose between a given list of descriptions in casting a comfort vote.

Environmental controls: Means by which the physical environment can be controlled: these may be mechanical, e.g. heating or cooling systems, fans etc, or passive, such as openable windows, blinds, etc.

Environmental variables (thermal environment): Thermal characteristics of the environment; generally the air temperature (T_a), the radiant temperature (T_r), the water vapour pressure (P_a) (or humidity) and the air velocity (V_a).

Free-running building: A building which is not being mechanically heated or cooled.

Heat balance model (of thermal comfort): A model of human thermal response based on the assumption that a necessary condition for thermal comfort is a balance between the metabolic heat production and the heat loss from the body (generally an analytical model).

Metabolic rate: The rate of heat production by the body when engaged in various tasks, often defined in terms of the resting metabolism (mets).

Micro-climate: The climate in the immediate vicinity of a building.

Preference vote: The response by a subject as to their preference at the time of asking; this may be a preference for a warmer or cooler environment, or for a particular response on a comfort scale.

Predicted mean vote: The average comfort vote predicted by a theoretical index for a group of subjects when subjected to a specified set of environmental conditions taking account of their clothing and metabolic rate.

Predicted percentage dissatisfied: The percentage of subject population who will be dissatisfied (uncomfortable) in a given environment as predicted by a theoretical index.

Steady-state model (of thermal comfort): A theoretical model of thermal response based on climate chamber measurements in conditions which are held constant in time.

Subjective response: The sensation caused by a physical stimulus (generally a comfort vote).

Survey (comfort survey, field survey): An experimental investigation of subjective responses of a group of subjects in the field, generally assumed to be undertaken in such a way as to disrupt the normal pattern of the subjects' lives as little as possible, and to leave subjects to decide their own dress and activity, use of environmental controls and so on.

Temperature standards: Recommended values for temperature (and other environmental parameters) in buildings or rooms; values generally defined by the expected use of the room.

Thermal comfort: The study of the relationship between our thermal sensation and the stimulus in the form of the thermal environment in conditions of moderate heat stress (generally taken to include thermal discomfort).

Thermal experience: The different thermal environments experienced by a subject, taking account of the order in which they occurred.

Thermal performance: The characteristic way in which a building reacts to the thermal climate.

Thermo-regulation: The various physiological means by which the core temperature is regulated: vasodilation/constriction, sweating and shivering.

Building-level indicators

Indicators for thermal comfort consistent with energy efficiency are:

- the availability of an appropriate method for relating comfort and the indoor environment
- the fall in the number of buildings which need air-conditioning in order to remain comfortable.

There are no context-free indicators for indoor climates; the conditions which people will find comfortable are influenced by the climatic, cultural, social and economic circumstances in which they find themselves. This is because the thermal environment is not something "out there" which we experience passively, but is part of a complex interaction between people, climate and buildings.

Given the chance, people make the indoor environment suit them, but not always in circumstances of their own choosing. For example, in buildings where the indoor climate is controlled by heating or air-conditioning, the comfort temperature will depend on the climate, the purpose of the space, management policy (e.g. the need for a dress code) and the flexibility of the heating/cooling system. It is possible to suggest appropriate indoor temperatures for various types of building purposes,[4] but these will depend on the social and climatic context.

When the indoor climate is produced by a heating or cooling system, occupants

Figure 9.2 Comfort temperature indoors as a function of outdoor temperature

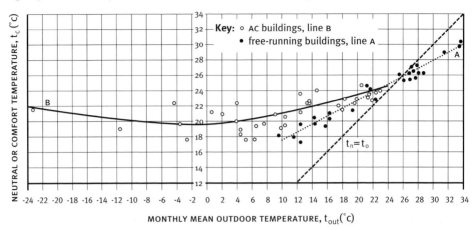

Source: "Outdoor temperatures and comfort indoors", Mike Humphreys, *Building Research and Practice* Vol 6, 1978

are often very critical of changes that are beyond their control. Tight control will be less important in a responsive system which occupants can change to suit their own requirements.

The comfort conditions in free-running buildings are quite different from those predicted using current methods (the PMV index, or "predicted percentage dissatisfied" (PPD) index).[5] Variable conditions may be acceptable or even advantageous where the variability is a result of conscious actions taken by occupants. It also means that in free-running buildings a range of temperature is possible without risking discomfort.

The comfort of occupants of free-running buildings depends on outdoor conditions (see Figure 9.2) according to the formula

$$t_c = 0.54t_o + 12.9$$

where t_c is the comfort temperature and t_o is the mean outdoor temperature.[6]

The value of the mean outdoor temperature, t_o, should reflect recent weather pattern as well as the current situation. The "running mean" of the outdoor temperature includes both. In early studies,[7] the monthly mean of the outdoor temperature was used because this was available from meteorological records world-wide. However, the comfort temperature can change more rapidly than is reflected by a monthly mean, and recent work[8] suggests that an exponentially weighted running mean is appropriate and easy to calculate from meteorological records (see Chapter 36, Climate data tools).

Predicting comfort temperature also allows us to predict a temperature above which people might begin to complain of overheating. This can be taken as 2°C above the comfort temperature suggested in the above equation. In many circumstances temperatures above this limit may be acceptable. An exceedance target could then be set as, say, a 10 per cent risk of exceeding this adaptive target during occupied hours.[9] However, we should note that a free-running building can be found too cool as well as too warm, so a simple answer is not available.

Some indicators are available from the work of thermal comfort researchers,[10] but they are generalised results that may not fit all circumstances. The only sure way to specify comfort conditions, or to ensure that comfort conditions are being provided, is to do a survey among your own particular population.[11]

References

1   Fanger PO (1970), *Thermal Comfort,* Danish Technical Press, Copenhagen

2   ISO 7730 (1994), *Moderate Thermal Environments: Determination of the PMV and PPD indices and specification of the conditions for thermal comfort,* International Organization for Standardization, Geneva

3   Humphreys MA and Nicol JF (1998), "Understanding the adaptive approach to thermal comfort" *ASHRAE Transactions* 104 (1), 991–1004

4   CIBSE (1999), *CIBSE Guide Volume A Part 1 Environmental criteria for design,* Chartered Institution of Building Services Engineers, London

5   Another problem with the PMV index and similar methods is that there is a tendency to categorise buildings into "free running" or "heated/cooled". Under this system many naturally ventilated buildings will fall into different categories at different times of year: for example, in the UK they may be free-running in summer but heated in winter.

6   See reference 3

7   Humphreys MA (1978), "Outdoor temperatures and comfort indoors", *Building Research and Practice*, 6 (2), 92–105

8   Nicol F and McCartney K (2001), *Final Report (Public) Smart Controls and Thermal Comfort (SCATs) Report to the European Commission of the Smart Controls and Thermal Comfort Project* (Contract JOE3-CT97-0066), Oxford Brookes University

9   In 1995, the UK government's Energy Efficiency Best Practice programme published *General Information Report 30: A performance specification for the energy efficient office of the future,* which gave specific performance requirements: "Internal environment (temperatures): not to exceed 28°C for more than 1% of working year; not to exceed 25°C for more than 5% of working year". See also Action Energy's *New Practice Case Study: The Environmental*

Building, Watford – feedback for designers and clients (not yet published), which describes the thermal comfort issues that arose when this specification was used.

10 deDear RJ and Brager GS (2002), "Thermal Comfort in naturally ventilated buildings: revisions to ASHRAE standard 55", *Energy and Buildings,* 34 (6), 549–561; and Nicol JF and Humphreys MA (2002), "Adaptive thermal comfort and sustainable thermal standards for buildings", *Energy and Buildings,* 34 (6), 563–572

11 Methodologies are suggested in: Nicol JF (1993), *Thermal Comfort: A handbook for field studies toward an adaptive model,* University of East London.

Building Regulations – related Approved Documents (see Appendix 2 for details)

A	B	C	D	E	F	G	H	I	J	K	L1	L2	M	N
											x	x		

Environmental indicators

Climate change

Definition

Climate refers to the average weather experienced in a region over a long period, typically 30 years. This includes not just temperature, but also wind and rainfall patterns. The climate of the Earth is not static, and has changed many times in the past in response to a variety of natural causes. The term "climate change" usually refers to the changes in climate that have been observed since the early 1900s. If the predictions of scientists from around the world are right, everyone, everywhere will be affected by the current pace of climate change, as we learn in other chapters of this book. To cope with these new demands, we must significantly improve the thermal performance of our buildings so that they will be cooler in summer, warmer in winter, use less energy and significantly reduce their impacts at every level.

Related indicators

Energy; Air pollution.

Related tools

Environmental impact assessment; Impact assessment in the UK – Ecopoints; BREEAM and Envest; Energy use in dwellings.

Background

Climate has always changed, and there have been several significant variations in global temperatures. It was only just over 10,000 years ago that the last Ice Age occurred, covering most of Europe with ice sheets. Then global temperatures were 3.5°C lower than today. From around AD 1400 to AD 1900 the 'Little Ice Age' occurred. Rivers froze regularly, and the ice-houses of Europe were filled each winter with pond and river ice. Global temperatures were only around 0.8°C lower than today, but now we rarely see ice on British ponds.

Observable changes in the global climate are caused by a combination of both natural and human actions. The Earth's climate varies naturally as a result of interactions between the ocean and the atmosphere, changes in the Earth's orbit, fluctuations in energy received from the sun, and volcanic eruptions. The main human influence on global climate is probably the burning of fossil fuels, which results in emissions of greenhouse gases such as carbon dioxide and methane. Changes in land use also result in a net annual emission of greenhouse gases. These gases act as a "blanket" over the Earth: they stop the Sun's heat from escaping from the atmosphere. Increasing concentrations of greenhouse gases in the atmosphere over the last 200 years have trapped more energy in the lower atmosphere, thereby altering the global climate. However, the picture is complicated by other pollutants from human activities, for example sulphurdioxide, which transforms into small particles (aerosols) that act to cool climate.

Buildings protect us against the climate. As *Homo sapiens* moved further from the equatorial regions to inhabit increasingly inhospitable climates so shelters, like clothes, had to offer ever greater protection against the differences in temperatures and extremes of wind and rain. The colder a region, the thicker the clothes humans must wear, the more insulation buildings must supply, and the more fuel is needed to keep people warm.

Small changes can make a large difference in the requirements for heating and cooling and the degree of shelter we demand from our buildings. The lesson for any aspect of building is: it's not how much warmer it gets that matters, but whether the temperature change crosses a threshold for performance – icehouses don't work if there is no ice.

By the end of the 20th Century, the widespread use of central heating and air-conditioning cushioned people from the climate. For around 100 years we have benefited from the miracle of oil and gas heating and cooling; and we have allowed artificial climate controls to dominate our lives to such a degree that we often no longer relate to the prevailing climate. But cheap comfort indoors is evaporating fast, for the following reasons:

- Fossil fuels are becoming scarce in relation to demand, so costs are rising.
- The total global populations is rising rapidly, increasing by almost 80 million people per year, about 10 times the average annual increment in the 19th Century. The world population has risen from 1.65 billion in 1900 to 6.08 billion in 2000.
- The per capita consumption of goods, services and energy is increasing significantly, and because there are more people, and their expectations are higher, we are depleting the world's resources more rapidly.

- "Modern" buildings, with their reliance on cheap fossil fuel, are poorly designed for the prevailing climate, leading to the excessive use of electrical equipment and energy to maintain comfort conditions, thus exacerbating problems of fossil fuel depletion and escalating fuel costs.

The burning of fossil fuels to power buildings is a main cause of climate change.

The energy efficiency of buildings first became an issue because of the dual concerns over how much oil remains that can be easily extracted and the political security of oil supplies. Concern dates back to the time when OPEC, the Organisation of Petroleum-Exporting Countries, began to limit their output of oil in the mid-1970s, driving up the price of a barrel of crude on the global market. But it was not until the 1980s that scientists generally alerted us to an even more urgent problem – the relationship between energy consumption and climate change.

At that time, the two key drivers of climate change were perceived to be:

- ozone-depleting gases
- greenhouse gases, particularly carbon dioxide (CO_2).

Ozone

Ozone is a molecule made of three oxygen atoms (O_3). Ozone in the upper levels of the Earth's atmosphere absorbs ultraviolet (UV) radiation from the sun's rays; without the ozone layer, land-based life could not have evolved. In 1985 a scientist with the British Antarctic Survey discovered a huge hole in this protective layer, and linked its presence with predictions made by US scientists in the 1970s that the release of man-made chemicals – in particular, chlorofluorocarbons (CFCs) – could cause such damage. The stunning images of the hole growing over the Antarctic stimulated unprecedented international meetings that culminated in the signing of the Montreal Protocol, which resulted in a ban on CFCs in 1996. Until the ban, CFCs were used as coolants in air-conditioners and refrigerators, or as aerosol propellants. A number of other substances, including halons used in fire extinguishers, were also covered by the ban.

Depletion of the ozone layer is now firmly linked with an increase in skin cancer cases in humans; it lowers production of phytoplankton, and thus affects other aquatic organisms; it can also influence the growth of terrestrial plants[1].

Over the next few years the concentration of ozone-depleting chemicals in the upper atmosphere is expected to reach a peak and then start to decline. The magnitude of the problem and the long life-expectancy of these chemicals means that it could take 50 years for the ozone layer to recover fully. Levels of ozone are now carefully monitored to assess whether recovery is taking place as expected, and to help verify compliance with the Montreal Protocol.

Carbon dioxide

There is strong scientific evidence that the increasing concentrations of green-house gases in the atmosphere over the last 200 years have had a direct and measurable effect on the global climate. Of all the greenhouse gases, carbon dioxide (CO_2) appears to be having the most significant impact on the climate; it is currently responsible for around two-thirds of the global warming effect. The atmospheric concentration of CO_2 has increased by 31 per cent since 1750 and has probably not been exceeded in the last 20 million years (see Figure 10.1).

Carbon dioxide is a by-product of the combustion of coal, oil and gas, and CO_2 levels have risen as a direct result of our ever-increasing need for energy since the Industrial Revolution (see Chapter 11).

Fossil fuels – coal, oil and gas – each contain different proportions of carbon and have different calorific (energy) values. This means that they each emit different amounts of CO_2 per unit of energy they produce when burnt. This is known as the "carbon emission factor", which is an important issue in the drive to cut CO_2 emissions. Calculations of CO_2 production need to correctly associate CO_2 production with each fuel used: this means taking into account emissions during the generation and distribution of fossil fuels, as well as those emitted at the point of use.

Figure 10.2 shows that the CO_2 emissions resulting from electricity consumption are much greater than those of other fuels; and that all the emissions per unit energy occur at the point of generation and none at the point of consumption. Electricity typically leads to two to three times more CO_2 emissions per delivered unit of energy than direct use of fossil fuels. This fact is a particularly important

Figure 10.1 Increasing concentration of carbon dioxide (CO_2) in the global atmosphere since 1870

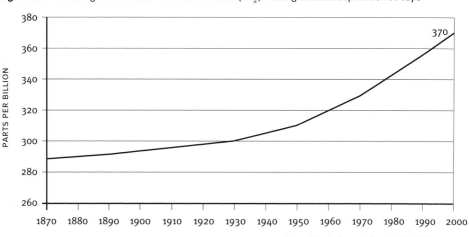

Source: Climate Change Information Kit, UNEP, 2001

Figure 10.2 Carbon dioxide emission factors for UK fuels (1994)

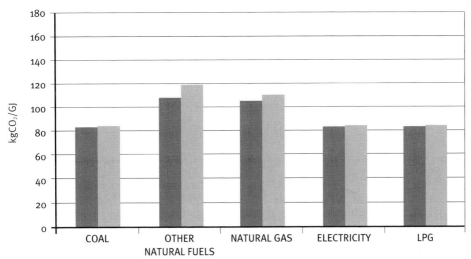

Source: *None domestic fact file*, Pout et al, BRE, 1998

when we begin to consider the energy use of buildings. Buildings use about two-thirds of the total electricity consumed in the UK and, when their fossil fuel consumption is added to that total, it turns out that buildings are responsible for about half of all the UK's carbon emissions.[2]

The issue of CO_2 emissions is now driving policy-making. Buildings are being targeted for major reductions in CO_2 emissions, and that means reductions in fossil fuel energy consumption, and an increase in the use of clean, non-carbon-emitting renewable energy sources.

The extent of the CO_2 problem was recognised by the UK Royal Commission on Environmental Pollution (RCEP). In 2000 the RCEP proposed that, because some human-induced climate change now seems inevitable, there is a real need to halt the rise in CO_2 concentrations to reduce the risks of catastrophic alterations to the climate. For the UK this would require a 60 per cent reduction of CO_2 emissions by 2050 and an 80 per cent reduction by 2100 (relative to 1997 levels) (Figure 10.3).[3]

Models of climate change

Many different organisations around the world are working on related projects to understand climate change, to predict future trends, and to develop impact mitigation strategies. The best known is the Intergovernmental Panel on Climate Change (IPCC), whose seminal studies have laid the groundwork for our understanding of the scale of the problem.[7]

A number of computer models have been developed to try to explain the recent

Concentration and convergence

The RCEP's CO_2 emission reduction targets, adopted by the UK government, are based on the "contraction and convergence principle" proposed by the Global Commons Institute (GCI). This principle states that every human is entitled to release into the atmosphere the same quantity of greenhouse gases.[4]

The current distribution of global carbon emissions is skewed between the developed and developing countries, so the principle of contraction and convergence ensures that, over time, each nation's emissions would shift towards a uniform per capita basis (convergence) and then begin to reduce (contraction).[5] The GCI's carbon dioxide emissions scenario (see Figure 10.3) is consistent with an outcome of carbon dioxide concentrations in the atmosphere of 450 ppm (parts per million) by the year 2100. This is a lower level of CO_2 in the atmosphere than the RCEP targets, which aims at 550 ppm. In the GCI scenario, an intermediate world target of 1 tonne of carbon per person is set for 2030 to aid contraction and convergence of countries. The final target is 0.2 tonnes of carbon per person, requiring a ten-fold decrease in the UK.[6]

Figure 10.3 GCI concentration and convergence

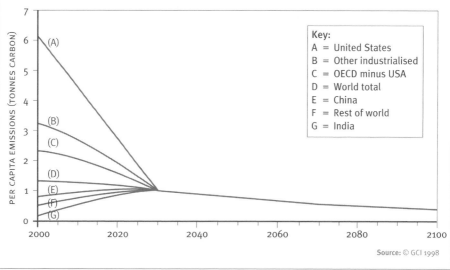

Source: © GCI 1998

changes in climate. Programs developed by the UK's Hadley Centre[8] simulate both past and future global climates from 1860 to 2000, and a range of future scenarios. Their models could only provide an adequate simulation of the course of global-average temperature over the entire period by adding both natural and human factors to the model (see Figure 10.4). This analysis is one of several

Figure 10.4 A good fit between observed and model-simulated global temperature is obtained only when both natural and human factors are included in the model simulation (Temperature change is relative to the 1880-1920 average)

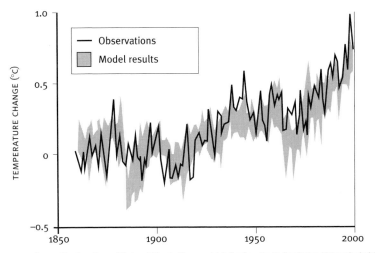

important pieces of evidence that point towards a substantial, and increasing, human influence on global climate.

The most useful index describing the state of the global climate is the average surface air temperature of the planet (see Figure 10.5). Estimates are compiled

Figure 10.5 The observed increase in global average surface air temperature anomalies, relative to the 1961-1990 average

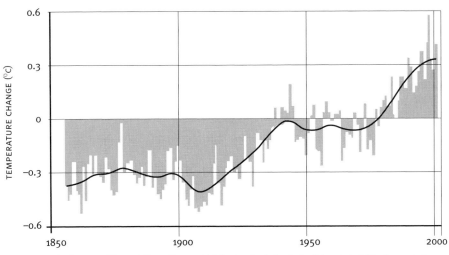

from millions of individual thermometer measurements taken around the world and dating back to 1860. The records show that global temperature has risen by about 0.6°C since the beginning of the 20th Century, with about 0.4°C of this warming occurring since the 1970s. 1998 was the warmest on record, and 2001 was the third warmest, but 2003 may well exceed all of these records. The 1990s were the warmest decade in the last 100 years, and it is likely that the last 100 years represented the warmest century in the last millennium.[9]

Other evidence for changes in the global climate include:

- an increase in night-time temperatures over many land areas at about twice the rate of day-time temperatures
- an increase in the length of the freeze-free season in many Northern Hemisphere mid-to-high latitude land areas
- more intense rainfall events over many Northern Hemisphere mid-to-high latitude land areas
- a near worldwide decrease in mountain glacier extent and ice mass
- a decrease in Northern Hemisphere sea-ice amounts and a substantial thinning of Arctic sea-ice in late summer.

Changes have also been observed in the climate of the UK, for which we have records extending back three and a half centuries. The 1990s were the warmest decade in central England since records began in the 1660s, and this warming of climate over land has been accompanied by warming of UK coastal waters.[10]

Analysis of other climate data has revealed the following changes in UK climate:

- The growing season for plants in central England has lengthened by about one month since 1900.
- Heatwaves have become more frequent, while there are now fewer frosts and winter cold spells.
- Winters over the last 200 years have become much wetter relative to summers throughout the UK.
- A larger proportion of winter precipitation in all regions now falls on heavy rainfall days than was the case 50 years ago.
- After adjusting for natural land movements, average sea level around the UK is now about 10cm higher than it was in 1900.

An enormous amount of work has been done by the UK Climate Impacts Programme (UKCIP), centred at the Hadley Centre and the Tyndall Centre for Climate Change Research at the University of East Anglia.[11] In particular, they have developed "climate change scenarios" for the UK. These present information on the possible changes in the UK climate over the 21st Century. The scenarios can be used to show future changes at a regional level, and provide an insight into potential changes in extreme weather events and sea level.

First published in April 2002, these scenarios present four different descriptions of how the world may develop in the decades to come.[12] They are based on four different emission scenarios from the IPCC: low emissions, medium-low emissions, medium-high emissions and high emissions. It is not possible to say which scenario is more likely, as this depends on the future choices made by society. Rather, the scenarios provide alternative views of the future, and they are particularly pertinent to the construction industry, which should already be creating buildings designed to deal with the likely changes.

Even under low emissions, the scenarios predict that by the 2080s the average annual temperature in the UK may rise by between 2 and 5°C. There will be greater warming in the south and east than in the north and west, and there may be greater warming in summer and autumn than in winter and spring. By the 2080s for the high emissions scenario, parts of the south-east may be up to 5°C warmer in summer.

Winters will become wetter and summers may become drier throughout the UK, and heavy winter precipitation will become more frequent.

The relative sea level will continue to rise around most of the UK's shoreline, although the rate of increase will depend on the natural vertical land movements in each region and on the scenario. By the 2080s, sea level may be between 2 cm below (low emissions) and 58 cm above (high emissions) the current level in western Scotland, but between 26 cm and 86 cm above the current level in south-east England, where the land mass is gradually sinking; and extreme sea levels will be experienced more frequently.

The implications of these predictions for the construction industry are discussed elsewhere in this book (see Chapters 14, 15, 21 and 22). However, the box (next page) gives two examples of the type of problem that must be addressed.

Our response to climate change

In the UK, the increasingly strict Building Regulations (Approved Document Part L1 and L2)[14] were introduced to attempt to respond to climate change. However, in the 1990s a move to have strong guidance to avoid any use of air-conditioning in buildings (except where essential e.g in laboratories or operating theatres) was dropped following heavy lobbying from industry. This was a grave mistake. Most excessive energy use in buildings is in air-conditioned offices – in this country air-conditioning is unnecessary in well-designed passive buildings.

Unfortunately the move to over-glazed "fashionable" modern buildings, spearheaded by some of our top design firms, has meant that air-conditioning is often

Heat islands

A built-up urban area is typically warmer than its suburban or rural surroundings, and studies around the world show that the air in the heart of large
cities can be as much as 10°C or more warmer that in the surrounding countryside. The actual fabric of the city – the cement and steel – absorbs and
stores not only the incoming radiation of the sun, but all the heat generated
by machines and people within the city. The difference between rural and
urban temperatures tends to be highest at night time when the open areas can
dissipate heat more rapidly than the monolithic mass of the city with its high
thermal capacity. Heat islands are very much affected by location, weather,
direction of winds and the weather history of a region.

Early surveys of London's heat island indicated that the peak usually lies
north-east of central London in Hackney and Islington, reflecting the density
of urban development, and the displacement of the heat island by prevailing
south-westerly winds. More recent monitoring has highlighted the mobility of
the peak in relation to hourly shifts in wind direction. The average nocturnal
heat island intensity for the period 1961 to 1990 was +1.8°C, ranging from
+10.0°C (on 14 January 1982) to –8.9°C (on 31 May 1970), with 5% of days
having an intensity of 5°C or more.[13]

As mean global temperatures rise, so the significance of the heat island
affect will increase. For example, if the maximum temperature rises to around
30–32°C and the heat island adds +3–5°C to this, summer conditions will be
even less comfortable, and people will clamour for the very air-conditioning
that is driving climate change in a vicious circle.

Groundwater

Groundwater levels are another of the factors that may be influenced by
climate change. In the Thames region groundwater is an essential source
of high-quality water, accounting for 40 per cent of public supply.
Groundwater discharges also contribute to the health of many rivers in the
upper catchment. Past abstractions have already resulted in a progressive
dewatering of the aquifer under London, and a fall in groundwater levels to
a minimum in the 1940s and 1950s. However, groundwater levels are currently rising at up to 2.5 m per year, threatening tunnels, buildings and
water sources in central London.

essential to keep spaces occupiable, not only on hot summer days, but simply whenever the sun is out.

At the moment there is a loophole in the UK in that planning permission is granted before the stage of performance-based assessment for the development proposals. If proper control is to be implemented then the performance of the building will have to be assessed at the stage when planning permission is given. The Town & Country Planning Association is already discussing a mandatory requirement for a "sustainability report" with every planning application. This does not necessarily mean that planners will have to become building performance experts, but they could have reports on performance either submitted with the proposal or supplied by the local building control officers, having seen the client's performance assessment, for larger projects.

Building designers should be concerned with the emissions of greenhouse gases from, or associated with, their buildings. But this is not just a question of CO_2 emissions; there are also emissions of methane, halogenated compounds and other potentially damaging gases. When preparing sustainability reports, care must be taken to ensure that the various emissions are put into their correct context. For example, as we have seen, electricity generates around four times the CO_2 per kWh compared with gas or oil, but even that must be qualified. Electricity's emissions depend on the "mix" at the power station, so CO_2 figures for electricity must always be quoted for a particular year.[15]

Global indicators

For every ecological niche, every species, every industry and every technology there will be a climate-related threshold that dictates whether it flourishes, perishes or merely survives. Again and again we hear of climate threats to the established order of the biosphere: the migration of Emperor penguins in the Antarctic; the failure of ski resorts without snow; and fish killed by warming water.

This book devotes a whole chapter to the impacts on biodiversity (see Chapter 12), but it is worth mentioning two examples here.

Rising sea temperatures associated with global warming are considered to be one of the leading causes of the destruction of about a quarter of the world's coral reefs. A 1000-page UN report[16] in 2001 warned that coral reefs in most regions could be wiped out in 30 to 50 years if sea temperatures reach such a point that the bleaching of the reefs becomes an annual event. Coral is a soft living organism – a combination of single-celled plant and animal tissues, which secrete a hard skeleton of calcium carbonate. Scientists say the increase in sea temperature obstructs the coral's production of natural sun-screen chemicals. This makes the coral more sensitive to light. This in turn leads the animal tissues to expel the single plant cells which give pigment to the coral. The coral then turns white (bleaches) and also starves because the plant cells provide it with its main source of food.[17]

An enormous amount of work has also been undertaken in the field of crop yields under the direction of people such as Martin Parry and Matthew Livermore of the Jackson Environment Institute, University of East Anglia. They suggest that, by the 2080s, climate change and CO_2 increases due to unmitigated emissions are estimated to increase cereal yields at high and mid-latitudes, such as Canada, China, Argentina and much of Europe. But at the same time cereal yields in Africa, the Middle East and, particularly, India are expected to decrease. The food system may be expected to accommodate such regional variations at the global level, with production, prices and the risk of hunger being relatively unaffected. However, some regions, particularly Africa, will be adversely affected, experiencing marked reductions in yield, decreases in production and increases in the risk of hunger. Reduction of emissions, leading to stabilisation of CO_2, appears to provide a way, in the short to medium term, of reducing the impacts of climate change on world food supply.[18]

The United Nations Framework Convention on Climate Change (UNFCCC) sets out targets for the return of greenhouse gas emissions to 1990 levels by 2000. The UK government states that it is on track to exceed its target of a cut in emissions to 12.5 per cent below 1990 levels by 2008–12,[19] but a number of observers think that this is wishful thinking, in which case in the future we will be faced with tougher measures to reduce emissions.

Figure 10.6 shows the CO_2 emissions from fossil fuels by continent in 1995.

The IPCC has pointed to a range of key indicators for the macro-climatic scale:

- Measurements have shown that atmospheric concentrations of many greenhouse gases are continuing to grow.
- Global temperatures have continued to rise, with 2003 and 2002 joining 2001 and 1998 as the top four hottest years on record.
- The Hadley Centre's ground-breaking carbon-climate model shows that carbon cycle feedbacks from forests and natural vegetation could strongly accelerate global warming in the future.
- The UKCIP climate change scenarios suggest a future of hotter, drier summers and warmer, wetter winters.

European indicators

Under the Kyoto Agreement, 38 industrialised countries agreed to aim for a total

Figure 10.6 CO_2 emissions from fossil fuels by continent in 1995

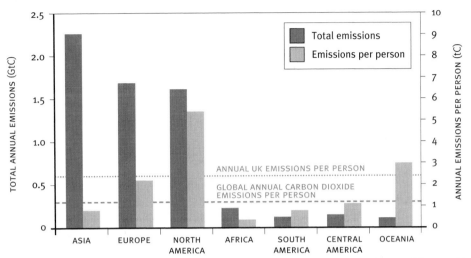

Source: *Energy – The Changing Climate: Summary of the Royal Commission on Environmental Pollution's Report*, RCEP, 2000. © Crown copyright

reduction of 5.2 per cent in greenhouse gases (with respect to the 1990 level) by 2008–12. The European Union agreed on a reduction of 8 per cent. In reality EU CO2 emissions are expected to show a 4 per cent increase by 2010.

Calculating total EU greenhouse gas emissions is not a straightforward business. The unit of measurement for the EU programme is tonnes per year and % variation (with respect to a reference year, preferably 1990), being measured annually. The measurements will be reported and presented per year, differentiated by sector. Consumption data disaggregate energy to reflect the various end uses:

- electricity
- gas
- district heating
- coal
- combined heat and power (CHP).

Emission data and emission factors are published for individual countries;[20] the data are also published through the national bodies responsible for producing emissions balance sheets at provincial level every five years.

Data analysis[21] considers:

- CO_2 equivalents – anthropogenic emissions (i.e. caused by human activity) of CO_2 and methane (calculated on the basis of 1990 figures). This indicator seeks to measure such emissions within an area of local authority control.

Table 10.1 UK CO_2 emissions and benchmarks at national, household and individual level ($MtCO_2$ = million tonnes of carbon dioxide; tCO_2 = tonnes of carbon dioxide)

	TOTAL UK CO_2 EMISSIONS		
YEAR	NATIONAL STATISTICS	DTI [b]	DETR [c]
1990 (base year)		604.3	616.0
1995	589.7	565.0	574.6
2000	605.4	559.5	565.8
2010			563.9
2020			589.2
2050			
UK PER HOUSEHOLD EMISSIONS PER YEAR (tCO_2)			
	Existing emissions in 1995		
Housing Energy Efficiency Best Practice Programme [f]	16.6 (for a 4 person household) *From house* 4.2 *Personal transport* 4.4 *Products, services, food* 8.0		
UK PER CAPITA EMISSIONS PER YEAR (tCO_2)			
Rising Tide [e]	8.2 *From house* 2.7 *Personal transport* 1.6 *Products, services, food* 3.9		
IEA [g]	9.0		

(a) National Statistics (2002), *Carbon Dioxide Emissions by 93 Economic Sectors 1990–2001*, The Stationery Office, Norwich

(b) DTI (2003), *UK Energy in Brief*, Department of Trade and Industry and National Statistics, London

(c) DETR (2000), *Climate Change: the UK programme*, The Stationery Office, Norwich

(d) RCEP (2000), *Energy – the Changing Climate: Summary of the Royal Commission on Environmental Pollution's Report*, HMSO, London

(e) Rising Tide (2003), *The Carbon Challenge: Living for the future*, Rising Tide, Oxford. This publication says: "The Intergovernmental Panel on Climate Change calculates that biological and chemical activity in oceans, forests and soils permanently removes around 4 billion tonnes of carbon from the carbon cycle each year. Then this is our global emissions target. With a current world population of around 6 billion, equal distribution would give each person a share of just two-thirds of a tonne of carbon each. The Carbon Challenge is to reduce our emissions to a maximum of two-thirds of a tonne of carbon per person per year."

(f) HEEBPP (1996), *Building a Sustainable Future: Homes for an autonomous community*, Housing Energy Efficiency Best Practice programme, Watford

(g) IEA (2002), *Carbon Dioxide Emissions from Fuel Combustion 1971–2000*, International Energy Agency, Geneva

- Local activities to be considered for measurement of such emissions should cover those which include the use of fossil fuels (coal, petroleum, natural gas) for energy purposes (including transport) and local waste management.

In fact, the Kyoto Protocol covers CO_2, nitrous oxide (N_2O), methane (CH_4), sulphur hexafluoride (SF_6), hydrofluorocarbons (HFCs) and perfluorocarbons (PFCs).

TARGETS FOR UK CO_2 EMISSION REDUCTION			REDUCTIONS ACHIEVED
KYOTO PROTOCOL (ON 1990 LEVELS)	UK GOVERNMENT TARGET (ON 1990 LEVELS)	RCEP TARGET[d] (ON 1997 LEVELS)	DETR[c]
			−8.2%
−12.5%	−20%		−8.4% (estimated)
			−4.4% (estimated)
		−60%	

UK PER HOUSEHOLD EMISSIONS PER YEAR (τCO_2)			
PER CAPITA EMISSIONS/YEAR CORRESPONDING TO VARIOUS TARGETS			
KYOTO PROTOCOL	DOMESTIC TARGET	RCEP TARGET	CARBON CHALLENGE[e]
14.5 (by 2010)	13.3 (by 2020)	6.6 (by 2050)	

UK PER CAPITA EMISSIONS PER YEAR (τCO_2)			
7.2 (by 2010)	6.6 (2020)	3.3 (2050)	2.5
7.9 (2010)	7.2 (2020)	3.6 (2050)	

Source: Rajat Gupta, Oxford Brookes University

Carbon dioxide emissions attributable to the energy sector (including energy production and energy consumption by industry, households, transport, etc.) are by far the most important factor responsible for climate change (industrialised countries contribute about 80 per cent of the total). However, the waste management sector is also relevant because of methane emissions.

There are many problems with measuring emissions:

- The city uses electricity that is produced with fossil fuel outside its boundaries: the emissions related to this production have to be accounted for as due to the city itself.
- The city makes use of natural gas that is produced elsewhere and transported up to the end users: the emissions related to the production and transportation activities have to be accounted for as due to the city itself.

- The city produces waste that is disposed of in a landfill outside its boundaries: the emissions related to such waste disposal have to be accounted for as due to the city itself. It can be useful to think of external emissions due to the import of energy or to the export of waste as "debt" emissions that have to be added to local emissions.

On the other hand, the city may export energy to and/or import waste from other cities. Thus emissions related to these activities should be subtracted from total domestic emissions. Thus the CO_2 indicator for a city includes emissions generated inside its boundaries (like typical national balances), plus "debt" emissions, minus "credit" emissions. If we limit the analysis to those emissions generated inside city boundaries, the emission accounting can be compared to national emission accounting according to the IPCC methodology, at least for the sectors and greenhouse gases considered in the European methodology.

UK government indicators

In February 2003 the Labour government published a White Paper on Energy.[22] This made clear the government's intentions to:

- protect citizens against the impacts of climate change
- minimise the CO_2 emissions from the UK that are helping to drive climate change.

The White Paper describes the government's strategy to reduce CO_2 emissions over the next 50 years, including a major expansion of renewable energy. The energy policy has four main goals:

- work towards cutting emissions of carbon dioxide by 60 per cent by 2050
- maintain the reliability of energy supplies
- promote competitive energy markets in the UK and beyond
- ensure that every home is adequately and affordably heated.

The government regularly publishes details of the nation's progress towards these aims.[23]

Every local authority must play its part in helping to achieve the national government's CO_2 emissions targets. Much of this work is to be achieved under the requirements of Agenda 21 (see Chapter 4). There are also many indicators and benchmarks relating to the various impacts of climate change. These are discussed in the other chapters of this book.

Table 10.1 puts the national and international CO_2 emissions targets into per-

Table 10.2 Climate related environmental trends in London and the wider Thames region

CLIMATE INDICATOR	RECENT TREND IN LONDON AND THE WIDER THAMES REGION
Air temperature	• Annual average has risen by +0.6°C since 1900s • Several of the warmest years on record have occurred since 1989 • Fewer 'cold' days and longer frost-free season • Growing season +30 days since 1900s • Nocturnal urban heat island intensifying
Rainfall	• Decreasing summer rainfall since 1880s and increasing winter rainfall over last 150–200 years • Two of three driest summers were 1995 and 1976 • Two of three wettest winters were 1989/90 and 1994/95 • More winter rain days and longer wet spells since 1960s • Heavy storms contribute more to winter rainfall totals since 1960s
Gales	• Record wind speeds in 1987 and 1990 • No long-term trend but cluster of severe gales in the 1990s
Groundwater	• Levels increasing by up to 2.5 m/yr in central London • Local declines due to unsustainable abstraction and dry weather
Tidal levels	• High tide levels rising by 6 mm/yr (includes subsidence) • Frequency of Thames Barrier closure increased during the 1990s
Air quality	• Air quality is failing standards in many parts of London principally due to traffic emissions • Weather patterns strongly affect ambient pollution levels
Biodiversity	• Decline in some species due to loss of habitat, e.g. Bumblebee • Loss of habitats due to redevelopment e.g. marshland and urban wasteland

Source: *London's Warming: The Impact of Climate Change on London*, London Climate Change Partnership, November 2003
© Crown Copyright

spective, and illustrates how far away we are from achieving the targets. It is worth noting here that data-gathering at this level is an extremely complex business. The apparent discrepancies between figures from different government departments are related to data collection methods. For example, each year the entire dataset is reviewed.

Local authority indicators

At the level of a single town or city climate change will have a wide range of impacts. The *London's Warming* report[24] identified four key environmental impacts:

- flood risk caused by inundation of floodplains by riverwater, local drainage flooding during heavy rains, and tidal surges in the Thames
- changes to soil moisture in summer, lower summer and higher winter river flows, and a rise in demand for domestic water
- changes in air quality and temperature, leading to health problems
- changes in the distribution of species and the places they inhabit.

Table 10.3 Strategies to protect buildings from the impact of climate change

CLIMATIC ATTRIBUTE	POSSIBLE MITIGATION STRATEGY
Air temperature	• Eliminate any direct solar gain into buildings in summer to avoid exacerbating overheating • Avoid excessive re-reflected light from adjacent surfaces into the building • Use night-time ventilation to minimise impacts of nocturnal urban heat island intensification. • Develop a strategy to adapt the building and its occupants to higher temperatures – more control of natural ventilation/external shading/high levels of thermal mass • Use evaporative cooling in extremis • Maximise the insulation values of exposed walls • All roofs should be very well insulated • Design for passive solar gain where appropriate to use the free heat of the winter sun while avoiding summer overheating • Never incorporate fixed windows: there will be times when power supplies may fail and if windows cannot be opened the building may become un-occupiable
Rainfall	• Provide rainwater storage (tanks and butts) for extra water for gardens, cleaning cars etc. • Provide wide, strong, storm-proof flood gutters • Design external landscape and drainage to cope with flood periods • Do not rely on water sinks and sumps that will, in flood times, be below the water table • Protect exposed walls from hard driving rain • Design strong foundations to avoid walls cracking in droughts • Cover new developments with "absorbent" surfaces such as grass, to delay surface flooding • Provide drying areas outside the main building for wet clothes
Gales	• Storm-proof roofs required as standard and in exposed areas • Use hurricane detailing to tie walls to floors • In very exposed areas, heavyweight building techniques should be used to avoid loss of buildings in gales
Relative humidity	• Avoid cold-bridging, or vapour barrier penetrations that may exacerbate damp and mould problems • Ensure that the vapour barrier is on the warm side of the insulation to avoid interstitial condensation
Groundwater	• Always check if the building is on a flood plain or at risk from flooding (see Chapter 15)
Biodiversity	• Check if an area has been, or is likely to be, a mosquito or termite area • Design houses to minimise the risk of dust mites • Plan buildings to create minimum disturbance to existing wild life, including destruction of micro-climates

Source: London's Warming: The Impact of Climate Change on London, London Climate Change Partnership, November 2003
© Crown Copyright

It also acknowledged that climate change would have a number of economic impacts. Flood risk, for example, could be a serious threat to economic assets including property and communication infrastructure; while weather-related disruption to transport has a very significant impact on profitability. However, on the plus side, the report acknowledges that the warmer weather in the summer might improve revenues from tourism.

Table 10.2 lists some of the climate-related changes already observed in the London area.

Building-level indicators

Most of us spend nearly all our lives in buildings or vehicles, both of them powered by fossil fuels; we are all guilty of driving climate change. And the scale of the potential impacts of climate change on our everyday lives is daunting.

Benchmarks for CO_2 emissions from buildings are directly related to energy use, and therefore are presented in Chapter 11. But designers should note that the dream of the "zero-carbon" building can be achieved – if renewable, clean, carbon-free sources of energy such as solar or wind power are used. There are already a number of "off-grid" buildings that are theoretically zero-carbon buildings. In fact, any building that uses renewable energy to some degree will have a reduction in its total CO_2 emissions.

Table 10.3 lists a range of options for mitigating the impact that climate change will have on buildings. The good thing about these options is that, not only will they make the buildings more comfortable for occupants, they will immediately contribute to reducing the impact of climate change.

References

1   For more details, see *www.theozonehole.com*
2   Pout CH, McKenzie F and Bettle R (2002), *Carbon Dioxide Emissions from Non-Domestic Buildings: 2000 and beyond*, Building Research Establishment, Garston, p 10
3   RCEP (2000), *Energy – the changing climate: Summary of the Royal Commission on Environmental Pollution's Report*, Royal Commission on Environmental Pollution, The Stationery Office, Norwich, pp 3–4
4   Ibid.; also Meyer A (2000), *Contraction and Convergence: The global solution to climate change*, Green Books, Totnes
5   GCI (1998), *Contraction and Convergence: a global solution to a global problem*. Available to download at: *www.gci.org.uk*
6   See 4
7   Visit *www.ipcc.ch*
8   Hadley Centre: *www.meto.gov.uk/research/hadleycentre*

9   Hulme M, Turnpenny J and Jenkins G (2002), *Climate Change Scenarios for the United Kingdom: the UKCIP02 scientific report*, Tyndall Centre for Climate Change Research, University of East Anglia, Norwich. Available at *www.ukcip.org.uk/scenarios*

10 Ibid.

11 Tyndall Centre for Climate Change Research at *www.tyndall.ac.uk*

12 Hulne et al (2002), op cit.

13 LCCP (2002), *London's Warming: The impacts of climate change on London*, London Climate Change Partnership, London

14 DETR (2002) *Building Regulations Approved Document L1 Conservation of fuel and power in dwellings, Approved Document L2 Conservation of fuel and power in buildings other than dwellings*, The Stationery Office, Norwich

15 National greenhouse gas inventories of emissions are calculated and reported for UNFCCC/Kyoto compliance in the tonnages of the actual gases (CO_2, CH_4, N_2O, HFCs, PFCs, SF_6) , but they are also aggregated as a total CO_2 equivalent number (CO_{2e}) – for which each metric tonne of non-CO_2 gas is converted to CO_{2e} using a "global warming potential" number. For example, each tonne of CH_4 is equivalent to 21 times the effect of a tonne of CO_2 over a 100 year time-frame. Emissions trading schemes for greenhouse gases follow this same method. For the UK emissions trading scheme, all greenhouse gases are potentially included, and quite a lot of the emissions traded are N_2O and HFCs as well as CO_2.

16 UNEP-WCMC (2001), *The World Atlas of Coral Reefs*, United Nations Environmental Program, World Conservation Monitoring Centre, Cambridge

17 For an academic study of the subject see: *www.coral.noaa.gov*

18 For further details, see Met Office (1999), *Climate Change and its Impacts; Stabilisation of CO_2 in the atmosphere*, The Stationery Office, Norwich. View on-line at *http://www.met-office.gov.uk/research/hadleycentre/pubs*

19 DEFRA (2002), *Global Atmosphere Research Programme Annual Report 2000–2002*, DEFRA, London. View the document at *www.defra.gov.uk/environment*

20 See: Trends in emissions of greenhouse gases (EEA sector classification and IPCC sector classification) (English version 3) at *http://dataservice.eea.eu.int*

21 See *Towards a Local Sustainability Profile; European Common Indicators; Methodology Sheets,* published by EC (Download from *www.sustainable-cities.org/indicators/index.htm*)

22 DTi (2003), *Our Energy Future: Creating a low carbon economy*, Government Energy White Paper, The Stationery Office, Norwich

23 DEFRA (2002), Op Cit.

24 LCCP (2002), Op Cit.

On-line resources

The UK's Environment Agency website carries a great deal of useful information about climate change and its likely impacts on buildings. Visit *www.environment-agency.gov.uk*

Further reading

Bartlett, PB and Prior JJ (1991), *The Environmental Impact of Buildings*, Building Research Establishment, Garston

DETR (2000), *Climate Change: The UK programme*, The Stationery Office, Norwich

Graves HM and Phillipson MC (2000), *Potential Implications of Climate Change in the Built Environment*, Foundation for the Built Environment, Garston

Henderson, G and Shorrock, LD (1990), *Greenhouse gas emissions and buildings in the United Kingdom*, BRE Information Paper, Building Research Establishment, Garston

Houghton JT, Jenkins GJ and Ephraums JJ (eds) (1990), *Climate change: the IPCC scientific assessment*, Cambridge University Press, Cambridge

Hulme M and Jenkins GJ (1998), *Climate Change Scenarios for the United Kingdom: Scientific report*. UKCIP Technical Report no 1, UKCIP, Norwich

IPCC (1996), *Climate Change 1995: The science of climate change: Contribution of Working Group I to the Second Assessment of the Intergovernmental Panel on Climate Change,* Cambridge University Press, Cambridge

IPCC (2001), *Climate Change 2001: The scientific basis: Contribution of Working Group I to the Third Assessment Report of the Intergovernmental Panel on Climate Change*, Cambridge University Press, Cambridge

Met Office (1999), *The Greenhouse Effect and Climate Change: A briefing from the Hadley Centre*, Meteorological Office Communications, Bracknell

Pout C, Moss S and Davidson P (1998), *Non-domestic factfile*, Building Research Establishment, Garston

Shorrock LD, Henderson G, Utley JI and Walters GA (2001), *Carbon Emission Reductions from Energy Efficiency Improvements in the UK Housing Stock*, The Stationery Office, Norwich

UNEP and UNFCCC (2001), *Climate Change Information Kit*, UN Environment Program Information Unit, Geneva

Watson TR, Zinyowera MC and Moss HR (1996), *Technologies, Policies and Measures for Mitigating Climate Change,* IPCC Technical Paper 1, IPCC, Geneva

Planning policy guidance – related documents (see Appendix 1 for details)

1	2	3	4	5	6	7	8	9	10	11	12	13
X						X			X	X	X	

14	15	16	17	18	19	20	21	22	23	24	25
X									X		X

Building Regulations – related Approved Documents (see Appendix 2 for details)

A	B	C	D	E	F	G	H	J	K	L1	L2	M	N
										X	X		

Energy

Definition

Dictionaries say that energy is the capacity of a physical system to do work, but that seems something of an understatement for the driving force behind the universe. In physics, the symbol for energy is E; and its importance is underlined by Einstein's famous equation $E=mc_2$ (where m stands for mass and c is the speed of light). This equation tells us that, at the atomic level, energy is at the very core of "matter" – a kilogram of anything conceals enough energy to boil a hundred billion kettles.[1] Physicists measure energy in two ways: as stored (potential) energy or as working (kinetic) energy. For example, the food we eat contains chemical (potential) energy, and the body stores this until it is released as kinetic energy when we work, walk or breathe. Energy is never destroyed; it is simply converted from one form to another – heat (thermal), light (radiant), mechanical, electrical, chemical, or nuclear energy.

Although we conveniently talk about the "energy" used in buildings, what we are actually referring to is the "power" that is driving various systems – "energy" is the capacity to do work, and "power" is the amount of energy used over a given time.

Related indicators

Climate change.

Related solutions

Building form and daylighting; The building envelope; Insulation and infiltration; Renewable energy and Photovoltaics; Energy-efficient equipment; Transport solutions; Green materials specification; Environmental management schemes.

Related tools

Impact assessment in the UK - Ecopoints, BREEAM and Envest; Ecological footprinting; Energy use in dwellings; Energy toolkit; Vital Signs; Post-occupancy evaluation.

Background

Energy production and use is, arguably, the single most important issue facing us today.

Most of the energy we use is derived from the burning of fossil fuels and generates the greenhouse gas carbon dioxide (CO_2) which we now know is causing climate change (see Chapter 10).

This is of concern to anyone involved in construction for two reasons:

- Buildings are the front line of our defence against the climate, and must shield us from the effects of climate change whether they be increased wind speeds, storm incidence or summer heat waves.
- Buildings currently account for 46 per cent of the UK's total energy consumption,[2] but they have the capacity to use much less, or even to produce their own energy, and thus lessen the impact of climate change.

At a time when gas, electricity and oil prices are steadily climbing, energy use is also of concern to the building user who has to pay for that energy. But pounds and dollars are not the only issue: we also pay the price for energy use because of the environmental damage and pollution that arise from energy generation and

---

Energy and design

The First Law of Thermodynamics (the law of the Conservation of Energy) states that energy cannot be created or destroyed. The Second Law (about entropy) explains that, while the total energy in the system is always constant, the system will tend towards a state of "disorder" – in energy terms, this means the energy "downgrades" from higher forms (e.g. light) to lower forms such as heat.

Understanding entropy is a fundamental lesson for building designers, who use their knowledge to ensure that heat energy, where needed, can be caught and used in many different ways in the building. The aim is to slow the process of downgrading so that heat energy is kept in the building for as long as possible – by preventing its escape using insulation and plugging the draught leaks, or by storing it as long as possible in the mass of the building. Conversely, the building could be cooled by opening all the windows to let the heat energy out, but an alternative would be for the designer to provide lots of building mass to absorb the surplus heat, resulting in a more constant comfortable temperature.

---

consumption. Impacts range from acid and toxic rains to the warming of oceans. In addition, as Professor Fergus Nicol has pointed out,[3] there is a direct link between high energy use in buildings, air-conditioning (over 40 per cent of all US electricity is consumed by air-conditioning), the United States' need for oil . . . and war (perhaps).

In the near future, three key issues will change the way we use energy in buildings:

- the rising cost of energy
- the reduced availability of energy
- climate change.

The internationally accepted (SI) unit of energy is the joule, J.[4] However, most energy-related calculations are concerned with the application of energy over a period of time – the power (measured in watts, W).

1 watt (1W) = 1 joule dissipated or radiated for 1 second (1s)
1W = 1J/s

One watt is a relatively small amount of power; for energy use in buildings measurements are usually scaled up to kilowatt-hours (kWh):

1kW = 1000W and 1h = 3600 seconds, so 1kWh = 3.6 x 10⁶J.

Most of the energy we use on Earth is, ultimately, derived from the Sun – for example, sunlight is needed for trees to grow; then wood or coal can be burnt to release the energy. Other sources include nuclear power, hydroelectric power, geothermal power, wind power and wave power. Primary sources of energy are those found "in nature". Secondary sources are those that are generated/converted from primary sources. Whatever the energy source, the power it provides can be measured in the same units, but before the advent of international measurement systems other units were used, and some persist today.[5] For example, horse-power was defined as the weight that a "standard horse" was supposed to be capable of lifting to a given height in a given time; and British thermal units (Btus), also known as "therms", are still used sometimes by the gas supply industry (1Btu is approximately equivalent to 1060J).[6] Table 11.1 lists primary and secondary sources of energy.

One of the main problems we encounter when we talk about energy sources is that it is difficult to compare the value of secondary sources because of the variability in the efficiency of extraction, transmission and operation. For example, if it takes 1 kWh (one unit) of "primary" gas to boil a large pan of water on a gas stove, then it would take three times as much gas to boil the same amount of

Table 11.1 Some primary and secondary of energy

ENERGY SOURCE	UNIT OF MEASUREMENT AT SOURCE/EXTRACTION	POWER (kWh) THAT CAN BE OBTAINED FROM ONE UNIT OF THE SOURCE*
Primary sources		
Sunlight	W/m2	0.001011
Wood	kg	3.8-4.2†
Coal	tonne	3800-4200†
Oil	tonne	2931
Gas	gallon	58.61
	cubic feet	0.0085
Secondary sources		
Land	hectare (Ha)	18,640,000 (total for one year)
Food	kg	2.608
Horse	horse-power	21.69
Man	man-hours	0.1011
Electricity	kW	1
Petrol	litre	13
Windmill	hours of wind	29

Source: Adapted from Fox, R. H. "Heat", in *The Physiology of Human Survival*, O.G. Edholme and A. L. Bacharach (Eds.), Academic Press, 1965

* These values are approximate, and do not account for, say, conversion or transmission losses.
† Energy content is variable and depends on the "quality" of the wood

water (i.e. to deliver 1 kWh) if that gas was first converted to electricity in a power station with a gas turbine that is, say, 50 per cent efficient and with attendant transmission losses.

The issue of comparing different energy sources and their environmental impacts is discussed in Chapter 31 (Ecological footprinting). Table 11.2 gives estimated man-power equivalents for a selection of primary and secondary energy sources (assuming 100% conversion efficiency), while Table 11.3 shows typical conversion efficiencies. Finally, Table 11.4 gives the typical cost per kWh for a range of energy sources.

Taken together,[7] these tables clearly illustrate why we are so addicted to oil. Burning oil is one of the most efficient ways of generating power. One gallon of oil will do the equivalent work of 580 man-hours, and could, say, push a car from Oxford to Manchester. (Of course, it depends on the sort of car – there's a huge difference between the power needed to drive a small light car and a great big "sports utility vehicle"! You can also see what sense it would make to run a very

Table 11.2 Comparing different energy sources

ENERGY SOURCE	EQUIVALENT TO ...
1 horse-hour	6 man-hours
1 kWh electricity	13 man-hours
1 traditional windmill hour	200 man-hours
1 gallon of oil	580 man-hours
1 barrel of oil	16 man-years (approx. 140,000 man-hours)
1 tonne coal	50 man-years
1 hectare of land	105,000 man-years
1000 kilocalories*	1.163kWh
1 hour of summer sunshine (1kWh)	1 hour of a one-bar electric fire

Source: Adapted from Fox, R. H. "Heat", in *The Physiology of Human Survival*, O.G. Edholme and A. L. Bacharach (Eds.), Academic Press, 1965

* Energy values of foods used to be quoted in "calories", but most are now presented as kcal.
For example, typical servicing of breakfast cereal contains 160-200 kcal.

Table 11.3 Typical conversion efficiencies of some primary and secondary fuel sources

CONVERSION OF ...	EFFICIENCY (%)
Primary energy to electricity	33
Petrol/diesel to mechanical (e.g. car)	35
Gas or oil to heating (domestic)	80
Food to work (human)	12
Food to work (human, nationally)*	6
Food to work (animal)	20
Electricity to mechanical	85
Sunlight to food	0.14
Sunlight to photovoltaic electricity	15

Source: Adapted from Fox, R. H. "Heat", in *The Physiology of Human Survival*, O.G. Edholme and A. L. Bacharach (Eds.), Academic Press, 1965

light solar vehicle!)

These figures also show what an incredibly powerful resource we are burning away, often for totally frivolous work – depriving future generations of the energy they will need just to survive, to say nothing of the environmental damage it causes.

Energy use in buildings

When did we first learn to depend on energy, on fire, to sustain life? All that remains to us of our ancestors' lives are glimpses in the early artwork – cave paintings or on rock walls. We can gain some insight into their lifestyle by looking at

Table 11.4 Typical cost per kWh for a range of energy sources (at 2003 prices, excluding tax)

ENERGY SOURCE	COST (£) FOR 1kWh OF USEFUL ENERGY (2003 PRICES, EXCLUDING TAX)
13 man-hours (@ £15 per hour)	195.00
Oil	1.56
Petrol	0.059
Coal	0.01
Gas	0.0184
Electricity	0.059
Food for humans	10.00

Source: Adapted from Fox, R. H. "Heat", in *The Physiology of Human Survival*, O.G. Edholme and A. L. Bacharach (Eds.), Academic Press, 1965

the wandering tribes that remain with us, travelling with family and flocks to take advantage of the richest pastures and avoid seasonally uninhabitable extremes of climate, from Mongolia and the Arctic wastelands to the deserts of Saudi Arabia and the African Savannah. Their energy needs vary enormously according to the climate and the availability of supplies. No doubt the armies of Alexander the Great feasted by fires fed from the ancient, now long-lost, forests of the Near East, a resource that, once used, cannot be easily replaced. Nomads today in the same region use amazingly little energy for their pleasant and often comfortable way of life. They only need fuel for a small fire in a tent, two or three times a day: for tea and warmth in winter, for cooking the milk products in spring (see Figure 11.1), and for cooking bread, rice and fattened lambs at feast times.

The wood they gather during the spring migrations may be branches, scrub or roots; on the barren summer hillsides water is sometimes boiled on fires of dried animal dung. A good pot of tea for many can be made with less than a kilogramme of properly prepared wood, and drunk from small glasses! The family goes to bed after sunset in winter when the fire has died down, beneath quilted covers, to keep each other warm through the colder nights – the obvious solution if you have no lights or warmth, and one used by the poor in Britain even after World War II. No doubt this still happens in winter in many parts of the world today.

In the villa of Julius Polybius (Figure 11.2), in the Roman city of Pompeii, which was buried by the great volcanic eruption of Etna in 79 AD, a single small oil lamp was found on the floor of every unearthed room. One small lamp would provide enough light to outline figures around it, and throw into sharp relief close objects, but would hardly give the light to read by. The oil used would have been pressed from olives or other vegetables or flowers. The house was heated in parts by a hypocaust warmed from a fire in the kitchen courtyard. Wood was already very

Figure 11.1 The spring milk is cooking on the tent fire in a Beiranvand camp

Figure 11.2 (a) The Villa Julius Polybius in Pompeii

Figure 11.2 (b) Plan of Villa Julius Polybius, Pompeii

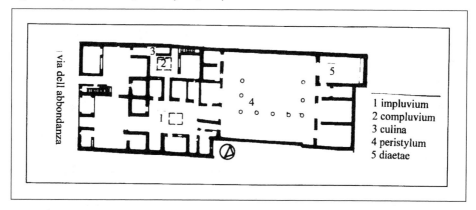

scarce in the area by then, and expensive. Travel was by horse, cart, donkey or boat. For a house such as this, the annual energy use was minimal, and much of the cooking may have been done in the local hot food shops. The citizens of Pompeii led, at best, an extremely pleasant and luxurious life, rich with gardens, art and the sensual pleasures afford by the public baths, theatres, poetry, academia and the delights of entertainments at the arena. I doubt there was ever recorded a case of sick building syndrome in Pompeii!

Seventeen hundred years later, by 1775, the neighbouring Neapolitan town of Herculaneum was home to some of the most sophisticated architects of all time. The Rococo-Baroque designers of the Herculaneum villas produced a large number of elegant confections of buildings that are some of the cleverest passive buildings in the world (see Figure 11.3). Again the occupants had only candles and oil lamps and wood for heating, but they invented numerous ways of increasing the value of the energy available, for example using highly reflective wall colours, mirrors and clever windows to re-reflect light. Their cross, stack and ducted ventilation systems were masterful, and they used glass not only to increase light but also for its thermal ability to keep out the cold while introducing the heat of the sun in passive solaria, or sunspaces. Ice stores in the basement, filled from winter ice and snow from the mountains, provided them with iced drinks and dishes, and cool for their rooms at night. These buildings represent the pinnacle of culture, delight, sensuality and luxury, and must rate amongst the greatest of human architectural achievement in terms of quality of life and energy efficiency.

They travelled using horses, donkeys and boats and, like the nomads, would change their abode, choosing the most pleasant climates for different seasons, returning to the less exposed city palaces for winter and occupying their seaside villas largely in summer.

Figure 11.3 (a) View of through the terrace at the Villa Campolietto in Herculaneum

Source: Sue Roaf/Energy Efficient Building Masters course, Oxford Brooks University, 1997

Figure 11.3 (b) section through the villa

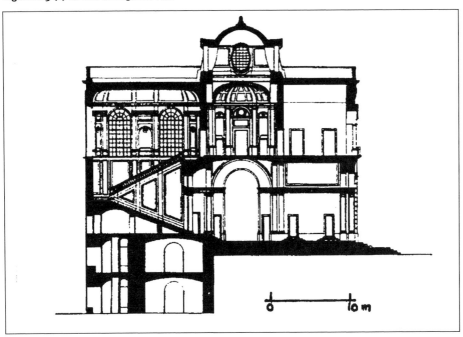

Source: Sue Roaf/Energy Efficient Building Masters course, Oxford Brooks University, 1997

Figure 11.3 (c) temperatures recorded in April at different levels in the building

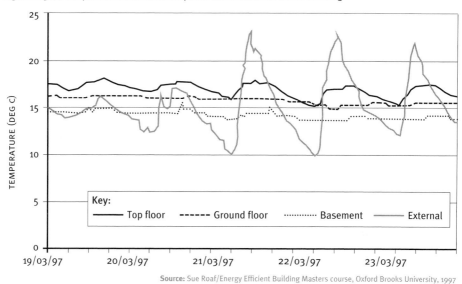

Source: Sue Roaf/Energy Efficient Building Masters course, Oxford Brooks University, 1997

Figure 11.4 UK CO$_2$ emissions since 1750. This graph is based on data of long-term trends collated by G Marland, TA Boden and RJ Andres of the Oak Ridge National Laboratory in the US

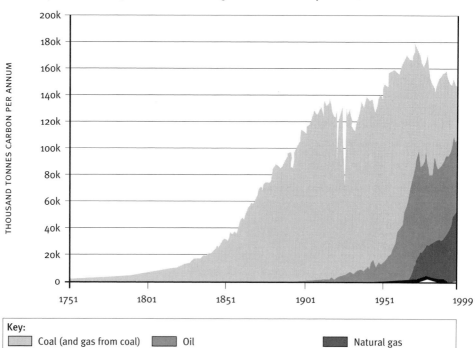

Source: UK National Energy Foundation and Oakridge National Laboratory, USA

Coal

In the late 18th Century, while the Italians were busily designing energy-efficient buildings, Britain was on the brink of the Industrial Revolution, and the factory fires were being stoked high with the power behind the revolution – coal.

Figure 11.4 shows the UK's CO_2 emissions since the start of the industrial revolution, much of it derived from burning coal. Although it is well down from its peak in the 1960s, the UK still uses a huge amount of coal, which is responsible for even more CO_2 emissions than oil. The high CO_2 emissions from coal – a "dirty" fuel – are related to the efficiency of the power generation process. Table 11.3 quoted 33 per cent efficiency electricity production, but this is actually an average figure. In reality, a gas-power turbine may be 50 per cent efficient, an oil-fired turbine could be 30 per cent efficient, and a coal-burning power station as low as 20–28 per cent efficient. Thus the CO_2 generated per kWh of delivered electricity depends on the type of fuel used at the power station. Table 11.5[8] shows typical 2003 CO_2 production for various energy-generation processes.

In Asia, electricity consumption has grown by 75 per cent in the last decade, in North America it has risen by nearly 30 per cent, and in Europe by 20 per cent.[9] In much of the world these increases have been fuelled by coal. For instance, in America, as the cost of oil rises that of coal continues to fall, and coal now costs

Table 11.5 These conversion factors can be used to calculate the carbon dioxide emissions (in kgCo2) associated with energy production

ENERGY SOURCE	CONVERSION FACTOR
Mains electricity, average (in kWh)	x 0.43
Coal-generated electricity (in kWh)	x 0.50
Gas-generated electricity (in kWh)	x 0.19
Oil-generated electricity (in kWh)	x 0.43
Natural gas (in kWh)	x 0.19
Petrol (in litres)	x 2.31
Low-pressure gas (LPG) (in litres)	x 1.51
Wood (in tonnes)	x 1800 to 2000
Coal (in tonnes)	x 2419
Miles in a petrol car	x 0.36
Miles in a train or bus	X 0.1
Miles in an aeroplane	x 0.29

Source: UK National Energy Foundation, *www.natenenergy.org.uk*

less than it did in 1970, while gas and oil prices have risen sharply over the last few years. The growing difference in costs is driving the steady growth of the coal market in the USA.

Oil

The use of oil increased significantly after World War II because of the rise of car use. In the early 1970s, approximately 40 per cent of global fossil fuel use was oil, but during the 1990s this figure has decreased. Improved energy efficiency has slowed down the rates of increase for oil consumption in some developed, industrialised countries, and shifts to other fuels such as natural gas and nuclear energy have occurred for environmental reasons and those of security of supply. Current estimates suggest that we have around 40 years of conventional oil reserves available, and that there remain around 10–20 years of "cheap", but increasingly costly, oil ahead.

Gas

There has been a dramatic increase in the amount of proven reserves of natural gas since the mid-1960s. Consequently, natural gas has become the fastest-growing energy resource in terms of accessibility. The present global use of natural gas accounts for approximately 20 per cent of all fossil fuel use, and this figure is predicted to rise in the future. Natural gas is a practical alternative to oil or coal, and in terms of CO_2 emissions and acidic pollution it is a cleaner fuel. Commonly accepted estimates indicate that reserves of natural gas may be readily available for around 60 years, although some people suggest longer. Unfortunately, where it is desperately needed – in the USA – reserves are almost exhausted.

The future

With the exponential growth in energy demand since the 1950s, the shock of the "energy crisis" in the 1970s, the rising costs of energy, plus the geopolitical drivers to increase security of supply and reduce dependence on troubled regions of the world, a new imperative has emerged – energy efficiency. If these reasons were not enough to make people want to use less energy, there is also now the increasingly urgent environmental need to reduce the greenhouse gas emissions resulting from energy generation that are driving climate change.

As Figure 11.5 demonstrates, while increasing the size of its economy (represented by an increase in gross domestic product, GDP) primary energy consumption in the UK has increased, but the "energy ratio" has fallen. The energy ratio compares the rate of change of GDP with the rate of primary energy consumption – the reduction in the energy ratio is a sign that we are producing wealth more energy-efficiently.

Figure 11.5 UK primary energy consumption compared with gross domestic product

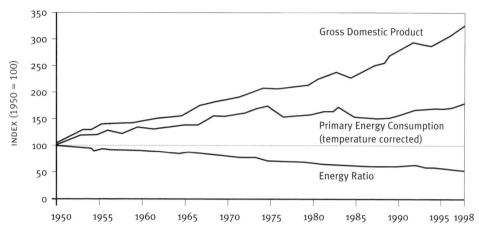

Source: *The Greenhouse effect and climate change: a briefing from the Hadley Centre*, Meteorological Office Communications, 1999

Unfortunately the need and the desire to reduce energy consumption are being outweighed by the increasing numbers of, and energy consumption trends in, cars and buildings. It is not simply a question of rising numbers; there is also the problem of fashion, which is driving the move to high-consumption sports utility vehicles and prestige air-conditioned offices.

An additional factor is that in the UK energy has, in fact, been getting cheaper in real terms as incomes have risen, so we do not feel a financial need to reduce consumption (see Figure 11.6).

What is clear is that the major power suppliers are preparing for a significant shift in the "energy mix". Shell International, for example, is predicting that if demand continues to grow at 2 per cent per year, energy from renewable sources is essential (see Chapter 23). The UK government also acknowledges this fact, offering support for research and implementation of renewable energy technologies.

Global indicators

For macro-level benchmarking of energy, the units of "millions of tons of oil equivalent" are most commonly used. However, global energy consumption is increasingly being mapped using tonnes of CO_2 emitted as the key indicator unit, taking into account the very different levels of related greenhouse gas emissions by fuel type.

Figure 11.7 illustrates the global disparity of energy use and hence CO_2 emissions. (It also highlights the developed world's obsession with air-conditioning.)

Figure 11.6 Average electricity (UK) and gas (GB) prices for domestic customers in real terms

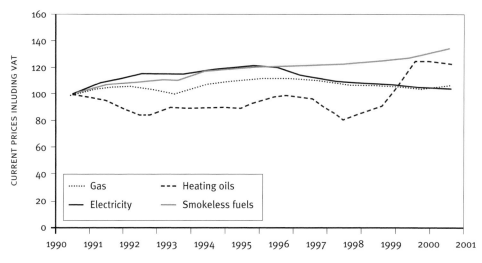

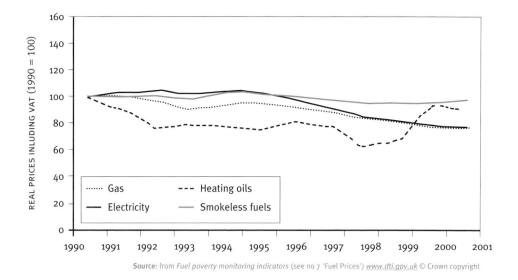

Source: from *Fuel poverty monitoring indicators* (see no 7 'Fuel Prices') www.dti.gov.uk © Crown copyright

There is a growing gap between global energy demand and dwindling oil and gas reserves (particularly in America), so it is essential to develop energy scenarios to aid planning of strategic energy-generating programmes. Planning now will make all the difference if we wish to maintain or improve the quality of life of the world population.

Figure 11.7 (a) and (b) are adapted by Michael Lindemann[10] from several publications of the Worldwatch Institute. The sources include: *United Nations Energy*

Figure 11.7 Scenarios for future energy demand, prepared by Michael Linderman (a) proballle energy demand, based on current requirements; (b) the preferred option (where 'Exoitic' includes energy generated by hydrogen fuel cells)

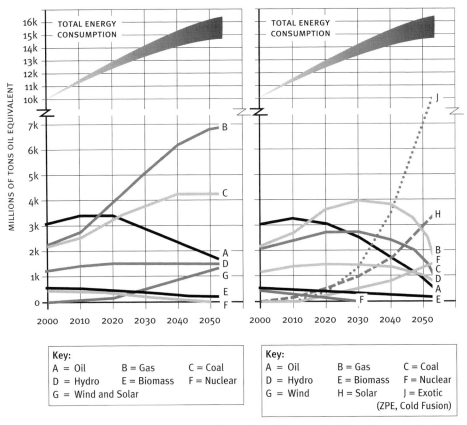

Key:
A = Oil   B = Gas   C = Coal
D = Hydro   E = Biomass   F = Nuclear
G = Wind and Solar

Key:
A = Oil   B = Gas   C = Coal
D = Hydro   E = Biomass   F = Nuclear
G = Wind   H = Solar   J = Exotic
                              (ZPE, Cold Fusion)

Source: Michael P Lindemann, Global Situation Report, www.gsreport.com

Statistics Yearbook (1997); *British Petroleum Statistical Review of World Energy* (1997); *United States Department of Energy International Energy Annual* (1996) and *Monthly Energy Review* (Jan 1998); *European Energy Report*; *Energy Economist*; *International Atomic Energy Agency*; *Nuclear News*; *New York Times*; and the *Financial Times*. The problem, as we have seen with carbon reporting in the UK (see Chapter 10), is the lack of compatibility of units and indicators. Despite the best efforts of Lindemann, the different reports and reporting methods arrive at different figures in virtually all categories, with variation in the range of ± 10 per cent. The numbers used for these figures are conservative extrapolations from a combination of sources.

UK government indicators

The need for benchmarks in buildings is clear: councillors, planners, clients, designers and the general public need access to commonly accepted measures for what is a high, medium or low energy-consuming building, not least so we know what to aim for, but also to begin to reverse the current trends for fashionable buildings to use more and more energy.

There is no reason today why a designer should not be able to provide an "eco-standard" building on virtually any site in the UK, for roughly the same cost, that will use a fraction of the energy required to power a prestige air-conditioned building. By making reference to benchmarks, we can make sure that the requirement for a low-energy, low-CO_2-emissions building is stipulated in every brief. Penalties can be written into the contract if the required performance standards are not met, as can methods of measuring the building consumption and performance at the point of handover and during specified post-occupancy periods. And, in particular, energy meters should be installed from day one, or retrofitted, to enable building owners and users to sub-meter different areas of the building.

The use of sensible and reasonable benchmarks, particularly in conjunction with occupant satisfaction monitoring, can be an excellent diagnostic tool for understanding where poor design and thermal performance occur in a building. Then efficient remedial actions can save a considerable amount of money – from both energy saved and a reduction in lost working days by occupants suffering from sick building syndrome (see Chapter 8).

Benchmarking energy performance in buildings is not a precise science. Buildings are idiosyncratic in their design, history and energy consumption patterns, so it is not until you begin to measure or predict consumption that the energy "personality" of the building emerges.

Factors that influence energy consumption in all building types are numerous, but include:

- building age – the older the better in terms of building form, although some more modern buildings can have more insulation in the envelope and be less draughty
- design features, footprint, daylighting, floor heights, opening windows
- thermal performance of the envelope, insulation and infiltration
- amount of mass in the building – typically more mass leads to lower running costs in buildings
- construction and integrity of the envelope, extent of the cold-bridging in the structure and in particular that of glass.[11]

- patterns of use in the building and hours of occupation
- effectiveness of the controls installed, clearly labelled and well positioned, with a high level of occupant control
- type and fuel of heating and cooling systems (e.g. in order to meet the carbon-equivalent benchmarks, electric heating has to be much better controlled in better insulated buildings than fossil fuel heating)
- air-conditioning – buildings with it can use four times or more energy than those with simple, naturally ventilated, cellular offices.

The benchmarks below (Table 11.6) are derived from the excellent work done by the government's Energy Efficiency Best Practice programme (now known as Action Energy), the buildings-related part of which has been managed by the Building Research Establishment's Energy Division since the programme's inception in the late 1980s. This programme commissions and carries out studies of energy consumption in, and energy efficiency opportunities for, many different types of buildings.[12]

The programme's reports and guides quantify building performance in terms of "typical" and "good practice" buildings. "Typical" energy consumption patterns are consistent with median values of data collected on the particular building type, while "good practice" represents examples where significantly lower energy consumption has been achieved using widely available and well-proven energy-efficient features and management practices. These examples fall within the lower quartile of the data collected.

It is important to note that the benchmarks are based on actual data, from the existing UK building stock: hence new buildings of all types should seek to exceed or significantly exceed such benchmarks.

The benchmarks published by Action Energy are given normalised annual energy consumption in terms of floor area ($kWh/m^2/year$), but in recognition of the increasing importance of CO_2 emissions from buildings, we present them here in terms of CCO_2 emission equivalents (see Table 11.5). The benchmarks for CO_2 emissions (kg/m^2) are derived by multiplying the energy consumption benchmarks with the CO_2 equivalents of each fuel used. The emissions are then summed to provide a single target.

All these benchmarks are subject to periodical revision as data collection and analysis techniques improve and the status of the building stock changes. The data presented in Table 11.6 are given here for illustration; you are strongly advised to regard these as minimum targets, and to seek the most recent figures.

Table 11.6 Good practice benchmarks for energy consumption and CO" emissions for a selection of building types

BUILDING TYPE	TYPICAL EXISTING CO_2 EMISSIONS (KGCO2/M2/YEAR)[A]		GOOD PRACTICE CO2 EMISSION (KGCO2/M2/YEAR)[A]		
	ELECTRICITY	FOSSIL FUEL (GAS)	ELECTRICITY	FOSSIL FUEL (GAS)	MOVEMENT FOR INNOVATION[B]
Offices:					20
• naturally ventilated, cellular	23	29	14	15	
• naturally ventilated, open plan	37	29	23	15	
• air-conditioned, standard	97	34	55	18	
• air-conditioned, prestige	154	40	101	22	
Schools:					
• primary	12	33	9	24	17
• secondary	13	33	10	26	17
Hospitals:					40
• teaching and specialist	52	78	37	64	
• acute and maternity	46	97	32	80	
• cottage	34	93	24	84	
• long stay	31	98	21	76	
Retail:					20
• DIY store	69	37	56	29	
• non-food stores	112	25	86	15	
Food retail					150
• department stores	125	42	103	29	
• small food shops	215	19	172	15	
• supermarkets	396	55	288	30	

DOMESTIC SECTOR CO2 EMISSIONS (KGCO2/YEAR)					
	TYPICAL HOUSE (1995 BUILDING REGULATIONS)[C]	HOUSING ENERGY EFFICIENCY PROGRAMME STANDARDS[C]			MOVEMENT FOR INNOVATION[B]
		ZERO CO_2	ZERO HEATING	AUTONO-MOUS	
Domestic	4241	2267	1414	663	30kgCO$_2$/m²/ year

Source: adapted from 'Energy efficiency in buildings', 1998 & 'Energy efficiency in buildings: draft report', 2002, Chartered Institution of Building Services Engineers, London

Local authority indicators

Energy consumption is the biggest single factor driving climate change and yet it is not covered in the current local authority planning policies. The only way energy can be factored into the planning process is if local authorities make energy consumption in, and CO_2 emissions from, buildings a "material consideration" in the local plan, thus giving some teeth, however weak, to the problem.

Energy use in buildings is the subject of regulation via the Building Regulations Approved Document Part L1 and L2.[13] However, the requirements are designed to prevent excessive energy consumption, rather than promote minimal usage.

Every local authority should discuss and establish what they consider to be appropriate standards for ecohouses, good practice and typical house standards for their region (this will vary with latitude and exposure). Then targets for numbers of ecohouses in new developments can be included in planning requirements, sanctioned under clauses in the local plans as material considerations. In addition, planners have similar powers to determine that all new houses in their region will be of "good practice" standards, to be approved in conjunction with proposed SAP ratings for new developments (see Chapter 33)

An excellent guide to the various options for dwellings is in *Insulation for Sustainability*.[14] This study sets out clearly the energy required to heat different standards of house. The Oxford Ecohouse, for example, uses:

- 6 kWh/m²/year gas to heat it
- 6 kWh/m²/year gas for hot water
- 6 kWh/m²/year gas for cooking
- 12 kWh/m²/year to run all the electrical equipment and the lighting.

Much of the electricity is provided by the $4kW_{peak}$ photovoltaic system on the roof. In all, the house uses around 20 kW//m²/year of fossil fuel energy. This is a good ecohouse standard, but I would say that for the conventional market acceptable general standards may be:

Ecohouse – 10–20 kWh/m²/year for heating
Zerohouse – 0 k Wh/m²/year for heating

A Adapted from CIBSE (1998), CIBSE Guide F: Energy efficiency in buildings, CIBSE, London.
B M4I (1998), Environmental performance indicators for sustainable construction: Sustainability Working Group Report, Movement for Innovation, London
C HEEBPp (1996), Building a sustainable future: homes for an autonomous community, Housing Energy Efficiency Best Practice programme, Watford

It is vitally important if we are to move towards sustainable developments that the planning system begins to incorporate performance standards, and ceases to be so largely concerned with the visual impacts of buildings.

Building-level indicators

The most energy-efficient buildings in the UK perform way in excess of the benchmarks shown in Table 11.6. Before setting the benchmark for a new build or refurbishment it is worth considering what is actually achievable with current technology, in real buildings.

One example of an excellent building, as identified by the PROBE project (see Chapter 39), is the Headquarters of Wessex Water, which won the "Building of the Year" award presented by the Royal Institution of Chartered Surveyors in February 2002.

Wessex Water's new operations centre on the outskirts of Bath (see Figure 11.8) is the workplace for over 500 staff.[15] It is a two-storey E-shaped building of area 10,000m² with three parallel wings of office space on the eastern side. The services are concentrated at the west side. The building received the highest possible BREEAM rating from the BRE (see Chapter 30). The architect was Bennetts Associates, and the building services engineer was Buro Happold.

This operations centre has been called the greenest office building in the UK. The green features of the Wessex Water operations centre include:

- high floor-to-floor height and orientation of building, enables utilisation of natural ventilation and daylighting through the manually operable windows and glazed walls
- highly insulated high thermal mass construction
- windows controlled by the building management system (BMS) to open at night to release excess heat and cool the concrete thermal mass, and to close when mechanical ventilation starts
- energy-efficient 2 x 26W T5 fluorescent luminaries with electronic dimming ballast down to 1 per cent of full output
- automatic lighting level adjustment and operation with light sensors and passive infra-red presence detectors.

The annual energy consumption of the building is 100 kWh/m², which is much better than some good practice offices (typically, 150 kWh/m²) and the "typical" office building (300 kWh/m²). The energy performance statistics are as follows:

- annual heating and hot water energy consumption, 50 kWh/m²

Figure 11.8 Wessex Water's Operations Centre in Bath has been called the greenest building in the UK

- annual mechanical ventilation and air-conditioning energy consumption, 10 kWh/m²
- annual lighting energy consumption, 12 kWh/m²
- annual small power energy consumption, 20 kWh/m²
- annual emission of CO_2, 36.36 kg/m²
- annual consumption of potable water, 4.48 m³/person.

References

1   Tallack P (ed) (2003),*The Science Book*, Weidenfeld & Nicolson, London, p 244
2   Pout CH, McKenzie F and Bettle R (2002), *Carbon Dioxide Emissions from Non-Domestic Buildings: 2000 and beyond*, Building Research Establishment and Department for Environment, Food and Rural Affairs, Garston, p 10
3   See *www.unl.ac.uk/LEARN/www/staff/fergus_prof_lec/index.htm*, the professorial lecture given by Professor Fergus Nicol, Deputy Director LEARN, at London Metropolitan University on 19 February 2003
4   One joule (1 J) is the energy resulting from the equivalent of one newton (1 N) of force acting over one meter (1 m) of displacement.
5   There are a number of websites that can do the mathematics of conversion. Try *www.convert-me.com/en* or *www.ex.ac.uk/cimt/dictunit/ccenrgy.htm*
6   Actually, quoting "Btu" is not strictly correct; when describing "power" we should talk about Btu per hour (Btu/h).
7   Source for tables: Fox RH (1965),"Heat", in *The Physiology of Human Survival*, Edholme OG and Bacharach AL (eds), Academic Press, London, Ch. 3
8   The UK National Energy Foundation's website has a facility to calculate an individual's annual CO_2 emission; the conversion factors in Table 11.5 are taken from here. View these, and more, at *www.natenergy.org.uk/convert.htm*
9   Keay M, McKee B and McCloskey G (2003), "Coal", *Oxford Energy Forum, Journal of the Oxford Institute for Energy Studies,* Issue 52, February 2003
10 Source: Michael Lindemann's article "Energy: can (the) world meet demand of the next 50 years?" at the Global Situation Report website on: *www.gsreport.com*
11 A key problem with many modern building is over-glazing. This leads not only to over-heating but also to discomfort and lower productivity because computers, for instance, cannot be used in high glare conditions.
12 Publications generated by this government-funded programme are free, and can be downloaded or ordered from *www.actionenergy.org.uk*
13 DETR (2002), *Building Regulations Approved Document L1 Conservation of fuel and power in dwellings and L2 Conservation of fuel and power in buildings other than dwellings,* The Stationery Office, Norwich

14 XCO2 (2002). *Insulation for Sustainability: A guide*, published by BING, the Federation of Rigid Polyurethane Foam Associations. See *www.XCO2.com*

15 Learn more about Wessex Water's Operations Centre at *www.wessexwater .co.uk/operationscentre/index.html*

On-line resources

For an excellent guide to how to do your own office energy audit see the factsheet: *Benchmarking & energy consumption* (1999), available at w*ww.uea .ac.uk/env*

See also: GCI (1998) *Contraction and Convergence: A global solution to a global problem* at *www.gci.org.uk*

Further reading

Bartlett P B and Prior JJ (1991), *The Environmental Impact of Buildings*, Building Research Establishment, Garston

Bartsch H and Muller B (2000), *Fossil Fuels in a Changing Climate*, Oxford University Press, Oxford

Beggs C (2002), *Energy: Management, supply and conservation*, Butterworth Heineman, Oxford

Campbell CJ (2003), "The peak of oil: an economic and political turning point for the world", in Low N and Gleeson B, *Making Urban Transport Sustainable*, published by Palgrave Macmillan, Basingstoke, pp 42–66

Hulme M et al (2002), *Climate Change Scenarios for the United Kingdom: The UKCIP02 scientific report.* Tyndall Centre for Climate Change Research, School of Environmental Sciences, University of East Anglia, Norwich, UK

Roaf S, Fuentes M and Thomas S (2003), *Ecohouse 2: A design guide*, Architectural Press, Oxford

Shorrock LD and Henderson G (1990), *Energy Use in Buildings and Carbon Dioxide emissions,* Building Research Establishment, Garston

Shorrock LD et al (2001), *Carbon Emission Reductions from Energy Efficiency Improvements to the UK Housing Stock*, Building Research Establishment and Department for Environment, Food and Rural Affairs, London

Biodiversity

Definition

There are three general kinds of biodiversity: species diversity, genetic diversity and habitat diversity. These are discussed in more detail below; suffice to say here that the survival of each is linked to the health of the other two, and together they comprise the wealth of ecosystems.

Year on year numerous species of flora and fauna become extinct, not just because of the impact of climate change and pollution, but also directly as a result of development.

Related indicators

Quality of life; Climate change; Energy; Land use; Flooding; Air pollution; Water pollution.

Related tools

Environmental impact assessment; Ecological footprinting; Regeneration-based checklist.

About this chapter

This chapter has been drafted with the assistance of John Harte of the American Defenders Organisation[1] and Peter Hakes of Essex Council Council.

Biodiversity is a wide-ranging subject; many books and articles have been written on the subject, and there is a vast wealth of research that we can draw on. We could not possibly do this vitally important subject full justice in the space available here, and instead have devoted this chapter to presenting a brief overview of the issues, backed up by a comprehensive list of references and information sources for readers who require more detail.

Background

Species diversity

Species diversity is what most people mean when they talk about biodiversity. The "species" is one level of classification in a taxonomic hierarchy that includes:

- the species
- the genus
- the family
- the order
- the class
- the phylum
- the kingdom.

Consider people, whose species name is *Homo sapiens*. *Homo* is the genus, and *sapiens* designates the species. We happen, now, to be the only living species in the genus *Homo*. We are in the family Hominidae (apes and man), the order of Primates (femurs, monkeys, apes, and man), the class Mammalia, the phylum Chordata (or vertebrates), and the kingdom animal.

There are several hundred classes and several dozen phyla. Individuals in different classes differ from each other far more than do those in the same class but in different orders, families, or species. For example, a downy woodpecker and a mallard duck (both in the class Aves, which includes all the birds) are more alike than a tiger salamander and a wood rat (which are in the classes Amphibia and Mammalia, respectively). And individuals in different phyla differ from each other far more than those in the same phylum but in different classes. For example, salmon and horses (both in the phylum Chordata, or organisms with a spinal cord) are more alike than are spiders and worms (in the phyla Arthropoda and Annelida, respectively).

There are about one and a half million named species on earth, but we know that many unnamed species exist, and the total number is probably between 5 and 15 million. Most of the evidence for numerous unnamed species comes from studies of insects in tropical forests: when the canopy of a tropical tree is fumigated and all the dead insects are collected, large numbers of hitherto unknown insects are frequently collected.

Tropical rainforests cover less than 2 per cent of the planet and yet are the only home of at least 50 per cent – possibly as many as 90 per cent – of all species on earth. The higher estimate is based on the assumption that a large share of the to-be-discovered species will be tropical because biological exploration of the tropics is so fragmentary. Other habitats are also poorly explored, though, and undoubtedly contain numerous species unknown to science today. Among these are the soils of temperate forests, such as the moist old-growth forests in the Pacific Northwest of the United States, where numerous new species of fungi, nematodes, beetles, and other equally warm and cuddly soil dwellers are likely to lurk.

It has been estimated that, in a typical acre of rainforest, there are likely to be more plant species than in all of Great Britain. Moreover, the geographic range of many species in the tropics is generally far smaller than it is in the temperate or polar latitudes. Thus, in the tropics, the species found in one acre differ from those in an adjacent acre far more than is the case elsewhere.

Each year, during the past several decades, people have been destroying enough tropical forest to cover an area half the size of Britain. Some of this lost forest, particularly in Central and South America, is burned and then used for cattle grazing or for crops; some, particularly in Asia, is clearcut for its timber; and, particularly in Africa, fuelwood gathering accelerates the pace of deforestation. During the 20th Century, between one quarter and one half of the rainforests on earth have been destroyed. At the current rate of destruction, there will be only tiny patches of rainforest left by the middle of the 21st Century.

Because of the tremendous concentration of species in the tropics and their often narrow geographic ranges, biologists estimate that tropical deforestation will result in the loss of half or more of the existing species on earth during the next 75 years. Humanity is now in the process of destroying roughly as many species during the next 50 to 100 years as were wiped out every 100 million years by natural causes. It takes only a few decades, as history shows, to drive a once-abundant species, like the passenger pigeon, to extinction. It is inconceivable that, during the coming millennia, evolution could replace with new species those lost to deforestation and other human actions.

Although deforestation in the species-rich tropics is currently a focus for out-rage, it must never be forgotten that deforestation in North America and Europe has destroyed even larger areas of old-growth forest than in the tropics. Virtually all the magnificent hardwood forests of the North Eastern United States were cleared prior to the American Civil War; the second-growth forests that have sprouted on abandoned farmland during the past century are a poor ecological substitute for what was lost. In recent years, clear-cutting in the United States is again destroying some of the most magnificent old-growth forest in the world.

Genetic diversity

Genetic diversity is about the "gene pool" of a population. A population is a col-lection of individuals who live together and choose mates from within the group. In the case of song sparrows, for instance, the sparrows in one population share more of their genes with each other than they do with other individuals from populations of the same species elsewhere, because individuals in one population rarely breed with those in another. Although each population within a species contains some genetic information which is unique to that population, individuals in all populations share in common the genetic information that defines their species.

Habitat diversity

Habitat diversity refers to the variety of places where life exists – coral reefs, old-growth forests, prairies, coastal wetlands, and many others. Each habitat is the home for numerous species, most of which are utterly dependent on that habitat. So when a type of habitat disappears, a vast number of species disappear as well. More often, an entire habitat does not completely disappear but instead is nibbled away, acre by acre, until only small patches remain. This has happened to old-growth forest and coastal wetlands in the United States and is now in full swing in tropical forests throughout the world.

Elimination of small patches of habitat can lead to the extinction of those species that live only in small regions of the habitat. Most damaging of all is the situation where only small patches of a habitat remain: this not only eliminates many localised species but also threatens those species that are dependent on vast acreages for their survival.

Habitat diversity is particularly vulnerable to damage from development. In a small country like Britain, new roads or railway routes can quickly isolate populations, cut wildlife off from food sources or obliterate ancient pathways. This problem has been acknowledged, and some areas now benefit from being designated as sites of special scientific interest (SSSIs); others, e.g. badgers' setts, are protected by law.

Global indicators[2]

Global biodiversity is changing at an unprecedented rate.[3] The current rate of extinction is many times higher than the "background" rate (i.e. that which has prevailed over long periods of geological time). However, over the past three decades, decline and extinction of species have emerged as major environmental issues, and there has been a concerted response to the biodiversity crisis. The diverse and increasingly sophisticated network of non-governmental organisations (NGOs) has been a major driving force behind this.

A number of international conventions have been developed that deal specifically with conservation of threatened species. Among the most notable are the 1973 Convention on International Trade in Endangered Species of Wild Fauna and Flora (CITES), and the 1979 Convention on the Conservation of Migratory Species of Wild Animals (CMS) (known as the Bonn Convention), which was developed to conserve terrestrial, marine and migratory bird species throughout their range. Inter-governmental agreements such as the African-Eurasian Waterbird Agreement (which aims to develop transboundary strategic measures necessary to conserve the network of critical wetland areas on which migratory waterbirds depend) are the primary tools for the implementation of the CMS.

Information on the conservation status of species is provided by the International Union for Conservation of Nature and Natural Resources (IUCN) which publishes the *Red List of Threatened Species*. The 2002 Red List[4] indicates that about 24 per cent (1,130) of mammals and 12 percent (1183) of bird species are currently regarded as globally threatened. Since the Red List assessment of 1996, the number of critically endangered species has increased from 169 to 180 mammals and from 168 to 182 birds. And some commentators suggest it is possible that over the next 100 years the extinction rate of vertebrate groups could be as high as 15–20 per cent.

Much of the relevant information on the status of species is qualitative or anecdotal, and it is therefore difficult to develop a quantitative overview of global trends. To assess trends in species loss or decline, indicators are required that provide quantitative estimates of change over time, using consistent methodologies for sampling and analysis. Ideally, such indicators should be based on data sampled explicitly for this purpose. Few such monitoring programmes have yet been established.

One approach is the Living Planet Index created by UNEP-WCMC in cooperation with WWF.[5] The index is based on estimates of population size of individual wild species available in the scientific literature, and takes 1970 as its baseline. The index covers three habitats — forest, freshwater and marine ecosystems. The prevailing trend of all three indices is downward.

The forest index, based on 319 populations of temperate and tropical species (mostly birds), shows a decline of about 12 per cent during 1970–99. The index for temperate species shows only little change over the period (most deforestation here having taken place before the 20th century). The tropical sample shows a downward trend, consistent with the continuing deforestation in many tropical areas.

The marine index, based on populations of 217 species of marine animals, shows a decline of about 35 per cent.

Inland water and wetland species, represented by a sample of 194 populations, have declined by 50 per cent.

Table 12.1 Impacts of biodiversity: direct and indirect

DIRECT IMPACTS	INDIRECT IMPACTS*
Loss of soils/vegetation	Soil pollution – leakage accident, substances deposited on or in land, polluted by precipitation or by migration of polluted groundwater soil conditions can affect toxicity of pollutants.
Loss or modification of habitats	
Severance or fragmentation of a habitat. For example, roads etc. may affect the movement of wildlife; if scarce species are separated the possibility of survival may be reduced.	Water pollution caused by accidental spillage or polluting discharges and changes to pH or nutrient levels.
Impacts on rare and protected species (e.g. badgers, otters, bats and barn owls) could include:	Altered flows in groundwater and river regimes.
• loss of roosting/breeding/hibernation sites	Air pollution – even apparently non-damaging materials can cause chemical changes e.g. alkaline dust from cement factories, and dust from haulage routes can smother plants.
• loss of foraging/hunting grounds	
• reduction in prey items/food supply	Micro-climate changes e.g. major urban areas tend to retain more heat than rural areas; release of heat in cooling water from power stations.
• interruption/bisection of traditional routes, and migration patterns etc	
	Noise, light and fire hazards from public activities e.g. war games and bike riding in woods, or simply caused by proximity to humans.
	Lateral migration of landfill gas some distance from landfill sites.

Source: courtesy of Peter Hakes, Essex County Council

* Indirect effects can be complex; effects can be cumulative and influenced by other factors such as temperature and sunlight.

European indicators

European law necessitates the recording, conservation and protection of endangered species and habitats, and every country in the European Union has its own related legislation to implement this. In the UK, for instance, this issue is covered by the UK European Protected Species Legislation, which in UK law is included in the Conservation (Natural Habitats etc.) Regulations 1994.[6]

There are a number of high-profile species in Europe that are becoming extinct: the Mediterranean Monk Seal, the Greater Horshoe Bat and the European Bison . . . and even "European Retail Banks" if an Internet search is to be believed!

Europe hosts a plethora of unique environments and climates, each with its own particular family of resident species. Nearly every region of Europe has a species that is mentioned in the Red List.[7]

Another excellent report, carried out under the auspices of the WWF (formerly the World Wide Fund for Nature) is "The Carpathian List of Endangered Species."[8]

Figure 12.1 One example of the many surveys carried out by the British Trust for Ornithology (BTO): Common birds census population trend for Skylark, 1962–1997

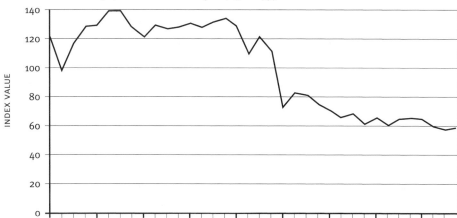

Source: British Trust for Ornithology

Issues of biodiversity are central to environmental impact assessments (see Chapter 27), and the European Union publishes clear guidelines on their application.[9]

UK government and NGO indicators

Nature conservation has a long and interesting history in the UK[10] but biodiversity has now become an important issue in planning and development because of the need to:

- avoid placing damaging development on or adjoining sensitive sites
- protect rare and protected species and habitats
- use the least sensitive areas for any necessary development
- seek to enhance nature conservation.

There is also a growing awareness that long-term management is essential if impact mitigation strategies are to be successful, and this should be accounted for early in the planning phase. For example, a relocated marshy grassland or wetland habitat will need to be regularly monitored to ensure that the site does not dry out, thus leading to a change in the species composition.

Development can have both direct and indirect impacts on biodiversity (see Table 12.1).

Any development proposals that are likely to affect a European Protected Species must seek a licence from the Department for Environment, Food and Rural Affairs (DEFRA), which will involve consultation with the relevant planning authority, and English Nature.

Figure 12.2 Suggested times of year for field surveys

	JANUARY	FEBRUARY	MARCH	APRIL	MAY	JUNE
Vascular plants				░	▓	▓
Bryophytes, lichens	▓	▓	▓	▓	▓	▓
Marine algae			░	░	▓	▓
Large fungi						▓
Wintering birds	▓	▓	▓			
Breeding birds			▓	▓	▓	▓
Terrestial invertebrates			▓	▓	▓	▓
Dragonflies						
Aquatic insects	▓	▓	▓	▓		
Ancient woodland surface features	▓	▓	▓	▓		

There are some exceptions, for example, hay meadows cannot be surveyed for vascular plants after cutting (usually June), and sand dunes should be visited to survey spring annuals before the middle of May.

Figure 12.3 Suggested times of year for surveying rare and protected species

	JANUARY	FEBRUARY	MARCH	APRIL	MAY	JUNE
Bats: Winter hibernacula Summer roosts (see note above)						
Badgers	░	░	░	░	░	░
Reptiles			▓	▓	▓	▓
Amphibians			▓	▓	▓	▓
Bees, ant and wasps (hymenoptera)			▓	▓	▓	▓
Woodland flora	░	░	░	▓	▓	▓
Grassland flora	░	░	░	░	░	▓

Bats: Should not be disturbed, whether during the winter when they hibernate or while roosting in the summer. Surveys will generally consist of looking for signs of bats rather than seeing the animals. If bats are thought to be present **English Nature** should be contacted so that an experienced person can assess the situation.

Badgers: Badgers breed in October and, as a result, setts should not be disturbed. Although survey work need not necessarily disturb sows or cubs at this time of year, care should be exercised, and encouragement given to survey work outside this period. Any work involving disturbance to a sett between the months of December and June will need to be licensed by **English Nature**.

Reptiles, amphibians and hymenoptera: No meaningful survey work will be practicable between the months of November and February. This is because these species will either be over-wintering as eggs/pupae or be holed up somewhere relatively warm and dark, waiting for warmer weather/spring and summer.

BIODIVERSITY

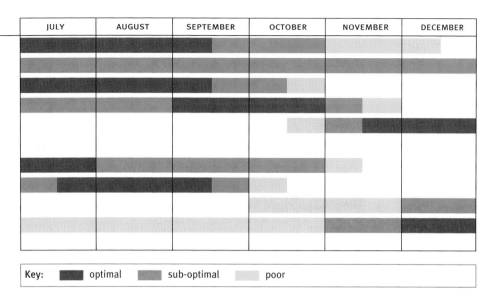

JULY	AUGUST	SEPTEMBER	OCTOBER	NOVEMBER	DECEMBER

Key: optimal sub-optimal poor

Source: Courtesy of Peter Hakes, Essex County Council

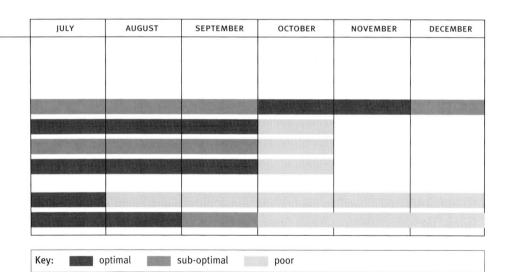

JULY	AUGUST	SEPTEMBER	OCTOBER	NOVEMBER	DECEMBER

Key: optimal sub-optimal poor

Source: Courtesy of Peter Hakes, Essex County Council

161

A vast array of NGOs in the UK collect data on the prevalence of species. For example, the Forestry Commission publishes an inventory of all trees and woodlands in Great Britain;[11] while the British Trust for Ornithology[12] has been tracking the decline of birds such as skylarks and song thrushes for over 30 years (see Figure 12.1)

Local authority indicators

Planning authorities are required to produce biodiversity action plans to protect and enhance priority habitats and species within their areas. Consult local authority websites for appropriate indicators.

Developers should also consult these local action plans to see whether the project is likely to affect habitats and species (including areas that might have the potential for habitat re-creation, or enhancement); and whether any of the actions identified in the plan can be delivered via the project.

Scope of biodiversity studies

Peter Hakes of Essex County Council writes: Studies of local biodiversity on sites may be required to cover:

- A habitat survey; to an appropriate level of detail. This should seek to cover fauna and flora at all relevant seasons, and, in particular, specialist surveys may be required for rare and protected species. Local specialists may be able to fill in details if time/season preclude new survey work. The weather can also determine visible species. Reference should also be made to long-term trends/previous records. Terrestrial and aquatic ecosystems should be considered; and also marine environs for example where pipelines are built to discharge effluent to tidal waters.
- Identification of designated areas, e.g. SSSIs, Ramsar sites (important wetlands) and special protection areas under the EC Birds Directive, and special areas of conservation under the Habitats Directive, National Nature Reserves and also local sites i.e. sites of importance for nature conservation (SINCS) (sometimes known as County Wildlife Sites), local nature reserves, wildlife corridors etc.
- Evaluation of sites and ecological features – in terms of size, species richness, and diversity, rarity, typicality and naturalness or ancientness or recreatability.
- Records of size and rarity. These should be set in the context of their surroundings and in terms of whether they are of international, national, regional or local importance.

Mitigation strategies

Table 12.2 lists some possible strategies to help avoid adverse impacts on local (or wider) biodiversity.

Table 12.2 Strategies to avoid adverse impact on habitats and species

AVOIDANCE	REDUCTION	REMEDIES/COMPENSATION*
Relocate away from high ecological interest Fence sensitive areas Time construction or lorry movements etc. to avoid sensitive periods Long-term management.	Modify design etc. e.g. reed bed silt traps to reduce polluted waste running directly into sensitive areas Conservation of wildlife corridors; tunnels for badgers etc	Seek to relocate species or recreate that which is lost; e.g. soil or turf transfers etc. However, there should be a presumption in favour of conservation in situ – ancient woodlands are not recreatable; new habitats take many years to achieve maturity. Only relocate species or habitats as a last resort, because success is very difficult to achieve and requires detailed monitoring; but new habitats can be a bonus! (They can take decades to achieve maturity.) Any new planting must be indigenous to the area.

Source: courtesy of Peter Hakes, Essex County Council

*   Note that water table levels, presence of landfill gas, nature of soil and micro-climate can all be crucial to survival of new planting/habitats.

- Identification of ancient woodland e.g. from county Ancient Woodland Inventories maintained and published by English Nature or from old maps.

Clearly these are complex issues, and any predictions of impacts or assessment of significance of impact should be undertaken by experienced ecologists. In particular, care must be taken to ensure that the biodiversity surveys are conducted at a suitable time of year – when the best data will be gathered, and when the least damage will be done to the species being recorded. Figures 12.2 and 12.3 outline suitable annual schedules for surveys.

References

1   The definition and general background to this chapter are based on an excerpt from Harte J (1993), *The Green Fuse: An ecological odyssey*, University of California Press. The full text, as published in *Defenders*, the house magazine of the US-based the Defenders of Wildlife, can be viewed at *www.defenders. org/bio-bio3.html* John Harte is an ecological scientist at the University of California, Berkeley.

2   Text for this section is derived from Chapter 2 of *Global Environmental Outlook (GEO) 3: Past, present and future perspectives*, published by the United Nations Environment Programme – World Conservations Monitoring Centre (UNEP-WCMC) project GEO. For the full text, visit *www.rolac.unep.mx*

3   For a list of the world's most high-profile endangered species see *www. quantum-conservation.org*

4   IUCN (2002), *2002 IUCN Red List of Threatened Species*. View the document at *www.redlist.org*

5   For more details, visit *www.unep-wcmc.org*

6   The Conservation (Natural Habitats, &c.) Regulations 1994 (Statutory Instrument 1994 No. 2716) (The "Habitats Regulations"), including a list of the European protected species, can be viewed at *http://www.hmso.gov.uk* See also: The Conservation (Natural Habitats, &c.) (Amendment) Regulations 1997 (Statutory Instrument 1997 No. 3055) and The Conservation (Natural Habitats, &c.) (Amendment) (England) Regulations 2000 (Statutory Instrument 2000 No. 192)

7   See IUCN (2002), op. cit.

8   Witkowski ZJ (ed) (2003) *Carpathian List of Endangered Species*, published by WWF, can be downloaded at: *http://www.carpathians.org* See also the WWF website at *www.panda.org/about_wwf*

9   Decision VI/07 "Identification, monitoring, indicators and assessments", of the COP 6 meeting; see *www.biodiv.org*

10 See *www.naturenet.net/status/history.html*

11 For example, oak is the most common tree; and there has been a 26 per cent increase in woodland cover since 1980. See *http://www.forestry.gov.uk/inventory*

12 BTO (1998), *The Common Birds Census*, British Trust for Ornithology, Thetford; view at *http://www.bto.org* See also the BTO index of surveys at *www.bto.org/survey/index.htm*

UK-specific references

British Government Panel on Sustainable Development (1994). *Biodiversity: The UK Action Plan*, Cm 2428, HMSO

Byron H (2000), *Biodiversity and Environmental Impact Assessment: A good practice guide for road schemes*, published by the RSPB, WWF, English Nature and the Wildlife Trusts, from the Royal Society for the Protection of Birds, Sandy

DETR (1996), *Reclamation of Damaged Land for Nature Conservation*, HMSO

Essex Guide to Environmental Impact Assessment (2000). Available from: *www.essexcc.gov.uk*

IEMAS (1995), *Guidelines for Baseline Ecological Assessment*, Institute of Environmental Management and Assessment, E & FN Spon, London

Nature Conservancy Council (1993), *Handbook for Phase 1 Habitats Survey: A technique for environmental audit*, 1st edn 1990, (See also the associated *Field Manual*)

Pryor SN and Smith S (2002), *The Area and Composition of Plantations on Ancient Woodland Sites*, The Woodland Trust. View at: *www.woodland-trust.org.uk/ policy/index.htm*

Ratcliffe DA (ed) (1989), *Guidelines for Selection of Biological SSSIs*, Nature Conservancy Council, Peterborough

RSPB (1997), *Guide to Mineral Extraction*, Royal Society for the Protection of Birds, Sandy

RSBP (1996), *Natural Conditions: Review of planning conditions and nature conservation*, Royal Society for the Protection of Birds, Sandy

RSPB/NRA/RSNC (1994), *The New Rivers and Wildlife Handbook: Guidance on the sympathetic management of watercourses*, Royal Society for the Protection of Birds, Sandy

RTPI (1999), *Planning for Biodiversity: Good practice guide*, Royal Town Planning Institute, London

Woodland Trust (2000), *Ancient Woods and Planning Applications, A guide for local authorities in England and Wales*, The Woodland Trust, Grantham. See also: *http://www.woodland-trust.org.uk*

Global references

Anderson DM (1994), "Red tides", *Scientific American*, August, 62–68

Bird Life International (2000), *Threatened Birds of the World*, Lynx Editions and Bird Life International, Barcelona and Cambridge

Bruner AG, Gullison RE, Rice R. and de Fonseca GAB (2001), "Effectiveness of parks in protecting tropical biodiversity", *Science,* 291, 125- 28

Costanza R et al (1997) "The value of the world's ecosystem services and natural capital", *Nature,* 387, 253–260

Etkin DS (1999), *International Oil Spill Statistics: 1998*, Cutter Information Corporation, Arlington, MA

FAO (1999), *State of the World's Forests 1999*, UN Food and Agriculture Organization, Rome. View the document at *www.fao.org* See also FAO (1999), *The State of the World's Fisheries and Aquaculture 1998*

Goreau T, McClanahan T, Hayes R and Strong AE (2000), "Conservation of coral reefs after the 1998 global bleaching event", *Conservation Biology* 14, 5–15

Green MJB and Paine J (1997), "State of the World's Protected Areas at the End of the 20th Century" Paper presented at the IUCN World Commission on Protected Areas Seminar *Protected Areas in the 21st Century: From Islands to Networks*, World Conservation Monitoring Centre, Cambridge

Groombridge B and Jenkins MD (2000), *Global Biodiversity: Earth's living resources in the 21st century*, The World Conservation Press, Cambridge

IPCC (2001), *IPCC Third Assessment Report: Climate Change 2001*. Working Group II: Impacts, Adaptation and Vulnerability, World Meteorological Organization and United Nations Environment Programme, Geneva. View the document at *www.ipcc.ch*

Loh J (2000), *The Living Planet Report 2000*, WWF-The Global Environment Network, Gland, Switzerland

Mace G M (1995), "Classification of threatened species and its role in conservation planning", In: Lawton JH and May RM (eds), *Extinction Rates*, Oxford University Press, Oxford

Mahony DE (1996), *The Convention on International Trade in Endangered Species of Fauna and Flora: Addressing problems in global wildlife trade and enforcement*, New England International and Comparative Law Annual. View the document at *www.nesl.edu*

Matthews E, Payne R, Rohweder M and Murray S (2000), *Pilot Analysis of Global Ecosystems: Forest ecosystems*, World Resources Institute, Washington DC

Milner-Gulland EJ and Mace R (1998), *Conservation of Biological Resources*, Blackwell Science, Oxford

Pimm S I, Russell G J, Gittelman J L and Brooks TM (1995), "The future of biodiversity", *Science*, 269, 347–50

Pounds AJ, Fogden MPL and Campbell J.H (1999), "Biological response to climate change on a tropical mountain", *Nature,* 398, 611–15

Sala OE et al (2000) "Global biodiversity scenarios for the year 2100", *Science*, 287, 1770–74

UNCCD (2001) *The United Nations Convention to Combat Desertification: An explanatory leaflet*. UN Convention to Combat Desertification. See *www.unccd.int*

UNDP, UNEP, World Bank and WRI (2000), *World Resources 2000-2001*, World Resources Institute, Washington DC

UNEP (1992), *World Atlas of Desertification*, Edward Arnold, London

UNEP (1995), *Global Biodiversity Assessment*, Cambridge University Press, Cambridge

Vitousek P et al (1997), "Human alteration of the global nitrogen cycle: causes and consequences", *Issues In Ecology* 1, 2–16

Vitousek PM and Hooper DU (1993), "Biological diversity and terrestrial ecosystem biogeochemistry", In: Schulze ED and Mooney HA (eds), *Biodiversity and Ecosystem Function*, Springer-Verlag, Berlin

Additional on-line resources

CREO, the Committee on Recently Extinct Organisms. *http://creo.amnh.org/index.html*

For an excellent bibliography of related publications see: *http://212.187.155.84/wnv/Subdirectories_for_Search/Glossary&References_Contents/BooksContents/BookRef93WetlandsIndustry&Wildlife/Appendix11.htm*

For a comprehensive list of documents and sites relating to protected species see *www.jncc.gov.uk/ProtectedSites/SACselection/references.htm*

Planning policy guidance – related documents (see Appendix 1 for details)

1	2	3	4	5	6	7	8	9	10	11	12	13
x	x	x	x	x	x	x		x	x	x	x	x

14	15	16	17	18	19	20	21	22	23	24	25	
x	x	x	x	x	x	x	x	x	x	x	x	

Transport

Definition

Transport is the movement of people or goods between places and the vehicular means of doing so. As the second largest generator of greenhouse gases (after buildings), as a consumer of a range of natural resources, and as the underlying reason for a significant proportion of all the world's construction projects, transport and its impacts should be high on any list that aims to tackle sustainability.

Related indicators

Quality of life, Community, Health, Climate change, Energy, Land use, Flooding, Air pollution, Waste.

Related solutions

Specifying for sustainability, Transport solutions, Environmental management schemes.

Related tools

Environmental impact assessment, Ecological footprinting, Regeneration-based checklist.

Background

Of all the environmental issues, transport has the greatest global and local impacts, after buildings, and is seen as an increasingly acute problem in many areas because it is a higher energy user and a significant source of carbon dioxide (CO_2) emissions, health impacts and pollution. It is also a consumer of raw materials and land for roads, and generates noise pollution too.

These problems are rapidly increasing around the world because, as Figure 13.1 shows, the richer we get, the more we travel, and the impacts of that travel multiply accordingly.

Figure 13.1 Trends in personal travel (cars) in the UK: 1974–1998

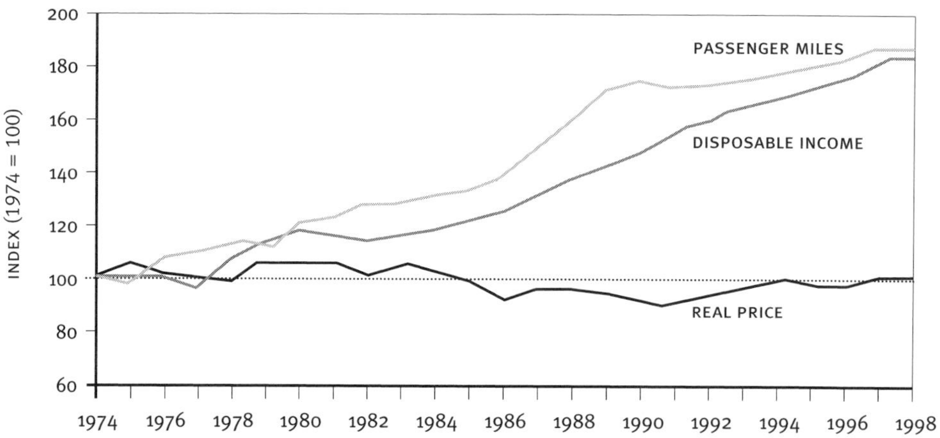

Note that the units on the vertical axis are ambiguous, although they do demonstrate trends well.

Source: www.sustainable-development.gov.uk © Crown Copyright

Today, our sophisticated methods of exploiting the high energy content of oil enable us to make journeys effortlessly, and we are in a position to take advantage of this. The increasing efficiency of our engines (as shown by the fact that the real price of travel has stayed constant as passenger miles rise) means that we spread the impacts of our travel far and wide, as we go further and further for the same price.

Transport and planning

Today, transport is a key issue in any planning process, but it has always been a dominant factor in the growth of settlements. People have always tended to congregate at "transport centres" – building cities such as London and Paris at river crossings; villages at crossroads; or hamlets at resting places between towns. Transport has always been a factor in city design – from the great circular walled cities of the Assyrians to the foursquare, four-gated Greek and Roman cities, and the 8th Century circular city of Baghdad. City planners traditionally designed to optimise route ways and travel distances for horses, carts and chariots alike, as well as taking into account the city's defences. How different these planned cities were from the un-planned higgledy-piggledy warrens of streets and passageways that characterised European and Eastern cities of the Middle Ages, and which grew around the church, temple, mosque and market place into surrounding fields and alleyways.

By the 18th and 19th Centuries industrial power and wealth gave the grand architects of Europe the opportunity to create great spaces, avenues and places, piazzas and parks, adorned by ornamental façades to be admired from the promenade or carriage. And with the growth of the railways in the 19th Century, many cities were restructured once more to accommodate the tracks and stations that serviced suburbs and empires alike.

But it was the invention of the car at the turn of the 20th Century that heralded a new, and unprecedented planning tyranny. Yet more roads were superimposed onto the faces of the cities, and the quality of the details of the built environment became less important. Indeed, the place and the façade often became irrelevant, often disrespected, as people sped through towns to reach ever more distant locations. One hundred years ago, who could have predicted the coming of dormitory villages, motorways and out-of-town shopping centres?

The car culture

One of the earliest plans for a motorised city was that of Chicago, in the heartland of the emerging motor industry of America. The 1906 Chicago Plan was undertaken by a private group of merchants belonging to the Commercial Club of Chicago. It was proposed:

"…for the moral up-building and physical beautification of Chicago, which included better living conditions for all people, reclaiming the lake front for the public, increasing the park areas and public playgrounds, and a scientific development of the arteries between the different sections of the city."[1]

In 1909, the City Council of Chicago authorised the appointment of the Chicago Plan Commission, which, by 1925, developed a comprehensive superhighway system, as well as the construction of the Outer Drive Bridge and additional straightening of the Chicago River. This venture provided the basis for the "scientific American model" for traffic planning that is still influential today in cities around the world, such as Canberra, the planned capital city of Australia.

Today in many cities like these the dominance of the car is affecting the sustainability of the city itself. For example, if oil prices were to rise sharply then Canberra and other cities, particularly in Australia, Canada and the USA, may be left with many people who cannot afford to use the car and yet very poor public transport systems for the workers who service such cities.

The impacts of our car dependency are far reaching:

- Vehicles are the largest source of air pollution in most cities.[2] This problem will become more significant because many pollutants react differently in warmer temperatures. Climate change may bring higher temperatures to many of the world's cities, and this could influence chemical reactions within and between pollutants, particularly where air is heavily polluted.

- Traffic noise and fumes are generally cited as the reason for fixing the windows of a building closed and introducing air-conditioning, with its high energy use and related environmental impacts (see Chapters 8, 9 and 10).
- We may experience increased urban flooding from large areas of hard surfaces for roads and parking as a direct result of our dependency on cars.

In the last 50 years the world has seen the growth of car dependent mega-cities, where travel times to and from work can be measured in hours rather than minutes, and where the phenomenon of "gridlock" has become common throughout the developed and the developing world. Table 13.1 lists some of the many problems associated with the car-dependent culture.

Not surprisingly, considerable research is now centred on how to reduce the impacts of transport on the lives and health of people in cities, and on future-proofing lifestyles against the inevitable end of the cheap oil that is, in the short term, fuelling the exponential trend towards more and more road and (particularly) airborne transport.[3]

Energy use for transport

Although we are addicted to our cars, they are not the most efficient mode of

Table 13.1 Some of the problems linked to our dependence on cars

ENVIRONMENTAL	ECONOMIC	SOCIAL
Oil vulnerability	External costs from accidents and pollution	Loss of street life
Photochemical smog	Congestion costs, despite endless road building	Loss of community
Toxic emissions such as lead and benzene	High infrastructure costs in new sprawling suburbs	Reduction in public safety
High greenhouse gas contributions	Loss of productive rural land	Isolation in remote suburbs
Urban sprawl	Loss of urban land	Traffic noise and fumes
Greater storm water from extra hard surfaces		Access problems for the car-less and those with disabilities
Traffic problems such as noise and severance		High levels of stress from traffic jams and gridlock
Related shift to air-conditioning in buildings and high resulting impacts		Shift to air-conditioning linked to sick building syndrome
Waste problem – tyres and scrap vehicles		

Source: Newman P and Kenworthy J, "Sustainable urban form: the big picture" in *Achieving Sustainable Urban Form*, K Williams et al, Spon, 2000

transport, as Figures 13.2, 13.3 and 13.4 show. The data in these figures is based on transport studies in Japan,[4] but clearly illustrates that rail travel is far more fuel-efficient than using the car.

There is also a strong correlation between wealth, the lifestyle of a culture and energy consumption in transport (see Table 13.2).

It is not surprising that there is also a very strong correlation between population density in these cities and transport energy consumption. An average Australian uses around twice as much energy as a European; while an American uses a staggering three times and more to fuel his travel than we do in Britain. In the agricultural city of Sacramento in California, for example, the citizens use 65,000 MJ/per person on transport, and there is a density of around 20 people per

Figure 13.2 Figures from Japan illustrate that cars use far more energy than other modes of transport

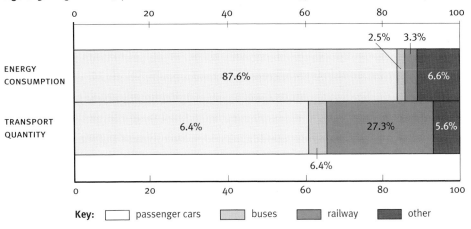

Source: 2000 Energy/Economy Statistics Summary, www.eccj.or.jp

Figure 13.3 The energy consumed when transporting one person 1 km using various vehicles (1998 figures)

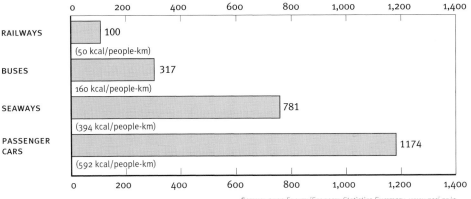

Source: 2000 Energy/Economy Statistics Summary, www.eccj.or.jp

Figure 13.4 Energy consumption for carrying 1 tonne of cargo for 1 km (1998)

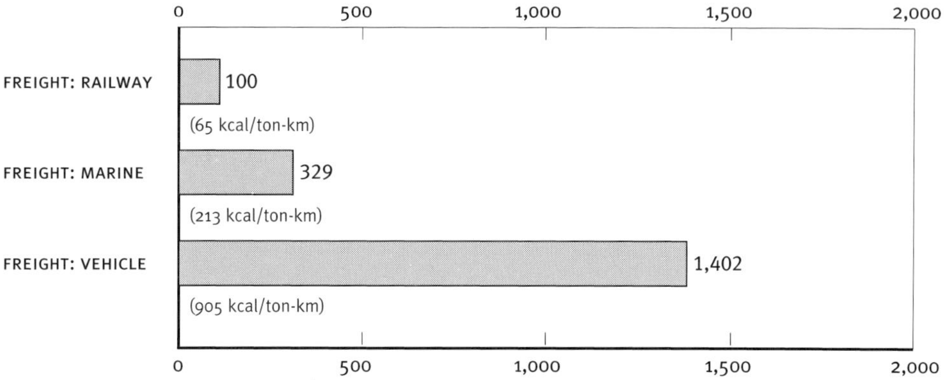

Source: 2000 Energy/Economy Statistics Summary, www.eccj.or.jp

hectare; at the other end of the scale in Hong Kong energy use is around 1,000 MJ/person per year and density is over 300 persons per hectare.[5]

Higher population densities are linked to lower energy consumption per capita on transport in several ways,[6] including:

- more people living closely together reduces the need to travel to see people for social contact, access to services, travel to work or shops
- shorter distances between places encourage walking or cycling and also make public transport options more viable due to the larger numbers available to use such systems.

Of course, in the case of Sacramento and Hong Kong, the actual cost of fuel is a major factor. Low petrol prices are a positive incentive to use cars in countries such as the United States, and also encourage the use of less fuel-efficient models. US travel energy consumption figures are undoubtedly influenced by the prevalence of large sports utility vehicles (SUVs) in America.

Table 13.2 Private passenger transport energy consumption per capita in 1990

COUNTRY	ENERGY CONSUMPTION (mJ/PERSON)
US cities	55,807
Australian cities	33,562
Canadian cities	30,893
European cities	17,218
Wealthy Asian cities	7,268
Developing Asian cities	5,832

Source: Newman & Kenworthy, 2000

Air travel

The last two decades of the 20th Century saw the introduction of another significant problem – cheap air travel – and concern is growing because of the damage it causes.

Aviation is the world's fastest growing man-made source of carbon dioxide in the atmosphere and is a major contributor to global warming. The world's 16,000 commercial jet aircraft pump out 600 million tonnes of carbon dioxide every year.[7]

A study by the eco-group Friends of the Earth found that one return London–Miami flight generates as much carbon dioxide as the average British motorist produces in a year. Jet fuel use, in the fabricated scenarios of global capitalists, is set to triple in the next half century.[8]

The main problem is the enormous amount of fuel it takes to keep an aeroplane in the air. Ten thousand new Boeing 747s, travelling for 10,880 miles and carrying nearly 200,000 litres of fuel, in a day use approximately equivalent to 1.25 million barrels of oil, and this represents a significant proportion of the 70 million barrels of oil a day we use around the world. The numbers are so big they are difficult to understand, but with the energy it takes to keep such a plane in the air every hour you could run 182,000 one bar electric fires, enough to heat a small town. The environmental impacts in terms of pollution and related emissions of greenhouse gasses are enormous. Air transport is responsible for around 3.5 per cent of contributions to climate change globally, a figure set to increase to between 4–15 per cent by 2050.[9] Many of the trips generated could quite easily be shifted to other forms of transport such as bus, rail or shipping, resulting in significant reductions to the atmospheric impacts of travel.[10] Table 13.3 gives the "ecological footprint" of typical plane journeys (see also Chapter 31).

There is also growing disquiet about the noise, traffic and pollution impacts of airports on local communities and the lives of the many people they affect.[11] While governments have been legislating to cut back on emissions from cars and buildings there is no tax on airline fuel, a move that would put restraints on the global economy. However, there is increasing pressure to impose such fuel taxes on the aviation industry as the impending severity of climate change becomes more apparent, but most doubt that governments, at the moment, have the will to act on this crucial issue.

Transport efficiency

So concerned are governments and local councils about transport, in terms of energy use, emissions and the implication of excessive fossil fuel dependence, that many cities have strong programmes for the promotion of transport efficiency. Chapter 25 discusses ways to avoid the worst impacts created by

Table 13.3 Ecological footprints for short and long haul flights for different plane types

Plane type	Boeing 737 (old)	Boeing 737 (new)	Boeing 747	Boeing 767	DC10 (old)	DC10 (new)
Passenger numbers	109	132	395	226	223	281
Fuel consumption (in litres per hour)	3,000	2,875	14,000	5,950	10,560	9,650
Speed (km/h)	835	835	920	865	890	890
Reach (km)	2,730	4,280	10,880	10,280	9,580	11,365
Fuel capacity (l)	20,000	20,000	197,000	91,700	138,000	145,000
Energy (mJ/passenger/km)	1.15	0.91	1.35	1.07	1.86	1.35
Embodied energy per km for new plane in 5 years	0.14	0.17	1.05	0.49	0.77	0.8
Ecological footprint per year per km for short flights (m²)	0.23	0.18	0.36	0.25	0.43	0.34
Ecological footprint per year per km for long flights (m²)			0.27	0.17	0.3	0.24

Source: Courtesy of Kevin Paulson

transport; but the extract from Melbourne City Council's website below neatly summarises the size of the problem that many cities are now facing.

"[Australian] Fact file:

- *Road transport costs $30 billion [Australian] per year in terms of congestion, accidents, pollution and noise*
- *Cars cost $2 for every $1 collected in road taxes and charges*
- *One third of our cities is made up of roads and car parks*
- *One train carrying 1000 people replaces 800 cars; one tram carrying 100 people replaces 80 cars*
- *One train carrying 1000 people = a line of cars 5 kilometres long; one bus carrying 50 people replaces 40 cars.*
- *A double track railway can move over 200,000 people per hour in each direction – a six lane freeway can move only a quarter of this volume*
- *A 6 lane freeway costs $6 million/kilometre, twice the cost of electrified double track railway*
- *Urban tram and train services keep 190 million car journeys off city streets each year, saving over 1 million tonnes of greenhouse gas emissions*
- *The average family car emits 6 tonnes of greenhouse gas emissions per year*
- *Australia has the third highest transport greenhouse gas emissions per capita in the world*

> • *Road transport greenhouse gas emissions comprise 89% of transport emissions, an increase of 18% since 1990*
> • *Just one freight train can keep 150 semi-trailers off highways."*[12]

The future?

What a difference a generation makes. It is increasingly rare, though not yet unheard, to hear of older people in Britain who say they have never been to the next big town, let alone the capital. Yet that was the norm for many people as little as 50 years ago in the UK, and it is still true for many people in the world. The car, bus, train, and now indeed the aeroplane, have democratised travel for even the poor in the richer countries, but travel by such means is still well out of the reach of the majority of the world's poor.

We are at the height of the car and plane age, and we should now be looking to see how to restructure our lifestyles and cities for the "post-fossil fuel age". Elements of the solution to this problem include:

- settlement planning
- public transport systems
- proper legislation and regulation to ensure the rights of all are catered for in relation to transport
- even the IT industries have a role to play – delivering a new way to bridge the gap between people without resorting to energy expensive car or plane use.

Global indicators

A number of international organisations are developing indicator sets for transport. One that has proved very popular is the Cities Environment Reports on the Internet (CEROI), established by the United Nations Environmental Programme (UNEP). These robust indicators, developed in response to Local Agenda 21, are being used on-line to provide an opportunity for cities around the world to compare their performance.[13] Table 13.4 gives one example of indicators in use.

European indicators

The EU's ten Common European Indicator sets for cities includes Indicators A.3, "Local mobility and passenger transportation".[14]
The indicators include:

- number of trips that, on average, each citizen makes during the day, where "trip" indicates a journey with a starting-point and a destination (number of daily trips per capita)

Table 13.4 Example of CEROI indicators for transport (data presented here for Prague)

INDICATOR	UNIT OF MEASUREMENT	DATA COLLECTED (1997)
Passenger cars	1/1000 persons	502
SO_2 air emissions	tonnes/year/km²	21.29
NO_x air emissions	tonnes/year/km²	9.62
Population affected by violation of air quality standards	%	–
Public transport seats	1/1000 persons	–
Work trips by public transport, bicycle or on foot	%	–
Total number of passengers carried by public transport	thousands	1,076,054

Source: www.ceroi.net

- reason for the trips and their regularity during the week, allowing for the trips to be classified as either "systematic" or "unsystematic" (percentage of systematic trips compared with the unsystematic ones)
- average distance covered by each citizen during the day (km/per capita)
- time taken by each citizen for his/her trips (minutes taken for the trips)
- modes of transport used for the trips and/or for the different distances associated with each trip (percentage relating to the different modes of transport considered).

The rationale for this indicator set is given as follows:

"The model of citizens' journeys or 'mobility' in an urban context is important with regard to both the quality of life of those directly involved (time devoted to trips, frequency of traffic congestion, costs, etc.) and the level of environmental pressure exerted by mobility. Data emerging from various surveys of urban mobility highlight developments that have taken place in recent years. There is a close linkage between mobility and other important themes in an urban context, including air quality and carbon dioxide emissions, noise, road safety, space consumption and urban landscape. It is desirable to achieve a progressive reduction in individual motorised mobility and at the same time achieve an increase in the use of alternative modes of transport."[15]

However, it may be worth making a distinction between discretionary travel and "forced" travel. There is a school of thought that considers that people may need cars for holidays but commuting is handled far better by public transport. There is also the problem that freight travel is being increasingly cited as a justification for road building, reflecting the trend towards just-in-time logistics systems that put more trucks on the roads to save space in storage depots.

Over the last decade the European Union has also developed these indicator sets under the transport and environment reporting mechanism (TERM) pro-gramme.[16] The headline indicators are:

- environmental consequences of transport
- transport demand and intensity
- spatial planning and accessibility
- supply of transport infrastructure and services
- transport costs and prices
- technology and utilisation efficiency
- management integration.

Under this scheme, each headline indicator has a number of subsets. For exam-ple, "environmental consequences of transport" includes:

- accidental and illegal discharges of oil by ships at sea
- energy consumption
- exposure of populations to exceedances of EU air quality standards
- fragmentation of land and forests (biodiversity and connectivity of nature)
- land taken by transport infrastructure
- proximity of transport infrastructure to designated areas (biodiversity protection)
- traffic noise: exposure and annoyance
- transport accident fatalities
- transport emissions of air pollutants (emissions reductions targets)
- transport emissions of greenhouse gases (Kyoto Protocol targets)
- waste from road vehicles (scrap reduction).

National indicators

Every country appears to have its own set of transport indicators. Presumably, one day, these will be synchronised so that performance can be compared inter-nationally. For the examples given below it is apparent that the indicator sets for different countries demonstrate different transport concerns. One worrying gap in the indicator sets is the lack of indicators for "road areas per capita" because in the latter days of the fossil fuel age populations will be increasingly burdened by paying tax to maintain acres and acres of road – not just linear lengths – in their annual dues to councils. I expect this is an issue that is being deliberately avoided by politicians around the developed world but may well be a key factor in the sustainability of cities in the 21st Century.

UK

A UK headline transport indicator is included in the UK Sustainable Development strategy plan published by the government in 1999 and updated in 2003.[17] There are actually four levels of indicator sets for transport: headline, national, regional, and local. For example, headline indicator no. 11 is "Road traffic", where the objective is to "improve choice in transport; improve access to education, jobs, leisure and services; and reduce the need to travel". As Figure 13.5 shows, in the UK, road traffic has increased from 200 billion vehicle kilometres in 1970 to nearly 500 billion vehicle kilometres today. Road traffic intensity (vehicle kilometres per GDP), however, fell by 9 per cent between 1990 and 1998 and by a further 3 per cent between 1998 and 2002, therefore showing some "decoupling" between road traffic and economic growth.[18]

However, the indicators give no clue as to how the need to improve access to services can be balanced by the imperative to reduce the need to travel. In Britain, policy appears to be very much influenced by the roads lobby, rather than by the desire to increase the sustainability of the UK population by reducing emissions from the transport sector. The UK government is stressing the need to balance factors, and ends up sounding very pro-car!

"The key objective of this indicator is to strike the right balance between transport's role in helping the economy progress and allowing people to travel wherever they need to go, while at the same time protecting the environment and improving quality of life. In the past traffic growth has been associated with economic growth, but the resulting volume of traffic leads to congestion, noise and air pollution and contributes to greenhouse gas emissions which cause climate change."[19]

Australia

The Australian government has a very strong set of indicators and targets for every sector of their economy, used originally to inform their National Greenhouse Strategy in the early 1990s.[20]

The transport-related indicators established in 1990 included:

- total emissions from transport sector
- emissions per passenger-km (total and by mode and fuel source)
- emissions per freight tonne-km (total and by mode and fuel source)

Figure 13.5 Trends in road traffic in the UK from 1970 to 2002

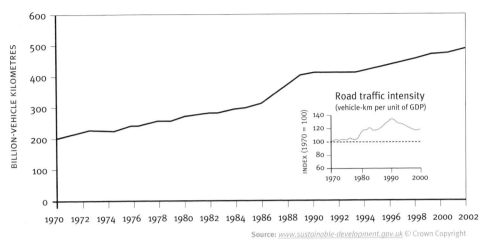

Source: www.sustainable-development.gov.uk © Crown Copyright

- emissions per km travelled in urban areas (by mode and fuel source)
- new vehicle national average fuel consumption for vehicles (by fuel type)
- overall fleet average fuel consumption (by fuel type)
- greenhouse gas emissions per passenger vehicle-km (by fuel type for fleet)
- total urban passenger-km per capita
- total passenger-km per capita
- share of passenger-km (urban and non-urban) (by mode and vehicle class)
- average commodity tonnes per vehicle-kilometre travelled (by freight vehicle class)
- greenhouse gas emissions per tonne-km for each class of freight vehicle by fuel type.

Despite such promising early beginnings the Australian government has, over the last few years, wound back any serious attempt at demand management relative to all sectors of greenhouse gas emissions including those resulting from transport. This illustrates the importance not only of having indicators but also using them to chart and control impacts – as if it matters.

New Zealand

The New Zealand government has declared a real intention to curb the impacts of transport using the following indicators:[21]

- transport energy use per kilometre
- vehicle fleet composition
- usual mode of journey to work

- total vehicle-kilometres travelled
- road congestion
- road run-off treatment on main arterial roads.

These indicators provide a good overview of the fleet composition, use, environmental impacts and energy consumption characteristics of the transport sector, and hence the pressure it exerts on the environment. For example, as Figure 13.6 shows, car journeys have nearly doubled in the past 20 years.

It is interesting to compare the transport miles/kilometres for the UK and New Zealand in terms of their rates of growth, and to speculate on a comparative figure for the change in vehicle miles/kilometres travelled per capita per annum in both countries.

Local authority indicators

In the UK, the national government has a stated strategy to reduce the impacts of transport (see above). Local and regional authorities are not required to monitor their own local and regional emissions of greenhouse gases, but they do bear a statutory requirement to monitor and control pollutants from vehicles. They are also responsible for planning and maintenance of the roads network.

National government recommends that local authorities collect data for a number of transport indicators,[22] but only one of these is directly related to the environment:

- the percentage of streetlights not working as planned
- percentage of repairs to dangerous damage to roads and pavements carried

Figure 13.6 Distance travelled by cars New Zealand showing the near doubling of kilometres travelled in 20 years by petrol cars and the small rise in the use of diesel fuel since 1990

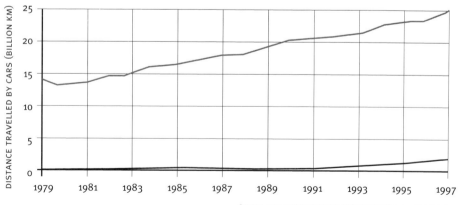

Source: www.environment.govt.nz/indicators/transport/vkt.html

out within 24 hours

- number of serious accidents per 1,000,000 miles travelled by a vehicle on principal roads
- percentage of principal roads at point at which repairs to prolong their future life should be considered
- number of days major council roadworks were in place per mile of busy road
- the cost of highway maintenance per 100 miles travelled by a vehicle
- the percentage of pedestrian crossings with facilities for disabled people
- the percentage of footpaths and other rights of way signposted where they leave a road
- net spending per head of population on public transport.

Nevertheless, local authorities are taking the lead by introducing sensible policies to reduce transport impacts. Every different region has different physical, social and economic characteristics, and every regional and local transport strategy will have different emphases, but their key headline concerns will be similar and include reducing impacts of:

- damage to the physical and ecological environment including landscapes and plant and animal populations
- air pollution, to which transport is a major contributor
- greenhouse gas emissions, for which transport in the UK accounts for around 23 per cent, and nearly half the oxides of nitrogen produced in the UK
- noise, which from roads is a growing problem, even in rural areas where the fastest growth in trips is from the leisure sector
- health
- other impacts such as the large use of aggregates in road building, a resource that requires careful management if its supply is to remain sustainable.

Unfortunately, local authorities have yet to develop a range of comparable indicators and targets on a single website that would make it possible to compare the performance of different local authorities. However, every region will have its own transport strategy. In Oxfordshire, for example, the comprehensive new Local Transport Plan 2001–2006[23] includes detailed plans for dealing with a range of key issues:

- climate change
- air quality
- health
- social inclusion

- disability
- road safety
- reducing the number of car journeys to work and school
- walking and cycling
- buses and taxis
- passenger and freight rail transport
- highways
- waterways
- parking
- traffic management.

The policy also includes details assessments for every different area within the county.

References

1 Find out more at *www.chipublib.org/oo4chicago/timeline/plan.html*

2 Newman P and Kenworthy J (2000), "Sustainable urban form: the big picture", in *Achieving Sustainable Urban Form*, Williams K, Burton E and Jenks M, E & F N. Spon, London, pp 109–120

3 Campbell C and Laherrere J (1998), "The end of cheap oil", *Scientific American*, 278(3), 80–86

4 Data for Figures 13.2, 13.3 and 13.4 are from ECCJ (2000), *Energy Conservation DataBook 1999/2000*, The Energy Conservation Center, Japan, which can be viewed on-line at *www.eccj.or.jp*

5 Newman & Kenworthy (2000), op cit.

6 Stead D, Williams J and Titheridge H (2000), "Land use, transport and people: identifying connections", in *Achieving Sustainable Urban Form*, op cit, pp 174–186

7 FOE (downloaded Sept 2003), *Aviation and global climate change*, Friends of the Earth Fact Sheet available from *www.foe.co.uk/campaigns/transport/case_studies/heathrow.html*

8 FOE (2002), *Flying into Trouble*, report compiled by Friends of the Earth, CPRE, AEF, NSCA and Transport 2000; see *www.aef.orf.uk*

9 Penner J, Lister D, Dokken D and McFarland M (1998), *Aviation and the Global Climate*, International Panel on Climate Change, available in full on *www.grida.no/climate/ipcc/aviation*

10 Whitelegg J and Williams N (2000), *The Plane Truth: Aviation and the environment*, edited by Chris Evans, commissioned by the Ashden Trust and

Transport 2000. available in full on *www.aef.org.uk*

11 FOE (2003), op cit.

12 Extract of information available to the public on the Melbourne City Council website at *www.everytripcounts.net.au/riding/1302.shtml* It is worth noting that this is information from a city with the longest per capita mileage of urban motorways in Australia, and where the government has just committed a billion $Australian to a ring road around the city (which many think will exacerbate the city's outward thrust) despite clear evidence that this was the least environmentally sustainable model of those on offer. The funding model in Victoria is also, in part, responsible for this decision: the federal government in Australia provides much of the funds for such programmes, the state government spends it, and local government has little power over transport issues, except local roads, and yet it has to pick up a hefty part of the bill for maintenance and for funding the infrastructural impacts of new roads. For more information see: Mees P (2000), *A Very Public Solution: Transport in the dispersed city*, Melbourne University Press, Melbourne

13 Details of the CEROI indicators can be found in: Denison N et al (2000), *Cities Environment Reports on the Internet: Understanding the CEROI template*, UNEP/GRID-Arendal, Arendal. Download the document from *www.ceroi.net*

14 Details of the EU indicators, plus methodology sheets, can be found at *www.sustainable-cities.org/indicators/index.htm*

15 Ambiente Italia Research Institute (2003), *Final Project Report: Development, refinement, management and Evaluation of European Common Indicators Project (ECI)*, Ambiente Italia Research Institute, Milan. For the full indicator, see *www.sustainable-cities.org*

16 See *http://themes.eea.eu.int/Sectors_and_activities/transport/indicators*

17 Published on-line at *www.sustainable-development.gov.uk/indicators*

18 For an excellent report with an overview of UK transport impacts see: AEA Technology Environment (2002), *Energy Efficiency in the UK (1990–2000)*, published on the Department of Trade and Industry's website at *www.dti.gov.uk/energy*

19 Source: *www.sustainable-development.gov.uk/indicators/headline/h11.htm*

20 Information gathered for most of these indicators for the period 1990 to 1998 is available at *http://www.greenhouse.gov.au/inventory*

21 See *www.environment.govt.nz/indicators/transport*

22 See, for example, UK local authority transport indicators (see: *http://www.local-regions.odpm.gov.uk*)

23 See *www.oxfordshire.gov.uk*

Further reading

Black W. (1999), "An unpopular essay on transportation", *Journal of Transport Geography*, 9, 1–11

Breheny M (1992), "The contradictions of the compact city: a review", in Breheny M (ed), *Sustainable Development and Urban Form*, Pion, London, pp 138–159

Chambers N, Simmons C and Wackernagel M (2000), *Sharing Nature's Interest: Ecological footprints as an indicator of sustainability*, Earthscan Publications Ltd, London

Gleeson BJ and Low NP (2000), *Australian Urban Planning, New Challenges, New Agendas*, Allen and Unwin, Sydney

Goodwin P, Hallett S, Kenny S and Stokes G (1991), *Transport: The new realism*, Report No. 624, Transport Studies Unit, University of Oxford

Goodwin P (1996), "Road traffic growth and the dynamics of Sustainable Transport Policies", in: Cartledge B (ed), *Transport and the Environment*, The Linacre Lectures 1994–5, Oxford University Press, pp 6–22

IIED, Nick Robbins (ed) (1995), *Citizen Action to Lighten Britain's Ecological Footprints*, International Institute for Environment and Development, Edinburgh

Mees P (1999), "A tale of two cities: urban transport, pollution and equality", in: Glover D and Patmore G, *New Voices for Social Democracy*, Pluto Press for the Australian Fabian Society, Sydney, pp 145–155

OECD (1995), *Urban Travel and Sustainable Development*, Organisation for Economic Co-operation and Development, Paris

Royal Commission on Environmental Pollution (1994), *Transport and the Environment*, 18th Report, The Stationery Office, Norwich

Sheller M and Urry J (2000), "The city and the car", *International Journal of Urban and Regional Research*, 24(4), pp 737–757

Wackernagel M and Rees WE (1996), *Our Ecological Footprint: Reducing human impact on the earth*, New Society Publishers, Gabriada Island, BC, Canada

Whitelegge J (1997), *Critical Mass: Transport, environment and society in the twenty first century*, Pluto Press, London and Chicago

Williams K, Burton E and Jenks M (2000) *Achieving Sustainable Urban Form*, E & FN Spon, London

Planning policy guidance – related documents (see Appendix 1 for details)

1	2	3	4	5	6	7	8	9	10	11	12	13
x	x	x	x	x	x	x				x	x	x

14	15	16	17	18	19	20	21	22	23	24	25
	x					x	x		x		

Building Regulations – related Approved Documents (see Appendix 2 for details)

A	B	C	D	E	F	G	H	I	J	K	L1	L2	M	N
											x	x		

Land use

> *Related indicators*
>   Quality of life, Community, Health, Climate change, Transport, Water quality
>
> *Related tools*
>   Environmental impact assessment, Ecological footprinting, Regeneration-based checklist

About this chapter

This chapter is written with Andre Viljoen and K Bohn, who both lecture on Sustainable Architecture at the School of Architecture and Design at Brighton University.

Focusing primarily on land use in cities, it presents a brief overview of the historical background to city development, assesses the likely impacts of climate change, and introduces a number of strategies that aim to mitigate these impacts and improve the quality of life for city dwellers.

Background

No city is truly "sustainable", because it is born of cultures and civilisations that come and go over time. The form of cities, and their relationships within regions, are heavily dependent on the prevailing transport systems and the productivity of the regional land, for agricultural, tourism, mining or industrial uses.

Climate change is already altering global demographics. As continents and islands dry up or flood, populations are moving to safer areas of the world, migrating northwards from Africa and the Middle East, where tracts of land are becoming less habitable through the process of desertification. Regional depopulation and the viability of climate-dependent industries such as tourism (in particular skiing in the Alps), agriculture and fishing are closely linked to the changes in the local and global climate.

We are only just beginning to understand the potential severity of these changes for continental, regional and local land use and settlement patterns. How, for instance, will the rising number of hurricanes and tornadoes on the US mainland, 562 in May 2003 alone,[1] influence settlement patterns, particularly in the central agricultural belts and the coastal zones? And maritime, estuarine and riverine cities may have to be redesigned to deal with the problems of rising sea level and increased intensity and frequency of flooding – a phenomenon that could see the re-engineering of population centres around the world to minimise the economic impacts of future inundations.

Transport

You can walk for hours across the levelled ruins of the ancient Mesopotamian cities of Ur, Babylon and Nineveh built three, four and five thousand years ago, on the once green but now desert brown plains of Iraq. Produce to feed these great cities was brought in from the agricultural hinterland by foot or on pack animals or carts, just as it still is today in many provincial Chinese cities. Traditional cities were divided by class, tribe and function,[2] and journey distances in and around the city were minimised because certain occupations were located in dedicated quarters, for instance for metalwork, or woodwork or the dealing of skins, wine and grains. As late as the 1970s Paris was similarly clearly divided into such artisans' and merchants' quarters.

During the industrial revolution the great drift of the rural poor from the country to the city to seek employment, money and a better life was aided by the railways, which extended the hinterlands of cities outwards and opened new market for goods and labour. The result was the great industrial cities of the 19th and 20th Centuries, with their squalor, putrid alleyways and mean streets to which the great visionary architects applied their skills, with great reforming zeal.

The Herculean efforts of Georges-Eugene Haussmann (1809–91), under the patronage of Napoleon III in Paris, managed to virtually destroy the old city and rebuild it as the first great city of the industrial age, cut through by broad roads lined with 8–10 storey apartment blocks in place of the lower, more cramped medieval city. The streets were designed to "assure the public peace by the creation of large boulevards which will permit the circulation not only of air and light but also of troops".[3] Another of Haussmann's principles was to "facilitate the circulation to and from railways stations by means of penetrating lines which will lead travellers straight to the centres of commerce and pleasure, and will prevent congestion and accidents".[4] In the 17 years between 1853 and 1869 Haussmann spent 2.5 billion francs on rebuilding Paris.

Railway and tram systems fitted well into the radial cities of the industrialised

Figure 14.1 The block layout of the University of Chicago in 1933, from a contemporary postcard printed by the university. As private ownership was still not universal, the buildings were designed to be served by public transport systems

pleasure". In Britain, at the turn of the 20th Century, Ebenezer Howard used a similar model. His plans were based on a set on concentric circles, at the centre of which are civic buildings grouped around a common, or central park. Midway between the centre and the outermost circle is a grand avenue 400 feet in width (the ring road) with trees and greenery, and the outermost circle is an agricultural belt (green belt). A "Crystal Palace" encircles the central park and recreation ground in which manufactured goods may be exposed for sale (the "mall"?). An area in the town is set aside for manufacturing. Thus began the garden city model that has been so influential in British planning and has served to influence urban densities, and to contain many UK cities within the tight noose of the "green belt" and the ring road system.

By contrast, in America, the dominant 20th Century model was that of the "urban block" city, designed to give optimum value to the car (see Figure 14.1). Residential blocks were bordered by wide highways grouped around a spine road that provided easy access into the city centre in a more linear city model. A similar model, propagated by a generation of highly skilled American urban transport consultants, has been used around the world. Surprisingly this model, developed originally in Chicago in the 1930s and 1940s, remains sacrosanct for some urban planning departments, such as in Canberra, Australia, where any modification of the plan to facilitate better public transport routes has been resisted.[5] With more and larger roads, different areas of the city were more readily accessible to vehicle drivers, and the trend in this model was to "zone" the city – to locate the different functions of the city (housing, commerce, industry and recreation) in separate areas.

The great dream of the car-driven city is being increasingly questioned. As early as 1967, the urban planning historian, Sigfried Gideon, wrote:

> *"It is easy to see why the original idea of the garden city 'where town and country are married' was doomed to failure. No partial solution is possible; only preconceived and integrated planning on a scale embracing the whole structure of modern life in all its ramifications can accomplish the task which Ebenezer Howard had in mind."*[6]

One strong current trend today is to try and do just that – to marry town and country through the weaving of green fingers through the city in a series of linked parks that not only act as wildlife corridors through the city but also increase the quality of life of citizens. The Canadian city of Vancouver is one of the foremost proponents of such integration and has an integrated parks strategy involving "green fingers" linking urban and regional parks set in live/work neighbourhoods.[7] Another emerging trend is to marry the two through the medium of "urban farming", of which more below.

The impacts of the car culture are discussed in Chapters 13 and 17, but it is worth noting here that fuel security is a major contemporary concern for cities built on the dispersed, car-dominated model. Petrol to fuel motor vehicles will become increasingly expensive and ultimately run out within the next half century,[8] bringing into question the sustainability of such cities unless new means of powering vehicles (e.g. hydrogen fuel cell technology) can be brought on stream in the near future.

Some traditional cities have resisted the move to carve up the urban landscape for freeways, having chosen instead to use efficient public transport systems – bus, metro or light railway systems. Other forward-looking cities, such as Curitiba in Brazil, have used the block system with urban spine roads to introduce a rapid, frequent and efficient bus system that builds on a range of strategies including freeways that route traffic away from the central city, and limited and expensive public parking in the partly pedestrianised city centre.[9]

There are also a number of social issues relating to city design and transport planning. For instance, quality of life can be a significant issue if citizens suffer

"severance", or alienation, from the rest of the community in dispersed, car-dominated, grid cities.[10] And the impacts of climate change – extremely hot summers,
floods and storms – will mean that road networks need more repairs, and more
frequent replacement at a time when, due to rising fuel prices, they will be
decreasingly used by the ordinary motorist who will be lumbered with the burden
of paying for their increasingly expensive upkeep.

Population and density

Density is probably the most hotly debated issue in the design of cities in the
early 21st Century.

The 20th Century was unprecedented in terms of city growth. It took London
from 1800 to 1910 to multiply its population by seven, from 1.1 million to 7.3 million; but in the 20th Century this growth rate was achieved by some African cities
within a generation. Many Asian cities increased fourfold in the same period. In
1950 there were just two cities in the world with a population of more than eight
million (London and New York) but by 2003 there were six such cities in industrialised countries, and there are 23 "mega cities" in the developing world, the
largest being Mexico City with a population of over 20 million in its metropolitan
area (see Table 14.1).

Population density in cities is closely related to the urban design strategies
upon which their form was predicated. There is currently a move to classify cities
by their archetypal urban geometries,[11] which relate to the patterns of population
densities:

- **dispersed city** – continued low-density suburban development of
  population, housing and jobs; infrastucture investment dominated by
  road transport; this for the most part is "business-as-usual" development
- **compact city** – increased population and density of an inner group of
  suburbs, with associated investment in public transport
- **edges city** – increased population, densities and employment at selected
  peripheral nodes within the city boundaries; increased investment in orbital
  freeways linking the edge cities
- **corridor city** – a focus of growth along linear corridors emanating from
  a central business district, supported by upgraded public transport
  infrastructure (one example is the radial city)
- **fringe city** – additional growth predominantly on the fringe of the city.

All of these forms of city, except the dispersed city, attempt to concentrate
development, and population, into particular sections of the city. Current trends
in the intensification of urban populations have increased the rate of redevelop-

Table 14.1 Population, car densities and urban road links in 12 cities

CITY	PEOPLE DENSITY (PER KM²)	CAR DENSITY (PER 100)	URBAN ROADS (TOTAL KM)
Houston	890	602	30,674
Brisbane	1,020	458	7,084
Perth	1,080	475	11,923
Adelaide	1,290	475	8,506
Melbourne	1,640	446	21,381
Sydney	1,760	412	19,812
Toronto	3,960	463	5,815
Stockholm	5,130	347	1,480
London	5,630	288	12,850
Munich	5,700	360	2,167
Singapore	8,320	65	2,356
Hong Kong	17,529	42	1,141

Source: Dean Graetz et al, *Looking Back: The changing face of the Australian continent 1972–1992* © CSIRO and the commonwealth of Australia, 1998

ment of brownfield sites and protected green areas and encouraged the use of public transport. However, levels of car use are still rising globally, even in more densely populated suburbs.

There is an extraordinary range of population densities in cities around the world, from the 890 people per km² in Houston to 34,221 people per km² in eastern Hong Kong. In Japanese cities, for instance, population densities are up to ten times higher than those in UK cities.

Urban planners often describe development in terms of "dwellings per hectare". Figure 14.2 shows the ground plans of the Hulme district of Manchester, where the 19th Century slum terraces (150 dwellings per hectare) were replaced with medium rise buildings in the mid-1960s (37 dwellings per hectare). However, this action, though reducing the number of dwellings in the area by over two thirds, destroyed communities, and significantly increased heating bills, rents and crime. At the time, issues of access into and out of the area were considerably less significant than the desire to adopt a fashionable design paradigm of the time, based largely on the ideas of Corbusier and his projects such as the "ilot insalubre no.6" designed in 1937 and "Unite d'Habitation" built in 1947–52[12] (see Figure 14.3). A surprisingly large number of the public housing developments of the 1960s and 1970s were based on this fashion, and many have already been demolished. The 1960s Hulme development was pulled down in the 1990s and replaced

Figure 14.2 (a) Ground plans showing the changing housing density patterns of Hulme, Manchester, from
(a) 1951, (b) 1991, and (c) proposed for 2000

Figure 14.2 (b)

Figure 14.2 (c)

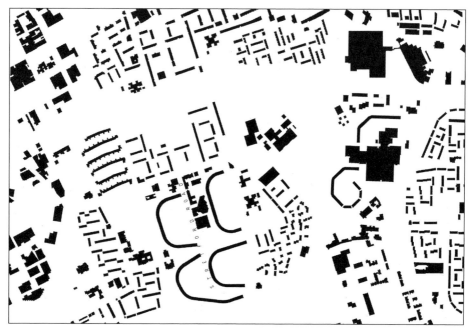

Source: MBLC Architects & Urbanists

– again by terraced housing, but this time at half the original 19th Century density (75–87 dwellings per hectare).

Planning issues

Today, land use planning should never be carried out without taking account of the potential impacts of climate change, but there are a number of other factors to consider, all of which are linked to the fundamental principle of improving the quality of life for city dwellers (see Chapter 5).

The importance of the ordinary citizen in the process of urban planning grew rapidly at the turn of the 20th Century, with the liberal philanthropic movements and ideas of the garden city. In the 1930s the Dutchman C. van Eesteren, an architect who was responsible for the planning of much of contemporary Amsterdam, redefined the role of the urban designer to include the emerging concern over population density:

"Above all he studies the different categories of people who have to be accommodated, each according to his manner of life; he finds out whether they are young, old, married or single, with few or many children. He must consider where these people work, the routes traffic must take, the distance there

should be between residential and industrial sections. He must also establish a control of the relationship between the communications of the city and its living quarters. He thinks no longer in linear terms of streets and axis, but in terms of population densities. His approach to the town is conditioned by this population ration, which in the Amsterdam extension plan, for example, was allowed to range between 110 and 550 inhabitants per hectare."[13]

People as human "units" were considered the currency of planning in the 1930s, but today the emphasis is on creating "sustainable communities" and places where ordinary citizens can enjoy a high quality of life. Much work has been done on why models of landuse and urban design do, and do not, work. In their book on creating *Responsive Environments*[14] Bentley et al identified a number of urban design issues that may cause the settlement dweller to be alienated from his or her environment. These include:

- **accessibility** – the ability to travel conveniently and economically to destinations
- **permeability** – the quality which affects where people can and cannot go
- **variety** – affecting the range of city functions available to people
- **resilience** – the degree to which people can use a given place for different purposes
- **resource efficiency** – the quality which affects the extent to which external resources have to be used to achieve high levels of usability of the city.

Qualities that offer psychological support for choice in the urban streetscape include:

- **legibility** – people's understanding of the opportunities that a place offers
- **transculturality** – the capacity to feel part of a larger ecosystem and to understand the part one plays in it
- **timelines** – the ability to feel rooted in the past but not stuck in it
- **empowerment** – the sense of being able to affect events, rather than merely reacting to them.

Intensification

Intensification of population in UK cities is occurring rapidly because the stranglehold of the greenbelts limits expansion into the countryside, because building costs are rising rapidly and, in particular, because demand for housing is growing. In addition, developers are being given incentives to re-use derelict industrial land (brownfield sites) within existing urban areas, in an attempt to optimise the use of urban land and avoid site wastage. The advantages of "compact cities" are thought to include a reduction of reliance on car transport, strengthening of public

Table 14.2 Common population densities in UK cities by dwelling type

HOUSE TYPE	DWELLINGS PER HECTARE	PERSONS PER HECTARE (APPROX.)
Estate housing	20-30	100-120
Four-storey walk-ups		92
Eight-storey flats		214
Taller apartment blocks		450+

Source: Andre Vilijoen

transport systems, increased investment in urban amenities and the rehabilitation of industrial and waste land within the city boundaries. However, the issue of intensification is politically sensitive. One survey[15] found that 72 per cent of respondents either had not noticed intensification, or perceived that it had either made no difference or made matters worse or much worse; only 28 per cent of respondents claimed that it had made matters better or much better. When questioned about their views on increased activity in a neighbourhood only 11 per cent said that it made the areas better or much better.

The influential architect Lord Rogers has suggested[16] that urban densities in the UK should increase significantly, with target densities possibly as high as 500 persons per hectare. However, such visions of piling people higher are seldom backed up by any indicators or benchmarks for the quality of life for such high-density, high-rise urban dwellers (although obviously a good view would be one of them!).

On this issue, in particular, it is important that we do not repeat the mistakes imposed on the poorest in society over the last 50 years by the grand visions of designers.

City height – limits to growth

The trend upwards was encouraged by the development of new iron and steel structures. The Empire State Building in New York, completed in 1930, is 102 floors and 443.2 m high, and is still one of the tallest buildings in the world. Skyscrapers are universally admired as a demonstration of technical skills and corporate machismo. The terrorist attack of September 11 2001 has caused some to question the need for these high-profile structures, but there are other equally good reasons for questioning their validity in the 21st Century.[17]

Cities that have significant clusters of tall buildings generate their own microclimate – the heat island effect, where heat reflected from acres of glass and concrete, plus fumes and heat from traffic exhausts and building services, cannot escape from the urban "canyons". Heat islands in inner cities can be 10–15°C hotter than their surrounding hinterlands. The higher the core of a city, the more

Figure 14.3 The brand new 32 storey Drake Tower Apartment block, next to the 800 room Drake Hotel, breaks through the urban canopy of 1933 Chicago as the city roofscape reaches for the sky

309   THE DRAKE, CHICAGO'S WONDERFUL HOTEL

50309

Source: S Ross Postcard Collection

intense, or hotter, the heat island. But such cities also have a "canopy", rather like the canopy of a rain forest (see Figure 14.4). Any building breaking through that canopy – like a tall poppy in a field – will not only be exposed to greater wind speeds and the potential for great storm damage, but will also cause higher wind speeds in the streets below, where the wind is channelled down the windward face of the building. Climate change will exacerbate the problem because higher wind speeds will increase the risk to these tall poppies, that may well face higher insurance premiums than those below the level of the urban canopy.

Another factor that will increasingly trim buildings down to the urban canopy level is that of "solar rights" – the need to ensure that buildings do not shade adjacent buildings from the sun, or reduce their potential to generate solar energy.

A solar access law has been introduced in Boulder, Colorado, to limit the height of new buildings to protect the solar rights of the citizens because:

> *"The city council finds that the public health, safety, and welfare of the citizens of this city are dependent upon reliable and affordable energy sources; the nation's conventional energy supplies are diminishing, and the long-term trend is toward depletion of the world's fossil fuel resources and higher energy prices; solar heating and cooling of buildings, solar heated hot water,*

199

and solar generated electricity can provide a significant contribution to the city's energy supply; a significant barrier to the use of solar energy is the concern among citizens that the solar radiation necessary for solar energy systems to function will be blocked by structures or vegetation located on property under the control of others, including the city; and existing laws and regulations are inadequate to provide the degree of protection needed. It is therefore the purpose of this chapter to regulate structures and vegetation on property, including city-owned and controlled property, to the extent necessary to insure access to solar energy, by reasonably regulating the interests of neighboring property holders within the city."[18]

Infrastructure

New concerns are emerging about the "invisible" city – the technical infrastructure that supplies and removes energy, water waste and information. Traditionally, stores of water, waste, energy (and its production) were kept outside the boundaries of the city, carried by pipes and cables to their destination. However, as the city expands wastes must be transported further, and the mechanisms needed to transport them need to be upgraded. The pumps and rotational speeds needed to move water and waste from 1,000 dwellings are very different from those needed to service 10,000 or 1,000,000 homes.

The energy, water and waste security of metropolitan districts should become a primary concern for city planners as we approach a period when historic technical infrastructure is beginning to fail.[19] Future planning of any area of a city should be required to include calculations of the impacts not only on the visible city, but also on its invisible networks. If, for instance, a new skyscraper is planned then the cost of upgrading the local water, waste and energy supply systems, and resizing of pumps, sewage farms, power station and reservoirs, should be agreed and met before the development is allowed to proceed. Infrastructure use planning is increasingly essential, using tools such as environmental impact assessment, life cycle assessment (see Chapters 27 and 28), and the Dutch Greencalc and TWIN models.[20]

Energy use and carbon dioxide reduction

There are a number of ways in which urban planning can influence energy use (and hence carbon dioxide emissions).[21] Every city should now be developing renewable energy strategies and, in particular, calculating the potential of the city to generate hot water and electricity from solar energy collected via the building roofs.

Germany demonstrates the need for, and success of, providing financial support and good information to stimulate emerging solar markets. As a result of the

"1,000 roofs" project in the early 1990s, the Germans now have tens of thousands of photovoltaic (PV) roofs, with a total installed capacity of over 260,000 kW$_p$ (see Chapter 23). Germany is now the European market leader, while the UK still has only 100 or so PV roofs.[22]

Research is ongoing to investigate the possibility of subdividing the city back into a local municipal grid that could be supplied by a combination of renewable and low emissions energy generation systems in a "micro-grid" system. Future local energy sources may include hydrogen fuel cells or combined heat and power (CHP) systems as well as renewables, with power gates between local grids to provide some energy security in cities in the future.

Eventually, all cities should have energy use plans, and these will be combined with land use plans and demand-side management strategies. In the UK many councils already have well-established plans and some, such as Watford City Council, have already tested micro-grids for electricity supply and embedded hydrogen fuel cell generators. These schemes are combined with a wide range of energy measures in the city, and within the county of Hertfordshire, which has achieved the highest rating out of the authorities in the UK for the management of energy in its buildings.[23]

Waterproofing cities

One of the very serious problems associated with climate change is that of flooding, which is particularly bad in urban areas where a high percentage of the city is covered in hard surfaces. Rain falls on these and quickly runs off to fill undersized gutters and drains, causing flash floods in many cities. The problem of urban run-off in the United States has proved so extreme that the Environmental Protection Agency (EPA) is advising that householders may consider using "green roofs" to absorb rain water, as well as using water butts and water stores to slow down the deluge. The problem is so great that in King County, Washington State, USA, the county has introduced taxes on water run-off to fund programmes to deal with the problem. Every property is charged a rate fee dependent on the area of hard surfaces in their development.[24]

In Germany, whole suburbs are adopting green roofs, in part as a storm prevention measure, and in the UK the government has developed a Sustainable Urban Drainage Systems (SUDS) to reduce the likelihood of flooding (see Chapter 15).

A GreenRoof project in Los Angles also proved that green roofs can mitigate the growing problem of urban heat islands. EPA computer simulations for Los Angeles suggest that increasing green space by 5 per cent and replacing dark roofs and asphalt with lighter surfaces could lower summer temperatures by four degrees, resulting in 10 per cent less smog and $175 million in energy savings per year. Secondary functions were listed as the ability of greened roofs to reduce storm-water run-off and create a weather buffer that helps the underlying roofs last much longer.[25]

Rain water collection from roofs may also become important as climate change reduces summer availability of water.

Urban farming

A key feature of future sustainable cities will be the ability of citizens to harness city land for food production. This may seem strange to us in an age of remote food production, with our green beans from Kenya and our pears from New Zealand, but the city forefathers who devised the allotment movement a century ago did so because they saw the potential of the city to feed itself. A strong case is now being made for urban design to include the possibility of city farming.[26] One study[27] suggests that, for settlements integrating local food production, optimum densities may be close to the UK norm, at 30 dwellings per hectare (approximately 120 persons per hectare).

Transportation, packaging, the use of fertilisers and mechanical production of food all contribute to the negative environmental impact of food production (see Box). The potential for locating food production within inhabited areas is greatest for fruit and vegetable production, because these require the minimum area for a given yield. For example, in Canada, the food production for one person requires about 1.3 hectares, of which fruit and vegetable production accounts for only 0.02 hectares,[28] while in Europe 0.01 hectares is considered adequate to supply all of an individual's fruit and vegetable requirements. Even within large urban centres such as London a significant percentage of open space exists, and

---

The impact of food production

The advent of supermarkets and the global markets for fruit and vegetables has had a significant impact on the environmental cost of food production. One source[30] estimates that, at 8 tonnes of CO_2 per year, the annual carbon dioxide emissions resulting from growing, processing, packaging and transporting food for an average family in the UK almost equal the total energy-related emissions of the family (for space heating, lighting, car usage etc). Even allowing for the possibility of error in these estimates (the CO_2 emissions for food production were based on published data from the 1970s) they do suggest that there is great scope for reducing emissions resulting from current methods of food production.

---

this could, in part, be utilised for commercially operated urban market gardens supplying locally produced organic produce to existing commercial outlets such as supermarkets.[29]

Figure 14.5 illustrates the difficulty of providing autonomy in fruit and vegetable and water requirements from within the curtilage of a site. However, a yield of 30 per cent of fruit and vegetable requirements could significantly reduce the environmental impact of remote food production, and dependence on the oil used to transport it. (From this analysis, it appears that density has relatively small impact on the potential for solar hot water generation. The potential for on-site electricity generation remains high for densities up to circa 200 persons per hectare.)

Available land in the city is, to an extent, a result of the site context and conditions. This will dictate the forms of urban agriculture that can be woven into a city, be it steep terraced sites, horizontal fingers in the landscape, or actually built into gardens and terraces on housing, apartment blocks, or roof gardens.

Other benefits of urban agriculture include:

- environmental benefits – development of ecological corridors and islands within urban areas, a means of promoting the local recycling of organic waste (composting)
- social benefits – development of local economies by means of generating a new local product (i.e. organic fruit and vegetables), promoting social inclusion through employment in market gardens, an educational amenity within a local area.

Figure 14.4 Site yield against density (persons per hectare). Yields have been calculated as a percentage of the total annual requirements for the entire population of each site. Outputs are presented for fruit and vegetable production (fruit & veg), rain water harvesting (r.w.h.), solar hot water (s.h.w.) for domestic hot water and Photovoltaics (p.v.)

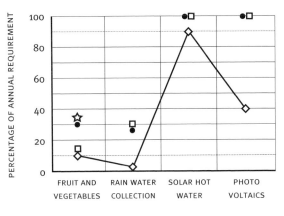

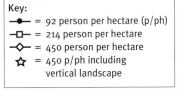

Key:
- ●— = 92 person per hectare (p/ph)
- ☐– = 214 person per hectare
- ◇ = 450 person per hectare
- ☆ = 450 p/ph including vertical landscape

Source: 'Urban intensification and the integration of productive landscape', Viligoen A, Bohn K, July 2000. Presented at the World Renewable Energy Conference, Brighton, U.K. Paper published in proceedings. 'World Renewable Energy Congress' VI, Part 1, pp 483-488

Global indicators

Ultimately, the ability to sustain life and settlements depends on the quality of the available soil and the access to adequate water to grow crops or raise animals. This is reflected in the core land use indicator of the Food and Agriculture Organisation (FAO) of the United Nations,[31] which measures "land condition change", i.e. the extent to which land is changed, including:

- physical soil condition
- diversity or density of vegetation cover
- thickness of topsoil (by erosion or, conversely, by good management)
- salinity or sodicity (alkaline conditions)
- terracing
- establishment of contour vegetation strips.

European indicators

Land use is No. 9 on the European Union's common indicators list,[32] although the other nine indicators each include issues relating to land use. Perhaps "land use" should now be replaced in planning systems by a more comprehensive term that covers all the sustainable land planning issues relevant to good city design in the 21st Century. The indicator says:

"A sustainable city is one that enhances the efficiency of land use within its territory, protects highly valued un-built land, biodiversity value and green areas from development and restores contaminated and derelict land [brownfield sites]. Most cities and urban-regional authorities implement policies aimed at increasing urban densities through targeted development. There is also a wide range of policies at all levels for protecting sites with agricultural, landscape and ecological value and able to sustain biodiversity, as well as European policies for the restoration of derelict and contaminated land."

The indicator is very clear on its priorities to restore land quality and value in the city and by so doing to enhance the lives of its citizens. Cities have to measure:

- artificial areas – artificial surfaces as a percentage of the total municipal area
- derelict and contaminated land – extent of derelict land (area, m²) and contaminated land (area, m²)
- intensity of use – number of inhabitants per km² of "urbanised land" area
- new development – quota of new edification taking place on virgin area (greenfield) and quota taking place on derelict and contaminated land

(brownfield in total area as soil projection) in per cent per year
- restoration of urban land, including renovation, conversion of derelict buildings (floor surface in m²), redevelopment of derelict land for new urban uses – including public green spaces (area, m²), and cleansing of contaminated land (area, m²)
- protected areas as a percentage of total municipal area.

An interesting feature of this indicator is that it does take into account the issues of urban flooding, and it is designed to revitalise and repair the historic cities of Europe, which may well be intrinsically more sustainable in form than the car-dependent cities of American and Australia.

UK government indicators

Strategies for sustainable cities are often linked both to the re-use of derelict industrial land (brownfield sites) within existing urban areas, and to the increasing density of urban areas. While the typical densities for housing in the UK are 20–30 dwellings per hectare (approximately 100 persons per hectare) Lord Rogers's report, for instance, suggested that densities should increase significantly.[33] Following the publication of this report, an architectural competition entitled "Living in the City" was launched, seeking proposals for utilising a brownfield site in London as a sustainable live/work development, with target densities of 500 persons per hectare. Some authors consider such densities may well exceed the "carrying capacity" of the city, and advocate a broader view of sustainability.

Social and economic trends are contributing to the lower size of the average household, placing more pressure on land use for development, and increasing the demand for housing. The UK government has set a target of building 3.8 million new houses by 2016, of which 60 per cent are to be on brownfield sites.

Local authority indicators

The city of Vancouver in Canada sets a good example with its policies, which aim to balance the needs of:

- wild and developed lands
- standard of living and quality of life
- environment and economy
- self-sufficiency and interdependence
- population and resources

Figure 14.5 The Vancouver Island Core Land Use Plan created in the early 1990s

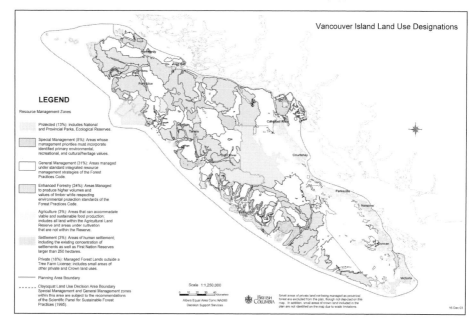

- environmental and social fairness
- rural and urban communities
- common good and private interest.

Regional indicators of land use are most useful when they are based on mapping and establishing percentage change in land use over time. The Vancouver Island Core Land Use Plan works in this way (see Figure 14.6).

Planners at the local authority level are in the strongest position to influence land use. A number of favourable land use strategies are emerging, and no doubt indicators and benchmarks will follow. Until then, planners are strongly advised to consider the following:

- Continuous landscapes through a city can connect otherwise disconnected existing pockets of open space, creating ecological corridors as well as alternative routes across the city for non-vehicular movement.
- Seek strong relationships between public open space and the public. (EU indicators on quality of life and community, discussed in Chapters 4 and 5, call for monitoring of the percentage of the population that lives within 300 m of a public open space of more than 5,000 m.)
- Design-out "severance". Plan land use in cities to optimise the connected-

ness of people to the landscapes, streets and places in the city to reduce the alienation of citizens and enhance the sense of community and place.

- Consider horizontal intensification, perhaps in "landscrapers". Vertical intensification has advantages: for example certain activities may be stacked above each other as a means of increasing density. However, at densities of about 100 persons per hectare this is unnecessary. At densities of 450 persons per hectare vertical intensification might be necessary, but it is essential to consider the environmental impacts of any high-rise buildings, and to plan for future climate change. Buildings being designed today will need to meet the climate and energy conditions in 2020 and 2050. For instance, suburbia may ultimately provide the most sustainable form of land use in the UK.
- Also consider solar access. This will become more important as renewable energy technologies become integrated into the "energy mix" at the local, regional and national levels. Shaded properties may, in future, suffer planning blight.
- Maximise the site yield (see Figure 14.5). A method for calculating the potential site yield has been described by Vale and Vale in a General Information Report published by the UK government.[34] This can be extended from food and energy to the collection and storage of water.[35]
- Waterproof cities. Reduction of hard surfaces to reduce urban flooding.
- Minimising the urban heat island effect by introducing more planting and green and reflective surfaces into the city, and by ensuring that buildings are not exposed to excessive re-reflection of solar incidence from the faces of other buildings, a problem that can cause severe internal overheating.
- Introduce policies on infrastructure use planning and management. Planners should ensure that developments do not exceed the carrying capacity of the city's visible and invisible infrastructures, and that all infrastructures can be well maintained.
- Cities should be planned to increasingly rely on public transport. Where urban spine roads exist they should be in part converted to rapid transit tram, bus and rail lines to avoid large areas of cities suffering from blight as the price of petrol rises. All new developments should only be given planning permission if they have a credible public transport plan.

References

1   Houghton Sir John (2003), "Global warming as a weapon of mass destruction", *The Guardian*, 28 July 2003, p 14

2 Roaf M (1990), *Cultural Atlas of Mesopotamia and the Ancient Near East*, Andromeda Press, Oxford

3 Gideon S (1967), *Space, Time and Architecture*, 5th edn (1st edn published 1941), Harvard University Press, Cambridge, USA, p 746

4 Haussmann G-E (1890–93), *Memoires*, Volume III, Paris, p 55

5 Mees P (2000), *A Very Public Solution: Transport in the dispersed city*, Melbourne University Press, Melbourne

6 Op cit, p 784

7 Howard R (2002), "Conference Summary", in *Proceedings of Cities and Transportation: Choices and Consequences*, February 2002, Simon Fraser University, Canada

8 Campbell C and Laherrere J (1998),"The end of cheap oil", *Scientific American*, 278(3), 80–86, and Bartsch U and Muller B (2000), *Fossil Fuels in a Changing Climate*, Oxford University Press, Oxford

9 See *www.bombayfirst.org/citymag/vol2no1/curitiba.htm*

10 Mees P (1999), "A tale of two cities: urban transport, pollution and equality", in: Glover D and Patmore G, *New Voices for Social Democracy*, Pluto Press for the Australian Fabian Society, Sydney

11 Newton P (2000),"Urban form and environmental performance", in *Achieving Sustainable Urban Form*, E & FN Spon, London, pp 46–53

12 Le Corbusier (1987), *The City of Tomorrow and Its Planning* (first published 1929), Dover Publications, Mineola, New York

13 Gideon S (1967), Op Cit, p 817

14 Bentley I et al (2001), *Responsive Environments*, Architectural Press, Oxford

15 Jenks M (2000), "The acceptability of urban intensification", in *Achieving Sustainable Urban Form,* E & FN Spon, London, pp 242–250

16 Rogers R and the Urban Task Force (1999), *Towards an Urban Renaissance*, E & FN Spon, London

17 Roaf S, Crichton D and Nicol F (not yet published), *Adapting Buildings and Cities for Climate Change*, Architectural Press

18 City of Boulder Land Use Regulations, Chapter 8 *"Solar Access"* at www. sustainable.doe.gov

19 Van Timmeren A, Kristensson WR and Roaf S (2003), "Reviewing energy concepts and technical infrastructure in urban planning and architecture", *Proceedings of the 20th Passive Low Energy Architecture Conference (PLEA)*, Santiago, Chile

20 *www.greencalc.com/en-materiaalmodule.html*

21 The Energy Smart Communities Network is an interesting place to explore related

ideas on the imaginative use of legislation and economic incentives to introduce embedded generation into city planning. See *www.sustainable.doe.gov*

22 See *www.re-focus.net*

23 See *www.hertsdirect.org.uk/environment* and *www.watford.gov.uk/information*

24 Ferrari L (1987) "Surface water fees used to reduce urban flooding" at
http://stormwaterfinance.urbancenter.iupui.edu

25 Source: *www.sunutility.com/html_pg/city.html*

26 See *www.cityfarmer.org*

27 Viljoen A and Tardiveau A (1998), "Sustainable Cities and Landscape Patterns",
in *PLEA 98 proceedings*, pp 49–52

28 Wackernagel M, Rees W E (1996), *Our ecological footprint. Reducing human
impact on the earth*, New Society Publishers, Gabriola Island, BC, Canada

29 Viljoen and Tardiven (1998), Op Cit

30 The estimates are: 4.2 tonnes CO_2 resulting from space heating, hot water,
cooking lights and appliances due to a four-person household living in a typical modern home; and 4.4 tonnes CO_2 resulting from typical family car use at
20 000 km/yr. See Viljoen A and Bohn K (2000), "Intensification and the integration of productive landscape", in *Proceedings of the World Renewable
Energy Congress*, Berlin. *www.stadtentwicklung.berlin.de/bauen/bauluecken-
management/en/planungsebenen.shtml*

31 See *www.fao.org*

32 Source: *www.sustainable-cities.org/indicators/index.htm*

33 Roaf, Op Cit

34 DETR (1998), *Building a Sustainable Future: Homes for an autonomous community*, General Information Report 53, Energy Efficiency Best Practice
programme, Department of the Environment, Transport and the Regions,
Watford. Download the document from *www.actionenergy.org.uk*

35 Roaf S, Fuentes M and Gupta R (2003), *Ecohouse2: A design guide*,
Architectural Press, Oxford

Further reading

Chambers N, Simmons C and Wackernagel M (2000), *Sharing Nature's Interest:
Ecological footprints as an indicator of sustainability*, Earthscan Publications,
London

Hall P (2001), *Cities of Tomorrow: An intellectual history of urban planning and
design in the twentieth century*, Architectural Press, Oxford

Hall P (2002), *Cities of Tomorrow*, Blackwell Publishing, Oxford

Keeping M and Shiers D (2003), *Sustainable Property Development: A guide to real estate and the environment*, Blackwell Publishing, Oxford

Low N and Gleeson B (1998), *Justice, Society and Nature: an exploration of political ecology*, Routledge, London

Newman P and Kenworthy J (2000), "Sustainable Urban Form: The big picture", in *Achieving Sustainable Urban Form*, Williams K, Burton E and Jenks M (eds), E & FN Spon, London, pp 109–120

Roaf S (in press), *Adapting Buildings and Cities for Climate Change*, Architectural Press, Oxford

Rudlin D and Falk N (2001), *The Sustainable Urban Neighbourhood: Building the 21st century home*, 3rd edn (first published 1999), Architectural Press, Oxford

Simmons C and Chambers N (1998), "Footprinting UK households: how big is your ecological garden?" *Local Environment*, 3 (3), pp 355–362

Syms P (2003), *Land, Development and Design*, Blackwell Publishing, Oxford

Viljoen A (1997), "The total environmental impact of low energy dwellings", *European Directory of Sustainable and Energy Efficient Building 1997*, James & James, London.

Walker LA and Rees WE (1998), "Urban density and ecological footprints – an analysis of canadian households" in Roseland M (ed) *Eco-City Dimensions: Healthy cities, healthy planet*, New Society Publishers, Gabriola Island, Canada, Chapter 8

Wackernagel et al (1999), "National Natural Capital Accounting with the Ecological Footprint Concept", *Ecological Economics*, 29 (3), pp 375–390

Williams K, Burton E and Jenks M (eds) (2000), *Achieving Sustainable Urban Form*, E&FN Spon, London

WWF (2002), *Living Planet Report 2002*, World Wide Fund For Nature, Gland

Planning policy guidance – related documents (see Appendix 1 for details)

1	2	3	4	5	6	7	8	9	10	11	12	13
		x	x	x	x						x	x

14	15	16	17	18	19	20	21	22	23	24	25	
	x		x	x						x		

CHAPTER 15

Flooding

Definition
In this chapter, flooding covers inundation from sea, river or urban run-off, but it may also arise from: sewage/drainage backup; rising groundwater; overflows from standing water, canals and waterways; blocked bridges, culverts and gully pots; and failure or overtopping of dams and raised embankments.

Related indicators
Health; Climate change; Biodiversity; Land use; Contaminated land; Water pollution.

Related tools
Environmental impact assessment; Ecological footprinting; Regeneration-based checklist.

About this chapter

This chapter focuses on the impacts of flooding in and around the British Isles. It is written with the assistance of David Crichton, who has also supplied a comprehensive bibliography. David is a Visiting Professor at the Benfield Hazard Research Centre at University College London and at Middlesex University Flood Hazard Research Centre, and a Research Fellow at the University of Dundee. He sits on a number of government and academic boards, and is a member of the UK Advisory Committee on Natural Disaster Reduction. He is also the author of the book *The Implications of Climate Change for the Insurance Industry*, first published in 2001, with sales around the world.

Flooding is on the increase, and results from urbanisation, poor planning and, of course, the impacts of climate change. Readers are recommended to see Chapter 10 for a more detailed discussion about climate change and the weather.

Background

There is good scientific evidence to show that global sea levels are rising as the world's oceans warm and expand. This trend is exacerbated by the melting of many land glaciers and the ice sheets of Greenland, but it is a complex situation. For example, meteorologists predict that the melting of the glaciers of Antarctica will actually reduce sea levels because snow fall there will be sequestered, at least until global temperatures have risen by around 10 degrees, whereas if the ice of Antarctica melted it is estimated that sea levels would rise by between 60 and 70 m. The "climate change scenarios" produced by the Tyndall Centre for Climate Change Research[1] (see Chapter 10) suggest that if we can curtail greenhouse gas emissions to a low level, then sea levels will rise by between 9 and 48 cm by 2080; but if emissions are high, the rise could be up to 69 cm. Because of the different rates of sinking and rising of the land mass in the UK, different regions of the coastline will experience different actual levels of sea rises. For instance, high emissions could result in an 86 cm rise in the London region (see Figure 15.1), while in southwest Scotland this may only be 59 cm by 2080.

Over 8 per cent of the land area of England – including 50 per cent of grade 1 agricultural land, parts of a number of major urban centres and areas of interna-

Figure 15.1 Central London and particularly the City and Docklands are in the risk zone for tidal flooding

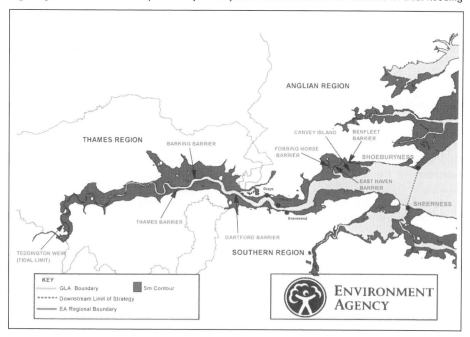

Source: 'Planning for flood risk management in the Thames Estuary', Environement Agency

tionally designated environment sites – are protected by river and coastal defences. In total nearly 5,000 km² of land in England and Wales are below sea level and protected from the sea alone by natural or artificial defences. Maintaining marine defences is very expensive, so there is a general government policy that areas liable to flood from the sea will, in many cases, be allowed to revert to the sea² (e.g. many areas of the Norfolk Broads).

Flooding in many areas of the UK is also predicted to increase significantly because of:

- increased winter rainfall
- higher sea levels, plus increased wave heights and bigger storm surges
- more intense and frequent winter storms.

It is difficult to predict storm incidence, and although the Hadley Centre model[3] predicts an increase, a number of other models do not. It is safe to say that storms will be wetter, however.

Each of the climate change scenarios suggests that winter precipitation will increase. By the 2080s, this increase ranges from 10–20 per cent for the low emissions scenario (depending on region) to between 15 and 35 per cent for the high emissions scenario. Conversely the summer pattern is reversed, and almost the whole of the UK may become drier, with summer rainfall half the reference level under the high emissions scenario. The highest changes in precipitation in both winter and summer are predicted for eastern and southern parts of England, while changes are smallest in the northwest of Scotland.[4] The problem of flooding in the southeast of England is already exacerbated by the fact that the land mass is sinking in that region and by the fact that relatively large areas in the southeast are already prone to coastal and riverine flooding.

Urban flooding

The move to cities has brought with it urban flooding problems as traditional streams are covered over and culverted and natural catchment areas are interrupted by new artificial landscapes. These new features of the increasingly "waterproof" city result in increased rates and volume of run-off, and a significant proportion of insurance claims for non-riverine floods are the result of inadequate urban drainage systems. Changes to future rainfall patterns, it is thought, will increase the likelihood of flash floods in the city. This will probably also increase the risk of the failure of urban sewage systems, leading to real problems of increased health risks to citizens who have to cope with flood-damaged cities.

The situation with flooding is already grave in England and Wales. Actual flood events – although inevitably influenced by natural fluctuation in the weather – do appear to be becoming more intense. For example, on 13 January 2003 the Environment Agency (EA) reported that the Thames Barrier at Woolwich had been closed a record 14 consecutive times between New Years' Day and 8 January 2003 because the combination of high incoming tides coupled with increased flows from upstream meant there was a real risk of flooding within the London area, especially underground transport and low-lying residential areas. The EA also reported that, at 261 mm, rainfall along the Thames Valley since 1 November 2002 was:

> *"...more than double the average (136 mm) and from 21 December to 31 December, 86 mm of rain fell in the region, more than the average for the whole month. This heavy rainfall pushed river levels on the Thames to their highest since 1947, and the third highest in 120 years. At their peak, river levels flowing over Teddington Weir were three times greater than average winter levels with over 9,000 million gallons of water a day flowing through the weir – the equivalent in volume of 220,000 Olympic swimming pools of water flowing through Teddington a day. High flows moving downstream combined with tidal flows over 1 m (3 ft) higher than a regular high tide, meant river levels in London rose 1.2 (4ft) above what would normally have been expected."*[5]

London suffers from the double whammy of threat from inundation from sea and river. Had the Thames Barrier not closed to hold back the high tide there was a very real risk of the Thames overtopping riverbanks, flooding riverside properties and causing havoc for London's transport network, not least the tunnels for London's underground train network (the Tube). In Greater London, riverside properties lying on tributaries of the Thames were also protected from flooding by the Barrier closures. Holding back the tide creates a reservoir on the Thames behind the gates, into which the rain-swollen tributaries can flow. An estimated 250 properties alongside the Thames and the River Crane would have been affected by flooding had the Barrier not closed. The government estimates that the value of the protected land and property within the Thames regional tidal flood risk area is around £80 billion, and in the event of a major flood in London well over a third of that sum would be incurred to cover flood damage, around £30 billion's worth.[6]

Planning considerations

Local authorities (LAs) are increasingly picking up the bill for emergency coverage during flooding by rivers or the sea, and for the rebuilding of infrastructures destroyed or damaged by flood events. LAs are also responsible (through the management of the local planning system) for the development and control of waste and polluted sites on flood plains and the safety of their citizens who dwell on them. Significant impacts will be:

- Cost of emergency services in times of floods. Emergency services should have a realistic and effective evacuation plan for every building in their area. Where properties are increasingly prone to flash floods these evacuation plans should be revised regularly.
- Cost of repairing infrastructure after events and funding preventative defences and strategies
- Co-ordination of evacuation planning within LA area.
- Implementation of sustainable urban drainage strategies (SUDS – see below).

Planning professionals and elected council members are responsible for what new developments take place in flood plains. Guidance on flooding supplied with planning proposals has, in some cases, been watered down, and there is still an ethos in the system in England and Wales that if adequate precautionary steps are taken then some development can occur in the floodplain. For example, Planning Policy Guidance 25, published in 2000 (see Appendix 1), introduced the "sequential principle", which basically says that building in the floodplain can be permitted if there is no other land available. However, this will hopefully change as planners and elected members come to realise what their decisions will actually mean for local people. A new motorway development, for instance, coupled with increased winter rainfall and rising sea levels, could result in more rapid urban run-off and the damming of natural river flows in catchment systems. Where there is a potential for flood, the planners must seek advice from the Environment Agency, but do not have to follow it, and frequently do not.

The position in Scotland is very different. The "precautionary principle" applies to planning decisions (see Chapter 7), and most authorities have taken advice from the insurance industry. For several years they have not allowed any residential building where the risk of flood exceeds the 1-in-200 year return period as at 2050, taking climate change into account. Since Devolution, there has been an active flood defence building programme, and defences have been completed or are in an advanced stage of preparation for all significant areas at risk.

In Scotland, too, councils are also responsible for watercourse maintenance, keeping and publishing detailed records of floods and action taken, and the construction of flood defences. This means that they are legally and democratically accountable, which gives an incentive not only to build defences, but also to prevent construction in flood hazard areas in the first place.

Scottish planners have the benefit of free advice from "flood appraisal groups"

– groups of experts and stakeholders who meet regularly to advise councils on planning strategies, major development proposals, SUDS, and flood defence schemes. They are often established on a catchment basis, enabling planners and engineers from all the relevant councils to meet together to ensure a river basin management approach to development. Such groups have been in operation in Scotland since 1996 and have been extremely successful in solving issues in a constructive and non-confrontational way. There is no reason why councils in England and Wales could not adopt a similar approach, which would help them to prepare for the imminent requirements of the EU Water Framework Directive.[7]

Insurance

Recent floods around the world have caused loss of life, loss of homes and livelihoods, illness, misery and stress, all of which are set to increase in the UK over coming years. The UK is unique in that private sector insurance companies guaranteed the availability of cheap flood insurance since 1961. This enabled people to buy houses in flood hazard areas, and people increasingly took insurance for granted. However, the growth in new housing in flood hazard areas which resulted means that it is no longer reasonable to expect property owners in safe areas to continue to subsidise those who choose to live in flood hazard areas.

When the second draft of the new English planning guidelines for flood (PPG 25) was issued in January 2000, it caused insurers a lot of concern for three reasons: it ignored insurers' comments on the first draft; it introduced the sequential principle; and it dropped the insurance template which had appeared in the first draft.[8] The immediate response of insurers was to cancel the 1961 price ceiling on insurance in flood hazard areas, which had kept prices artificially low, so from February 2000 insurers were free to increase prices to the "technical rate" (the rate that would have existed without the cap). In some cases, the technical rate was so much higher than the rate being charged that most decided to do this in stages, increasing the price each year. Typical increases in the first year were around 250 per cent, but each year there will be more price increases until the technical rate is reached. For an average house in a 100 year floodplain, the annual premium will need to increase by around £700. In higher risk areas the increases could be greater, and there have been cases where premiums have increased from £300 per year to £300 per month.

The main change happened on 1 January 2003, when insurers withdrew the 1961 guarantee of availability of insurance for all. They replaced it with a short-term guarantee for properties where the risk is less than the 75–year return period. This is to give the government more time to build flood defences. It will be reviewed every year and will expire in 2007.

With this in mind, developers, clients, architects and engineers should note that they are the perpetrators of high or low flood risk buildings, and are strongly advised to educate themselves on the risks of various building forms, strategies to reduce flood impacts through good design, and the potential risks of placing buildings in vulnerable locations. The opportunity to evacuate building occupants in an emergency is created at the design stage and is the responsibility of the designers. No doubt in the not too distant future designers and developers whose buildings cause financial loss or distress to their occupants or the general public in the event of flooding will be sued for recompense.

Surveyors must also be aware of the impacts of flooding. Money can be easily made or lost by missing a flood risk warning on a site. The value of a property can be almost wiped out by a single flood, so a knowledge of flooding is an increasingly important attribute in the current market place. The Royal Institution of Chartered Surveyors (RICS) has commissioned and published various studies in this field,[9] as they are responsible for advising their customers on where to move to and from.

Everyone pays the price

It is the general public that eventually has to pay for the increasing risk of floods in the UK through considerably reduced building values, higher or unobtainable insurance premiums, and the repair work to buildings and lives. Council taxes will inevitably be affected by the need to reinstate infrastructure. We may even see a significant influx of climate refugees over the next decade.

The average insurance flood loss for a domestic residence is over £30,000, because even after quite a shallow flood much of the fabric and finish of a building has to be ripped out and replaced. Landfill taxes will make it more expensive to demolish buildings, so it is more sustainable to reinstate the building using more resilient materials, and this would also reduce the costs of repair for future floods.[10] In Scotland, the Buildings (Scotland) Act 2003 gives power to the Scottish Executive to introduce regulations to make resilient reinstatement compulsory after a flood or storm.

Global indicators

While regional increases in localised river flooding will vary with changing regional climates, one source of flooding that will have a relatively similar impact around the world will be global sea level rises. Since the end of the last Ice Age, 18,000 years ago, the sea level has risen by over 120 metres. Geological data suggests that global average sea level may have risen at an average rate of 0.1–0.2

mm/yr over the last 3,000 years. However, tide gauge data indicate that the global rate of sea level rise during the 20th Century was 1–2 mm/yr, and in the 21st Century this will rise to 2.5–4.5 mm/yr on average, although this may happen in catastrophic stages if whole ice sheets reach their phase change temperature at one time.

This is occurring as a result of:

- Melting of land ice, such as mountain glaciers and polar icecaps. Current evidence of global warming includes the widespread retreat of glaciers, huge water stores, on five continents, and the major ice-sheets in Greenland and Antarctica.
- Melting of sea ice. Even at very high northern latitudes, large reductions are predicted in the fraction of ocean area covered by sea ice. A less dramatic decrease in sea-ice amount is predicted for the southern oceans around Antarctica.
- The thermal expansion of water within the oceans. As the temperature of the waters in the oceans rises and the seas become less dense, they will spread, occupying more surface area on the planet. Increased temperature will accelerate the rate of sea level rise.

Along relatively flat coastlines, such as coastlines bordering fertile, highly populated river deltas, a 1 mm rise in sea level causes a shoreline retreat of about 1.5 m.

In addition to the relatively slow inundation of low-lying coastal areas as the global mean sea level rises, an increase in the frequency of short-lived extreme high water events is expected. It is these events, which are associated with storm surges, that will present the greatest immediate threat to populations, particularly those of low-lying countries such as:

- the Atlantic Coast of the USA
- Denmark, Holland and Sweden
- island nations including the Cook Islands, Tuvalu (nine coral atolls east of Australia with their highest point just 5 m (15 feet) above sea level) and the Marshall Islands, where the island of Majuro lost up to 20 per cent of its beachfront during the 1990s
- Bangladesh, where a 1 m rise in sea level would inundate half of that country's rice land.
- other highly populated countries including Viet Nam, China, India, Thailand, the Philippines, Indonesia and Egypt, where relatively small areas of inundation would displace a disproportionate number of climate refugees.

Absolute rises in sea level are also influenced by geological movement of landmasses. For instance, in Britain, the north west of the country is rising, while the south east is sinking and will be more prone to flooding as a result by both sea and river.[12]

UK government indicators

In England and Wales the Environment Agency is responsible for flood fore-casting, and prevention and reduction strategies. No site that is vulnerable to flooding should be granted planning permission without having first been vetted by the EA. Currently 27 per cent (by value) of all new housing in England and Wales is being built in flood hazard areas, against the advice of the EA.[11] The corresponding figure in Scotland is zero.

Priorities should include:

- no new development in flood plains
- action by local councils and the EA to protect properties from the likelihood

---

Mitigation strategies

Many cities are experimenting with SUDS.[13] These are "soft" engineering solutions which are not, in fact, restricted to urban areas. SUDS rely on gravity to drain the surface water run-off from hardstanding areas into the drainage system during storms (peak-lopping or shaving) and increase significantly the time it takes for the rainfall to reach watercourses. Attenuating the flow, and thereby reducing the risk of flooding, also provides time for the natural processes of sedimentation, filtration and biodegradation, which reduces the pollutant load in the surface water runoff.

SUDS can be designed to fit into their environmental setting, adding considerably to local amenity or local biodiversity through systems of streams, ponds and lakes that are managed to ensure that the final discharge will not pollute rivers, or create flooding downstream. However, caution should be used in relying on SUDS, because they only work outside the floodplain. The water table must not be near the ground surface, so that any "holding areas" for water can provide temporary stores during flood periods.

Other flood-prevention techniques include the use of absorbent surfaces in cities, and a number of cities in Germany and Switzerland have adopted green roof policies (for example, in Kassel, Germany, the roofs of a suburb are key components in the flood reduction strategies of the planners). Collecting rain water for reuse in WCs etc. also increases the storage capacity of a city.

---

of flooding, including appropriate measures to reduce the risk of death from flooding in vulnerable properties

- education of building users on the risks of flooding, including warning systems and how to use them, and flood risk mitigation strategies they can use in their own buildings and lives
- encouraging the use of SUDS (see box).

Building-level indicators

Anyone who owns a property or wants to rent or buy should first check whether that property is at risk from flooding. The EA's website[6] has simple-to-use flooding maps that check risk based on postcodes in England and Wales. But the EA raises a number of other considerations:

- Is the site vulnerable to flooding by sea, river or urban flood waters today?
- Will the site be vulnerable to flooding by sea, river or urban flood waters in five, ten, twenty or fifty years' time?
- Is it possible to get building insurance for this building that covers flood risk?

If there is a risk of flooding, other questions must be addressed:

- Can the property be evacuated sufficiently rapidly?
- Will evacuation routes be blocked by water?
- Are the evacuation routes large enough to handle the number of people who will be trying to evacuate the building or area?
- Are the evacuation routes safe? For example, do they rely on escaping by cars parked in basement car parks that will be flooded, or do escape routes go through tunnels that will also be flooded? Also, does the building have a closed skin with no opening windows and the only exit doors being on the ground floor or basement levels – unusable during flooding? Bungalows, for instance, should have "means of escape" skylights.
- Can services such as gas, electricity and water be turned off safely in the event of a flood i.e. from a location above maximum flood height?

References

1   Hulme M, Turnpenny J and Jenkins G (2002), *Climate Change Scenarios for the United Kingdom*. The UKCIP 02 Briefing Report, Tyndall Centre for Climate Change Research, University of East Anglia, Norwich. Download from *www.ukcip.org.uk/scenarios*

2   Office of Science and Technology (1999), *Environmental Futures: Foresight Programme*, Department of Trade and Industry, London, March 1999. For more details see *www.foresight.gov.uk*

3   Met Office (1999), *The Greenhouse Efect and Climate Change: A briefing from the Hadley Centre*, Meteorological Office Communications, Bracknell

4   Hulme et al (2002), op cit

5   See *www.thamesweb.co.uk/floodrelief/2003effects.html*

6   For more information about flooding in any area of England and Wales, consult the Environment Agency's website at *www.environment-agency.gov.uk* Alternatively try a website that gives information for the whole of the UK, *www.home-envirosearch.com*

7   See: Crichton D (2001), *The Implications of Climate Change for the Insurance Industry*, Building Research Establishment, Watford, and also WWF (Sept 2002), *Managing Floods in Europe: The answers already exist*, a WWF background briefing paper available at *www.panda.org*

8   This template shows what levels of flood risk are acceptable to insurers for different types of development.

9   See, for instance: RICS Working Party (2001), *Flooding: Issues of concern to chartered surveyors*, RICS, London, available for downloading from *www.rics.org*

10 Building Research Establishment (2003), *Assessment of the Cost and Effect on Future Claims of Installing Flood Damage Resilience Measures*, Association of British Insurers, London, available from *www.abi.org.uk*

11 Lord Renton of Mount Harry, House of Lords Debate, Hansard, 18 Dec 2001: Column 215. See also: Crichton D (2003), *Flooding Risks and Insurance in England and Wales: Are there lessons to be learned from Scotland?*, April 2003, available in pdf on *www.benfieldhrc.org*

12 Source: *www.metoffice.gov.uk/research/hadleycentre/pubs/brochures/B2000/predictions.html*

12 More details on SUDs can be found at *www.sepa.org.uk* or *www.ciria.org.uk*

Further information

This reading list is mainly designed to assist and inform people whose properties may be liable to flooding and to help designers and students studying flood or flood-related topics or wishing to design flood risks out of their scheme. It is limited to sources that are readily available in the public domain, and most of the information is free. If you have any suggestions of items which could be added to this list, please email: *david@crichton.sol.co.uk*

Insurance issues

ABI (2001), *Flooding: A partnership approach to protecting people*, Association of British Insurers, London. Download from *www.abi.org.uk*

ABI (2002), *Renewing the Partnership: How the insurance industry will work with others to improve protection against floods*, Association of British Insurers, London. Download from *www.abi.org.uk*

Clark M, Priest S, Treby EJ and Crichton D (2002), *Insurance and UK Floods: A strategic reassessment,* A research report for TSUNAMI, University of Southampton, Southampton. Available free from *office@theriskgroup.org*

Crichton D (2003), *Flood Risk and Insurance in England and Wales: Are there lessons to be learned from Scotland?* University College London, Benfield Greig Hazard Research Centre. Download from *www.benfieldhrc.org*

Green C and Penning-Rowsell E (2002), *Flood Risk and Insurance: Strategic options for the insurance industry and government*, Middlesex University Flood Hazard Research Centre, London. Available free from *office@theriskgroup.org*

Environment Agency Booklets

The following are available free of charge from Floodline (Tel: 0845 988 1188):

Caravans and Flood Risk: Advice for caravan and camping park owners
Damage Limitation: How to make your home flood resistant
After a Flood: How to restore your home
Flood Management Research in England and Wales
Living on the Edge: An updated guide to the rights and responsibilities of a riverside owner. (NB English law only, but still of interest)

Damage and costs of flooding

Black A and Evans S (1999), *Flood Damage in the UK: New insights for the insurance industry*. University of Dundee, Dundee. (Price £250, but may be available free to bona fide researchers). E-mail: *paul.miller@aon.co.uk*

BRE (1996), *Design Guidance on Flood Damage to Dwellings*, Building Research Establishment, Watford.

Garvin SL, Phillipson M, Sanders CH, Hayles CS and Dow GT (1998) *Impact of climate change on building*, Building Research Establishment, Watford.

DTLR (2002), *Preparing for Floods: Interim guidance for improving the flood resistance of domestic and small business properties*, Department of Transport, Local Government and the Regions, London. Available free from SEPA, or by telephoning Floodline (see above).

Kelman I (2002), *Physical flood vulnerability of residential properties in coastal Eastern England*, PhD Dissertation submitted September 2002 to the

University of Cambridge. Available for free download from *http://www. arct.cam.ac.uk/curbe/ilanphd.html#ilanphddownload*

Ogunyoye F and van Hereveld M (Posford Haskoning Ltd) (2002), *Temporary and Demountable Flood Protection: Interim guidance on use*, DEFRA and Environment Agency, R&D Publication 130. Available free from E-mail: *publications@wrcplc.co.uk*

UKCIP and EPSRC (2003), *Building Knowledge for a Changing Climate: The impacts of climate change on the built environment*. A research agenda, UKCIP, Oxford. Available free from *www.ukcip.org.uk*

Bowker P (2002), "Making properties more resistant to floods" *Municipal Engineer,* 151, 197–205. This issue was published in December 2002, and contains a number of excellent articles on flooding. Most local authority roads departments should have a copy, and most universities will subscribe to the journal, either in hard copy or have an electronic subscription. For more details, including abstracts of papers, see "Municipal Engineering Papers" at *www.t-telford.co.uk/ME.htm*

Hazards and climate change

BBC Radio Scotland "Fresh Air" series broadcast weekly from 19 February to 26 March 2003. The accompanying book *After the Flood* can be downloaded from *http://www.bbc.co.uk/scotland/radioscotland*

Price DJ and McInally G (Babtie Group) (2001), *Climate Change: Review of levels of protection offered by flood prevention schemes*, Scottish Executive Central Research Unit Report No 12. Edinburgh. Available from *www.scotland.gov.uk/ cru/resfinds*

Werritty A, Black A, Duck R, Finlinson W, Shackley S and Crichton D (2002), *Climate Change, Flood Occurrences Review*, Scottish Executive Environment Group Research Programme Research Findings No. 19, Scottish Executive, Edinburgh. Available from *www.scotland.gov.uk/cru/resfinds*

Dawson AG, Smith DE and Dawson S (2001), *Potential Impacts of Climate Change on Sea Levels Around Scotland*, Scottish Natural Heritage, Edinburgh

Entec Ltd and JBA Ltd, with contributions from Crichton D and Salt J (October 2000), *Inland Flooding Risks,* General Insurance Research Report No 10, Association of British Insurers, London

European Environment Agency (2001), *Sustainable Water Use in Europe. Part 3: Extreme Hydrological Events: Floods and droughts*, Report No. 212001, European Environment Agency. Download from *http://reports.eea.eu.int/ Environmental_Issues_No_21/en/enviissue21.pdf*

Historic flood events

There are many publications recording details of flood events. Some recent examples are:

Thomas A (2001), *The Lewes Flood*, S B Publications, Seaford

Welsh Consumer Council (1992), *In Deep Water: A study of consumer problems in Towyn and Kinmel Bay after the 1990 floods*, Welsh Consumer Council, Cardiff

Lawson Wood (2002), *The Great Borders Flood of 1948*, Tempus Publishing, Stroud

Non-structural solutions

Institute for Catastrophic Loss Reduction (October 2001), *Proceedings of a Conference on Non-Structural Solutions to Water Problems*, Ontario, Canada. (Placed on the web in November 2001.) Download from *www.engga.uwo.ca/ research/iclr/Post -ws/default.htm*

Drainage and SUDS

EA and SEPA (1999), *Sustainable Urban Drainage: An introduction*, Environment Agency and Scottish Environmental Protection Agency. See *www.sepa.org.uk/ guidance/urban-drainage*

North East Scotland Flood Appraisal Group (2002), *Drainage Impact Assessment: Guidance for Developers and Regulators*, Aberdeenshire Council, Stonehaven. Available from Hilary McBean, Aberdeenshire Council. Tel: 01569 768300, E-mail: *hilary.macbean@aberdeenshire.gov.uk*

Crichton D, *Floods and SUDS: A guidance note for local authorities on SUDS issues*, (not yet published). For details contact *david@crichton.sol.co.uk*

Shot in the Dark Centre for Environmental Communications (2002), *Designs That Hold Water: Sustainable urban drainage systems explained*, Video production (25 minutes) sponsored by SEPA, The Environment Agency, and the Institution of Civil Engineers. Available from SEPA or EA.

Scottish Executive (2001), *Planning Advice Note 61: Planning and Sustainable Urban Drainage Systems*, Scottish Executive, Edinburgh.

Scottish Water (2002), *Sewers for Scotland*, Scottish Water, [Sue: place?]

CIRIA guidance notes

The following are available via *www.ciria.org.uk*:

Report C506 *Low Cost Options for Prevention of Flooding from Sewers*, 1998.

Report C521 *Sustainable Urban Drainage Systems: Design manual for Scotland and Northern Ireland*, 2000.

Report C523 *Sustainable Urban Drainage Systems: Best practice manual*, 2001.

Report C539 *Rainwater and Greywater Recycling in Buildings: Best practice guidance*, 2001.

Advice

Fleming G et al (2001), *Learning to Live with Rivers*, The Institution of Civil Engineers Presidential Commission Report, London. Download from *www.ice.org.uk/rtfpdf/ICEFlooding.pdf*

Aberdeenshire and Aberdeen City Council (2002), *Guidance Note – Works to Watercourses and their Banks – Flooding Issues*. Available from either Council.

Federal Emergency Management Agency publications such as:
Reducing Flood Losses *www.fema.gov/hazards/floods/fldlosses.shtm*
Avoiding Flood Damage *www.fema.gov/pdf/hazards/flddam.pdf*
Floodplain Construction Technical Bulletins *www.fema.gov*

Managed realignment

See: "Feasibility and implications of managed realignment of Skinflats, Forth Estuary, Scotland" at *www.forthestuaryforum.co.uk*

Planning issues

Scottish Office (1995), *National Planning Policy Guidelines: 7 – Flood*, (NPPG 7), Scottish Office, Edinburgh

Crichton D (2002), *Flood Appraisal Group Guidelines*. Revised regularly: latest edition available by email free from *david@crichton.sol.co.uk*

RICS Working Party (2001), *Flooding: Issues of concern to chartered surveyors*, RICS, London. Download from *www.rics.org/downloads/flooding.pdf*

Crichton D (2001), "Flood news from the insurance front line" and "A Scottish lead in managing flood risk" *Town & Country Planning Journal,* 70, 183–185 and 188–189

Crichton D (2001), "Flooding, insurance and planning", *Scottish Planning and Environmental Law Journal,* 84, 29–31

Managed retreat issues

D'Arcy BJ et al (2001), *Diffuse Pollution Impacts: The environmental and economic impacts of diffuse pollution in the UK*, Chartered Institution of Water and Environmental Management (funded by EA, SEPA and SNIFFER). Available from SEPA (see above).

Reservoir risks

Babtie Group and the Centre for Ecology and Hydrology (2002), *Climate Change Impacts on the Safety of British Reservoirs*, Report commissioned by the

Department of the Environment, Transport and the Regions (DETR) now DEFRA, through their reservoir safety research programme.

Hughes A et al (2000), *Risk Management for UK Reservoirs*, Research project report C542, Construction Industry Research and Information Association (CIRIA), London

River restoration

River Restoration Centre (2003), *Manual of River Restoration Techniques*, Download from *http://www.therrc.co.uk/manual.php*

Planning policy guidance – related documents (see Appendix 1 for details)

1	2	3	4	5	6	7	8	9	10	11	12	13
x			x	x		x			x	x	x	

14	15	16	17	18	19	20	21	22	23	24	25	
x				x					x		x	

Building Regulations – related Approved Documents (see Appendix 2 for details)

A	B	C	D	E	F	G	H	I	J	K	L1	L2	M	N
		x					x							

Noise

About this chapter

This chapter explores the relationships between noise, planning, building design and climate change. It was written in consultation with John Hinton of Birmingham City Council, UK. John is chair of the EC Working Group 4 on Noise Mapping, and author of several books about noise and buildings. There is a short glossary of terms at the end of the chapter.

Background

Noise can have profound effects on our mental well-being, our health, our sleep patterns, and our ability to work; it can cause both psychological and physical damage; it can wreck marriages, families and communities.

As any councillor or environmental health officer knows, it is perhaps the most common nuisance reported by members of the public (see Table 16.1). Despite this, it is surprisingly low on the agenda of most building designers, even though it should be considered at the briefing or development stage of any project.

Table 16.1 Noise nuisance complaints in England and Wales (1995/96)

SOURCE OF NOISE	NUMBER OF COMPLAINTS
Domestic premises	164,115
Industrial and commercial premises	49,543
Construction noise	7,716
Vehicles, machinery, equipment in streets	7,427
Street noise	3,636
Total	232,437

Source: *Pollution Handbook*, Loveday Murley, National Society for Clean Air and Environmental Protection, 2003

Unfortunately, it is also a subject which is often poorly taught in many schools of architecture.

It is difficult to define and legislate against noise because the nuisance is different for each situation and for each person. Levels of noise in a disco may be fantastic for dancers, but are way beyond anything that could be tolerated by a family in a home. It's a personal thing: some people can adapt to being quite happy in high noise levels; for others, trying to go to sleep under comparatively low levels of sound can cause real distress. Indeed, in offices where noise has been almost eliminated its absence causes distress, and noise machines have had to be introduced to improve the working environment!

The extent of noise annoyance, however described or reported, is clearly influenced by numerous non-acoustic factors such as personal, cultural, attitudinal, and situational factors in addition to the amount of noise per se (see Figure 16.1).

Climate change may bring a wide range of physical and social adaptations that could affect noise levels, particularly in cities. For example, the growth of the "café society" may increase street activity at all times of year, so it would seem sensible to pre-plan open air eating facilities in relation to residential areas.[2] Thought should also be given to the greater need to open windows in warmer weather and for ventilation cooling. But the noise impacts of street life and traffic noise will have an impact on mixed-mode and non-air-conditioned buildings. The increased need for traffic-free zones in open restaurant areas of a city may become a feature of future inner city planning strategies, to ensure that local office buildings can be naturally ventilated without excessive noise levels.

Sources of noise

Noise can be internal or external. Table 16.2 lists common sources.[3]

Figure 16.1 Factors that contribute to noise annoyance in communities

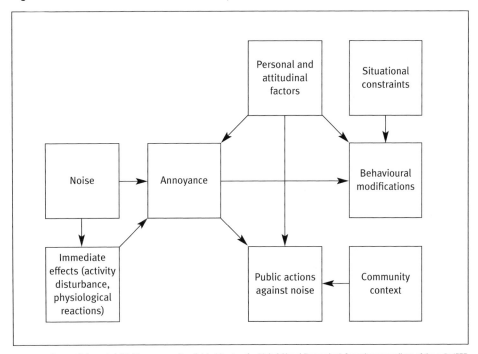

Source: Nelson et al, 'Multiprogramme Parallel Architecture for Digital Signal Processing', from the proceedings of the 1987 IEEE International Conference on Acoustics, Speech and Signal Processing, April 1987

At the upper end of noise nuisance is "speech interference" i.e. being unable to hear speech because of background noise. However, even in environments where communication is essential, such as the trading floor of the Stock Exchange, where noise levels are very high and people shout to be heard, the traders have invented a system of manual communication to overcome the problem, perhaps considering noise as an acceptable aspect of earning such high salaries on the floor. No doubt noise is a major contributory factor to the "burnout" experienced by many on the trading floors, but this particular business environment includes the opportunity to take early retirement because of the

Table 16.2 Typical sources of noise

EXTERNAL NOISE	INTERNAL SOURCES
Road traffic Industry Trains Construction Street Aircraft	Industrial processes Machines including TVs and radios Human noise from speech or movement

> ## Noise in the workplace
>
> Some years ago Oxford Brookes University undertook an occupant satisfaction survey on the County Hall building in Oxford, where extremely high energy bills and high numbers of complaints about the indoor environment resulted in the County Council taking out the air-conditioning and replacing all the fixed windows with opening windows to the cellular, now naturally ventilated offices.
>
> Despite the fact that County Hall is right beside a busy road, and the opening of windows introduced far higher levels of road noise, there was a marked increase in occupant satisfaction with the indoor environment, not least because the natural ventilation provided them with more control over their indoor environment and a much more pleasant source of fresh air and summer cooling. Occupant surveys showed that, generally, people expressed a definite preference for natural ventilation through opening windows even though the noise level in some rooms increased considerably. The response to the additional noise was mixed – a cocktail of perceptions and emotions about comfort, control, health and a sense of relationship to the wider environment. A similar response has been recorded by a number of researchers.[5]
>
> The solution in Oxford was also complemented by strategies for reducing traffic levels in the city centre that also improved the air quality as well as reducing general noise levels from traffic.

inherent high rewards, so maintaining the sustainability of the trading floor system. In factories, where people do not have the option to retire early, such choices are not an issue and legislation to protect the individual is essential.

Noise in the workplace can contribute to both temporary and permanent hearing loss, although current evidence suggests that the risks at the typical exposure levels associated with environmental noise are low.[4] Noise-induced hearing loss often occurs at higher frequencies first, at around 4,000 Hz. Hearing damage can then extend to lower frequencies and become relatively more severe after increasing exposure at higher levels. Temporary hearing loss after short-term exposure may be associated with permanent hearing loss even though the physiological mechanisms may be quite different. Noise-induced hearing loss can contribute directly to increased stress and annoyance, particularly in situations where speaking and listening are important. Low frequency noise in particular can be very disturbing. Stress, including noise-related stress, can manifest itself in many forms, including hypertension and heart disease.

Measuring noise

The most common unit of measurement for noise is that of the decibel – dB. One decibel is the smallest perceptible change in sound level that the human ear can detect. The decibel measures the intensity of sound (the sound pressure level) on a logarithmic scale, i.e. there is not a linear relationship between levels.[6] Noise levels are often quoted as "dB(A)", where A indicates "weighted average", to account for the frequency response of the average human ear.

Some examples of sound pressure levels are:

whisper – 20 dB
normal speech – 70 dB
passing tube train – 100 dB
large jet plane – 120 dB

The threshold of pain is around 120 dB.

Noise is measured with a sound level meter – an instrument designed to respond to sound in approximately the same way as the human ear and therefore to give objective, reproducible measurements of the sound pressure fluctuations present at the measurement position. There are two main types available:

- A sound level meter will display the instantaneous sound level in dB(A). This type of instrument can be used to perform simple checks but is not sufficient to carry out a noise-at-work assessment or survey.
- An integrating-averaging sound level meter will measure L_{eq} dB(A) , where L_{eq} is the equivalent continuous sound pressure level, or a measure of the average sound pressure level during a period of time.[7]

It is actually very difficult to study and measure noise, let alone set standards for it. Think of the difference between your own emotional response to the crying of your baby and that of the person next door hearing it through a thin wall. How do you compare the noise levels of different types of road traffic, aircraft, railways and industrial or construction noise? Research shows that people find different levels of noise annoying, but there is a pattern to the levels of annoyance (see Figure 16.2).[8]

Noise and the law

For some reason noise was not thought to be a legislatable problem until the 1960s. The first law setting out the guidance for acceptable noise levels was the Noise Abatement Act of 1960. Prior to this, noise was largely dealt with locally as

Figure 16.2 Percentage highly annoyed versus noise level

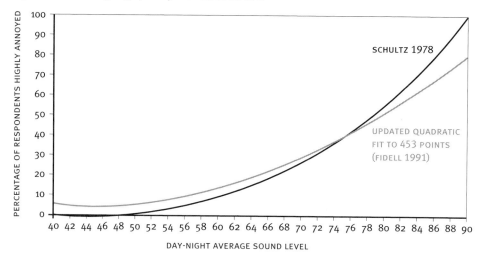

Source: adapted from Fidell, 1991 and Schultz, 1998

a nuisance and either under local bye-laws or under the Laws of Tort, because nuisance at law is a tort, i.e. a civil wrong for which courts can provide a remedy, usually damages.

In any action for noise nuisance the key factor is the need for an aggrieved person to establish that their occupation of land or property is affected by noise, and each case is considered on its merit. Nuisance is a criminal offence and provides powers to confiscate noisemaking equipment.

It is apparent that noise is now being taken more seriously, and local authorities are taking up the challenge of trying to quantify noise levels in their localities and developing strategies for improving them where necessary. One of the most interesting new developments is the mapping of noise (see local authority indicators, below).

There are various other approaches to the control of noise covered under the legislation[9] including the planning controls, particularly PPG 24, which suggests how noise should be taken into account in the planning process – including the need for special attention to proposed developments that could affect "quiet enjoyment" of areas of outstanding natural beauty, national parks etc. PPG24 suggests that:

- Noise need not be considered as a determining factor in granting planning permission, although the noise level at the high end of the category should not be regarded as a desirable level
- Noise should be taken into account when determining planning applications

---

Related legislation and standards

The Control of Pollution Act 1974, Part III covers construction site noise and certain noise in the street

The Environmental Protection Act 1990

The Noise and Statutory Nuisance Act 1993, which, as well as amending the EPA and COPA, also covers noise emitted from vehicles or equipment on the street, and burglar alarms.

The Noise Act 1996 makes certain night-time noise a criminal offence and provides powers to confiscate noise-making equipment.

British Standard 5228, Noise Control on Construction and Open Sites, provides guidance to enable compliance with Section 60 of the 1996 Act, and is applicable throughout the UK. It is in five parts.

---

and, where appropriate, conditions imposed to ensure an adequate level of protection against noise.

- Planning permission should not normally be granted where noise levels are predicted will be excessive.

Global indicators

The World Health Organization (WHO) suggests[10] that:

- Daytime noise levels of below 50 dB cause little annoyance
- Daytime levels should be no more than 55 dB for outside noise in residential areas
- The recommended level for undisturbed sleep should be no more than 35 dB.

European indicators

In a Green Paper of 1996[11] on future noise policy the European Commission estimated that between 17 per cent and 22 per cent of the population of the EU suffered from environmental noise levels it considered "unacceptable" (daytime levels greater than 65 dB(A) L_{eq}). It was also claimed that 90 per cent of this problem was caused by road traffic.

On 21 May 2002, the Council of Ministers formally approved the EU Environmental Noise Directive (Directive 2002/49/EC), and this is now being implemented in the EU member states. The Directive is a direct result of the 1996 Green Paper, which includes the following targets:[12]

- exposure to more than 65 dB(A) Leq should be phased out and at no time should 85 dB(A) L_{eq} be exceeded
- those exposed to levels of between 65–55 dB(A) L_{eq}, and those currently exposed to less than 55 dB(A) L_{eq}, should not suffer any increase.

To achieve these levels the Commission proposes wide-scale implementation of noise abatement strategies including the production of noise maps and action plans (noise policy) for:

- agglomerations with populations greater than 100,000
- major roads with more than 3,000,000 vehicles a year
- major railways with more than 30,000 trains a year
- major civil airports with more than 50,000 operations year.

Many different types of noise are considered within the European context, and in general priority is given to the effect of noise on citizens. Noise is number 8 of the European Commission "Sustainable Communities" Indicators.[13] This indicator is designed to identify the share of population exposed to long-term high levels of environmental noise from road, rail and air traffic, and from industrial sources in their homes, in public parks and other relatively quiet areas.

The proposal for the Community Environment Action Programme 2000–2009[14] includes a target of reducing the estimated 100 million people regularly affected by long-term high levels of noise by 10 per cent within 2010 and by 20 per cent within 2020. The long-term objective is to reduce them to a statistically insignificant number.[15] The units of measurement for this indicator are:

- percentage of population exposed, broken down into different value bands of Lden[16] and Lnight
- percentage of measurements corresponding to different value bands of indicators Lden and Lnight
- existence (yes/no) and level of implementation of noise action plan/pro-gramme (%).[17]

The European Commission made three further important recommendations:

- mapping of noise climate and noise exposure
- a common noise exposure index to be used throughout Europe
- harmonised measurement methods to be developed for Europe for environmental noise sources.

While the need for noise maps and harmonised measurement methods is clear, it is very difficult to see how the Swedes, the British and the Italians could ever agree on what are acceptable levels for, say, domestic or street noise. It may be one more thing on which Europe will never agree!

For cities with more than 100,000 inhabitants maps and associated data must be produced within ten years of the Directive coming into force. Similarly, from the information produced, action plans for noise reduction must be drawn up and approved within just one more year. The data to be sent to the European Commission will include:

- number of people living in dwellings exposed to noise levels divided into 5dB bands of Lden on the most exposed façade (55 to >75 dB)
- total number of people living in dwellings exposed to noise levels divided into 5dB bands of Lnight on the most exposed façade (50 to >70 dB)
- "where available and appropriate", the total number of people living in dwellings with "special insulation" that fall into the different bands of Lden and Lnight on the most exposed façade
- "where available and appropriate" the number of people living in dwellings with "a relatively quiet façade" that fall into the different bands of Lden and Lnight on the most exposed façade.

UK government indicators

We know that around 56 per cent of the population of England and Wales[18] are exposed to daytime noise levels exceeding 55 dB(A) L_{eq} and that around 65 per cent are exposed to night-time noise levels exceeding 45dB(A) L_{eq} (as measured outside the house in each case). The value of 45 dB(A) Leq night-time outdoors is equivalent to the 1995 WHO guideline value of 30 dB(A) L_{eq} night-time indoors (allowing 15 dB attenuation from outdoors to indoors for a partially open window for free-air ventilation to the bedroom).

Based on these figures, very drastic action would be needed to reduce the percentages of the population exposed above the WHO guideline values – it would take the virtual elimination of road traffic noise and other transportation noise (including public transport) from the vicinity of houses. The social and economic consequences of such action would probably be far greater than any environmental advantages of reducing the proportion of the population annoyed by noise. In addition, there is no evidence that anything other than a small minority of the population exposed at such noise levels find them to be particularly onerous in the context of their daily lives.

UK efforts to control noise pollution are probably about two years behind efforts to control air pollution.[19]

Local authority indicators

Many cities in the UK are already developing air pollution maps, but only a few have begun their noise mapping exercise. Noise mapping is a method of presenting complex noise information in a clear and simple way either on a physical map or in a database.[20] This mapping information can be either calculated or measured using a variety of techniques and methods, and the results of such exercises can be presented in many different ways and used for a number of different purposes.

To produce the required noise exposure data, noise mapping information must provide noise levels outside buildings. These noise levels then need to be linked to building occupancy. Preliminary results from the Birmingham noise mapping project suggest that the following percentages of the population of Birmingham are living in dwellings where the daytime L_{eq}(16 hr), or Lday, free field noise levels outside the most exposed façade exceed 60 dB, 65 dB and 70 dB:

- 20.6% over 60 dB
- 12.5% over 65 dB
- 2.5% over 70 dB.

Action plans may be developed simply by studying the noise maps to determine the most appropriate areas for action. Alternatively, so-called conflict maps may be produced which take account of the number of persons exposed to unacceptably high levels of noise in different areas. Through this process priorities can be identified when budgets for noise reduction actions are limited.

However, some actions, e.g. reducing road width, reducing speed limits and implementing lorry bans, can reduce noise levels in the targeted areas but increase noise in other areas. In some circumstances, therefore, it may be appropriate to take a more holistic approach and evaluate the effects of action plans across an entire city or agglomeration.

Such a project is currently under way in Birmingham. This project involves changing the relevant source and geographical information system (GIS) input data to evaluate the effect of possible action plans on the number of people exposed to various levels of Lday and Lnight. So far two noise reduction scenarios have been modelled. In the first scenario it was assumed that the speed limit on motorways was reduced to 50 mph and that bus-only lanes were installed on all dual carriageways in the city, along with an associated 30 mph speed limit. The second scenario evaluated the effects of introducing workplace car parking charges.

Building-level indicators

When recommending or deliberating upon a proposed development, planners must take into account the current and future levels of noise adjacent to a site. Where high levels exist, recommendations for development should be tempered by an understanding of the health and quality of life implications of the noise in relation to the proposed function of the building or its adjacent development. Very high levels of localised noise are a contra-indication for schools, residential homes, housing, a number of workplaces, and historic and natural environments.

Architects will need to know the location and levels of noise adjacent to, and within, sites in order to inform the design. The Building Regulations Approved Document E 2003 (see Appendix 2) requires significantly higher levels of sound insulation than the previous Document E, particularly between the walls and floors of individual dwelling units. There are a number of factors to be considered:[21]

- External noise will have a different effect on internal noise levels, depending on the distance of the room from the source of the noise: ground and first floor levels typically experience the highest levels of noise intrusion.
- The morphology of adjacent buildings is important because noise can arise from, and be reflected from, façades of adjacent buildings, a particular problem in narrow urban "canyons".
- The orientation of a building towards, or away from, a noise source influences the risk of noise disturbance. The risk can be reduced by the erection of solid barriers between the source and the building, but again the effectiveness of the barrier is influenced by its height, density and permeability, because noise will travel readily through any openings in the barrier.
- The transmission and reverberation properties of the materials of the building envelope are significant. For instance, sound travels more easily through a single-glazed window or façade than through double-glazing.
- The air-tightness of the envelope is important because noise travels through, and can be amplified by, air passages through the construction (see Chapter 22).

Glossary

There are a number of different measurement systems, indices and acronyms used to describe noise. Common terms are described below,[22] confusingly, of which the following are in common use:

dB (decibel) – a unit for expressing the relative loudness of sound on a logarithmic scale. 1dB = 10 log (P_1/P_2), where P_1 = measured power level (e.g. in watts), and P_2 = reference power level (e.g. in watts)*.

dB(A) – weighted average unit, often used to take account of the frequency response of the average human ear.

f – frequency

I – sound intensity

Lden – day-night average-sound level

Lday – day average-sound level over 16 hours

Lnight – night average-sound level

Le – aircraft exposure level

Leq – equivalent continuous sound pressure level

LPN – mean peak perceived noise level

NEF – noise exposure forecast

NI – noiseness index

NNI – "noise and number index", developed to quantify airport noise

NPL – noise pollution level

PNL – perceived noise level

SIL – speech interference level

TNEL – total noise exposure level

TNI – traffic noise index

*According to the National Physical Laboratory: "The use of the decibel in many descriptors stems from some observations about human reaction to sound, particularly that the ear is a non-linear transducer. For example, it is observed that the minimum detectable increase in sound pressure is not a constant but depends on the existing pressure, and is approximately 1 dB (or 12 per cent). Essentially, the ear reduces its sensitivity as the input increases, behaving as a logarithmic detector, and consequently some users find a logarithmic scale convenient. Other users find the consequences of a decibel scale more confusing (e.g. if there are several identical noise sources in a room, and a measurement is made of the noise when one source is operating and then a second source is turned on the level will increase by 3 dB. It would take two more sources to be activated to increase the level by a further 3 dB and four more to increase it by yet a further 3 dB)."[23]

References

1 WHO (1980), *Noise*, published by the United Nations Environmental Programme and the World Health Organization, Geneva at *www.inchem.org*

2 Warmer evenings may well pre-date the adaptation of populations to higher street noise levels.

3 For more information on the range of noise sources and legislation see *www.defra.gov.uk/environment/noise*

4 Murley L (2003), *Pollution Handbook*, National Society for Clean Air and Environmental Protection, Brighton

5 See: Wilson M, Nicol F and Singh R (1993), "Background noise levels in naturally ventilated buildings, associated with thermal comfort studies, initial result", *Journal of the Institute of Acoustics*, 15 (8), 283–295; Dubiel J, Wilson M and Nicol F (1996), "Decibels and discomfort – an investigation of variation in noise tolerance in offices", *Proceedings of CIBSE/ASHRAE Joint National Conference*, vol. II, 184–191; and Nicol J, Wilson M and Dubiel J, (1997), "Decibels and degrees – interactions between the thermal and acoustic comfort in offices", Proceeding of the CIBSE National Conference, pp 206-214

6 For example, when measuring in dB (a logarithmic scale), 20 dB is twice the sound level of 10dB, but 30 dB is twice as loud as 20 dB. That makes 40 dB twice the sound level of 30 dB, and so on.

7 Details of sound measurements and measuring instruments are at *www.cirrus research.co.uk/work.html*
Calculate your own noise-at-work measurements using the spreadsheet at *www.hse.gov.uk/hthdir/noframes/noise/noisecalc.xls*

8 Some of the problems of measuring noise are discussed at *www.npl.co.uk/npl/acoustics/publications/articles/29.html*

9 Murley L (2003), op cit, pp 185–228

10 See *www.who.int/peh/noise/noiseindex.html*

11 See *http://europa.eu.int/en/record/green/gp9611/noisesum.htm*

12 Source: *www.bksv.com/2766.htm*

13 A full list of indicators can be found at *www.sustainable-cities.org/indicators/index2.htm*

14 See: *http://europa.eu.int/comm/environment/newprg*

15 More information on EU action to combat noise can be found at *http://europa.eu.int/comm/environment/noise/home.htm*

16 Lden is short for Lday-evening-night

17 Commission of the European Communities (2000), *Proposal for a Directive of the European Parliament and of the Council relating to the Assessment and Management of Environmental Noise*, COM(2000) 468 final

18 BRE (2001), *The UK National Noise Incidence Study (NIS) 2000/2001*, at *www.defra.gov.uk/environment/noise*

19 See *www.defra.gov.uk/environment/consult/noiseambient*

20 See *www.defra.gov.uk/environment/noise/birmingham/report*, and an excel-

lent website on noise mapping, developed by John Hinton, who has pioneered these techniques in the UK and Europe, is at *http://reports.eea.eu.int/NOS02/ en/eu_noisewg4.pdf*

21 Lord P and Templeton D (1995), *Detailing for Acoustics*, Taylor & Francis, London
22 Source: *www.inchem.org*
23 Source: *www.npl.co.uk/acoustics/techguides/soundmeasurements/quantities .html*

Further reading

BRE (1974), *Traffic Noise and Overheating in Offices*, Digest No. 162, Building Research Establishment, Watford

Clausen G et al (1993), "A comparative study of discomfort caused by indoor air pollution, thermal load and noise", *Proceedings of the Indoor Air Conference*, vol. 3, pp 255–262

Fidell S, Barber D, Schultz T (1991), "Updating a dosage-effect relationship for the preference of annoyance due to general transportation noise", *JASA (Journal of the American Statistical Association)* 89, 15–28

Nelson P M (ed) (1987), *Transportation Noise Preference Book,* Butterworth & Co, London

Oseland N and Raw G (1996), "The interrelationship of effect of temperature, air quality and noise on perceived acceptability", *Proceedings of the Indoor Air Conference*, vol. 3, pp 1043–1048

Parkin H and Humphreys H (1979), *Acoustics, Noise and Buildings*, Faber, London

Saunders D, Templeton D, Mapp P and Sacre P (1997), *Acoustics in the Built Environment Advice for the Design Team*, 2nd edn, Architectural Press, Oxford

Schultz T J, 'Synthesis of the Social Surveys on Noise Annoyance', *Journal of the Acoustical Society of America*, 84 (2)

Planning policy guidance – related documents (see Appendix 1 for details)

1	2	3	4	5	6	7	8	9	10	11	12	13
		x	x	x	x						x	x

14	15	16	17	18	19	20	21	22	23	24	25	
	x		x	x						x		

Building Regulations – related Approved Documents (see Appendix 2 for details)

A	B	C	D	E	F	G	H	J	K	L1	L2	M	N
				x									

Air pollution

About this chapter

This chapter draws heavily on the excellent work of the National Society for Clean Air and Environmental Protection (NSCA)[1] and in particular their excellent publication *The Pollution Handbook*, edited by Loveday Murley. The NSCA's objectives are to promote clean air and environmental protection through the reduction of air, water and land pollution, noise and other contaminants, while having due regard for all aspects of the environment, and their work provides a very high standard of indicators and benchmarks on these subjects for the UK.

Background

Clean air, like clean water, is a fundamental requirement for sustaining life. As most of us spend 80–90 per cent of our time indoors, the air quality in buildings is vitally important. But indoor air pollution is intimately linked with the outdoor air pollution (sometimes called ambient air pollution) that occurs in both urban and rural areas.

It should be noted that the elderly, people with chronic heart and lung conditions, asthma sufferers, and young children are most at risk from the effects of airborne pollution, so remedial strategies are just as important as mitigation. This is particularly relevant given the current drive to increase land utilisation in towns and cities (see Chapter 14), which will mean more people living in areas where air pollution is already a significant health hazard.

Outdoor air quality

As early as the 13th Century air quality was a much talked about subject in London. This was the time when the first laws were passed to prevent the burning of coal in the City of London because of the injurious effect smoke was having on the health of citizens. Yet it is only 50 years since the last great "pea-souper" blanketed London with its lethal yellow/black fog of soot particles and sulphur dioxide, through which people could not even see their own hands. This event lasted for five days and resulted in approximately 4,000 more deaths than usual.[2] In response, the government passed the first Clean Air Act in 1956, which aimed to control domestic sources of smoke pollution by introducing smokeless zones, which in turn led to a reduction in sulphur dioxide pollution. The combination of this Act and the increased use of electricity and gas, and the locating of power stations away from towns, all helped to reduce the very high levels of air pollution in cities.

The next Clean Air Act, of 1968, required tall chimneys to be used for industries that burnt coal, liquid or gaseous fuels so that industrial pollution would be dispersed in the upper air streams. (It was considered too expensive to remove such pollutants from industrial emissions.)

Levels of pollution experienced by cities and buildings can be greatly influenced by location, morphology and the local climate. My own grandmother used to say that you could always tell when you were approaching Sheffield because "the sheep were black" – they were constantly bathed in the domestic and industrial smog that drifted outwards from in a cold air inversion within the city's basin of hills.

At that time, there was a different mix of air pollutants in the countryside. But from the 1970s onwards emissions from vehicles were beginning to take over as the major source of air pollution. These included emissions of carbon monoxide, particulates, oxides of nitrogen and volatile organic compounds (VOCs) such as hydrocarbons (see below for details of pollutants).

Since then, many strategies have been employed to combat harmful vehicle emissions – reducing car use in city centres, introducing lead-free petrol, public transport incentives, using smaller, lighter cars with lower emissions. Catalytic convertors, mandatory since January 1993 in all new cars sold in the European Union, led to a dramatic reduction in emissions of nitrogen oxides, as well as other harmful pollutants. More recently, we have seen the introduction of electric vehicles and those powered by alternative fuels that are less harmful to the environment.

It is important to note that concentrations of pollutants vary significantly even

Figure 17.1(a) Predictions of pollution in Melbourne in 2011 compared with the baseline year (1990) for different urban configurations

Exposure to fine particles

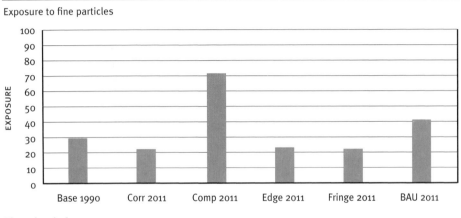

Photochemical smog

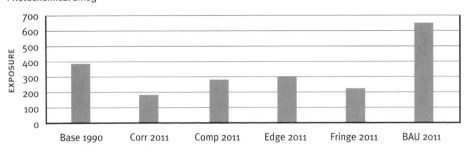

Figure 17.1(b) Key to configuration types

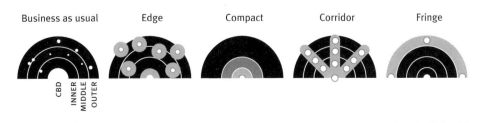

Source: *Reshaping Cities for a More Sustainable Future*, PW Newton (Ed), Australian Housing and Urban Research Institute, Melbourne, 1997.
www.ahori.edu.au

within a city, according to location and the weather at a particular time. For example, air quality predictions for the City of Melbourne, Australia, in 2011, when the population is expected to rise from 2.5 million to 3.0 million, show a dramatic impact on urban air quality in different parts of the city (see Figure 17.1). Worst-case scenarios relating to summer photochemical smog showed that by far the worst pollution would result if present urban development remained, i.e. business as usual (a 71 per cent increase in population exposed to levels of pollution above nationally accepted levels). The best performer under these conditions was the "corridor model" (55 per cent decrease). And worst-case scenarios relating to windy conditions with air particle build-up showed that the "compact model" fared worst (160 per cent increase), with the business as usual model second worst (61 per cent increase). (See also Chapter 14.)

Waste incineration is another significant source of air pollution. Most local authorities have now banned incineration near urban areas for this reason, and many have banned the construction of new incineration plant altogether. However, the next generation incinerators that burn rubbish to create useful heat for, say, community heating systems use much cleaner technology.

Indoor air quality

Common indoor air pollutants include carbon monoxide and nitrogen dioxide from faulty gas heaters and cookers, carbon monoxide and benzene from cigarette smoke, and VOCs from synthetic furnishings, vinyl flooring and paints. (All are discussed in more detail below.) In addition, there are biological pollutants such as dust mites and mould.

In developing countries, concerns over air quality differ significantly from those in the UK. For instance, indoor air pollution from the open fires used for cooking and heating is a serious problem. The World Health Organization[3] (WHO) estimates that about 2.5 million people in developing countries die annually because of exposure to high concentrations of suspended particulate matter in the indoor air environment of rural areas.

Air pollution and climate change

Air pollution is already a growing health problem in many cities, including London, and it will become worse in large urban areas under conditions of climate change. (See Chapter 10 for a more detailed discussion of climate change impacts.)

Predicted future increases in the number and intensity of hot anti-cyclonic weather in summer will favour the creation of more temperature inversions, which trap pollutants in the near-surface layer of the atmosphere. For example, it is estimated that a 1°C rise in summer air temperatures in London will result in a 14 per cent increase in surface ozone concentrations.[4] In cities, temperature increases will also be exacerbated by the "heat island effect" (see Chapter 10).

Thus it is important for architects to understand and therefore compensate for the effects of increasing levels of air pollution. For example, they should investigate any sources of airborne pollution adjacent to a site in order, where necessary, to inform the design of the ventilation systems and location of opening windows and ventilation intake ducts.

The pollutants

The WHO cites three types of air pollution:

- stationary sources, e.g. power stations and industrial plant
- mobile sources, e.g. road transport
- indoor sources, e.g. from paints and finishes.

Pollutants are also categorised as "primary" (released directly into the atmosphere) and "secondary" (formed in the air as a result of chemical reactions that occur between the products of other pollutants). Ozone, for example, is a secondary pollutant, as is acid rains which forms when the primary pollutants sulphur dioxide and nitrogen oxides are transformed into sulphuric and nitric acid.

The key ambient air pollutants covered by UK legislation are described below (in alphabetical order).[5] (Ammonia is also considered to be a serious pollutant but it is produced largely by the agricultural sector.)

Benzene

Benzene is a volatile organic compound (VOC) and is a member of the chemical compound family known as the "aromatics" (characterised by a "ring" of carbon atoms). It is a minor constituent of petrol (about 2 per cent) by volume. The main sources of benzene in the atmosphere in Europe are unburnt fuel via petrol vehicles exhausts (64 per cent) and industrial emissions (15 per cent). Benzene is also a product of the decomposition of other aromatic compounds. Benzene is a known human carcinogen, and because of its negative health effects EU legislation was passed to ensure that the amount of benzene in petrol was reduced from 5 per cent to 1 per cent by 2000.

1,3-Butadiene

1,3 Butadiene, like benzene, is a VOC emitted into the atmosphere principally from petrol and diesel vehicles. It is not a constituent of the fuel, but is produced as a result of the combustion of olefins. 1,3 Butadiene is also an important chemical in some industrial processes (e.g. the production of rubber). It is a known and potent human carcinogen.

Carbon monoxide

Carbon monoxide (CO) is a colourless, odourless, poisonous gas produced when fuels containing carbon are burned where there is too little oxygen. It also forms as a result of burning fuels at too high a temperature. CO burns in air or oxygen with a blue flame and is slightly lighter than air.

If there is an adequate supply of oxygen, most CO produced during combustion is immediately oxidised to carbon dioxide (CO_2). However, in many vehicles, especially under idling and deceleration conditions, there may not be enough oxygen available and carbon monoxide is formed instead. This is the cause of around 90 per cent of UK CO emissions, and hence the highest concentrations are generally close to busy roads and in enclosed spaces such as multi-storey car parks. Smaller contributions come from processes involving the combustion of organic matter, for example in power stations and waste incineration. However, one of the most dangerous sources of CO is from naked flames – on stoves, boilers or open fires. If there is insufficient ventilation to provide the necessary oxygen to form CO_2, CO builds up in the room. Carbon monoxide poisoning is an all-too-common cause of death in the UK, and often occurs in rented accommodation where heating appliances have not been regularly serviced. Inhaled CO combines with haemoglobin, the oxygen-carrying substance in red blood cells, and prevents the cells from taking up oxygen from the air. CO is also a constituent of tobacco smoke!

Dioxins and furans

Dioxins and furans are the terms generally used in referring to polychlorinated dibenzodioxins (PCDDs) and polychlorinated dibenzofurans (PCDFs) – classified chemically as halogenated aromatic hydrocarbons. The most widely studied compound of this family is 2,3,7,8-tetrachlorodibenzo-p-dioxin (TCDD), considered to be one of the most toxic substances known. Of the 75 known PCDDs only seven are thought to be toxic, and of the 135 compounds among the PCDFs, only 10 are toxic.

Dioxins and furans are members of a group of persistent organic pollutants (POPs) that can be found in the air, earth and soil, and build up in the fat cells of animals, particularly fish. Although POPs are not very soluble in water they can travel over long distances in the air, so they tend to migrate into regions where their effects on the environment and human health have an impact on populations, even though their uses, production, and marketing are prohibited or severely restricted. They have a serious effect on human health, with impacts such as birth defects, cancer, and dysfunctions of the immune and reproductive systems.

Dioxins and furans are not usually produced on purpose, but occur as a consequence of thermal processes, particularly combustion processes that involve chemical compounds containing chlorine. These sources include the incineration of household, hospital, and hazardous waste; metallurgical processes, such as steel production at high temperatures, foundry operations and metal recovery; and combustion of wood, coal, and petroleum derivatives. They can also be generated as by-products in the production of chlorine and its compounds, in for instance paper pulp bleaching factories. Some pesticides are contaminated with dioxins and furans as a consequence of the manufacturing process.

In the UK, road traffic, vandals burning cars and bonfires now produce more dioxins than incineration, but the largest single source of dioxins is the iron and steel industry, followed by the non-ferrous metal industry; both are now subject to stringent new emissions laws.

There is considerable debate as to the most effective way to dispose of these highly toxic compounds,[6] because they are difficult to destroy (the process requires high temperatures, typically 850–1000° C).

It is estimated that around one third of people in the UK are eating or breathing in more dioxins than the recommended maximum dose. Children and pregnant women are particularly vulnerable to the dangers of dioxins. In January 2003 strict measures were introduced by the government to cut the emissions of dioxins in 15 municipal and other incinerators by ten times. There are around 950 existing large and small incinerators in the UK. In addition, plans for many new incinerators have been abandoned because of the potential health risks of their emissions, and only six now await permission of the 100 or so originally planned. A preferred solution is to use rubbish digesters that produce gas to make electricity, with the residue then being composted; this avoids the risk of creating the dioxins in the first place.

Lead

Lead is the most widely used metal in the world, apart from iron. It is most commonly used in batteries (60–70 per cent) and also in paints, glazes, alloys, radiation shielding, tank lining, roofing and piping. As tetraethyl lead, it has been used for many years as an additive, in petrol and most airborne emissions in Europe do now originate from petrol. However, with the increasing use of unleaded petrol, air-borne emissions and concentrations have declined steadily in recent years. Lead is a fairly toxic poison to the system.

Oxides of nitrogen

Nitric oxide (NO) is an odourless, colourless gas that is produced during high temperature fuel combustion, and over 50 per cent of it in Europe comes from road traffic, as well as heaters and cookers. Once it is mixed with air NO quickly combines with oxygen, forming nitrogen dioxide (NO_2). NO and NO_2 are collectively known as NO_x. NO_2 is also present in tobacco smoke and is a reddish brown, non-flammable, gas with a detectable smell.

In significant concentrations NO_2 is highly toxic, causing serious lung damage with a delayed effect, exacerbating asthma and possibility leading to infections. Other health effects include shortness of breath and chest pains. This is especially important when designing buildings to be used by the vulnerable, the old and the young.

Nitrogen dioxide is a strong oxidising agent that reacts in the air to form corrosive nitric acid, as well as toxic organic nitrates. In the presence of sunlight, it combines with hydrocarbons to produce photochemical pollutants such as ozone or smog.

NO_x also has a lifetime of around one day, but once it is converted into nitric acid it can be deposited directly onto the ground, or be transferred in tiny droplets of water as acid rain.

Figure 17.2 Annual average background NO_2 (ppb) in the Thames Valley, indicating that concentrations are particularly high close to major roads

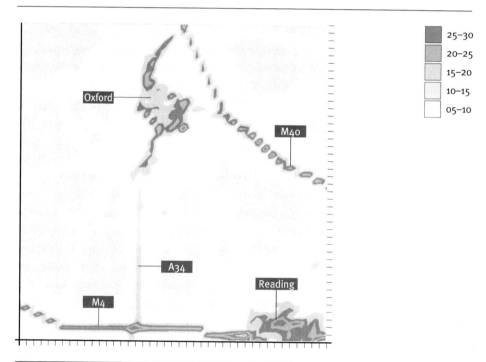

Source: *Stage 1 & 2 Air Quality Review and Assessment*, a report produced for Oxford City Council, AEA Technology plc, 1998

Nitrogen dioxide is largely a traffic-related pollutant, so emissions are generally highest in urban rather than rural areas (see Figure 17.2). Levels are also high around power stations, heating plants and industrial processes. The highest concentrations of the gas occur in stable weather conditions such as high pressure systems when there is insufficient air movement to disperse them. Annual mean concentrations of nitrogen dioxide in urban areas are generally in the range 10–45 parts per billion (ppb), and lower in rural areas. Levels vary significantly throughout the day, with peaks generally occurring twice daily as a consequence of rush hour traffic, when concentrations can be as high as 200 ppb.

Many town centre locations do now, and increasingly will, exceed the specified objectives by 2005, and local authorities are looking at ways in which NO_x pollution can be controlled, typically by reducing the number of vehicles on particular stretches of road and introducing traffic management strategies. Local authorities can supply measured or estimated data of NO_x levels to property developers.

Ozone

Ozone (O_3) is a toxic, bluish, unstable gas, with pungent odour, found naturally in the atmosphere, particularly in the stratosphere 19–30 km above the Earth's surface, where it forms the ozone layer (see Chapter 10). At these altitudes, ozone filters out the incoming ultraviolet (UV) radiation. Near ground level, however, it can impair lung function and cause irritation to the respiratory tract, so it is particularly harmful to asthmatics. Irreversible damage to the respiratory tract and lung tissue can occur if O_3 is present in sufficiently high quantities.

There are no direct man-made emissions of ozone to the atmosphere; only about 10–15 per cent of ground-level O_3 is transported from the stratosphere.

Most ground-level O_3 is formed indirectly by the action of sunlight on VOCs in the presence of nitrogen dioxide. As O_3 concentrations are particularly dependent on sunlight, episodes are always likely to develop following sustained periods of warmth and calm weather.

Particulate matter

Airborne particulates vary considerably in source, composition and size. PM10 particles (being less than 10 μm in size) are a major concern at the moment because they are so small they penetrate deep into the lungs, where they can pose a serious health risk. Some estimates have suggested that fine particles are responsible for up to 10,000 premature deaths in the UK each year. (Larger particles are not so readily inhaled and tend to settle either on the outside or are filtered out inside the body, while fine particulates travel right into the lung with the air.)

Particulate matter (PM) is categorised as:

- primary particulates, emitted directly to the atmosphere
- secondary particulates, formed by reactions involving other pollutants.

In the urban environment, most secondary particulate matter occurs as sulphates and nitrates formed in reactions involving sulphur dioxide (SO_2) and NO_x. The atmospheric lifetime of particulate matter is related to the particle size, but may be as long as 10 days for particles around 1 μm in diameter.

Particulate matter is emitted from a wide range of man-made sources, the most significant primary sources being road transport (25 per cent), non-combustion processes (24 per cent), industrial combustion plants and processes (17 per cent), commercial and residential combustion (16 per cent) and public power generation (15 per cent). Natural sources are less important; these include volcanoes and dust storms.

Fine particulates pose a significant health problem in many towns and cities. Anyone wanting to build in areas with high particulate levels should seek expert advice, and care should be taken to ensure that indoor air is sourced away from the highest particulate concentrations.

Sulphur dioxide

Sulphur dioxide (SO_2) is a colourless, non-flammable gas with a penetrating odour that irritates the eyes and air passages. It is a corrosive acid gas that combines with water vapour in the atmosphere to form acid rain, which has been shown to destroy vegetation, soils, building materials and watercourses. SO_2 in the ambient air is associated also with asthma and chronic bronchitis.

Sulphur dioxide pollution is considered more harmful when particulate and other pollution concentrations are high – the "cocktail effect". The health effects of sulphur dioxide pollution were exposed graphically during the "Great Smog" of London in 1952, which resulted in approximately 4,000 premature deaths.

High-level movement of acid rain has meant that emissions from UK sulphur coal burning plants have caused the decimation of forests in Norway and Sweden, but in the last 20 years emissions of SO_2 have been significantly reduced because fuel sources changed in the UK away from the most common sources of sulphur dioxide (coal-fired power stations). However, we should not underestimate the impact of emissions from power stations. In Oxford, for example, under adverse meteorological conditions, the emissions from the nearby Didcot power station may cause concentrations to rise above 100ppb in the city.

Coal burning is the single largest man-made source of sulphur dioxide, accounting for about 50 per cent of annual global emissions, with oil burning accounting for a further 25–30 per cent. Other sources include industrial plants dealing with smelting, manufacture of sulphuric acid, conversion of wood pulp to paper, incineration of refuse and production of elemental sulphur. The most common natural source of sulphur dioxide is volcanoes.

Tobacco smoke

Environmental tobacco smoke is made up of the smoke that comes from the burning end of a cigarette, pipe or cigar, and the smoke that is exhaled by the smoker. It contains tar droplets and various harmful chemicals including carbon monoxide (CO), nitric oxide (NO), ammonia, and hydrogen cyanide. Tobacco smoke also contains small amounts of some substances which have been shown to induce cancer in animals, including polycyclic aromatic hydrocarbons (PAHs) and benzene.

In 1998 the UK government published a White Paper, *Smoking Kills* and in July 1999 issued a policy document, *Saving Lives: Our Healthier Nation*. Tackling the effects of tobacco smoke, particularly "passive smoking", is an issue that all building designers should become acquainted with in these litigious times.[7]

Volatile organic compounds

Many VOCs are produced by the burning of coal, oil and petrol and as a by-product of the evaporation of petrol on service station floors. These and other sources, such as solvents, cleaners and paints, all contribute to the level of different VOCs found in outdoor air. Some VOCs are also released from tobacco smoke.

VOCs are of special concern because they react in sunlight to cause ozone or smog. VOC levels in urban areas like London or New York City fluctuate considerably at different times of day, peaking at rush hour. One of the most serious sources measured in the USA came from smoke plumes on building sites, where concentrations were up to 4,000 times higher than in the surrounding streets. Workers on these sites were provided with respirators and other protective gear.[8]

Controlling air quality

The WHO clearly defines the need for an effective process to enforce air quality standards by developing control actions on emission sources that will deliver compliance with the standards.[10] The instruments used to achieve this goal are the Clean Air Implementation Plans (CAIPs), and the WHO recommends that these plans should be defined in regulatory policies and strategies. CAIPs were introduced in several developed countries during the 1970s and 1980s.

As we have seen, air pollution comes from a very wide range of sources, so it is extremely difficult to assess the public health risks associated with a single source, or even a group of sources. As a consequence, on the basis of "the pol-

---

Radon

Radon is an invisible, odourless, tasteless radioactive gas that comes from the natural radioactive decay of uranium in soil, rock and water. Although not strictly a "pollutant" (because it is naturally occurring) radon should be taken into account during the early stages of a project, and particularly during the design phase. It can build up in the room air of buildings, and this makes it responsible for thousands of deaths every year around the world. In America it is the second highest cause of lung cancer deaths after smoking.

The main source of radon is the ground below a building, particularly granitic geology. Radon is present in all parts of the UK, but in the most populous areas the levels are typically quite low. The highest levels in the UK have been found in some homes on or near granite in southwest England. However, not all granites give high levels, and some other rocks, but not clays, also cause high radon levels.

Radon levels in homes vary during the day, from one day to the next, and from winter to summer, mainly because of temperature differences between indoors and outdoors. They are generally higher at night and during the winter. Although radon enters homes all the time, some is carried away by the natural ventilation. Even in a home with good draught-proofing and double-glazing, the air changes several times a day. Increasing the ventilation, especially on the ground floor will, in most cases, cause a moderate reduction in the radon level.[9]

---

luter pays" principle, researchers have developed sophisticated techniques to assess the sources, air pollutant concentrations, health and environmental effects and control measures, and make a causal link between emission, air pollution and the necessary control measures.

A typical CAIP includes:

- a description of the area
- an emissions inventory
- an air pollutant concentrations inventory – monitored and simulated
- a comparison with emissions and air quality standards or guidelines
- an inventory of the effects on public health and the environment
- a causal analysis of the effects and their attribution to individual sources
- control measures and their costs
- transportation and land-use planning

- enforcement procedures
- resource commitment
- projections for the future.

In May 2001 the European Commission formally adopted the Clean Air For Europe (CAFÉ) programme in a move that hopes to integrate air quality strategy for Europe, and to act as an umbrella under which the various strands of pollution legislation can be coordinated by 2005.[11]

Current legislation has three aims:

- to control climate change emissions (see Chapter 10) (to be covered by the EU greenhouse gas emissions trading scheme by 2005)[12]
- to control air quality standards (UK legislation on air quality is largely dominated by EU legislation based on the EU Directive on Ambient Air Quality Assessment and Management (96/62/EC) adopted in September 1996 and implemented by member states by May 1998)[13]
- to implement local air quality management objectives (LAQM).

Today, in England and Wales, the Environment Agency (EA) plays a major role by regulating the release of pollutants into the air from over 2000 of the larger or more complex industrial processes. Through its powers in pollution control, the EA works with local authorities, the Highways Agency and other organisations to deliver the government's Air Quality Strategy in England and Wales.[14]

Local authorities control air pollution from the 20,000 or so smaller industrial processes. Emissions from some other major sources of air pollution, such as transport, are controlled through a combination of measures at European, national and local level. In particular, Europe has very strict controls governing the production and transport of airborne pollution across national boundaries, with specific protocols for sulphur, oxides of nitrogen and VOCs.[15]

On 28 December 2002 Regulations were introduced in the UK to implement the European Waste Incineration Directive 2000/76/EC, which includes stringent operating conditions and sets minimum technical requirements for waste incineration and co-incineration. The main aim of the Directive is to prevent and limit negative environmental effects by emissions into air, soil, surface and groundwater, and the resulting risks to human health, from the incineration and co-incineration of waste.[16]

At ground level, there are stringent statutory urban air quality requirements that are monitored in many cities by local authorities under the National Air Quality Standards programme.[17]

When recommending or deliberating upon a proposed development, planners must take into account the levels of airborne pollution adjacent to a site.[18] Where high levels exist, recommendations for development should be tempered by an understanding of the health implications of those emissions in relation to the proposed function of the buildings. For example, very high levels of localised air borne pollution are a contra-indication for schools, residential homes or housing.

Global indicators

The World Health Organization's Air Quality Guidelines[19] set out the range of ambient concentrations and give guideline values that define a concentration of air pollutant below which no adverse effect to human health is expected (see Table 17.1). Guideline values for 38 non-carcinogenic compounds and some carcinogens are set in relation to different exposure times.

The WHO clearly states that the application of these Guidelines should help significantly reduce the number of people who die or are disabled from this highly preventable source of ill-health however, they are much lower than the UK standards (see below), and relate more to the less regulated countries. It should be remembered that many of these standards are for single pollutants in isolation, and their impacts can be exacerbated when in combined with other airpollutants and with, for instance, gas emissions from landfill sites.

Table 17.1 Some examples of the WHO guideline values for common gaseous pollutants

POLLUTANT	ANNUAL AMBIENT AIR CONCENTRATION (μG/M^3)	GUIDELINE VALUE (μG/M^3)	CONCENTRATION AT WHICH EFFECTS ON HEALTH START TO BE OBSERVED (μG/M^3)	EXPOSURE TIME
CO	500–7000	100 000	Not applicable	15 min
		60 000		30 min
		30 000		1 hour
		10 000		8 hours
Lead	0.01–2.0	0.5	Not applicable	1 year
NO$_2$	10–150	200	365-565	1 hour
		40		1 year
O$_3$	10–100	120	Not applicable	8 hour
SO$_2$	5–400	500	1,000	10 min
		125	250	24 hour
		50	100	1 year

Source: Air pollution Factsheet no 187, World Health Organisation, revised 2000, www.who.int

Table 17.2 EU target values for ozone

EU TARGET VALUES (2002/3/EC)	OZONE IN AMBIENT AIR	COMMENTS
For the protection of human health	120 μG/M³	Maximum daily 8 hour mean to be achieved by 2010, not to be exceeded on more than 25 days per calendar year averaged over 3 years Long-term objective of 120 μg/m³ (daily maximum for an 8 hour mean within a calendar year), to be met by 2020, "save where not achievable through proportionate measures"
For the protection of vegetation	18000 μG/M³.H	(AOT40, calculated from 1 h values from May-July), averaged over 5 years, "to be attained where possible" by 2010. Long-term objective of 6000 μg/m³.h (AOT40, calculated from 1 hour values from May-July), to be met by 2020, "save where not achievable through proportionate measures"

Source: *Pollution Handbook*, Loveday Murley, National Society for Clean Air and Environmental Protection, 2003

European indicators

The European Environment Agency (EEA) is responsible for setting the basic indicator standards within the European Union (see Tables 17.2 and 17.3). The EEA says that ozone in the troposphere (the lowest layer of the atmosphere) and particulate matter pose the greatest threat to human health, with acidification and ozone as the main threats to ecosystems. It also says that a small number of pollutants (SO_x, NO_x, NH_x, and VOCs) and fine particulates are the main causes of these problems.[20] This is now reflected in EU policy, which has shifted to a multi-pollutant, multi-effect air pollution abatement strategy, because reducing a group of pollutants can have a positive effect on various air pollution problems.

This approach has led to international legal instruments that impose nationally differentiated targets for emission reductions of four main pollutants. For instance, a substantial proportion of the emissions result from the burning of fossil fuels, so an effective measure is to reduce the use of fossil energy sources. In this way, the measures that will be required to reach the Kyoto Protocol targets for greenhouse gas emissions (see Chapter 10) will also result in reductions in air pollution – a neat example of the virtuous circle that underpins all truly "sustainable development".

The EU's indicator on quality of local ambient air is based on:

Table 17.3 Basic indicator standards for the EU

LIMIT VALUES FOR NAMED PARTICULATES	EXPOSURE OBJECTIVES
Sulphur dioxide* Limit values (to be met by 1.4.83): • 120 µg/m³ if smoke less than 40 µg/m³; 80 µg/m3 if smoke more than 40 µg/m3 – one year median daily values. • 180 µg/m³ if smoke less than 60 µg/m³; 130 µg/m3 if smoke more than 60 µg/m3 – winter (median of daily values). • 350 µg/m³ if smoke less than 150 µg/m³; 250 µg/m³ if smoke more than 150 µg/m³ – year, peak (98 percentile of daily values. Guide values: • 100-150 µg/m³ – 24-hour mean. • 40-60 µg/m³ – one year mean.	**Sulphur dioxide** • *Hourly limit value for the protection of human health:* 350 µg/m³, not to be exceeded more than 24 times per calendar year (pcy) target date: 1.1.05. • *Daily limit value for the protection of human health:* 125 µg/m³, not to be exceeded more than 3 times pcy; target date: 1.1.05. • *Alert threshold:* 500 µg/m³ measured over 3 hours. • *Annual limit value for the protection of ecosystems:* 20 µg/m³; target date: 2 years after Directive enters into force.
Smoke* • 80 µg/m³ – one year (median of daily values). • 130 µg/m³ – winter (median of daily values). 250 µg/m³ – year, peak (98 percentile of daily values).	**Particulate matter (PM$_{10}$)** Stage 1: • *Daily limit value for the protection of human health:* 50 µg/m³, not to be exceeded more than 35 times pcy; target date: 1.1.05; • *Annual limit value for the protection of human health:* 40 µg/m³; target date: 1.1.05. Stage 2: • *Indicative daily limit value for the protection of human health:* 50 µg/m³, not to be exceeded more than 7 times pcy; target date: 1.1.10. • *Indicative annual limit value for the protection of human health:* 20 µg/m³; target date: 1.1.10.
Nitrogen dioxide** *Limit value (to be met by 1.7.87)* • 200 µg/m³ – one year (98 percentile of 1-hour mean). *Guide values* • 50 µg/m³ – 1 year (50 percentile of 1-hour mean). • 135 µg/m³ – 1 year (98 percentile of 1-hour mean).	**Nitrogen dioxide** • *Hourly limit value for the protection of human health:* 200 µg/m³, not to be exceeded more than 18 times pcy; target date: 1.1.10. • *Annual limit value for the protection of human health:* 40 µg/m³; target date: 1.1.10. • *Alert threshold:* 400 µg/m³ measured over 3 hours. • *Annual limit value for the protection of vegetation:* 30 µg/m³; target date: 2 years after Directive enters into force.
Lead in the air*** *Limit value (to be met by 9.12.87)* 2 µg/m³ annual mean	**Lead** *Annual limit value for the protection of human health:* 0.5 µg/m³; target date: 1.1.05

Source: © European Communities, 1998-2003

* Sulphur Dioxide and Suspended Particulates: EU Directive 80/779/EEC ** EU Directive 85/203/EEC *** EU Directive 82/884/EEC

- the number of times that the limit values for selected air pollutants are exceeded
- the existence and level of implementation of an air quality management plan.

This indicator focuses on the main sources of air pollution in urban areas, mainly linked with combustion processes in mobility, heating systems and industries.

UK government indicators

In the UK responsibility for monitoring air pollution rests with the Environment Agency and the local authorities. The government publishes a list of standards on key pollutants. Table 17.4 presents a summary of these standards, with notes. Readers are strongly advised to view the full details on the Department for the Environment Food and Rural Affairs' website.[21] Individuals may also check the location of local sources of pollution on the Environment Agency's website.[22]

In July 2002 the new Road Traffic (Vehicle Emissions) (Fixed Penalty) (England) Regulations 2002 came into force, giving significant statutory powers to local authorities to enforce emissions standards on all vehicles and roads within their jurisdiction.

Local indicators

The objectives of the local air quality management (LAQM) policy are set nationally in England, Wales and Scotland to provide protection for human health against excessive local levels of air pollution. These objectives for each pollutant are currently given statutory force under the Air Quality (England) Regulations 2000 and

Figure 17.3 Days of air polution (UK) recorded between 1987 and 1997 in the UK (measured as average number of days per site where air polution was recorded as moderate or worse)

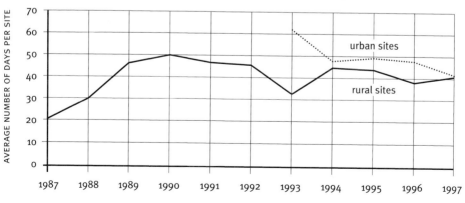

Source: DETR, 1998 © Crown Copyright

Table 17.4 UK standards for a range of pollutants

POLLUTANT	OBJECTIVE	MEASURED AS
Benzene		
All authorities	16.25 µg/m³	Running annual mean
Authorities in England and Wales only	5 µg/m³	Annual mean
Authorities in Scotland and Northern Ireland only	3.25 µg/m³	Running annual mean
1,3-Butadiene	2.25 µg/m³	Running annual mean
Carbon monoxide		
Authorities in England, Wales and Northern Ireland only	10.0 mg/m³	Maximum daily running 8-hour mean
Authorities in Scotland only	10.0 mg/m³	Running 8-hour mean
Dioxides and furans	12 picogrammes	The maximum permitted daily dose
Lead	0.5 µg/m³	Annual mean
	0.25 µg/m³	Annual mean
Nitrogen dioxide (provisional)	200 µg/m³	1-hour mean (not to be exceeded more than 18 times per year)
	40 µg/m³	Annual mean
Ozone	100 µg/m³	Running 8-hour mean (Daily maximum of running 8-hour mean not to be exceeded more than 10 times per year)
Particles (PM$_{10}$) (d)		
All authorities	50 µg/m³	24-hour mean (not to be exceeded more than 35 times per year)
	40 µg/m³	Annual mean
Authorities in Scotland only (as set out in the Air Quality (Scotland) Amendment Regulations 2002)	50 µg/m³	24-hour mean (not to be exceeded more than 7 times per year)
	18 µg/m³	Annual mean
Sulphur dioxide	266 µg/m³	15-minute mean (not to be exceeded more than 35 times per year)
	350 µg/m³	1-hour mean (not to be exceeded more than 24 times per year)
	125 µg/m³	24-hour mean (not to be exceeded more than 3 times per year)

TO BE ACHIEVED BY	COMMENTS
31/12/2003 31/12/2010 31/12/2010	If air-conditioning is to be used, ensure that the air intake vents are located so as to avoid exposure to high levels of car exhaust fumes.
31/12/2003	
31/12/2003 31/12/2003	Natural background levels of carbon monoxide fall in the range of 10-200 parts per billion (ppb). Levels in urban areas are highly variable, depending upon weather conditions and traffic density.
–	The average intake is 1.8 picogrammes.(a picogramme is a millionth of a millionth of a gram) Recent studies indicate that the highest intake is around 3.5 picogrammes.
31/12/2004 31/12/2008	Levels of air-borne lead pollution should be requested for any sites adjacent to industrial premises such as industrial lead smelters
31/12/2005 31/12/2005	These standards may be difficult to achieve by major roads or congested roads where levels of NO_x are actually rising due to the relentless increase of traffic on our roads ** Assuming NO_x is taken as NO_2
31/12/2005	NB: Ozone is not included in the Regulations
31/12/2004 31/12/2004 31/12/2010 31/12/2010	
31/12/2005 31/12/2004 31/12/2004	Hourly peak values can occasionally be as high as 750 ppb. Natural background levels are about 2 ppb.

its subsequent Amendments. Local Authorities must taken the objectives into account when reviewing local air quality and, where necessary, draw up an air quality management plan if standards are being breached, or at risk of being breached in the future. In February 2003 DEFRA and the National Assembly for Wales published revised policy guidance on the implementation of the LAQM policy.[23]

London, the seat of the evil miasmas that killed so many as late as the 1950s, has its own stringent legislation to control levels of air pollution within the capital enshrined in the Greater London Authority Act of 1999,[24] which includes the requirement to assess and manage, current, and future, air quality in the city. Road vehicles in London are the greatest source of pollution, and the current Mayor has instigated far-reaching strategies to reduce related pollution by trying to increase the use of public transport, introducing congestion charging and encouraging the use of cleaner vehicles in the city. He is also proposing to reduce emissions resulting from poor energy use in buildings, promoting improved fuel and energy efficiency.[25]

References

1   *www.nsca.org.uk*

2   See *www.doc.mmu.ac.uk/aric/eae/Air_Quality/Older/Great_London_Smog.shtml*

3   Bruce N, Perez-Padilla R and Albalak R (2002), *The Health Effects of Indoor Air Pollution Exposure in Developing Countries*, WHO, Geneva (view at *www.who.int/peh/air/Indoor*)

4   London Climate Change Partnership (2002), *London's Warming: The impacts of climate change on London*, Technical Report, Greater London Authority, London, p. 63 (view the full report at *www.ukcip.org.uk*)

5   The following descriptions are based on more detailed information available from *www.defra.gov.uk/environment/airquality/index.htm*

6   For more details on dioxins, visit *www.lancashire.gov.uk/environment/waste/condoc/technical/dioxine9.htm*

7   For a full list of EU and UK legislation and programmes related to smoking see *www.ash.org.uk*

8   See *www.epa.gov/wtc/voc*

9   BRE (1999), *Radon: Guidance on protective measures in new dwellings*, Building Research Establishment, Watford; see also *www.nrpb.org/understand/radon/radon.htm*

10 For details of WHO air quality policies, visit *www.who.int/peh/air/airindex.htm*

11 The CAFE umbrella covers everything from climate change emissions and waste incineration to the "Control of Auto Oil" programme. Details of the Clean

Air For Europe (CAFÉ) programme (COM(2001) 245) are at *http://europa. eu.int/comm/environment/air/cafe*. For a full description of the complex related legislation see Murley (2003)

12 See *http://europa.eu.int/comm/environment/docum/0087_en.htm*

13 The Directive and its Daughter Directive have been implemented in England through the Air Quality Limit Values Regulations 2001 with similar legislation in Scotland, Wales and Ireland

14 See *www.airquality.co.uk*

15 A full list of related EU legislation is at *http://europa.eu.int/comm/environ-ment/air/legis.htm*

16 See Waste Incineration Directive at *www.defra.gov.uk/environment*

17 DEFRA (2002), The Air Quality (England) (Amendment) Regulations 2002, The Stationery Office, Norwich

18 PPG23 *Planning and Pollution Control* is currently being revised to take account of the statutory regime introduced by the government in 2000. A new style Planning Policy Statement will be published at the end of 2003, accompanied by two annexes, one on pollution control, air and water quality and one on land affected by contamination.

19 WHO (1999), *Air Quality Guidelines*, World Health Organization, Geneva at *www.who.int/en*

20 Further details from *http://themes.eea.eu.int/Environmental_issues/air_quality /indicators*

21 See 5

22 The Environment Agency website at *www.environment-agency.gov.uk* includes a postcode-based pollution information system

23 See *www.defra.gov.uk/environment/airquality/laqm/guidance*, and for a review of the related legislation see Murley (2003).

24 *www.hmso.gov.uk/acts/acts1999*

25 *www.london.gov.uk/mayor/strategies/air_quality*

Further information

The UK Air Quality information service was established to advise the public on air quality, and not only is there extensive information available on *www.airquality .co.uk* but for anyone who is concerned about local levels of pollution there is also an information hotline available on freephone 0800 556677.

Further reading

AEA Technology PLC (1998), *Stage 1&2 Air Quality Review and Assessment*, a report produced for Oxford City Council, *www.aeat.com*

Curwell S, Marsh C and Venables R (1990), *Buildings and Health*, RIBA Enterprises, London

Murley L (2003), *Pollution Handbook,* National Society for Clean Air and Environmental Protection, Brighton

Planning policy guidance – related documents (see Appendix 1 for details)

1	2	3	4	5	6	7	8	9	10	11	12	13
	x	x	x	x	x	x			x	x	x	x

14	15	16	17	18	19	20	21	22	23	24	25
x	x			x			x	x	x		

Building Regulations – related Approved Documents (see Appendix 2 for details)

A	B	C	D	E	F	G	H	J	K	L1	L2	M	N
			x		x		x	x					

Contaminated land

Definition

The European Environmental Agency defines contaminated land as:

"A location where as a result of human activity an unacceptable hazard to human health and ecosystems exists. Local contamination (contaminated sites) is a problem in restricted areas (or sites) around the source, where there is a direct link to the source of contamination." [1]

This definition is sufficient for the purposes of this chapter, but it should be noted that a more detailed statutory definition exists.[2] This links the contamination with the degree to which it is likely to cause a problem to humans, ecosystems and property.

Related indicators

Quality of life; Health; Biodiversity; Air pollution; Water pollution; Waste.

Related tools

Environmental impact assessment; Regeneration-based checklist.

Background

People have always polluted land. The toxic spoil heaps from Roman lead and silver mines, for instance, are still visible in parts of North Wales.

The effects of pollution on soil should not be under-estimated. Soil contaminated by toxic chemicals may have a direct effect on human health if homes and gardens are built on the land in question, even many years after the contamination occurred. Particles of soil handled or ingested by adults or children may carry irritants or poisons, and inhaling particles or vapours from the pollutants is another route for absorption. For example, vegetable gardens sited on polluted land may produce crops contaminated by the direct uptake of toxins, as was seen recently, where zinc extraction in Shipham, Somerset, resulted in high levels of cadmium in soil which, in turn, produced a very particular cadmium-resistant range of home-grown vegetables.[3]

Once a pollutant reaches the soil a number of things may happen to it:

- It may break down or be neutralised.
- It may be washed out by rain or, if volatile, evaporate.
- It may remain in the soil, building up to high concentrations with successive additions.

An additional problem of contaminated land is that pollutants tend to move from the place where they were first deposited by a process known as "leaching". Leaching will occur if the pollutants are soluble in water at the prevailing pH. The various substances react together to form "leachate", a noxious liquid that can spread into surrounding soils. The type of soil and its permeability affect the rate of leaching. For example, sandy soils that are low in organic content tend to give a higher leaching rate, while leaching through clay soils, and those with large amounts of humus, is much slower because contaminants tend to be more tightly bound to soil particles.

Leaching is already a complicating factor in tackling contaminated land, but this is likely to become more significant under the wetter and stormier weather conditions predicted by climate change models (see Chapter 10). The worst conditions will be provided by a combination of contaminated land and regularly inundated sites. For example, any sites on flood plains that have a history of toxic substances being dumped on them may become more toxic if the soil is flooded. If flooding is a regular event, pollutants may leach through the new top soil towards the surface, even if a portion of the top soil has been removed and replaced.

The UK government has recently set a target that 60 per cent of all new houses should be built on "brownfield" sites to relieve the pressure on greenfield sites and preserve the countryside. Most of these sites will be "contaminated", but it is not clear just how contaminated they are.

Remediation

The fate of a pollutant and its concentration in the soil depend on the balance between the rate of input and the rate of removal. Removal mechanisms are, in turn, determined by the chemical, physical and biological properties of the contaminant and of the soil medium, together with the presence and the nature of any other materials subsequently deposited.

Pollutant breakdown, by various chemical and microbiological processes, can be an important removal mechanism. Phenols, for instance, can be destroyed by micro-organisms provided that the concentration is not too high. Certain herbicides can also be decomposed microbiologically, and their frequent use leads to the establishment of populations of soil flora particularly adept at breaking them down. Materials that are not broken down by micro-organisms, and the products of those that are, may leach out.

Contamination from industrial processes can be treated in a number of ways:

"Solidification, where a binder (e.g. cement) is used to enclose the contaminated soil in a solid form reducing its solubility, mobility and toxicity (suitable for dealing with heavy metals but not mercury or organic compounds).

Physical, where contaminants are isolated or concentrated, but not destroyed, e.g. by vapour extraction or soil washing.

Chemical, where reactants are used to destroy, immobilise, extract or neutralise contaminants.

Thermal treatment at 800–2,500°C.

Biological methods to produce degradation of organic contaminants; to transform to less harmful or mobile forms; or convert to more mobile forms to allow separation." [4]

Along with the growing requirement for reclamation and redevelopment of brown field sites comes the need to understand what are acceptable levels of contamination for different uses. The total restoration of contaminated land to an unpolluted state is rarely achievable and, in many cases, unnecessary. Instead, a remedial approach tailored to the intensity and extent of the contamination found and the intended end-use of the site is adopted. In some cases it may be necessary to "zone" the land for specified non-residential purposes, endorsing the title deeds to that effect. For example, it may be possible to use lightly contaminated land for amenity purposes if the materials present are largely inorganic and a sealing sward of tolerant grasses can be planted to prevent both human contact with the soil and the windborne transport of polluted dust.

More heavily contaminated sites may only be usable for purposes such as car parks, warehouses and other industrial developments where a layer of tarmac or concrete could be laid on the surface, thereby sealing off the pollution. In certain instances, such as the occurrence of highly contaminated pockets in otherwise fairly clean sites, or small sites badly contaminated throughout, the polluted soil may be removed in its entirety to a licensed waste disposal site and replaced with cleaner material.

The UK government's Interdepartmental Committee on the Redevelopment of

---

Landfill

Depositing both industrial and domestic wastes into landfill sites can, in some instances, result in contamination of ground or surface waters because of leaching. However, leaching can be prevented by properly lining landfill sites and covering them to prevent rainwater penetration.

If, on the other hand, the contaminants are not broken down, or leaching does not occur to any great extent, or if material is added frequently, contaminants can accumulate in the upper layers of the soil. This build-up may not be permanent because subsequent changes in conditions may cause the remobilisation of some materials bound to soil particles, but in most instances soil contaminated with persistent materials remains damaged indefinitely.

A more serious problem with landfill sites is the build-up of methane gas to potentially explosive levels, posing a danger to nearby housing. Large quantities of methane and carbon dioxide are produced if biodegradable material is buried, because it will decomposes anaerobically (i.e. without the presence of oxygen). Depending on the geology of the area, these gases can seep underground or rise to the surface. Methane from landfill sites can be either vented off to the atmosphere, collected and used as a fuel supply, or simply burned off.

Contaminated Land publishes guidance on the redevelopment and after-use of contaminated land, based on the "suitable for use" principle.[5]

Legislation

Historically, the problems of contaminated land were dealt with almost exclusively in the context of redevelopment, where there was the objective of economic benefit linked to environmental enhancement. Today, priorities are changing, as the government grapples with the issue of sustainable land use (see Chapter 14).

The main difficulty now is knowing where contamination has occurred. Some sites will have title deeds that go back to the Domesday Book with a complete record of the use of its land over centuries, but for others records may be patchy or even non-existent. Even if records do exist, the land may have been used for illegal dumping.

The Environment Agency estimates that there could be between 5,000 and 20,000 contaminated sites in England and Wales that may have an impact on human health or the wider environment. Recent legislation[6] has introduced a requirement for local authorities to proactively inspect their areas and ensure the remediation of any contaminated land.[7] This includes keeping registers to record land that is classed as contaminated using the statutory definitions. So far only 33 sites had been determined in England by March 2002, but the first round of inspections are not expected to finish until about 2006 in some local authority areas.[8]

Under the legislation, only land that is assessed as likely to cause "significant harm" (and therefore in need of remedial action) will be noted in the register. This means that a key activity is assessing the level of risk related to the contaminated land.

Many factors will influence risk of contamination spreading, including:

- soil texture, where runoff may cause a risk to ponds, wetlands or coastal waters, or where infiltration may present a risk to groundwater
- soil depth
- bedrock height
- depth to water table
- proximity to surface water
- gradient.

Many sites may have some degree of contamination but fall outside the statutory definition – i.e. there may not be a risk of "significant harm" – and these sites could need action if or when the land is put to a new use. These sites will continue to be dealt with within the planning regime at the point the land is redeveloped, which is not always satisfactory.

Having registered any contaminated land, the local authority also has a statutory responsibility to decide:

- who is responsible for the remediation of that land
- what remediation is required on that land, and ensure it is carried out with voluntarily or by enforcement
- who should pay towards the cost of that remediation, and how much.

Once an area of land has been designated as contaminated, the enforcing authority (the local authority or the Environment Agency) will serve a Remediation Notice on the owners of the site to enforce them to clean it up.

However, landfill sites have been singled out within the planning legislation for specific attention. Since 1988 waste disposal authorities (WDAs) have to inform local planning authorities of all sites used for the deposit of refuse or wastes during the past 30 years, i.e. they have registers of such sites. Moreover, local planning authorities are now required to consult the WDAs on any applications for development within 250 m of a landfill site.

Planning Policy Guidance 23: *Planning and Pollution Control* (June 1994)[9] high-

---

Radioactive waste

Radioactive materials are used in the generation of electricity, for military purposes, in industry, including the food processing industry, medicine, and in research. Their use results in gaseous, liquid and solid radioactive wastes that can be divided into three categories:[11]

- high-level (or heat-generating) waste, which results from reprocessing of spent nuclear fuels; about 97 per cent is recycled
- intermediate-level waste, which includes scrap metal, sludge and residues from fuel storage ponds, plutonium-contaminated materials and fuel cladding
- low-level waste, which includes paper towels, protective clothing, laboratory equipment and soil that has come into contact with radioactive waste

Disposal of radioactive waste must comply with strict safety standards. The National Radiological Protection Board (NRPB)[12] advises the government on radiological protection criteria to be applied to the disposal of all types of solid radioactive waste.

---

lights the need to be aware of the previous use of land in considering development plans. Where contamination is suspected, developers should investigate the land to determine what remedial measures are necessary to ensure its safety and suitability for the purpose proposed.[10]

European indicators

The cleaning-up of land has become a key issue in Europe. Sustainable development, restoration and protection of land and sites, and the need for brownfield development are powerful drivers for new approaches to sustainable city planning. In EU guidance, "restoration" refers to the regeneration of disused, derelict or contaminated land; and "protection" addresses protection of sensitive ecological sites. Indicator 9 of the Common European Indicator Set[13] covers land use:

" *a) urbanised or artificially modelled land: the size of the artificially modelled area as a percentage of the total municipal area;*
b) derelict or contaminated land: the size of the derelict or contaminated area (m^2);
c) intensity of use: number of inhabitants per km^2 of the area classified as

"urbanised land";

d) *new development: new building on virgin area (greenfield sites) and new
building on contaminated or derelict area (brownfield sites) compared to
the total area (%);*

e) *restoration of urban areas:*

1. *renovation and conversion of derelict buildings (total number);*

2. *renovation and conversion of derelict buildings (total of m² of each floor);*

3. *redevelopment of derelict areas for new uses, including public open
spaces (area in m²);*

4. *cleansing of contaminated land (area in m²).*

f) *protected areas: size of the protected area as a percentage of the total
municipal area."*

National indicators

Every country has a different approach to the problems of the resulting con-
taminated land. It is fitting that the greatest consumerist society in history, the
United States of America, should be home to some of the most contaminated land
in the world! The most toxic abandoned waste sites in the US are listed on the
Superfund National Priorities List (NPL),[14] which provides an indication of the
extent of the most significantly contaminated sites (see Table 18.1). The
"Superfund" is a program that operates under the legislative authority of the
Comprehensive Environmental Response, Compensation, and Liability Act
(CERCLA). It funds and carries out the US Environmental Protection Agency's solid
waste emergency and long-term removal and remedial activities. Some Americans
consider that this system causes a "contaminated land blight" – the result of a
legal system that encourages hitting the deepest pocket in order to pay for clean-
up, so large corporations are required to pay for the land pollution they are

Table 18.1 Numbers of the most toxic abandoned waste sites in the United States from the Superfund
National Priorities List (2003 data)

STATUS	NON-FEDERAL (GENERAL)	FEDERAL	TOTAL
Proposed sites (i.e. untreated)	60	6	66
Final sites (those that meet the qualifications to be cleaned up under the Superfund Program)	1,075	158	1,233
Deleted sites (i.e. cleanup is complete)	260	13	273

Source: EPA's Superfund NPL Assessment Program (SNAP), US Environment Protection Agency, *www.epa.gov*

responsible for. The average NPL site in the USA costs around $40 million to clean up, giving an idea of the scale of the problem and the pollution that has been perpetrated. (In the UK the "polluter pays" principal dominates.)

Netherlands

In Britain the underlying philosophy is "fitness for use", i.e. contaminated land should be restored according to the planned usage. In the Netherlands, the "New" Dutch List, which grades contaminated sites, is based on the need for land to be multi-functional after cleaning.[15] (Under the UK system, a site that will become a light industrial redevelopment will have a different burden of cost than a site that is to be used for agricultural purposes.) Both the Dutch and the Americans adopt the approach of multi-functionality, leaving a site of a standard suitable for any possible use.

In part the Dutch approach is a function of the geology of the Netherlands, which has granular sands and soils with a high water-table, permitting easy groundwater movement. The geology of the UK permits a more pragmatic approach, because glacial clay capping tends to lock the potential pollutants in place.

UK

The government publishes a list of acceptable levels of common contaminants and "trigger levels" which, if observed, will require that the land be considered as contaminated (see Table 18.2).

References

1 From: *http://glossary.eea.eu.int/EEAGlossary/C/contaminated_site*

2 See Contaminated Land (England) Regulations 2000 (Statutory Instrument 2000 No. 227), at: *www.hmso.gov.uk/si/si2000/20000227.htm*

3 See MOD (2001) *Report by the Academy of Medical Sciences to the Chief Scientific Adviser, Ministry of Defence on the Zinc Cadmium Sulphide dispersion trials undertaken in the United Kingdom between 1953 and 1964* on the Ministry of Defence website at *www.mod.uk/publications*

4 RCEP (1996), *19th Report: Sustainable Use of Soil, Royal Commission on Environmental Pollution*, The Stationery Office, Norwich, Chapter 8

5 See *www.contaminatedland.co.uk*. See also Construction Industry Council (2003), *Brownfields: Building on previously developed land*, *www.cic.org.uk* This guide will help companies to develop a strategy, and offers advice on grants, tax allowances and planning as well as how to tackle contaminated land.

6 See 2 and The Contaminated Land (England) (Amendment) Regulations 2001,

Table 18.2 Trigger concentrations for UK soil contamination

CONTAMINANT	PLANNED USE	TRIGGER VALUES (MG/KG AIR-DRIED SOIL)	
GROUP A (MAY POSE HAZARDS TO HEALTH)		THRESHOLD	ACTION
Arsenic	Domestic gardens, allotments	10	–
	Parks, playing fields, open space	40	–
Cadmium	Domestic gardens, allotments	3	–
	Parks, playing fields, open space	15	–
Chromium (hexavalent)	Domestic gardens, allotments	25	–
	Parks, playing fields, open space	No limit	No limit
Chromium (total)	Domestic gardens, allotments	600	–
	Parks, playing fields, open space	1,000	–
Lead	Domestic gardens, allotments	500	–
	Parks, playing fields, open space	2,000	–
Mercury	Domestic gardens, allotments	1	–
	Parks, playing fields, open space	20	–
Selenium	Domestic gardens, allotments	3	–
	Parks, playing fields, open space	6	–
GROUP B (PHYTOTOXIC* – BUT NOT NORMALLY HAZARDOUS TO HEALTH)		THRESHOLD	ACTION
Boron (water-soluble)	Any uses where plants are grown	3	–
Copper	Any uses where plants are grown	130	–
Nickel	Any uses where plants are grown	70	–
Zinc	Any uses where plants are grown	300	–
GROUP C - (ORGANIC CONTAMINANTS)		THRESHOLD	ACTION
Polyaromatic hydrocarbons	Domestic gardens, allotments, play areas	50	500
	Landscaped areas, buildings, hard cover	1,000	10,000
Phenols	Domestic gardens, allotments,	5	200
	Landscaped areas, buildings, hard cover	5	1,000
Cyanide (free)	Domestic gardens, allotments, landscaped areas	25	500
	Buildings, hard cover	100	500
Cyanide (complex)	Domestic gardens, allotments	250	1,000
	Landscaped areas	250	5,000
	Buildings, hard cover	250	No limit
Thiocyanate	All proposed uses	50	No limit
Sulphate	Domestic gardens, allotments, landscaped areas	2,000	10,000
	Buildings	2,000	50,000

Table 18.2 (continued)

CONTAMINANT	PLANNED USE	TRIGGER VALUES (MG/KG AIR-DRIED SOIL)	
GROUP C - (ORGANIC CONTAMINANTS) *CONTINUED*		THRESHOLD	ACTION
Sulphate *continued*	Hard cover	2,000	No limit
Sulphide	All proposed uses	250	1,000
Sulphur	All proposed uses	5,000	20,000
Acidity	Domestic gardens, allotments, landscaped areas	pH<5	pH<3
	Buildings, hard cover	No limit	No limit

No limit: the contaminant does not present a particular hazard for this use. (For details of sampling method, please refer to the source document: ICRCL 59/83, available from *www.contaminatedland.co.uk*)

* Pure rainwater is slightly acidic, with a pH of about 6.5 (due to dissolved carbon dioxide). If the pH falls, the toxic effects of uptake of these elements will increase. Grass is more resistant than most other plants to phytotoxic effects, hence its growth may not be adversely affected at these conditions. Note also that the phytotoxic effects of copper, nickel and zinc may be additive. The trigger values for these elements are those applicable to the "worst-case'" phytotoxic effects, which may occur at these concentrations in acid sandy soils, but are not likely in neutral (pH=7) or alkaline soils at these concentrations.

Source: *ICRCL 59/83 Trigger Concentrations,* www.contaninatedland.co.uk

    SI 663 (View on-line at *www.environment-agency.gov.uk*)

7 The New Forest District Council, for example, has produced a good plan of action. See *www.nfdc.gov.uk/media/adobe/contam_draft_ind.pdf*

8 Of the 33 sites, 11 were designated as "special" sites, which require special attention and are under the direct regulation of the Environment Agency, and for 7 of these remediation statements or plans have been agreed. The number of registered "contaminated" and "special" sites is expected to increase as the inspection of whole areas is completed.

9 PPG 23 is currently being revised to take account of the statutory regime introduced by the government in 2000. The consultation document was issued in June 2002 and is at *www.planning.odpm.gov.uk/consult/contamin/01.htm*

10 The Environmental Protection Act 1990 Part II Section 34 (effective 1 April 1992) places a "duty of care" on all those involved in dealing with waste from its generation to its disposal, under the "polluter pays" principle. (The duty of care extends to closed landfill sites where the site operator remains responsible for the site until it has been declared safe and a "certificate of completion" issued.)

11 Murley L (2003), *Pollution Handbook*, National Society for Clean Air and Environmental Protection

12 See *www.nrpb.org*

13 See *Towards a Local Sustainability Profile – European Common Indicators*, Indicator 9. Download the full document from *www.sustainable-cities.org* (go to "outputs").

14 See *www.epa.gov/superfund,* where you can also view the document *Better Protected Land*, in the Draft Report on the Environment

15 *Intervention Values and Target Values: Soil quality standards*, published by Ministry of Housing, Spatial Planning and Environment, Directorate-General for Environmental Protection, Department of Soil Protection, The Hague, The Netherlands

On-line resources

www.nsca.org.uk

www.environment-agency.gov.uk/subjects/landquality

A good bibliography on reclaimed land can be found at *www.nottingham.ac.uk /sbe/planbiblios/bibs/vacant/03.html*

Further reading

Thanks to Dr. Carol Dair of Oxford Brookes University for help with assembling this list.

Adams D and Watkins C (2002), *Greenfields, Brownfields and Housing Development*, Blackwell Scientific Publishers, Oxford

Cairney T and Hobson DM (eds) (1998), *Contaminated Land: Problems and solutions,* 2nd edn, E & FN Spon, London

HBF (1998), *Urban Life: Breaking down the barriers to brownfield development*, House Builders Federation, London

Hester T and Harrison RM (eds) (1997), *Contaminated Land and Its Reclamation*, Royal Society of Chemistry, Cambridge

Laidler D, Bryce A and Wilburn Associates (2003), *Brownfields: Building on previously developed land*, Construction Industry Council, London

Petts J, Cairney T et al (1997), *Risk-based Contaminated Land Investigation and Assessment*, John Wiley & Sons, Chichester

POST (1998), *A Brown and Pleasant Land: Household growth and brownfield site*, Parliamentary Office of Science and Technology, London

Taylor AG, Gordon JE and Usher MB (eds) (1996), *Soils, Sustainability and the Natural Heritage*, The Stationery Office, Norwich, ISBN 0 11 495270 1

And a range of publications by the Construction Industry Research and Information Association (CIRIA), including:

Remedial Treatment for Contaminated land Volume III: Site Investigation and Assessment

Remedial Treatment for Contaminated land Volume IV: Classification and Selection of Remedial Methods

Remedial Treatment for Contaminated Land Volume XI: Planning and Management

Remedial Treatment for Contaminated Land Volume XII: Policy and legislation

Planning policy guidance – related documents (see Appendix 1 for details)

1	2	3	4	5	6	7	8	9	10	11	12	13
x			x	x		x			x	x	x	

14	15	16	17	18	19	20	21	22	23	24	25
x				x					x	x	x

Building Regulations – related Approved Documents (see Appendix 2 for details)

A	B	C	D	E	F	G	H	I	J	K	L1	L2	M	N
		x	x				x							

Water quality

Definition
   In this chapter, "water" relates to drinking water, river water and bathing water and the re-use of water in grey water systems, while "quality" is concerned with human consumption. However, there are two other factors that relate to quality: one is the availability of decent water; the other is how the manipulation and pollution of water supplies can impact on ecosystems (see related indicators, below).

Related indicators
   Climate change; Biodiversity; Land use; Flooding; Contaminated land.

Related tools
   Environmental impact assessment; Regeneration-based checklist.

Background

The access to clean drinking water is one of the fundamental necessities of life. Globally, around 1.1 billion people do not have access to water supplies that have been treated to an acceptable standard, and 2.4 billion people do not have access to any type of acceptable sanitation facility. About 2 million people die every year due to diseases linked to poor water quality and inadequate sanitation most of them are children under five years of age.[1]

After air, water is the easiest substance to pollute. Add a drop of colour to a swirling bowl of water and the colour quickly taints the clear liquid; so it is with the common pollutants that foul the water we drink and bath in. The less water there is, the more concentrated the pollutants become. We constantly tip poisons into water supplies, confident that because there is so much water out there this little drop of pollutant will be diluted and will not threaten the quality of the water on which we ourselves depend.

Sewage, shampoo, fertilisers, paints, chlorine from the domestic cleaners and left-over medicines – all go down the drains and escape into rivers and eventually the sea. But there comes a point where water systems can no longer support this level of abuse, especially during dry summers when there is simply less water in the system.

Climate change could have a dramatic effect on water quality:

- Decreases in summer rainfall will affect water availability and quality, increasing also the concentrations of carbon dioxide and pollutants in river, dams and lakes.
- Higher sea levels will interfere with natural drainage patterns, coast lines and water and sewage supply networks.
- More intense and frequent winter storms may pollute water supplies.
- Changing ground water levels will affect the water supply.
- Increased water temperatures will accelerate the growth of water-borne bacteria, plants and fungi, while decreasing oxygen levels in water with higher temperatures combined with less water in rivers may kill river species including fish, which are also particularly sensitive to the temperature of their habitats.
- High levels of rain water run-off from increased levels of rain fall and storm incidence will exacerbate pollution incidences in built-up areas.

Controlling water quality

There are three separate, but related, issues to be addressed:

- drinking water
- river water
- bathing water.

The provision of drinking water of an adequate quality is one of the most important statutory obligations that a government has. Failure to provide effective treatment of water sources and safe distribution of treated drinking water can expose the community to the risk of outbreaks of diseases and other adverse health effects. The quality of drinking water has to be controlled through a combination of protection of water sources, control of treatment processes, and management of the distribution and handling of water.

However, it is actually the quality of river water that makes it into the UK government's list of top 15 indicators for "quality of life".[2] Over the last two decades, stricter regulations have resulted in much greater control of what is dumped into rivers, and gradually stretches of our rivers are repopulating with species that had previously abandoned whole reaches of the water ways – otters, fish, birds and water voles. Though enormous progress has been made, the quantity of water we

Figure 19.1 A provocative campaign image from the home page of the Surfers Against Sewage website

Source: www.sas.org.uk

each use is rising rapidly, and the amount of chemicals, and their complexity and toxicity (particularly in beauty and cleaning products), is also on the rise.

While the preservation of drinking water standards remains a primary function of government, in the UK the bathing water standards have been the focus of much attention, primarily due to the tireless efforts of pressure groups such as "Surfers Against Sewage"[3] (see Figure 19.1) This group campaigns for clean, safe recreational waters, free from sewage effluents, toxic chemicals and nuclear waste, and uses solution-based arguments – using viable and sustainable alternatives to highlight the inherent flaws in current practices, attitudes and legislation, and to challenge industry, legislators and politicians to end their "pump and dump" policies.

In the UK, the Environment Agency (EA) is responsible for maintenance of water quality standards, under the auspices of the Department for the Environment, Food and Rural Affairs (DEFRA). The EA is responsible for local control and maintenance of water quality, water resources and flood defence in England and Wales, whereas DEFRA oversees water policy and sets the framework within which the EA operates.[4]

The Drinking Water Inspectorate (DWI)[5] regulates public water supplies in England and Wales, and takes enforcement action if standards are not being met. The legal standards are laid out in the Water Quality Regulations.[6] Most of these standards come directly from a European law and are based on World Health Organization guidelines, but there are additional standards over and above the general standards to safeguard the already high quality of water in England and Wales. These standards are strict and generally include wide safety margins, covering:

- bacteria
- chemicals such as nitrates and pesticides
- metals such as lead
- the way water looks and how it tastes.

OFWAT is the economic regulator for the water and sewerage industry in England and Wales, while Water Voice represents water customers in England and Wales.[7]

Quantity is also an issue

In his excellent paper for the World Health Organization,[8] Guy Howard, Programme Manager at the Water Engineering and Development Centre at Loughborough University, UK, lists what we expect from our water supplies and how standards ensure that as many people as possible have enough water of a decent quality as possible. He quotes studies that show that 7.5 litres a day of water is sufficient to meets the basic needs of most people under most conditions in the world today – for drinking, cooking and personal hygiene – and yet in the UK water consumption averages around 160 litres a day per person. Indeed, in the US state of Florida, they believe they have a cause for celebration because, over the past 16 years, per capita water consumption has declined by 7 per cent from 685.2 l per resident per day in 1980 to a mere 639.7 l per resident per day in 1995![9]

Unfortunately, the once swampy Florida County is in the hands of government officials who have developed the local "comprehensive plans", designed using "effective growth-management tools" that predict nearly 90 million residents for the State where roads, schools and water supplies are already straining to deal with 16 million people. The population of the state in 1950 was just 2.8 million people and by 2020 it is expected to rise to 21 million, a 30 per cent increase on today. The water wars are already starting in town near you, or at least in Florida. Commenting on the policies, Eric Draper, policy director for Audubon of Florida, said:

"There's almost a cruel joke being played on the people in Florida. They'll be asked to take shorter showers and water less, so the water-management district can give water to the next developer that shows up."[10]

Grey water systems

There is concern about the high per capita water consumption in developed countries. Water metering, which would have an impact on consumption, is a contentious issue in the UK because there are public health issues similar to those of fuel poverty (see Chapters 8 and 9): i.e. it is perceived that those least able to pay would suffer the most from an inadequate supply.

There are two main issues relating to "domestic" water use – toilet flushing and "external uses" such as car washing and watering gardens. (Domestic in this context refers not just to water used in dwellings, but the water we use in all buildings for things like flushing toilets, washing hands and dishes, and preparing food.)

Even though people are supposed to have a special licence to run a garden hose in the UK (i.e. they pay an additional fee for this extra use of water) this remains an extremely wasteful use of high-quality (drinking) water. Many local authorities now run campaigns to encourage people to collect rainwater for use on the garden. Rainwater collection has also been introduced for this purpose, and for toilet flushing, in some public buildings (e.g. the award-winning BedZed settlement in South West London).

Although capturing rainwater for gardens is to be encouraged, there are implication for sewerage systems, and in any case it is always preferable to minimise use or maximise the value of existing usage. That is why there is a growing interest in the use of "grey water". Around one third of the domestic water that is thrown down the drains – from baths and showers and sinks – could be recycled for the garden or for flushing toilets. (Waste water from kitchen sinks, dishwashers and washing machines is often much dirtier. It can contain emulsified fats and many chemicals, and is still considered by some to be "black water", and much more difficult to recycle.)

A third of the water used in homes is for toilet flushing. At present, this high-grade water is supplied from the mains – it's good enough to drink! There is no reason why grey water could not be used for this purpose. However, currently there are no standards. Attempts to write workable standards in the mid-1990s set unrealistically high benchmarks because the debate was influenced by the idea that children or dogs might drink water from the WC bowl! It seems reasonable to apply the bathing water standards to grey water systems on the assumption that one would never ordinarily drink from the bowl but a child may accidentally swallow some, as it might also swallow sea-water or river-water.

The truth of the matter is that the State of Florida does not have enough water to supply its own population today, and with the added wild card of climate change I think the lawns will definitely be suffering sooner rather than later!

Florida will have to learn from other US states, where water companies have, under law, a duty to reduce per capita consumption. For example, in Arizona, the State water utility (Tucson Water) is now required by law to reduce per capita consumption, although how the company achieves this is not specified. Failure to reach specified targets results in fines of up to $10,000 per day.[11]

While there is some comfort in the fact that it is only the residents of Florida who will eventually suffer from over-exploitation of the water resource in their own region, it is a fact that, as with energy consumption, the impacts of such excessive demand are, inevitably, global.

In the UK, water usage is a complex issue linked to public health, planning and land use and, in particular, infrastructure (see Chapter 14), where many water supply companies are battling to plug up the leaks in the antiquated supply system.

Global indicators

The World Health Organization (WHO) is the leading player in the field of water quality standards. Their Guidelines present five key components for water quality monitoring:[12]

- management plans documenting the system assessment and monitoring against targets
- system assessment to determine whether the water supply chain (from source through treatment to the point of consumption) as a whole can deliver water of a quality that meets the above targets
- operational monitoring of the control measures in the supply chain, which are of particular importance in securing drinking-water safety
- management plans documenting the system assessment and monitoring, and describing actions to be taken in normal operation and incident conditions including upgrade and improvement documentation and communication
- a system of independent surveillance that verifies that the above are operating properly.

The WHO's Standards also deal in detail with individual substances, and have a comprehensive list of guidelines for the levels in water of 70 chemicals.[13]

European indicators

Water problems, like many other environmental issues, know no geographical boundaries, and European water policy has resulted in legislation that provides minimum standards for all countries in the Union.

The production of legislation on water pollution and water quality by the EU has been extensive, and includes:

- Surface Water Directive (Directives 75/440/EEC and 79/869/EEC)
- Bathing Water Directive (Directive 76/160/EEC)
- Dangerous Substances Directive (Directive 76/464/EEC, as amended by Directive 91/692/EEC, and "daughter" Directives 82/176/EEC, 83/513/EEC, 84/156/EEC, 84/491/EEC and 86/280/EEC)
- Fish Water Directive (Directive 78/659/EEC)
- Shellfish Water Directive (Directive 79/923/EEC)
- Groundwater Directive (Directive 80/68/EEC)
- Drinking Water Directive of 15 July 1980 (Directive 80/778/EEC)
- Urban Wastewater Treatment Directive (Directive 91/271/EEC)
- Nitrate Directive (Directive 91/676/EEC)
- Drinking Water Directive of 3 November 1998 (Directive 98/83/EC).

UK government indicators

Table 19.1 summarises the drinking water quality benchmarks, as specified in Schedules 1 and 2 of the 2001 Water Supply (Water Quality) Regulations. (Please refer to the Regulations for full details.)

The UK government reports that, in England, 94 per cent of river lengths were of good or fair chemical quality in 2001, compared with a mere 43 per cent in 1990, and in Wales 98 per cent were of good or fair chemical quality in 2001, compared with the much higher 86 per cent in 1990.[14] However, the latest data for biological river quality in England and Wales will not be available until late 2003.

It should be noted that, even in this technical field, the measurement techniques and standards used in England and Scotland cannot be compared, not to mention techniques used abroad. So the key lesson is that it is important to have not only published indicators, but also details about the method of measurement used when ensuring that the standards are met.

Table 19.1 Microbiological paramenters/Chemical parameters

MICROBIOLOGICAL PARAMENTERS

PARAMENTERS	CONCENTRATION OR VALUE (MAXIMUM)	UNITS OF MEASUREMENT (AT CONSUMERS' TAPS)
Enterococci	0	number/100ml
Escherichia coli (E. coli)	0	number/100ml

PART II NATIONAL REQUIREMENTS

PARAMENTERS	CONCENTRATION OR VALUE (MAXIMUM)	UNITS OF MEASUREMENT (AT CONSUMERS' TAPS)
Coliform bacteria	0	number/100ml
Escherichia coli (E. coli)	0	number/100ml

CHEMICAL PARAMENTERS
PART I: DIRECTIVE REQUIREMENTS

PARAMENTERS	CONCENTRATION OR VALUE (MAXIMUM)	UNITS OF MEASUREMENT (AT CONSUMERS' TAPS, UNLESS STATED)
Acrylamide (see *16* for compliance details)	0.10	$\mu g/l$
Antimony	5.0	$\mu gSb/l$
Arsenic	10	$\mu gAs/l$
Benzene	1.0	$\mu g/l$
Benzo(a)pyrene	0.010	$\mu g/l$
Boron	1.0	mgB/l
Bromate	10	$\mu gBrO_3/l$
Cadmium	5.0	$\mu gCd/l$
Chromium	50	$\mu gCr/l$
Copper	2.0	$mgCu/l$
Cyanide	50	$\mu gCN/l$
1, 2 dichloroethane	3.0	$\mu g/l$
Epichlorohydrin (see *16* for compliance details)	0.10	$\mu g/l$
Fluoride	1.5	mgF/l
Lead	(a) 25 from 25th December 2003 until immediately before 25th December 2013 (b) 10 on and after 25th December 2013	$\mu gPb/l$ $\mu gHg/l$ $\mu gNi/l$ $mgNO_3/l$ $mgNO_2/l$
Mercury	1.0	$\mu g/l$
Nickel	20	$\mu g/l$

Table 19.1 Microbiological paramenters/Chemical parameters (continued)

PARAMENTERS	CONCENTRATION OR VALUE (MAXIMUM)	UNITS OF MEASUREMENT (AT CONSUMERS' TAPS, UNLESS STATED)
Nitrate	50	µgNi/l
Nitrite	0.50	mgNO3/l
(at treatment works)	0.10	mgNO2/l
Pesticides:	0.030	µg/l
Aldrin		
Dieldrin		
Heptachlor		
Epoxide		
Other pesticides	0.10	µg/l
Pesticides (total)	0.50	µg/l
Polycyclic aromatic hydrocarbons	0.10	µg/l
Selenium	10	µgSe/l
Tetrachloroethene and Trichloroethene	10	µg/l
Trihalomethanes (total)	100	µg/l
Vinyl chloride (see *16* for compliance details	0.50	µg/l

PART II NATIONAL REQUIREMENTS

PARAMENTERS	CONCENTRATION OR VALUE (MAXIMUM)	UNITS OF MEASUREMENT (AT CONSUMERS' TAPS)
Aluminium	200	µgAl/l
Colour	20	mg/l Pt/Co
Hydrogen ion	10.0 6.5 (minimum)	pH value
Iron	200	µgFe/l
Manganese	50	µgMn/l
Odour	3 at 25°C	Dilution number
Sodium	200	mgNa/l
Taste	3 at 25°C	Dilution number
Tetrachloromethane	3	µg/l
Turbidity	4	NTU

Table 19.1 Microbiological paramenters/Chemical parameters (continued)

PARAMENTERS	SPECIFICATION CONCENTRATION OR VALUE (MAXIMUM) OR STATE	UNITS OF MEASUREMENT	POINT OF MONITORING
Ammonium	0.50	mgNH4/l	Consumers' taps
Chloride	250	mgCl/l	Supply point*
Clostridium perfringens (including spores)	0	Number/100ml	Supply point*
Coliform bacteria	0	Number/100ml	Consumers' taps
Colony counts	No abnormal change	Number/1ml at 22°C	Consumers' taps, service
		Number/1ml at 37°C	Reservoirs and treatment works
Conductivity	2500	µS/cm at 20°C	Supply point*
Hydrogen ion	9.5	pHvalue	Consumers' taps
Sulphate	250	mgSO4 /l	Supply point*
Total indicative dose (for radioactivity)	0.10	mSv/year	Supply point*
Total organic carbon (TOC)	No abnormal change	mgC/l	Supply point*
Tritium (for radioactivity)	100	Bq/l	Supply point*
Turbidity	1	NTU	Treatment works

* May be monitored from samples of water leaving treatment works or other supply point.

Source: *The Water Supply (Water Quality) Regulations* 2001 No. 3911. © Crown copyright

In view of the fact that many industries, such as tourism and fishing, depend on local sea and river water quality, publishing any monitoring results is seen as a priority in the UK, and as an indication of the economic value to Britain of maintaining its own water quality standards. UK bathing water standards are, by and large, predicated upon those of the EU.

There has been a significant improvement of the quality of water at British beaches since 1990 and the de-regulation of the water companies. The number of beaches that are now getting the "Blue Flag" awards is impressive. Bathing water quality in England in the 2002 season was the best ever, with 98.5 per cent of bathing waters in England (401 out of 407) complying with the EC mandatory coliform bacteria standards.[15] Water quality necessary for a Blue Flag was 70 per cent compliance in 2002, compared with 60 per cent in 2001 however, this is not considered good enough by many, including Surfers Against Sewage. (The Annex to the EU Bathing Water Directive contains information on the requirements for monitoring programmes, lists the 19 parameters and values which apply to

Table 19.2 Compliance rate for bathing water quality standards in England

YEAR	% COMPLIANCE (ENGLAND)	% COMPLIANCE (UK)
1991	74	76
1992	79	79
1993	79	80
1994	83	82
1995	89	89
1996	89	89
1997	88	88
1998	90	89
1999	90	91
2000	95	94
2001	98	95
2002	98.5	98

Source: *UK bathing water results, www.defra.gov.uk* © Crown copyright

bathing waters, and states how results should be interpreted.[6])

Table 19.2 shows compliance over the last decade in England, and the UK as a whole, with the EC mandatory coliform bacteria standards for bathing waters. It is possible to argue that the use of this indicator makes the situation look as rosy as possible, whereas if they had used the compliance figures the data would not have been so favourable.

References

1 See "water-related diseases" at *www.who.int/water_sanitation_health/en* and also Gleick P (1993), *Water in Crisis*, Oxford University Press, Oxford, pp 170–179

2 See *www.sustainable-development.gov.uk/indicators*

3 See *www.sas.org.uk*

4 See *www.environment-agency.gov.uk* and *www.defra.gov.uk/environment/water/quality/index.htm*

5 See *http:/www.dwi.gov.uk/index.htm*

6 The Water Supply (Water Quality) Regulations 2001 No. 3911 (available from *www.hmso.gov.uk/legislation*)

7 See *www.ofwat.gov.uk*

8 Howard G (2003), *Domestic Water, Service, Level and Health*, World Health Organization, Geneva. Download the document at *www.who.int/water_sanita-*

tion _health/en

9 These figures include residents in the hotels that house the many visitors to the "Sunshine State". Source: *www.state.fl.us/eog/govdocs/gapcomm/ critical/section_six/sect_six_percapita.html*

10 Salamore D (2002) "Paving it over", in Orlando Sentinel, 26 May 2002. Read the full story at *www.orlandosentinel.com/news*

11 Kulakowski S and Martin WE (1991), "Water price as policy variable in managing urban waste water use: Tucson, Arizona", *Water Resources Research*, 27 (2) 157–166

12 See World Health Organization (WHO) *Framework for Safe Drinking-water*, at *www.who.int*

13 WHO (2003), *Guidelines on Drinking Water Quality*, 3rd edn, World Health Organization, Geneva

14 Source: DEFRA news release "River water quality headline indicator for sustainable development: 2001", 3 October 2002

15 For a full list and maps of beach water quality see *www.seasideawards.org.uk*

16 EU Bathing Water Directive 76/160/EEC is discussed in more detail at *www. sepa.org.uk/data/bathingwaters/1998bathingseason/bwinterpretation.htm*

On-line resources

The Construction Industry Research and Information Association (CIRIA) publishes a number of relevant documents on water standards, water pollution from construction sites, water quality standards and a forthcoming publication on key performance indicators for the water industry. See *www.ciria.org.uk/acatalog*

A very good source group on the subject is the Water Save Network based at Imperial College London, who can be contacted on *www.watersave.uk.net/ About_network*

For a more detailed reading list on water quality and pollution see also *http://lib5.leeds.ac.uk/rlists/environ/envi2170.htm*

Further reading

Aitken C et al (1994), "Residential water use: predicting and reducing consumption", *Journal of Applied Social Psychology*, 24 (2), 136–158

Barty-King H (1992), *Water: An illustrated history of water supply and wastewater in the United Kingdom*, Quiller Press, Norwich

Baumann D, Boland J and Hannemann W (1998), *Urban Water Demand Management and Planning*, McGraw-Hill, New York

Butler D (1991), "A small-scale study of wastewater discharges from domestic appliances", in *J.IWEM (Journal of the Institution of Water and Environmental Management)*, 5, 178–185

Butler D, Friedler E and Gatt K (1995), "Characterising the quantity and quality of domestic wastewater inflows", *Wat.Sci.Tech.*, 31 (7), 13–24

Butler D et al (1996), "Local water conservation, reuse and renovation combined greywater and rainwater recycling." *21 AD: Water. Architectural Digest for the 21st Century,* School of Architecture, Oxford Brookes University, Oxford, 20–23

Butler D and Davies JW (2000), *Urban Drainage*, E & FN Spon, London

Davis S (2001), "The politics of water scarcity in the Western states", *Social Sciences Journal*, 38, 527–542

DeSena M (1999), "Public opposition sidelines indirect potable reuse projects", *Water Environment & Technology*, May

Diaper C et al (2000), "Small scale water recycling systems – risk assessment and modelling", *1st IWA Congress*, Paris, France, April

Dixon A, Butler D and Fewkes A (1999), "Water saving potential of domestic water re-use systems using greywater and rainwater in combination", *Wat.Sci.Tech.*, 39 (5), 25–32

Dixon A, Butler D and Fewkes A (1999), "Guidelines for Greywater reuse – health issues", *J. CIWEM (Journal of the Chartered Institute of Water and Environmental Management)*, 13 (5), 322–326

Edwards K and Martin L (1995), "A methodology for surveying domestic consumption", *J.CIWEM*, 9, 477–488

Environment Agency (2000), *On the Right Track: A summary of current water conservation initiatives in the UK*, Environment Agency, Bristol

Environment Agency (2001), *Water Resources for the Future: A strategy for England and Wales*, Environment Agency, Bristol

Center for Environmental Research Information (1992), *Guidelines for Water Reuse*, US Environmental Protection Agency, Ohio, EPA/625/R92/004,

Griggs J, Shouler MC and Hall J (1996), "Water Conservation and the Built Environment." *21 AD: Water. Architectural Digest for the 21st Century,* School of Architecture, Oxford Brookes University, Oxford, 3–14

Hall MJ, Hooper BD and Postle SM (1988), "Domestic per capita water consumption in South West England", *J.IWEM*, 2 (6), 626–631

Herrington P (1997), "Pricing water properly", in O'Riorden, T (ed) *Ecotaxation*, Earthscan Books, London

Herrington PR (1996), *Climate Change and the Demand for Water*, HMSO, London

Jeppesen B (1996), *Model Guidelines for Domestic Grey Water Reuse for Australia,*

Urban Water Research Association of Australia, Melbourne, Research Report No. 107

Mazmanian D and Kraft M (1999), *Towards Sustainable Communities*, MIT Press, Cambridge, USA

McDaniels TL, Axelrod LJ and Cavanagh N (2000), "Public perceptions regarding water quality and attitudes towards water conservation in the lower fraser basin", *Water Resources Research*, 34 (5), 1299–1310

Murley L (2003), *Pollution Handbook*, National Society for Clean Air and Environmental Protection, Brighton

Mustow S et al (1997), *Implications of Using Recycled Grey Water and Stored Rainwater in the UK*, BSRIA, Bracknell, Report 13034/1

OFWAT (2000), *Patterns of Demand for Water in England and Wales 1989–1999*, Office of Water Services, Birmingham

POST (2000), *Water Efficiency in the Home*. POST Note 136, Parliamentary Office of Science and Technology, London

Rose J et al (1991), "Microbial quality and persistence of enteric pathogens in grey water from various household sources", *Water Research*, 25 (1), pp 37–42

Strang V (2001), *Evaluating Water: Cultural beliefs and values about water quality, use and conservation*, Water UK, Suffolk

Surendran S and Wheatley A (1998), "Grey-water reclamation for non-potable reuse", Journal of the *Chartered Institution of Water and Environmental Management*, 12 (6), pp 406–413

WHO (1989), *World Health Organization Guidelines for the Use of Waste Water in Agriculture and Aquaculture*, World Health Organization, Geneva, WHO Technical Report Series 778

Planning policy guidance – related documents (see Appendix 1 for details)

1	2	3	4	5	6	7	8	9	10	11	12	13
x	x	x	x	x	x	x				x	x	x
14	15	16	17	18	19	20	21	22	23	24	25	
	x					x	x		x			

Building Regulations – related Approved Documents (see Appendix 2 for details)

A	B	C	D	E	F	G	H	I	J	K	L1	L2	M	N
											x	x		

Waste

Definition

Wastes are generated by a wide range of human activities – from basic metabolism, to the creation of highly sophisticated consumer goods. In particular, wastes may be generated during the extraction of raw materials, the processing of raw materials into intermediate and final products, and the consumption of final products.

Buildings account for a significant proportion of all waste generated, whether from the design construction processes, refurbishment, renovation, or demolition, or as a result of the indoor activities that result in effluents – water and sewage and materials – and the food stuffs and products that enter buildings and leave as waste.

Related indicators

Land use, Air pollution, Contaminated land, Water pollution

Related solutions

Specifying for sustainability

Related tools

Environmental impact assessment, Life cycle assessment, Monitoring waste

Background

Every year we consume more and more goods and products, generating more and more waste. The UK alone produces over 400 million tonnes of solid waste per year, enough to fill London's Albert Hall every hour:[1]

- Domestic waste alone increased in volume by 14 per cent between 1991 and 1998.
- It is estimated that households, industry and commerce produce between them up to 50 per cent of the national waste – around 170 and 210 million tonnes each year in the UK.

Municipal waste, largely from households, was over 29 million tonnes in 1999/2000. It is growing at 3 per cent a year as households consume more goods and throw away more rubbish and, it is estimated, will double by 2020.[2]

For individual businesses, waste can account for over 4 per cent of business turnover, and it has been estimated that by tackling waste minimisation the majority of companies can save up to £1,000 per employee.[3]

Figure 20.1 shows that mining and quarrying (largely for the construction industry and road building), agriculture and the construction industry are among the largest producers of waste.

Just as buildings are responsible for over 50 per cent of energy consumption in the UK, so a very high proportion of waste results either from the construction industry or from buildings in use. National data differ considerably because of the efficiency of the various construction industries. In the USA, for example, it is estimated that 25–30 per cent of all landfill waste comes from buildings in construction or demolition, whereas Canada's constructors produce only 20 per cent of the national waste, but in Australia the figure could be as high as 44 per cent. The UK building industry is at the higher end of these figures.

The bottom line is that we are using vast quantities of non-renewable natural resources with reckless abandon, and in so doing we are also creating an ever-

Figure 20.1 Estimated annual waste arisings in the UK by sector

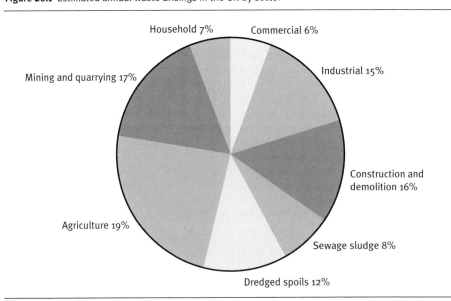

Source: *Quality of Life Counts*, DETR, *www.sustainable-development.gov.uk* © Crown Copyright

increasing problem of how to dispose of mountains of the resulting unwanted, sometimes toxic, wastes. The building industry is a significant player in this unsustainable profligacy. Globally, the industry consumes three billion tonnes of raw materials annually, 30–40 per cent of the total material flow in the world economy, excluding food.[4] For instance, North America, Europe, and Japan, with less than 20 per cent of the world's population, use over 50 per cent of its wood and over 65 per cent of its paper.[5]

Ultimately, we all pay the price. We pay over the odds for products that could have been developed and manufactured more thoughtfully; we pay the price, through taxation, for the increasing cost of disposing of waste; and we all suffer when waste is not managed correctly.

Every local authority in the UK is affected by the growing problem of the servicing and disposal of waste, not least because of new financial penalties imposed for the dumping of waste to landfill. Before 2010, the issue of transporting and disposing of waste will be near the top of local authority costs, and all councils should be putting in place early strategies to minimise the future cost and environmental impacts of this growing problem.

To make matters worse, climate change could well exacerbate the problems of waste management. Higher summer temperatures could lead to an unacceptable increase in outdoor odour problems associated with waste disposal; and heavy rains and floods will bring new containment problems.

Two key issues will have to be dealt with using well-thought-out long-term strategic planning:

- Increasing pressure on available land for development, particularly in the south east of England, means that landfill sites will have to be identified for the next 30–50 years and their environs protected from adjacent development.
- Strategic planning for waste will need to be an open process now that pressure groups and professional organisations are succeeding in educating the public about the problems. Any plans will need to bring people on board because decisions may be highly contentious.

The construction industry must also make a concerted effort to address the waste issue. Indeed, the industry has much to gain from so doing: lower construction costs, savings in business/administration costs, and a marketing advantage because the resulting buildings will save clients money too. All schemes should incorporate strategies for waste management during design, construction, use and demolition.

Figure 20.2 Waste arisings and management (UK) 1997/8

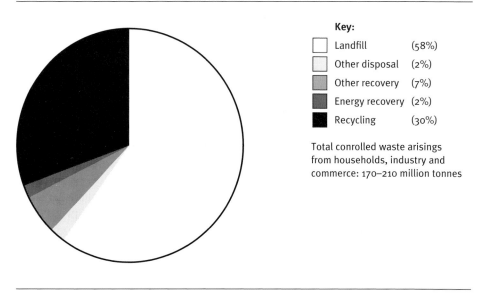

Key:

☐	Landfill	(58%)
☐	Other disposal	(2%)
▨	Other recovery	(7%)
▨	Energy recovery	(2%)
■	Recycling	(30%)

Total conrolled waste arisings from households, industry and commerce: 170–210 million tonnes

Source: Headline Indicators for Sustainable Development (H15), www.sustainable-development.gov.uk © Crown Copyright

Landfill

As Figure 20.2 shows, a high proportion of waste is currently deposited in landfill sites, and it is increasingly difficult to identify acceptable locations for new landfill sites. This has led to the introduction of very stringent laws to penalise what is considered to be the excessive dumping of waste to landfill – a move that was also spurred on by growing concerns about the high levels of greenhouse gases produced at landfill sites (see Chapter 18), and the health effects of living close to landfill sites, which are poorly researched at present, but potentially very serious.[6]

In 1996 the UK government introduced the Landfill Tax and associated with it the Landfill Tax Credit Scheme (LTSC), which enables landfill site operators to donate up to 6.5 per cent of their landfill tax liability to environmental projects in return for a 90 per cent tax credit.[7] The LTCS was designed to help mitigate the effects of landfill upon local communities. It encourages partnerships between landfill operators, their local communities and the voluntary and public sectors.[8] As a result, the cost of dumping in landfill in the UK is expected to rise from around £10 a tonne to £15 a tonne and maybe even rise to £20 a tonne excluding tax.

Some 1,400 landfill sites currently operate[9] in the UK, and these must apply to the Environment Agency (EA) for permits to continue to treat waste.

Control and minimisation

In 2000 the UK published a new Waste Strategy, which included a very clear definition of the problems, the indicators to be used, and a strong monitoring programme for immediate implementation,[10] and in July 2001 the European Union's Landfill Directive came into force[11] setting up even tighter waste management standards for members of the EU over the next 18 years. This includes slashing the amount of biodegradable waste that can be landfilled, and the need to separate out the most hazardous materials for safe treatment rather than dumping.

The EU and UK policies are based on a strategy known as the "waste hierarchy". This acknowledges that waste cannot be completely eliminated, but that its environmental impact can be minimised in three ways:

- *Reduce* – waste should be reduced in the first place. Waste minimisation by industry involves examining alternative processes and each stage of a production process to find ways of cutting resource use and waste.
- *Reuse* – discarded products, materials or buildings.
- *Recycle* – value can and should be recovered from the material by recycling, composting or energy production. Energy can be recovered from waste by generating heat and electricity from waste incineration or by capturing and burning methane released from landfill sites.

Only if these routes have failed is the waste disposed of, usually to landfill.

Another factor related to minimisation is the "proximity principle", which states that waste should be disposed of near to where it was produced in order to minimise the impacts of its transport. This principle has to be set against practical factors such as the economies of scale (particularly with specialist materials and products such as fridges and cars) and the higher standards of processing that are possible in larger waste facilities serving a wider area. With cars, for instance, the End-of-Life Vehicles Directive[12] makes the car industry responsible for scrapping and recycling old cars, but the location of the appropriate disposal facility may become an impediment to local disposal practices.

Reduction

Once waste becomes a real issue – with financial implications – then many different players become involved in the challenge of reducing wastes. For instance, dramatic reductions have been achieved in the amount of packaging going to waste through involving manufacturers, who also gain by having to pay for less packaging:

- J Sainsbury plc has reduced the gauge of its carrier bags from 30 to 25 μm, and thus reduced the amount of plastic used by 1,450 tonnes a year.
- A corrugated case used in a closed loop for the transport of plastic tubs has been developed by Rexam Plastics, Deeside, and SCA Packaging. This replaces single-trip corrugated cases and has been shown to be capable of at least ten trips.
- Standard 400g food cans have reduced in weight by 21 per cent since 1970, which means that for every 1 million cans made today, there is a typical saving of 250 tonnes of steel compared with 1970.

These achievements should be seen against the general target level for recycling of packaging in a recent EU Directive:

- minimum recovery of packaging waste – 50 per cent
- minimum recycling of packaging waste – 25 per cent
- minimum recycling of each material – 15 per cent.

Packaging is one area of construction where much could be achieved, but savings must be sought during the design and tender stages – either from the client's brief, during tendering or when selecting materials suppliers.

Refrigerants

Around 3 million domestic refrigeration units (fridges, fridge-freezers and freezers) are disposed of in the UK each year, and up to half a million commercial refrigeration units are also replaced annually. ODS may be found in the circulating coolant system of a fridge, or they may have been used as a blowing agent for the polyurethane foam used to insulate the unit.

Prior to 1994 almost all appliances used CFCs as both refrigerant and as foam blowing agent. Modern fridges are generally manufactured using HFC or hydrocarbon refrigerants and hydrocarbon blowing agents. Most are also marked with an appliance rating plate that carries information about the appliance, for example model and serial number. In most cases it will also state what refrigerant was used in the appliance. Fridges that are marked with R12 or R134a on the plate will most probably have CFC or HCFC in the insulation foam and should be treated accordingly, unless there is evidence to suggest otherwise.

The UK currently has no facilities capable of extracting CFCs from insulation foam before the refrigerators are recycled.

Designers and specifiers can also play a significant part in reducing the amount of hazardous waste. Under the European Hazardous Waste Directive (91/689/EEC),[13] substances such as corrosives or solvent-based liquids – including a number of building materials such as solvent-based paints and treatments – will require treatment at specially licensed plants, which will be heavily policed by the Environment Agency.

Air-conditioning and refrigeration systems are also in the spotlight – during specification but, perhaps more significantly, during renovation or demolition. European Council Regulation No. 2037/2000 on ozone-depleting substances (ODSs), which came into effect in October 2001, requires Member States to remove ODSs including chlorofluorocarbons (CFCs) and hydrochlorofluorocarbons (HCFCs) from refrigeration equipment before such appliances are scrapped (see Chapter 17).[14] The key message here is to avoid refrigeration and air-conditioning, but where it cannot be avoided, to ensure that the systems put in place are as environmentally benign as possible.

Reuse and recycling

Composting of biodegradable waste will become an important factor in meeting the UK's Waste Strategy targets. The government has set targets to recycle or compost at least 25 per cent of household waste by 2005, rising to at least 33 per cent by 2015.

Composting is classified as a waste recovery operation under the Waste Framework Directive. In practice, this means that large-scale composting is carried out under a waste management licence issued by the Environment Agency or a licensing exemption registered with the Agency; the aim is to protect the environment and human health, while producing a useful substance.

Compost can be used as a soil conditioner, to improve soil structure and to enhance its biological activity, and as a growing medium for the horticultural industry. The use of compost reduces harmful emissions of the greenhouse gas methane from landfills, it reduces the need for scare natural resources such as peat, and it returns organic matter to the soil.

The majority (92 per cent in 1998) of municipal waste comprised green wastes collected from civic amenity sites or local authority parks and gardens, with only 7% of organic municipal wastes collected at the kerbside.

Where catering or household waste contains meat or other products derived from animals then, although it may be composted, it may not, currently, be used on land for fear of transmission of diseases such as BSE through the waste. The Animal By-Products Order prohibits the use of this mixed compost on land where animals (including wild birds) may have access. However, this position, is chang-

---

Sewage

Sewage, largely in the form of effluent from buildings, is a major waste. Most of the sewage in England and Wales is treated, leaving sewage sludge. Because dumping sewage sludge at sea was banned in 1998, it is usually applied to farmland, incinerated or sent to landfill. Recycling sewage sludge to soil provides valuable nutrients and organic matter; the Environment Agency regulates the process to ensure that pathogens do not enter the food chain and to avoid the build-up of harmful substances in soils.

---

ing with the current EU Regulation on Animal By-Products, which allows for the use of properly composted mixed waste on all land except pasture used for the grazing of cattle or sheep.[15]

A number of local authorities in the UK already promote composting, either by offering kerbside collections of garden waste, or by offering low-cost domestic compost bins. Most also collect separated domestic wastes – plastics, tins, paper etc – from the kerbside.

The practice of recycling via kerbside collections is likely to increase, and designers of both domestic and industrial buildings would serve their clients well by allocating space for the storage of recyclable materials between collections.

There is enormous potential for reuse of construction materials, many of which can be reclaimed without further processing, lessening environmental impacts and possibly bringing a cost saving. Sometimes materials can be re-used on the same site; failing that, there are a range of outlets for many building materials.[16]

Waste minimisation in construction

The benefits of waste management have been well demonstrated by the UK company Carillion, whose waste strategy has demonstrated the benefits of not only good site practices, but also the incorporation of waste issues into the design process.[17]

Their recently completed Great Western Hospital project significantly exceeded the target to reduce waste sent to landfill by 50 per cent, against their previous best practice benchmarks. This was achieved by examining the major waste arisings on similar projects, then working with the supply chain to minimise these. For example, the design and procurement teams ordered plasterboard cut to either optimised or exact sizes to fit the required areas, and working with the supply chain led to the implementation of the UK's first plasterboard "take-back and recy-

Figure 20.3 Great Western Hospital Swindon – landfill waste target

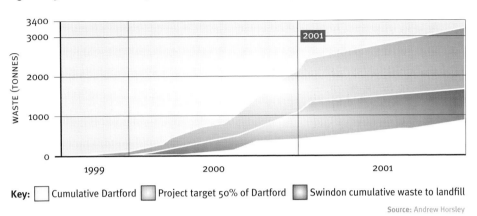

Key: ☐ Cumulative Dartford ☐ Project target 50% of Dartford ☐ Swindon cumulative waste to landfill

Source: Andrew Horsley

cling" scheme to deal with any damaged or remaining offcuts.

The final part of the chain was to set up a waste management system to ensure the segregation of all waste on site (see Chapter 38 for more details on waste segregation techniques). Only a very small proportion was sent to landfill, materials with viable recycling routes was recycled, and all organic waste was composted on site and used as a valuable part of the landscaping process (see Figure 20.3).

Global indicators

The simple UN Global Compact Indicators set for 2002 has the simple headline indicator of "Total amount of waste by type and destination"[18] – a good start!

European indicators

The European Environment Agency states that the cornerstones of the EU's strategy to coping with waste are to:

- prevent waste in the first place
- recycle waste
- turn waste into a "greenhouse neutral" energy source
- optimise the final disposal of waste, including its transport.

Although the EU has a number of targets and Directives supporting these aims, the data is patchy due to a lack of consistency across the EU. What is abundantly clear, however, is that some of these targets are not being met.

To begin with, a wide range of different waste streams are increasing in volume, from consumers generating too much household waste to more wastewater treatment plants producing larger amounts of sewage sludge. What is more, waste disposal methods are not coping with the increased loads, with several countries increasing the amount of biodegradable waste sent to landfill.

Finally – and most importantly – waste generation is still linked to economic activity, meaning that, as Europe's economy grows, the waste problem will grow with it.[19]

National indicators

Canada

The Canadian construction industry seems to be a real world leader in terms of best practice for sustainable development – you only have to look at their high-performance windows to see that! Over 20 per cent of waste in Canada going to landfill is generated from new construction, renovation and demolition projects, already much lower than Australia's 40 per cent. The boom years of the 1980s fuelled incredible economic expansion, but unfortunately left behind the philosophy that waste generation was an acceptable by-product of growth and development. In 1994 The Government of Ontario passed Bill 102, made under its Environmental Protection Act, which places the construction industry under increased pressure to divert materials from landfill. This Bill deals with solid waste from residential, industrial, commercial and institutional sources including those generated by the construction and demolition industry, and sets ambitious targets to decrease the amount of waste going to disposal by at least 50 per cent by the year 2000, compared with the base year of 1987.

The Canadian Environmental Protection Act requires that any project of over 2,000 m² (by floor space) requiring a building permit, must submit a waste audit (see Chapter 38) and waste reduction work plan. The plan should include a detailed inventory of materials that are being sent to landfill, what efforts are being made to reduce waste, and what will be salvaged for reuse. This programme has offered an opportunity to rethink the practices that have generated waste and to develop new means of diverting construction materials from the traditional waste stream.

UK

Waste is listed in the UK Headline Indicators of Sustainable Development.[20]

The objective of H15 is to move away from disposal of waste towards waste reduction, reuse, recycling and recovery, and the indicator that is used is that of household waste, all arisings and management (see Figures 20.1 and 20.4). These targets are derived from European legislation such as the Landfill Directive and

Figure 20.4 Household waste and recylcing: 1983/4 – 2001/2

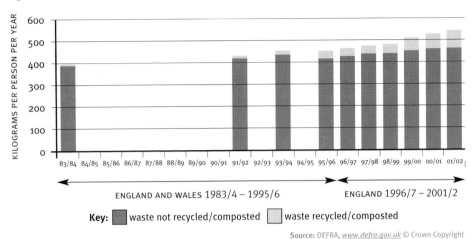

the Packaging Directive, and pressure for change is being passed down through local authorities to building owners, users, and in turn to designers.

Local authority indicators

The Audit Commission monitors the performance of local authorities, and has two waste indicators,[20] the first to monitor incidence of dog fowling bins per square kilometre and the second (no. 143) concerning domestic waste, which sets out to measure how much waste is:

- recycled
- composted
- used as an energy source or
- sent to landfill.

This indicator is also included as a Best Value Performance Indicator 82, a measure of the efficiency of service provision, and as a Quality of Life Indicator 32, a measure of the importance of proper waste measurement to the well-being of the community.

The Office of the Deputy Prime Minister (ODPM) has issued detailed guidance to local authorities on how to prepare a waste management strategy.[22]

Community indicators

Although European and national legislation is necessary to regulate recycling and waste management there is still much that can be done by citizens working alone, or even more effectively working cooperatively in a community group, be it a street, neighbourhood, school, government department, works canteen or professional office.

Starting and developing a community recycling scheme is not difficult, and there are a number of UK agencies at national and local level to encourage and support local agencies to do just that. The rewards can be defined as a community dividend, which can be not only environmental but also financial and educational, and lead to a community enrichment. A good example of active citizenship is through the linking of such projects to the teaching of citizenship in schools, now a compulsory part of the National Curriculum in England, up to the age of 16. The skills learnt in such projects are transferable into the wider society, which will be essential if there is to be the proposed increase in the recycling of domestic waste.

Such a scheme was set up in 1989 in the village of Lower Wolvercote, outside Oxford, based on experiences of two residents, Christopher and Ruth Gowers, in village co-operatives in India and Victoria in British Columbia. The group was also helped by the local Friends of the Earth team, which used a milk float to collect paper locally, long before the local authority took any interest in recycling domestic waste. In 1989 a group of locals got together and formed a village-wide scheme. The scheme had a number of components:

- Paper and glass for recycling were collected from dwellings and the local school, taken to a local collection depot (often one in each street), and then disposed of to the bottle bank or via Friends of the Earth
- Local traders joined the scheme, collecting and sorting and selling to waste merchants including metal, rags and skip loads of paper
- Envelope labels were reused
- A newsletter for 300 members was published
- Public meetings and talks were organised
- Stalls at local events for selling recycled stationary (proceeds were used to help finance a school exchange with Tanzania) were set up
- A community compost heap was made
- A community garden shredder was purchased
- Expertise was contributed to local and national committees
- Carpentry tools were collceted for refurbishment, and then use by students from a local school to build a village school in Uganda

A campaign by this group and others in the city eventually led Oxford City Council to adopt a kerbside green box collection scheme for every house for papers, glass, tins and rags.

This scheme demonstrates how important individuals are in achieving the goals of sustainable development in any country and for any issue.

Building-level indicators

An excellent example of waste reduction was set by Fletcher Construction in the Australian State of Victoria, where construction industry waste accounts for a staggering 44 per cent of total landfill. In 1992, the local authority agreed to provide developers Fletcher with A$40,000 to contribute to a trial waste minimisation programme based on the idea of good housekeeping using both waste minimisation and waste management strategies.[23]

A plan and programme were written, and workers were briefed on the first day of work about the waste minimisation goals and how they would be achieved. Initiatives included the use of recycled materials in the design and the separation of waste on site into bins in order to maximise reuse and recycling during construction. Data was collected and benchmarks were established so that outcomes could be measured and so that the process could be reviewed and continuously improved.

Recycled concrete, bricks and paper were purchased for use in the project, and there was an 8% saving on paper costs alone. On-site recycling of the metals, roof tiles, bricks and structural steel of the existing police, court and community buildings saved around A$10,500 on waste removal.

Waste materials were separated and recycled wherever practical and economical. Waste volumes generated, the percentage of the waste stream recycled, and their treatment were as follows:

- Plasterboard: the high percentage of plasterboard waste was directly related to the lack of flexibility in the delivery of required sheet sizes. No recycling plant for plasterboard exists in Victoria. Some plasterboard was stockpiled for a planned plant. Percentage of waste stream 19.6 per cent. Percentage recycled 7.1 per cent.
- Cardboard: for packaging and office amenities, cardboard was recycled at a credit of 20 cents per kilogram. Percentage of waste stream 17 per cent. Percentage recycled 78.8 per cent.
- General sweepings: mixed waste that was not considered cost effective to separate, was cleaned up on a regular basis. Percentage of waste stream 15.2 per cent. Percentage recycled 0 per cent.
- Excavated soil: excavated soil is usually a major component of landfill, but it was not evaluated for the pilot project because of difficulties in

comparing different topographies. Topsoil was sold to nurseries. The remaining soil was used for road base or building up land in other construction projects.

- Timber: timber in non-standard sizes was ordered from suppliers, rather than cutting it on site and throwing away the offcuts. Outlets for recycling are not well established. Percentage of waste stream 13.8 per cent. Percentage recycled 17.4 per cent.
- Metals: metals are easily recycled and offer a cash return, from 75 cents per kilogram for ferrous metals to A$3 per kilogram for non-ferrous metals such as copper. Percentage of waste stream 9.5 per cent. Percentage recycled 100 per cent.
- Plastics: many different types of plastic are used in construction. Separation is difficult because there are no large volumes of any particular type. Percentage of waste stream 6.9 per cent. Percentage recycled 8.7 per cent.
- Concrete: 75 per cent of tip fees were saved by sending concrete to the crusher for re-use as road base. In Sydney, 30 per cent of the cost of concrete can be saved through the purchase of recycled concrete. In Melbourne, savings are only marginal on purchase costs due to an abundance of cheap quarry rock. Percentage of waste stream 6.7 per cent. Percentage recycled 80.6 per cent.
- Carpet: no recycling outlets for carpet were found, although they are common overseas. Percentage of waste stream 6.7 per cent. Percentage recycled 0 per cent.
- Insulation: larger scraps of insulating material were taken by site workers for their own use. Percentage of waste stream 3 per cent. Percentage recycled 30 per cent.
- Paper (first quality): first quality paper collected from site offices included computer paper and plan prints. Percentage of waste stream 1.2 per cent. Percentage recycled 100 per cent.
- Glass: all bottles from site amenities were recycled. Percentage of waste stream 0.4 per cent. Percentage recycled 100 per cent.

Fletcher Construction cut its waste removal cost by more than half, and that was without land fill tax advantages. The measures did not involve any capital cost, but they have resulted in substantial savings to both the company and the environment:

- The total volume of waste was reduced by 15%.
- Over 30 per cent of the remaining waste volume generated was recycled.

- 55 per cent savings were achieved on waste removal costs through recycling and input reduction.
- 43 per cent less volume of waste sent to the landfill.

Fletcher Construction has set a benchmark of 25 per cent for waste reduction on all future building sites in its new "green" national policy. Its sister company in Seattle, Washington, has implemented similar measures.

References

1 For reports, statistics and information on waste in the UK, see *www.defra. gov.uk*

2 Source: *www.esauk.org*

3 Source: Scottish Environmental Protection Agency at *www.sepa.org.uk/ wastemin*

4 Altenpohl D (1980), *Materials in World Perspective*, Springer-Verlag, Berlin

5 Worldwatch Institute (1998), "Accelerated demand for land wood, and paper pushing world's forests to the brink", press notice issued 4 April 1998. See www.worldwatch.org

6 Dolk H et al (1998) "Incidence of congenital anomalies near hazardous waste landfill sites in Europe", Lancet, 352, August, 423–427

7 ACBE (August 2001), *Resource Productivity, Waste Minimisation and the Landfill Tax*, Advisory Committee on Business and the Environment, download from *www.defra.gov.uk/environment*

8 See *www.ltcs.org.uk* and for help on individual schemes see *www.contaminated land.co.uk*

9 Check the location of local landfill sites by postcode at *www.environment agency.gov.uk* (choose "What's in your backyard")

10 DEFRA (2000) *Waste Strategy 2000 for England and Wales*, Parts 1 & 2, Department for Environment, Food & Rural Affairs, London. See *www.defra. gov.uk/environment/waste*

11 See *www.defra.gov.uk* and Murley L (2003), *Pollution Handbook*, National Society for Clean Air and Environmental Protection, 163–219

12 Directive 2000/53/EC of the European Parliament and of the Council, End-of-Life Vehicles, *OJEC (Official Journal of the European Communitites*, 18 September 2000. Download the document at *www.dti.gov.uk/environment/ consultations/elv.htm*

13 See also the Special Waste Regulations 1996 (at *www.legislation.hmso. gov.uk*), which set out procedures to be followed when disposing of, carrying

and receiving hazardous waste

14 Further information can be found in the joint DTI/DEFRA guidance available at *www.dti.gov.uk/access/ozone.htm*

15 For an excellent article on composting see "Occurrence and survival of viruses in composted human faeces", by the Danish Environmental Protection Agency, only available on-line at *www.mst.dk/homepage*

16 See the Waste and Resources Action Programme (*www.wrap.org.uk*), a not-for-profit company supported by the government, which is working to creating stable and efficient markets for recycled materials and products. See also Salvo Materials Information Exchange – a place to trade large volumes of reusable, reclaimable, recyclable and recoverable materials (*www.salvomie.co.uk*)

17 See *www.carillionplc.com/home.asp*

18 UN Global Compact (2002), *The nine UN Global Compact principles and selected 2002 GRI Sustainability Reporting Guidelines core performance indicators*, available online at *www.globalreporting.org*

19 See *http://themes.eea.eu.int/all_indicators_box*

20 UK indicators can be found at *www.sustainable-development.gov.uk*

21 See, for example, Audit Commission (October 2003), *Waste Management Services*, Staffordshire County Council Inspection Report; Audit Commission (2003) *Local Authority performance Indicators in England 2001/2002*; and the Audit Commission's *"Library of local performance indicators"* – all available at *www.audit-commission.gov.uk*

22 DTLR (May 2002), *Guidance on Policies for Waste Management Planning*, The Stationery Office, Norwich, available from *www.odpm.gov.uk*

23 See *www.environment.gov.au/net/environet.html*

On-line resources

A detailed pre-2002 reference list is at *www.wasteguide.org.uk/referenceguide/mn_references.stm*

There are a number of organisations that can help develop a clear waste policy, including:

www.smartwaste.co.uk
www.wastewatch.org.uk
www.crn.org.uk (Community Recycling Network)

For specific advice on recycling:

www.recycle.mcmail.com/wood.htm (wood products)

www.recycle.mcmail.com/architec.htm (architectural salvage)
www.recycle.mcmail.com/furnrec.htm (furniture)
www.envocare.co.uk/electrics_phones.htm (telephones, mobiles, electrical and electronic goods)

Municipal Waste Bulletins can be viewed at *www.defra.gov.uk*

Further reading

Department of the Environment (1992), 1992 Environmental Protection Act (Control of Wastes Regulations), Statutory Instrument No 588. HMSO, London

Department of the Environment (1996), The Special Waste Regulations, 1996, HMSO, London

Environment Agency (2000), *Strategic Waste Management Assessment 2000* (reports on each of the nine planning regions of England and a single report for Wales), WRC, Swindon

DEFRA (2001), *Municipal Waste Management 1999/2000*, Department for Environment, Food and Rural Affairs, London

Gutt W and Nixon P (1979), *Use of Waste Materials in the Construction Industry*, Building Research Establishment, Watford

Murray R (1999), *Creating Wealth from Waste*, Demos Publishing, London

OECD (1995), *The OECD System for Transfrontier Movements of Hazardous Wastes Destined for Recovery Operations: Guidance manual,* Environment Monographs No 96. OECD, Paris

World Metal Statistics (monthly), World Bureau of Metal Statistics, Ware.

Wise A and Swaffield J (2002), *Water, Sanitary and Waste Services for Buildings*, 5th edn, Architectural Press, Oxford

Williams P (1998), *Waste Treatment and Disposal*, John Wiley & Sons, Chichester

Planning policy guidance – related documents (see Appendix 1 for details)

1	2	3	4	5	6	7	8	9	10	11	12	13
	x					x			x	x	x	

14	15	16	17	18	19	20	21	22	23	24	25	
x				x					x			

Building Regulations – related Approved Documents (see Appendix 2 for details)

A	B	C	D	E	F	G	H	I	J	K	L1	L2	M	N
		x	x			x	x							

Solutions **4**

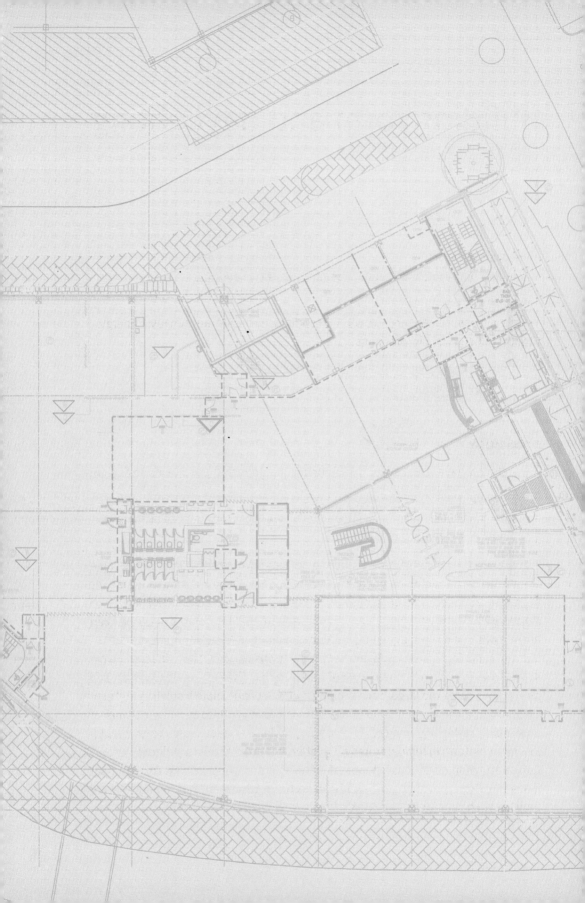

Building form and daylighting

Related indicators
   Quality of life; Health; Thermal comfort; Energy; Land use.

Related tools
   Impact assessment in the UK – Ecopoints, BREEAM and Envest; Energy toolkit; Energy use in dwellings.

Introduction

The British have always had a feel for the weather and good climatic design:

"'You have a very small park here,' returned Lady Catherine, after a short silence.'This must be a most inconvenient sitting-room for the evening in summer: the windows are full west.'"

These are the words of Lady Catherine de Burgh to Elizabeth Bennett, heroine of Jane Austin's novel *Pride and Prejudice*, which was first published in 1813. Lady Catherine was well known for giving free, and largely uncalled-for, advice to anyone who crossed her path, and it is unfortunate that the custom of taking heed of the skills and knowledge of our forebears has been largely forgotten.

   It was shocking to see how many people in Europe could not remain comfortable in their own homes in the heatwave of August 2003. Their discomfort was caused by windows being too large, poor shading and lack of adequate insulation and ventilation. But if the climate change predictions prove to be correct the summer of 2003 was just the beginning of much worse problems ahead. Imagine how a building might perform in temperatures 5°C higher. It is not difficult to maintain comfort temperatures in such heat – people do it around the world with no cooling – but many building types that are common in northern Europe today will perform very badly in such conditions and should be avoided by sensible investors.

Climate change may bring more sunshine hours, more intense radiation and higher air temperatures (see Chapter 10). This will have a significant impact on the thermal and lighting performance of buildings, resulting in overheating of those buildings that are highly glazed and un-shaded, and increased levels of glare that will impair productivity.

The extremes of weather, either much hotter, colder or windier, will influence the height of buildings (see Chapter 14). At the same time, higher fuel prices and prohibitive taxes on carbon emissions, coupled with insecure energy supplies will make new laws governing the form of buildings essential, not least to optimise the potential of the built environment to generate clean renewable energy.

New York on 16 August 2003 provided us with a nightmare vision of the future for our unsustainable buildings. When power supplies failed across the city, the appalling reality struck home: these buildings, without electricity to run them, became un-occupiable within minutes because their air became un-breathable.

Yet here is a city that until 100 years ago had no electricity in most buildings, and occupants were able to live quite happily through the summers with the building windows open and through the judicious use of blinds, awnings and shades. The really worrying thing about the New York incident was that this happened in mid-summer when people could survive by sleeping on the streets, but what would happen if it occurred in a cold spring, autumn or winter? Then the old, young, vulnerable would have died in their hundreds on the steps of buildings because they simply could not occupy the buildings all around them. The great dream of air-conditioned America has shown us its dark side in a city that, without power, could become a graveyard.

One of America's leading teachers of architectural building science was asked last year what one lesson he would like to pass on to future generations. His reply was:

"No more deep plan buildings."

If today's buildings are being built as if they will still be around by 2050 – as all buildings should be – then selection of building form, envelope and openings is the most crucial first decision.

This can only be achieved by reverting to a more traditional form of low-energy, shallow plan building, with opening windows, natural ventilation and daylight. The intelligently written, far-sighted local building codes of the city of Berlin in Germany (see Figure 21.1) point the way to a more sustainable – and comfortable – future.[1]

The traditional approach

Form played a large part in the comfort of traditional buildings.

Figure 21.1 Model of a building block of Berlin, demonstrating the shallow footprint of the buildings

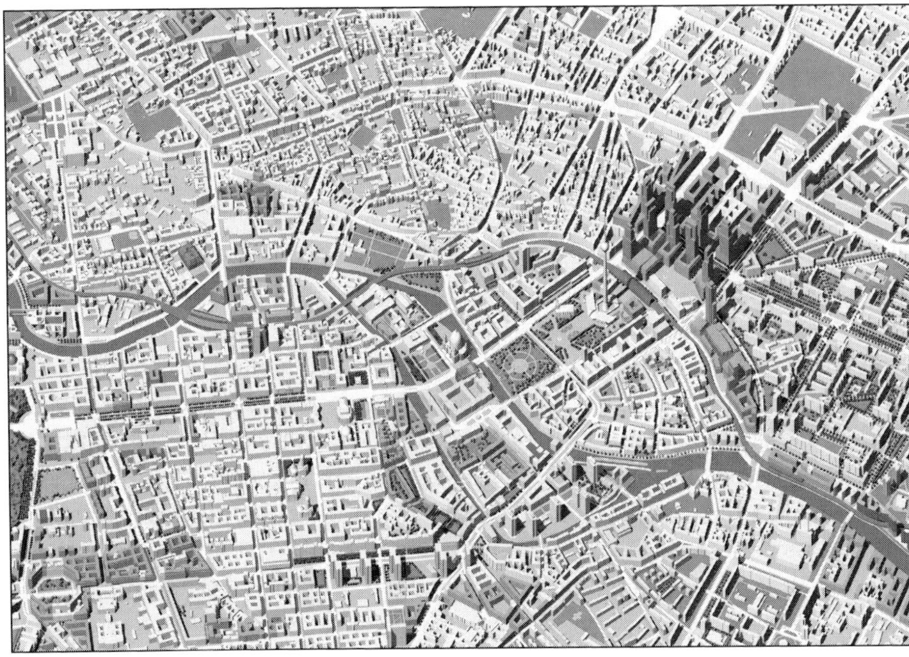

Source: Seratsverwaltung für Stadtentwicklung

A hundred years ago most buildings were lit by daylight, candles or lamps. Only a few homes had electricity, though more had gas, but very few had modern central heating, let alone air-conditioning. Windows had to provide adequate light during daytime, but they also had to maximise solar gain and minimise ventilation losses in winter, and minimise solar gain and allow for good natural ventilation in summer. The building forms used to achieve this varied according to the external climate – dictated by latitude, altitude, location, exposure, weather and the ambient environment.

Buildings evolved over time to optimise their effectiveness for their climate, and by the mid-19th Century central Paris boasted apartment and office blocks of up to eight or ten storeys,[2] while in the USA large office blocks of 12–23 storeys, with natural ventilation and daylighting, began to appear in the late 1800s.[3] Many of these buildings were shallow enough to allow for cross-ventilation and adequate light, and many were built around large central ventilated atria and light wells.

A local historic building type provides a good indication of what is particularly appropriate for the local climate, from the eaves details to the roof height and slope, orientation and size and location of windows, but we should remember that what was comfortable for our grandparents may not be so comfortable for us today.

The following brief summaries give an indication of the importance of designing for different climates. Suggestions for further reading about each solution are listed in Table 21.1 (see Further reading).

Very hot climates

In extremely hot countries such Saudi Arabia and Iraq it was important to "couple" the building to the cooler earth during the day and in summer, and to the cooler sky at night and in winter. In the heat of the summer the top floors of buildings were abandoned during the day, and they acted as a thermal buffer against the power of the sun. Buildings were also surrounded by thermal buffer spaces, such as the timber *mushrabiyeh*, to protect the building wall and windows from the direct sun while allowing the cooling breeze to enter the rooms behind. The "stack effect" was used in tall rooms and buildings to drive the hot air upwards out of the house and draw the cooler air from basements and lower rooms. So height, shade, breeze and the use of thermal buffers, as well as the thick insulating mud walls, were important to keep people inside comfortable in temperatures acceptable inside when the temperature outside was over 50°C. Courtyards, where they existed, were used to draw some light inside the building, enable cross-ventilation to take place and allow some loss of heat from the courtyard's walls to the night sky, being careful not to allow too much summer sun into the house at the same time. Thick roofs protected against the gruelling overhead sun.

Hot climates

In hot climates, where mean outdoor temperatures are more in the early 40s Celsius, courtyards could expand to allow more of the summer breeze into the house and buildings were lower, because thermal buffering from the roofs was not so essential, although they still need to be very efficient insulators. As the outdoor temperature approaches body temperature (37°C), then more breeze is introduced into buildings. Cool night air draws some of the heat from the thermal mass of the fabric, making it a far cooler radiant environment, and using the breeze for evaporative cooling the skin can be particularly effective at temperatures above skin temperature (32–35°C). (Below skin temperature people are easily cooled by convection where the passing air, at a lower temperature, draws heat from the surface of the skin.) Adapted populations can be quite comfortable at such temperatures. Indeed, in the right conditions, many would find this thermally delightful. Thermal mass is used here mainly for night cooling, but in high hot climates winter warmth is also a precious commodity.

Warm climates

There are many regions of the world with almost perfect climates, warm enough but not too hot, from Malawi to the Caribbean, and from the Maldives to Tamborine Mountain in Queensland. Buildings here have good roofs to keep off the overhead sun and are sprawled to encourage cross-ventilation, with high ceilings to keep the hottest air away from seated occupants. Even in such regions exposed thermal mass can be useful for night cooling on the hottest summers days.

Cold climates

In cold climates it is important to minimise the surface area of a building and with it heat loss. Buildings are sheltered against the most exposed directions for wind and rain and, where possible, use passive solar energy to heat the building. Even in the largest buildings there will be winter snugs, smaller spaces, with lower ceilings so the heat does not escape, where occupants can get near to the sources of heat such as a fire or a cooker, avoiding the draughts.

Solutions

Though not yet widespread, post-occupancy evaluation (see Chapter 39) is beginning to highlight the attributes of a building that promote quality of life, health and thermal comfort. These social indicators of sustainability are strongly linked to building performance – in particular, indoor temperature and access to daylight. Post-occupancy evaluation asks basic questions about people's feelings when they are in the building:

- How comfortable is the building?
- Is it too hot or too cold in summer?
- Is it too hot or too cold in winter?
- Is the air in the building fresh or stuffy?
- How much direct sunshine do you get in your space in (season)?

The answers to these questions, together with our current knowledge about the likely effects of climate change, point firmly in one direction: i.e. buildings with natural ventilation and as much daylight as possible, coupled with solar shading to avoid glare and overheating.

This ought not be too great a challenge for architects and engineers; after all, it wasn't until the 1970s in the UK that air-conditioning became a prerequisite for office buildings, mainly to counteract the effects of overheating caused by the trend for excessively glazed buildings. But, bearing in mind that extreme weather conditions, including higher summer temperatures, are predicted, there is a need for urgent action.

This re-focus can be driven by all parties in the construction process, particularly clients, who should be demanding buildings that are more sustainable. Local authorities – through the planning process – can also wield considerable influence. Planning officers and council members who sit in deliberation on proposals should be trained to understand about the performance of the buildings they decide on. The London Boroughs of Brent and Enfield are leading the way, with well-developed training and information programmes, and a requirement for "sustainability statements" to be associated with all larger planning developments.[4]

When recommending or deliberating upon a proposed development, planners must take into account future needs for naturally ventilated and daylit buildings, plus the current and future levels of noise and pollution adjacent to a site.

The rest of this chapter discusses potential solutions. Suggestions for further reading on each design issue are given in Table 21.1 (see Further reading).

Natural ventilation

When it comes to comfort, the last thing we should think is that installing air-conditioning is an appropriate solution. Heating and ventilation engineers may well find it easier to do their calculations for the air-conditioning systems if the windows are fixed closed but to do this in the 21st Century is utterly irresponsible.

When I worked for York, Rosenberg and Mardell (YRM) on the Basra Teaching Hospital in Iraq in the early 1980s I begged the engineers to put opening windows in the building. They refused and put fixed windows everywhere, saying: "In this climate you have to have air-conditioning, and we've designed in a good back-up generator system". In the summer of 2003 I looked in horror at images of the hospitals in Basra. They have no electricity, and little fuel for the back-up systems. Think of the waste – when the air-conditioning goes off the building very quickly becomes unoccupiable, as we saw in New York in August 2003. Are the Americans now going to go in and fill the country of Iraq with even more of these unsustainable buildings that are unusable as soon as the electricity fails?

No building should be built, anywhere in the world, without opening windows in the 21st Century. To do otherwise is to condemn it to a very short life. And existing buildings should have the fixed windows replaced with opening ones. We've done it here in Oxford when, in the 1990s, County Hall was refurbished. The result has confirmed the theory – post-refurbishment evaluation showed that people felt the indoor environment was more comfortable, not less!

With an eye to the future and the long-life of any sustainable new building, the brief should specify that the building must be naturally ventilated, or mixed-mode (using some air-conditioning at the hottest times of year), and the brief should also state that windows will be shaded from the sun in summer and excessive glazing levels be avoided (see box, opposite).

This will require a temporary revolution in the building design profession, as architects and engineers re-educate themselves on how to design passively cooled buildings but it will pay dividends. A study we conducted in 1998[5] showed that even by 2050, when the British climate may have changed considerably, it will still be possible to be comfortable in well-designed passive buildings.

What makes a successful naturally ventilated building? Emerging strategies include:

• careful window sizing and design

The LT method

The LT method[6] can be used to investigate strategic design decisions, particularly those relating to building form, façade design and building use, and to make comparisons of a number of design options. It is a simple manual procedure requiring no more than a pencil and calculator, and results are combined onto a single worksheet. Figure 21.2 shows a typical LT method analysis.

The LT method can be applied to a range of building types including schools, offices, institutional buildings and health buildings; and various versions exist for UK and European climates.

Figure 21.2 Numerous refurbishment strategies were being considered for a 17th Century dwelling. Using the LT method revealed the relative energy savings of each option, and the results clearly demonstrated the importance of 'form' issues such as buffer zones

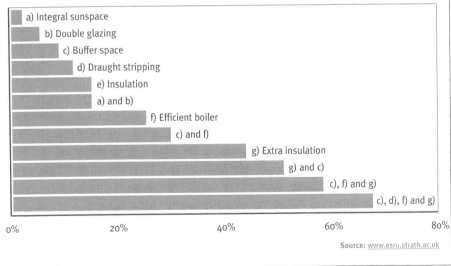

Source: www.esru.strath.ac.uk

315

- window shading
- room heights
- orientation
- shading
- building mass
- envelope design
- careful design of ventilation pathways for cross and stack ventilation.

Avoid glass roofs

A recent refurbishment scheme at the HM Treasury building in London showed how quickly problems can arise when climate and location have been overlooked. At the Treasury, an internal courtyard had been a key element in the natural ventilation strategy of the original building; but during refurbishment this courtyard was covered over during refurbishment with a clear roof. This roof helped to make it so hot in the building as a whole that it was impossible to occupy during August 2003. All the staff had to be sent home early because they could no longer work in the building.[7]

This same problem is experienced during hot spells in the much-celebrated covered court of the British Museum. Here, conditions become extremely uncomfortable on a hot afternoon, due largely to the radiant effect of the hot walls and ceiling and also the feeling of a lack of moving air in the space. The glass roof provides no protection from the strong overhead sun, and the curved shape of the roof exposes the maximum surface area to the direct rays of the sun. With a pitched roof or a see-saw roof at least large parts of it would be shaded during the morning or afternoon, but a dome maximises exposure. (That is why thick, well-insulated domes are used in hot climates, where they intercept nearly all of the incoming sun, keeping it out, and then dissipate the incoming heat so far above the head that its effects are minimised.)

The trouble with making a dome of glass is that very little in coming heat is filtered out, as fixed tight-skin transparent buildings, so they both act rather like a great big cucumber cloche or greenhouse – both of which would be unfit for human habitation during hot spells.

Even in the UK, avoiding the cucumber effect should be top priority. Thin tight skins made New York's buildings un-occupiable in August 2003.

So, glass roofs should be avoided at all costs, but we should also begin to question the use of high atria, where similar problems can occur. Hot countries have a better solution: a section of the insulated roof is lifted and surrounded with openings that draw the hot air out of a space, driven by the stack and the Venturi effect, while still allowing light to enter the space below, and air to leave it.

Radiant temperature and air temperature

A mistake some modern designers make – both architects and engineers – is to associate air temperature, in isolation, with comfort.

This is a significant error: the air may be at a perfect temperature but the radiant environment can be unbearable. I once saw a TV programme about a team of scientists building a cabin in the Antarctic. It was a beautiful warm day with hot sunshine, and while nailing a slat onto the cabin one team member made the automatic gesture of putting the nails he was not using into his mouth. The nails promptly froze to his lower lip and had to be surgically removed, as a result of the very bad frost bite. In the sun, his skin temperature was very warm, but the air temperature was well below freezing, and the metal nails formed a cold bridge from the air to his skin. In the same way the air in a room can be comfortably cool, but if the sun is streaming in to heat skin and surfaces it can create a very uncomfortable thermal environment.

A further location-dependent issue is that of re-reflected solar incidence. If heat and light reflect off an adjacent building, a pavement or a road onto another building, this can bring with it significant extra heat or glare (as anyone who has walked through a light beam reflected off a façade will have realised). Often this is overlooked in the original building design calculations.

Thermal mass

The issues of form, choice of materials, envelope and openings all influence the performance of the building at different seasons of the year and in different weather conditions. In addition the location of "thermal mass" in a building is important in relation to opening windows and glazed areas.

Thermal mass is basically any building material with a high thermal capacity that can store heat or coolth for periods of time according to its density, the amount of it in the building and its degree of exposure to sunlight, heating or cooling breezes. In good passive buildings with lots of well-insulated thermal mass the internal temperature can remain constant day and night, and throughout the year, running at around the average of the mean between daytime and night-time temperatures.

In winter, taking advantage of low winter sun angles, solar gain can be positively encouraged into the building and stored in the thermal mass to be evenly re-radiated back into that space during the night – a free source of winter warmth, like the brick in a storage radiator, only the energy used to heat it is clean and free.

317

Solar shading

Though thermal mass and good insulation are welcome, if such a building receives high levels of solar incidence in summer then it will heat up like an oven. This is where solar shading is so important, and increasingly so with climate change. There is an argument to be made that all windows should now be provided with external shading against the summer sun, particularly in buildings for the old and the young, because these people are the most vulnerable to heat stroke. Now may even be the time to ensure that every south-facing room designed for older people is provided with external shading. (It has to be shading outside the window, because if it is on the inside the heat has already entered the space and can't get out again.)

Appropriate planning guidance is needed on this issue, and eventually legislation will eventually have to be introduced to protect vulnerable people from the impacts of heatwaves, just as today there is legislation relating to cold and fuel poverty.[8]

One question remains: is solar gain and shading part of the envelope or the building form? The orientation of a building clearly relates to form. Distances between buildings, their slopes and orientation are crucial, in order to optimise the efficiency of passive solar systems, solar hot water and photovoltaic systems. If properly arranged, the building can also provide shading for itself by turning its back on the worst of the sun during summer.

Daylight

What was considered adequate light in the pre-electrical world would often now be considered unacceptable. Different cultures also have very different expectations for levels of light.

In the last 50 years or so lighting standards, developed by the artificial lighting industry, have become more and more prescribed but often appear to be unnecessarily high, leading to the image of empty city skyscrapers fully lit – powerful beacons symbolising the irresponsible consumption of finite fossil fuels by an unrepentantly profligate society. Contrast this with the sheer force of impact that can be achieved with small shafts of natural daylight, illuminating an altar or an *objet d'art* in a museum.

Careful design and management of a sensible daylight strategy for buildings is a key requirement for sustainable cities, settlements and societies.

The goal of providing light for a building, whether it is daylight or artificial light, is to enable building occupants to see and do what they want or need to, and to ensure an adequate, or heightened, quality of life in a building, but sustainable lighting strategies will have more ambitious goals including:

- minimising the use of fossil-fuel-generated energy for artificial lighting
- minimising the use of fossil-fuel-generated energy for associated heating and cooling cost resulting from poor fenestration design
- reducing discomfort to building occupants due to poor lighting design
- increasing productivity in building through good lighting design
- reducing health risks, such as eliminating excessive exposure to UV radiation in many parts of the world.

As with solar gain, the availability of light depends on may factors such as latitude, altitude, the local landscape and obstructions. The path of the sun over the year determines the availability of natural light at any one place as well as the characteristics of that light, which are also influenced by the local landscape features. Climate, weather and pollution also play a part. In Europe we receive typically between 20 and 70 per cent of what we might expect because of clouds, and in some areas of South-East Asia a similar reduction in available radiation occurs due to air pollution in cities.

The availability of light inside is also influenced by the form of the room, its orientation, and its fenestration. Whether that is adequate will depend on what tasks need to be performed where in the room.

The success of the lighting in a building depends on many different factors including:

- Glare – is it possible to work on a computer with the ambient glare levels?
- View – what are the outside views that one would want to capture?
- Need for privacy
- Ambience – what does it feel like inside?
- Security – can the windows be protected, how attractive is the building to thieves, and how likely is it to be vandalised?
- Safety – will excess glare endanger people, e.g. in swimming pools where glare affects the view of others?
- Exposure of a wall to the elements – will driving wind, rain or snow influence the window design and indoor comfort?
- Productivity –will the window design enhance or minimise the productivity of the occupants, e.g. by providing too much glare for computer users or not enough light for them to complete their tasks efficiently etc.?
- Will the lighting strategy make occupants feel more comfortable or delighted?
- Will the light make people more healthy? Studies have shown that naturally lit wards in hospitals with pleasant views increase the rate of patient recovery. (Some modern PFI hospitals are providing internal, windowless

consulting rooms that are making even healthy doctors fall prey to sick building syndrome!)
- How easy/possible is it to clean and maintain the windows?
- Heat loss and gain – will the windows make the space too cold in winter or too hot in summer?
- Orientation towards or away from the sun – which way are windows facing?
- The local requirement for breeze – how do the windows perform in the ventilation strategy of the building?
- Noise – location, size and composition of windows are important depending on whether you need to keep noise in or out.

Lighting quality cannot just be measured in "amount" alone, and indicators of good lighting should include:

- visual comfort
- visual delight
- average illuminance on the working plane
- uniformity of illuminance on the working plane
- luminance ratios within the space
- glare levels in the space
- direction of light and the effects of shadows
- colour temperature of light
- colour rendering of light.

The LT method can give a good feel for the success of a lighting scheme, and there are several, quite complex lighting programs to prepare the detailed lighting design of spaces, but equally it is possible to follow a few simple "rules of thumb":

- South light (in the northern hemisphere) is generally abundant and relatively uniform, and excess solar gain from the south can be controlled by overhanging shades. South is the preferred aspect for windows.
- North-facing rooms (in the northern hemisphere) are the next most desirable alternative, because of their exposure to less abundant, but more diffuse uniform skylight. However, the large net heat loss through north-facing glazing is still a disadvantage.
- East and west rooms (in the northern hemisphere) may only have half a day of direct sunlight, then at low angles that penetrate deep into the building, and for the western façade incoming sun coincides with the hottest time of the afternoon, creating a problem for the overheating of spaces.
- The "5/10 rule" for open plan offices (with high windows and a minimum

3 m floor-to-ceiling height): the first 5 m zone of a building with careful fenestration can be task lit largely by daylight, the next 5 m zone, taking you to 10 m from the window, can be partially daylit with supplementary artificial light, and the remainder of the floor will require entirely artificial light.

- A 12 m width of floor plan works well for daylighting a wing with cellular offices each side and a central corridor or circulation zone. This is the type of footprint that is now required under planning laws in Berlin for all new offices (see above).

References

1 *www.stadtentwicklung.berlin.de*
2 Gideon S (1967), *Space, Time and Architecture*, 5th edn (1st edn published 1941), Harvard University Press, Cambridge, MA, pp 739–775
3 Ibid p. 390
4 See Circular SPG 19 from the Director of Environment, London Borough of Brent to all wards: "Supplementary design & planning guidance on sustainable design, construction & pollution Ccontrol", issued Monday 28 April 2003 (download from *www.brent.gov.uk*; see also *www.enfield.gov.uk*
5 Roaf S, Hawes P and Orr J (1998), "Climate change and passive cooling in Europe", *Proceedings of PLEA Conference*, Lisbon, James & James, London, pp 463–466
6 For full details on how to use this method see *www.esru.strath.ac.uk/ Courseware/Design_tools/LT/how_to_use.htm*
7 *The Guardian*, 9 August 2003, p 3. See also *www.betterpublicbuildings.gov. uk/hm_treasury.htm*
8 Rudge J (2000), "Winter morbidity and fuel poverty: mapping the connection", in Rudge J and Nicol F (eds), *Cutting the Cost of Cold: Affordable warmth for healthier homes*, E & FN Spon, London, 134–143

Further reading

Table 21.1 summarises appropriate further reading for specific issues. More general reading is listed below.

Baker N and Steemers K (2000), *Energy and Environment in Architecture*, Routledge, London (includes a technical design guide, the latest version of LT and case study projects)
Littlefair P and Oscar Faber (1999), *Daylighting and Solar Control in the Building*

Regulations, CR 398/99, Building Research Establishment, Watford (Download this document from *www.odpm.gov.uk*)

Givoni B (1998), *Climate Considerations in Buildings and Urban Design*, John Wiley & Sons, New York

Loe D and Mansfield K (1998), *Daylight Design in Architecture*, BRECSU, Watford

Majoros A (1998), *Daylighting*, PLEA Notes No. 4, published by the University of Queensland, Department of Architecture (contact e-mail: *s.szokolay@mail-box.uq.edu.au*)

Moore F (1991), *Concepts and Practice of Architectural Daylighting*, Van Nostrand Reinhold, New York

Humphreys MA (1978), "Outdoor temperatures and comfort indoors", *Building Research and Practice*, JCIB, 6 (2), 92–105 (reprinted as BRE Current Paper CP53/78)

Humphreys MA and Nicol JF (1998), "Understanding the adaptive approach to thermal comfort", *ASHRAE Transactions*, 104 (1), 991–1004

Nicol JF and Humphreys MA (2002), "Adaptive thermal comfort and sustainable thermal standards for buildings", *Energy and Buildings*, 34 (6), 563–572

Rudge J (1995), "Why does it appear that the British have traditionally cared so little for energy efficiency and warmth in the home?" *Proceedings CIBSE 1995 National Conference*, Chartered Institution of Building Services Engineers, London, 2, 1–9

Rudge J (1996), "British weather: conversation topic or serious health risk?" *International Journal of Biometeorology*, 39, 151–155

Stack A, Goulding J and L J Owen (2001), *Solar Shading For European Climates* Energy Research Group, Dublin (for a copy, send an e-mail to: *erg@erg.ucd.ie*)

Tregenza P and Loe D (1998), *The Design of Lighting*, E & FN Spon, London

Building Regulations – related Approved Documents (see Appendix 2 for details)

A	B	C	D	E	F	G	H	I	J	K	L1	L2	M	N
					x						x	x		

Table 21.1 These publications provide more detailed guidance on the topics specified

DESIGN ISSUE/ SOURCE OF GUIDANCE	CLIMATE				NATURAL VENTIL- ATION	THERMAL MASS	SOLAR SHADE
	VERY HOT	HOT	WARM	COLD			
Roaf S, Fuentes M and Thomas S (2003) *Ecohouse 2: A design guide*, Architectural Press, Oxford	X			X	X	X	X
Edwards B, Sibley M, Land P and Hakmi M (2000), *Courtyard Housing*, Spon Press, London	X	X					
Szokolay S (2003), *Introduction to Architectural Science: The basis for sustainable design*, Architectural Press, Oxford	X	X	X			X	X
Hyde R (2000), *Climate Responsive Buildings*, E & FN Spon, London		X	X				
Mazria E (1970), *The Passive Solar Energy Book*, Rodale Press, Emmaus, PA				X			
Lawson T (2001), *Building Aerodynamics*, Imperial College Press, London					X		
Allard F (ed) (1998), *Natural Ventilation in Buildings*, James & James, London					X		
DETR (1998), *Planning for Passive Solar Design*, Energy Efficiency Best Practice programme, Reference ADH010, Action Energy, Watford. Download from *www.actionenergy.org.uk*						X	X
Thomas R (1999), *Environmental Design: An introduction for architects and engineers*, 2nd edn, E & FN Spon, London (reprinted 2001)							X
Stack A, Goulding J and Owen Lewis J (2000), Shading Systems, Energy Research Group, Dublin. *http://erg.ucd.ie*							X

The building envelope: insulation and infiltration

Related indicators

Quality of life; Health; Thermal comfort; Energy; Air pollution.

Related tools

Energy toolkit; Energy use in dwellings; Climate data tool; Post-occupancy evaluation.

Introduction

With the miracle of air-conditioning, predicated on the dream of endless cheap energy, came the belief that whatever the climate, any building type could be made comfortable by turning on the heating or cooling system. This worked well enough for over 50 years, but it is a dream that is about to end, as energy costs, insecurity of supplies and climate change become a reality.

From the late 1950s onwards building envelopes have become:

- thinner, with less insulation and, at worst, little more than a glass skin
- "tighter": offices around the world tend not to have opening windows
- more highly glazed
- less adaptable.

Poor envelope design is one of the main reasons why many UK offices became difficult to occupy during the summer of 2003, with enormous financial impacts on the business sector. One poll in London suggested that a third of workers would stay away from their offices during the heatwave,[1] and during a week when temperatures reached an all-time high the staff at HM Treasury in central London were sent home early (see Chapter 21 for details). Absenteeism costs UK industry around £1.75 billion a year, and peaks in summer.[2]

When temperatures soar, it is cities that fare the worst: one problem is that temperatures rise even more because of the "heat island effect" (see Chapter 10); another is that pollution increases significantly (see Chapter 17), and air pollution can enter buildings through open windows, and through air-conditioning system ducts and filters. In fact, in these conditions air-conditioning systems can magnify the pollutants, creating worse air quality than in a building where you simply open the window (see Chapter 8). In addition, air-conditioned buildings with sealed windows prevent occupants from feeling the benefit of a breeze, which is such an important factor for cooling the skin by convection or evaporation.

Temperatures soar in thin, tight-skinned, highly glazed buildings, but also the indoor air quality can become very poor. A heady cocktail of polluted outdoor air mixes with pollutants rising from internal finishing materials, machines and body odours, and can cause a serious increase in the incidence of sick building syndrome (see Chapter 8).

Conversely, in winter, the heat that is generated internally by people, machines and heating systems is often dissipated into the environment by radiation through poorly insulated and excessively glazed walls and by high levels of air leakage through the envelope.

In addition, modern building envelopes often have more "thermal bridges" – highly conductive pathways from the inside skin of a building to the outside climate across which heat can travel either inwards in the summer, or outwards in the winter.

Good building envelope design is absolutely essential for sustainable buildings, and the very poor standards of most modern buildings mean that they will become white elephants that will either have to be pulled down or be re-enveloped with more climatically robust facades.

The idea that sustainable building design depends on the design of the fabric of the building itself, and that a sustainable solution can be achieved by an integrated process where architects and structural and environmental engineers work together, will be hotly disputed by some architects (many of whom have few skills in the field of performance-related building design), and by engineers, who are typically paid on contracts by the amount of machinery they can fit into a building. Nevertheless, it is the truth, and the sooner this is recognised the sooner we will be able to develop new building types, able to resist all that climate change will throw at us, using less energy and contributing less to the problem itself.

What steps should be taken on the road to the desired high-quality building envelope? Ironically, the first step is to listen and learn from occupiers of current buildings – find out what they like and dislike.

Though not yet widespread, post-occupancy evaluation (see Chapter 39) is beginning to highlight the attributes of a building that promote quality of life, health and thermal comfort. These social indicators of sustainability are strongly linked to building performance – in particular, indoor temperature and access to daylight. Post-occupancy evaluation asks basic questions about people's feelings when they are in the building:

- How comfortable is the building?
- Is it too hot or too cold in summer?
- Is it too hot or too cold in winter?
- Is the air in the building fresh or stuffy?
- How much direct sunshine do you get in your space in (season)?

It is already clear that there are several key factors to the design of passive low-energy buildings in the future – building form, integrated thermal mass, glazing levels, and better building envelopes. The first three factors are discussed in more detail in Chapter 21. This chapter deals with the building envelope:

- insulation
- thermal bridging
- infiltration
- adaptability (opening, ventilation and shading options).

The section on insulation was written with Rajat Gupta, who works as a building performance consultant to local architectural practices and local authorities. He is also pursuing doctoral research at Oxford Brookes University on the subject of mitigating domestic carbon dioxide emissions, using a combination of energy-efficiency measures and renewable energy technologies.

The section on infiltration was written with Paul Jennings, who is a building enclosure integrity specialist with Retroke (Europe) Ltd.

Insulation

Buildings are sometimes described as the "third skin", and just as the Inuit people of the Arctic choose extremely good insulating material for clothes to enable them to survive in the extreme cold, so they also choose buildings that are made of good insulating material, and which are built to withstand bitterly cold winds. The British, being a pragmatic and economical nation, had a fairly simple solution to the problem of keeping warm – they didn't! They lived in draughty cold houses, often made of walls only the thickness of a single brick, and relied on radiant heat from fires for warmth.

As expectations of comfort, health and wealth for the ordinary citizen rose, so too have the indoor temperatures expected in buildings in the winter, fuelled by the growth of central heating, which is currently used in 92 per cent of UK homes[3]

Figure 22.1 Annual carbon dioxide emissions per annum from houses build to the 1976, 1982, 1990,1995 and 2000 Building Regulation Standards respectively. Note the reduction in emissions relating to space heating, while other usages has remained almost static

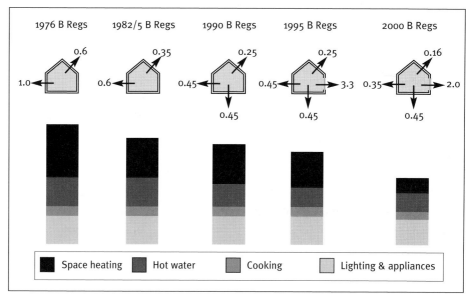

Source: John Willoughby

Figure 22.2 Insulation of the UK housing stock 1987-1998

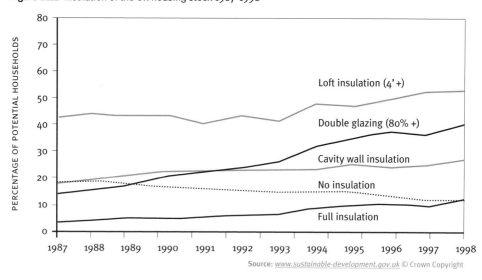

Source: www.sustainable-development.gov.uk © Crown Copyright

(although only 85 per cent of people over 65 have it). Equally, the minimum U-value – the thermal resistance, or insulation level – of floors, walls and roofs has risen incrementally with each new revision of the Building Regulations over the past 30 years. Government publicity initiatives, plus an increase in the knowledge of the general population on such issues and greater wealth, have encouraged people to insulate, double-glaze and otherwise improve their own homes (see Figure 22.2).

The UK government plans to continually upgrade the U-value requirements of buildings to the types of levels shown in Table 22.1. These standards have already been demonstrated in other countries, so they are already achievable in the UK, but changes in design and construction practice will be needed to achieve the cost reductions that will allow such standards to become routine practice. However, the advance notice being given by the government does give industry time to pre-pare for such changes.[4]

The UK government's principal domestic energy efficiency information, advice and research programme, the Housing Energy Efficiency Best Practice Programme (HEEBPp),[5] sets out standards for achieving best practice insulation standards in new as well as existing dwellings. There are three standards for new dwellings:

- "good" – a standard which will ensure that the statutory/regulatory minimum is achieved with specific additional constraints
- "best" – a standard that will involve the adoption of technically proven, cost-effective products and techniques that are already established on the market, and able to save energy without incurring undue risks

Table 22.1 The UK government's intention is to gradually increase fabric insulation standards (U-valves)

LONGER TERM INDICATIVE STANDARDS FOR FABRIC INSULATION – U-VALUES (W/M^2K)			
	STAGE 1		STAGE 4
	T*	T + 18 MONTHS	(AFTER ANOTHER 5 YEARS OR SO)
Roof (insulated between/over joists): all sectors	0.20	0.16	0.16
Roof (integral insulation in roof structure): dwellings	0.25	0.20	0.16
Roof (integral insulation in roof structure): non-domestic	0.35	0.25	0.16
External walls	0.35	0.30	0.25
Ground floors	0.30	0.25	0.22
Average of all windows, doors and rooflights	2.2	2.0	1.8

Source: Rajat Gupta

* T is the date when the new Building Regulations Approved Document L1 and 2 came into effect i.e. 1 April 2002 for England and Wales, and 4 March 2002 in Scotland.

- "advanced" – a standard for those who specifically wish to address sustainability issues and produce dwellings that are capable of achieving a minimum impact on the environment.

However, there is only one standard set for improvement of existing dwellings.[6] This is the same as the good standard for new dwellings, and is also the minimum standard as laid down by Approved Document Part L1. These standards are shown in Table 22.2; they indicate that future standards are already being exceeded by

Table 22.2 Comparison of the energy efficient standards for existing and new dwellings with that of a typical UK dwelling

ENERGY EFFICIENT IMPROVEMENTS	IMPROVED FABRIC U-VALUES (W/M^2K)		
	BUILDING REGULATIONS PART L1 2000/ ENERGY EFFICIENT STANDARDS FOR EXISTING HOUSING	BEST PRACTICE ENERGY EFFICIENT STANDARDS FOR NEW HOUSING	ADVANCED ENERGY EFFICIENT STANDARDS FOR NEW HOUSING
Cavity wall insulation	0.52	0.25	0.15
Internal wall insulation	< 0.45	0.25	0.15
External wall insulation	< 0.35		
Insulation between rafters	0.20	0.13	0.08
Insulation between ceiling joists	0.16	0.13	
Insulation above structural deck	< 0.25	0.13	0.08
Insulation above or below concrete slab	0.2-0.25	0.20	0.10
Insulation between joists of timber floor			
Low-e double-glazed windows with integrated draught stripping	< 2.0	1.80	1.50
ALL DOORS AND WINDOWS TO BE DRAUGHT STRIPPED			
Airtightness (at 50 Pa)	4 $m^3/h/m^2$ for houses with HRV* 7 $m^3/h/m^2$ for other houses	3 $m^3/h/m^2$	1 $m^3/h/m^2$
Ventilation system*	Extract and trickle, PSV, aPSV, HRV	PSV, aPSV, HRV	MVHR

Source: Rajat Gupta

Abbreviations: heat recovery ventilation system (HVR); passive stack ventilation system (PSV); assisted passive stack ventilation system (aPSV); mechanical ventilation with heat recovery (MVHR).

advanced buildings in the UK. Methods of achieving these standards are described in Chapter 33.

Thermal bridging

Thermal bridges are areas of the building fabric where, because of the geometry or the inclusion of high-conductivity materials (i.e. metals), the heat flow is higher than through the adjacent areas. Thermal bridges normally occur at junctions between plane elements of the fabric and around penetrations such as doors and windows, but in fact they can occur anywhere in the building envelope. There are often hundreds of thermal bridges in a building, in the form of metal wall ties, metal lintels that span across cavities and the many other metal elements visible on the facades of modern buildings. Besides leading to what can be significantly increased energy demand, the higher heat flow through thermal bridges lowers the internal surface temperatures, often creating local discomfort and commonly being associated with damp patches on walls and the occurrence of condensation and mould growth.

In current Building Regulations the effects of thermal bridging at junctions and openings are recognised in qualitative terms only, through encouraging the use of proven "standard details". The government has supported the development of an "atlas" of building details which shows their thermal behaviour in two-dimensions and using steady state calculations. Known as KOBRA, the atlas is available as a computer program.[9]

However, the UK government is currently developing a linear transmittance concept as a way of quantifying the effect of heat loss at junctions. This concept[10] may well be used in future regulations to quantify the effects of thermal bridges, a step thought to be necessary because, as general insulation standards improve, the importance of the thermal bridges becomes relatively much more significant.

Infiltration

Air infiltration is a term that describes the uncontrolled air movement through cracks, gaps and openings in the envelope of a building, driven by wind pressure and the stack effect. Air leakage (i.e. excessive infiltration) is a severe problem in buildings, where it is important to contain heat or coolth inside the building. Infiltration can account for between 30 and 50 per cent of heat loss or gain in buildings with poor infiltration performance. In pre-1960s buildings this figure was only around 30 per cent because the thermal performance of the envelope was generally poor, but in buildings built to 2002 regulations infiltration can account for more than 50 per cent of heat losses due to the significant improvements that have occurred in rest of the envelope efficiency since then.

British houses were known for being cold, draughty and poorly insulated compared with northern continental homes, which were much more snug, even in colder climates. It is difficult to justify the continuing low priority given to energy efficiency in construction.[11] One particular problem is that the existing legislation for controlling draughts relates largely to new construction, but the current rate of building replacement means that most people actually live in existing housing stock – much of which was built before energy efficiency requirements were introduced. Unless something is done to improve these dwellings, they will be draughty for many years to come.[12]

Today, many ventilation problems relate to inadequate air movement. This encourages damp, condensation, dust mites and mould, particularly in lightweight buildings with gas heating, where temperatures surge up and down (see Chapter 8). Installing new PVC windows, not opening them often enough, not insulating the walls so they remain cold, and then increasing the indoor air temperatures can result in almost immediate mould growth. Current Building Regulations require windows to incorporate small trickle ventilators, but what is really needed is to return to window systems with small areas that can be easily opened to provide background ventilation without chilling a whole room.

Excessive air movement, either through the building or within it (by convection), is probably the most widespread reason for the inadequate performance of the building envelope. The usual air change rate used in calculating heat loss is one air change an hour (1 ac/h) in the house itself, although this is modified if, for example, a balanced ventilation is installed with heat recovery system. The ventilation rate depends on the degree of air-tightness achieved in designing and building the envelope, the vagaries of the weather and the habits of the occupants. If, for example, people smoke or have pets the ventilation rate can be double or trebled (because of more frequent opening of doors and windows).

Not all air movement that affects the performance of thermal insulation connects with the inside of the house, so it will not be detected by pressure testing. It can travel from the outside, up through the outer wall construction and out again in most types of construction. Within the fabric itself very narrow cracks and very low air velocities can be important in increasing heat loss. It is common to see lengths of gaping vertical joints in insulation in the inner leaves of cavity walls, resulting in a very "leaky" wall. Partial cavities have an open cavity that is vented to the outside by weep holes and voids in the mortar, and these can form an effective air path from the inside to the outside of the building.

Infiltration is exacerbated when joints exist between any two materials with very different coefficients of expansion – so putting a plaster finish against a metal element that expands and contracts much more will result in a gap between the materials through which air can leak.

Timber, of course, is an organic material that moves according to the ambient humidity and temperature. With the moving air through the structure comes moisture that can condense out on cold surfaces, causing timber rot or mould growth. An important source of draught is likely to be below timber window sills, and special care should be taken with timber bay windows and dormer windows.

The use of dry linings of plasterboard instead of wet plaster finishes is increasingly common, but these two materials have other differing characteristics. Wet plaster keys into a wall and seals most draughts, except for the un-plastered perimeter strip at first floor thickness where fissures and draughts persist; but plasterboard is typically fitted proud of the wall, seated on dabs of mortar, allowing air flows behind it that can escape at ceiling junctions and around skirting boards.

There are also numerous services which penetrate the surfaces of rooms and so potentially lead to added ventilation – water pipes, gas pipes, electricity cables, telephone cables, heating controls, flues and chimneys, plumbing wastes and soil vent pipes, fan ducts and air bricks. They are installed by tradesmen, subcontractors or by public utilities, none of whom are normally concerned with considerations of energy conservation or even making good the hole they drive.

Controlling unwanted ventilation

A rule of thumb is that if you can feel the draught it is a problem; but even if you can't feel it, there may still be a problem, affecting your energy bills, your health and your comfort. So it is important to test a building, not only to see if the designer's predictions are met but to provide proof to the building owner or occupier that no infiltration problems exist. It is not uncommon for consultants to be called out to investigate why newly occupied buildings are almost impossible to get warm, and the answer is usually excessive air infiltration.

Pressure testing is done using equipment consisting of a fabric that is fixed onto a frame fixed to the external wall. The frame is adjustable in size, and fills an open external doorway, where it is clamped to the door frame. A powerful variable speed electric fan is fitted through an aperture in the fabric, together with devices to measure inside and outside air pressure and air flow through the fan (see Figure 22.3). All other external doors and windows are closed. Extract fans, waste plumbing and flues are sealed. The internal volume of the house is measured and the fan speed varied to give the relationship between air change rate and internal pressure.

Figure 22.3 Paul Jennings fits hi infiltrations test door onto the front door of the Oxford Ecohouse

A real advantage of testing is that by using a smoke puffer in the building during the test individual leaks can be identified and dealt with, considerably improving the air permeability of the building. An experienced person is needed to run the test and to interpret the results. Pressure test measurements are taken in m^3/hour/m^2 total surface area at 50 Pa pressure, and the Building Regulations (Part L1) require a proportion of all new dwellings to be tested. With smaller buildings such as houses this can roughly equate to the air changes per hour, but because the surface area of a building typically increases at a greater rate than the volume they are different for larger buildings.

For houses the following air change rates could provide an adequate rule-of-thumb:

- 1980s build – 7 ac/h at 50 Pa maximum
- 1990s – 5 ac/h at 50 Pa (max.)
- 2000s – 4 ac/h at 50 Pa (max.)
- 2010s – 3 ac/h at 50 Pa (max.).

At these pressures a higher air change rate means that the house is too leaky. Anything less is a bonus.

Adaptability

The need to adapt for climate change is all too apparent to those who have sweltered though the hottest summer in recorded history, in 2003. It is a subject that is rapidly becoming more important as the flaws of the fixed window, thin, tight-skinned building become apparent. The range of adaptive opportunities in the design of envelopes may include:

- opening windows
- windows of different sizes to provide background ventilation, comfort cooling, dilution of the polluted indoor air and give the occupants a feeling of control over their environment (an important factor in building user satisfaction)
- window shading to keep out the summer sun, awnings, shades etc.
- window shutters
- wall shading
- wall planting and trellises
- light shelves to keep the sun out while throwing reflected light into the building.

There are a number of constraints on the use of adaptive opportunities in buildings:

- Are they available?
- Can they be easily used?
- Do they interfere with each other (e.g. not being able to open the window when the blind is down)?
- Are there problems raised in their use (e.g. introducing street noise or pollution)?
- In a multi-occupied space do people disagree with their use?

It should also be noted that adaptive opportunities in buildings allow for considerable cultural difference in attitudes and habits of building occupants in different countries, as is shown by the results of a study by Nicol, Wilson and

Table 22.3 Why do people not wish to open a window? Clearly locations and cultural differences play a part

REASON FOR NOT OPENING A WINDOW	UK (% OCCUPANTS)	PAKISTAN (% OCCUPANTS)
Noise	56	28
Air quality	20	20
Other people	40	25
Air movement and/or temperature	2	26

Source: *The Dialectics of Thermal Comfort*, Furgus Nicol, *www.unl.ac.uk*

Dubiel in 1997.[13] People in a range of buildings in the UK and Pakistan were asked if they would rather have the window open, and those who said "yes" were then asked why they did not have it open. The responses are shown in Table 22.3.

References

1 Paul Peachey and Genevieve Roberts "Summer sun puts heat on British business", *The Independent*, 9 August 2003, p 5

2 Ibid.

3 Source: *www.ageconcern.org.uk*

4 Note that, currently and as proposed for Stage 1, the standard for roofs with insulation at rafters level is less demanding than if the insulation is between/over the joists. The current thinking is that there should be a progressive move towards roof standards that result in equivalent rates of heat loss wherever the insulation is placed. Such a change has not been thought practical for Stage 1 because the technical solutions are not yet in place to achieve U-values of 0.2 W/m²K or better, so innovation will be necessary before such future standards can be met. See Roaf S, Fuentes M, and Thomas S (2003), *Ecohouse 2: A design guide*, Architectural Press, Oxford, pp 75–99

5 This programme is managed by the Energy Saving Trust: see *www.est.org.uk/bestpractice* See also the non-domestic programme at *www.actionenergy.org.uk*

6 HEEBPp (2002), *Energy Efficiency Standards for New and Existing Dwellings*. General Information Leaflet 72, Housing Energy Efficiency Best Practice Programme, Watford

7 BRE (1998) *Domestic Energy Fact File*, Building Research Establishment, Watford, Chapter 3

8 Sources are Housing Energy Efficiency Best Practice Programme publications including General Information Leaflet 72 (op cit.); General Information Leaflet 59; Good Practice Guide 79; and Good Practice Guide 155

9   Copies of KOBRA and the EUROKOBRA atlas are available from Eurisol (the UK Mineral Wool Association), in conjunction with BRE. The Eurokobra atlas contains over 3,000 building details on which a thermal bridging analysis can be carried out including the condensation risk and the increased heat loss due to the thermal bridge. See: w*ww.eurisol.com/pages/eurokobra.html*

10 This methodology is described in BS EN ISO 14683, and is discussed in the ODPM document "Current thinking on possible future amendments of energy efficiency provisions", which can be viewed at *www.odpm.gov.uk*

11 Rudge J (2000), "Winter morbidity and fuel poverty: mapping the connection", in Rudge J and Nicol F (eds), *Cutting the Cost of Cold: Affordable warmth for healthier homes*, E & FN Spon, London

12 Boardman B (1993), *Proceedings of Neighbourhood Energy Action Conference*, Birmingham, National Energy Action (NEA), Newcastle upon Tyne

13 Nicol JF et al (1994), *A Survey of Thermal Comfort in Pakistan toward New Indoor Temperature Standards*, Oxford Brookes University, Oxford

On-line resources

An excellent discussion of the UK Building Regulations and insulation can be found at *www.eurisol.com/pages/building_regs.html*

The full text of the UK Building Regulations can be viewed and downloaded from *www.odpm.gov.uk*

For information on window opening and comfort, visit Prof. Fergus Nicol's Professorial Lecture at *www.unl.ac.uk/LEARN/www/staff/fergus_prof_lec/index.htm*

Further reading

Humphreys MA (1978), "Outdoor temperatures and comfort indoors" *Building Research and Practice, J CIB*, 6 (2), pp 92–10

Humphreys MA and Nicol JF (1998), "Understanding the adaptive approach to thermal comfort", *ASHRAE Transactions*, 104 (1), 991–1004

Nicol JF and Humphreys MA (2002), "Adaptive thermal comfort and sustainable thermal standards for buildings", *Energy and Buildings*, 34 (6), 563–572

Humphreys MA and Nicol JF (2002), "The Validity of ISO-PMV for predicting comfort votes in every-day thermal environments", *Energy and Buildings*, 34, 667–684

Jennings P (2003), "Infiltration" in Roaf S, Fuentes M, and Thomas S, *Ecohouse 2: A design guide*, Architectural Press, Oxford, 90–96

Mould A (1992), "Designing effective domestic insulation" in Roaf S and Hancock M (eds) *Energy Efficient Building: A Design Guide*, Blackwell Scientific

Publishers, Oxford

Rudge J (1995), "Why does it appear that the British have traditionally cared so little for energy efficiency and warmth in the home?" *Proceedings CIBSE 1995 National Conference* Chartered Institution of Building Services Engineers, London, 2, 1–9

Rudge J (1996), "British weather: conversation topic or serious health risk?" *International Journal of Biometeorology*, 39, 151–155

Szokolay S (2003), *Introduction to Architectural Science: The basis for sustainable design*, Architectural Press, Oxford

Thomas R (1999), *Environmental Design: An introduction for architects and engineers*, 2nd edn, E & FN Spon, London

Building Regulations – related Approved Documents (see Appendix 2 for details)

A	B	C	D	E	F	G	H	J	K	L1	L2	M	N
				x						x	x		

Renewable energy and photovoltaics

Related indicators
  Climate change, Energy, Land use

Related tools
  Life cycle costing, Energy use in dwellings, Climate data tools

---

Introduction

As climate change begins to take hold and fossil fuel reserves diminish, the world will need to be powered by clean, green renewable energy.

Over 160 countries have signed the Kyoto Treaty[1] – a testament to the seriousness of the global environmental problems we face. Notably, the United States, with just 4 per cent of the world's population, produces over 25 per cent of the world's greenhouse gases (see Chapter 10) but has not signed the Treaty.

Annex B of the Kyoto Protocol[2] lists 39 nations (including the United States, the individual EU nations, Japan, and many of the former Communist nations) and states the percentage by which each must cut its emissions of greenhouse gases (with 1990 generally taken as the base year). For example, most European countries should aim for an 8 per cent reduction. Under this list, the United States would be committed to a reduction of 7 per cent, to be achieved as an average over the five years 2008–12. Even if it eventually signs up to the Treaty, this target will be impossible to achieve, because energy use is growing rapidly in all the States of the Union.

The behaviour of the United States demonstrates either the hopelessness of the global situation or the importance of renewable energy for our global futures!

In fact, as early as 1992 some influential players in the energy industry realised that the future will be powered by renewable energy, as demonstrated by this very influential graph (Figure 23.1) developed by the Futures section of Shell International.

Figure 23.1 Projection of the 'sustained growth scenario' of renewable energy in the global energy mix made by Shell International in 1992, showing almost 50% of world demand met by renewables by 2060

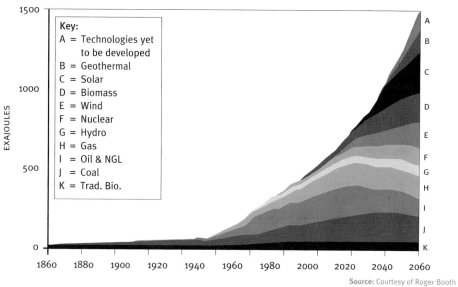

Key:
A = Technologies yet
    to be developed
B = Geothermal
C = Solar
D = Biomass
E = Wind
F = Nuclear
G = Hydro
H = Gas
I = Oil & NGL
J = Coal
K = Trad. Bio.

Source: Courtesy of Roger Booth

Most European countries are expecting to meet a minimum of 10 per cent of their energy to be generated from renewable resources by 2010. For example, Britain is hoping to meet this target and also a second, widely discussed, target of 20 per cent renewables by 2020. Denmark, however, is already on line to achieve the excellent target of generating 50 per cent of its 2030 energy needs from renewables, largely from wind power.

In the UK, Planning Policy Guidance 22 (PPG 22) addresses renewable energy, but this guidance is not yet sufficient to drive the massive change required.[3] For example, there is general agreement that PPG22's annex on photovoltaics is vague and does not give clear guidance to planning officers on the criteria for planning and photovoltaic installations, a problem which leads to substantial inconsistencies between different planning authorities, especially with regard to conservation areas and listed buildings.

However, many local authorities are now including guidance on the use of renewable energy in their local plans, suggesting that the use of renewables may constitute a "material consideration" when deliberating on planning applications, and schemes that use solar technologies, for example, will be favourably considered in the process. Oxford City, for instance, has ambitious plans to become the first Solar City in Britain, and has launched the Oxford Solar Initiative.[4] The Council's Second Draft Local Plan state that the City Council particularly encourage the use of solar panels, photovoltaics and, where appropriate, wind generators on all developments (both new and existing) and on residential and non-residential build-ings. And Cambridge City Council has gone one step further by including the stated requirement that all new developments should be designed so that at least 10 per cent of their required energy should come from renewable energy.[5]

The rest of this chapter concentrates on photovoltaics, or solar electric systems. These are potentially the easiest of all renewable electricity sources to embed in cities, and have the added advantage that they provide electricity at the point of use, on the actual buildings where the demand for energy is generated.

A brief introduction to photovoltaics

Edmund Becquerel discovered the photovoltaic (PV) effect in 1839, but it was not until 1954 that the first modern PV cell was created in the Bell Laboratories in the USA. Today we are all familiar with the idea that a watch or calculator can be powered by a PV cell; and improved production techniques are making larger-scale PV applications more affordable.

PV cells convert sunlight directly into electricity. They are made of semicon-ducting materials similar to those used in computer chips. When sunlight is absorbed by the semiconductor, the solar energy knocks electrons loose from their atoms, allowing the electrons to flow through the material to produce elec-tricity. This process of converting light (photons) to electricity (voltage) is called the photovoltaic effect.

Although solar cells were used to power the 1958 space satellite, *Vanguard I*, it was not until 1973 that "Solar one", the first PV house, was built by the University of Delaware using a PV-thermal hybrid system.[6]

PV solar cells are typically combined into modules that hold about 40 cells con-nected together to provide a "standard voltage" of 12 Vdc.[7] A number of these PV modules, or panels, are then combined to form a PV array. The flat-plate PV array can be mounted on vehicles and buildings, either at a fixed angle facing south (or north depending on which hemisphere you are in), or on a tracking device that fol-lows the sun, allowing it to capture more sunlight over the course of a day.

The amount of energy that a module and array can produce depends on the type of solar cell used. Common cell types include are mono-crystalline, poly-crys-talline and thin film amorphous cells,[8] with published manufacturer efficiencies of 15–17 per cent, 13–15 per cent and 10 per cent respectively.[9]

There is now a wide range of product types and colours, including:

- modules
- glass laminates

- sun slates
- solar shingles
- flat roof systems.

The actual size of the PV system will depend on where it is located, where it is to be installed, how efficient the panels are, what the electricity demand is, and how it will be used over the day and year. It will also depend on whether the PV system uses batteries or the National Grid to store the excess electricity generated for use later when it is needed. Electricity can be exported back out into the grid in a two-way metering system if so designed.

In construction applications the PV array can be designed as:

- the base load power system, generating only enough electricity to cover the loads in the building that are always on and producing no extra electricity for storage
- a partial system, where enough electricity is generated to cover the baseload, plus an extra amount that can be used for peak loads or to be stored in batteries or the National Grid
- a whole-building system,[10] where the array generates enough electricity over the year to cover all the annual loads and selected peak loads.

Figure 23.2 The PV roof of the Oxford Solar House was installed in 1995

In 1995 the first PV roof was put onto a UK house in Oxford (see Figure 23.2), more than five years behind the widespread adoption of the technology by the leaders in the field, Germany and Japan. The Oxford Solar House relies on solar power for electricity, hot water and space heating, and the PV roof can provide a maximum of 4 kW of power under ideal conditions – more electricity than the house uses over a year – and is responsible for emitting only 200 kg of carbon dioxide per year, whereas similar houses in the same road produce 3,000–5,000 kg.

Ten reasons why you should use PVs

1. PV systems provide *CLEAN* electricity without producing carbon dioxide (CO_2), the main greenhouse gas. It is estimated that for every kWh of PV electricity that is produced 0.6 kg of CO_2 is saved, with this figure rising to 1 kg/kWh when the PV replaces off-grid diesel. Energy efficiency measures can save up to 60 per cent of CO_2 emissions in ordinary UK houses, but using the sun's free energy this can rise to over 90 per cent.[11]
2. As global fossil fuel reserves diminish, solar energy provides an inexhaustible, universally available and increasingly cheap energy source.
3. Solar energy is the most acceptable of the renewable energies. The public like it, and want it on their buildings. A survey in Oxford found that 92 per cent of those questioned wanted more energy-efficient homes, 65 per cent wanted solar hot water systems, and around 20 per cent wanted PVs, even at current market costs.[12]
4. With PV, the energy supply is located at the point of demand so there are no losses incurred in transporting the electricity.
5. PVs can supply electricity to locations remote from a traditional grid.
6. PV electricity supply can be isolated from the grid supply and so provide a reliable back-up at periods of grid failure. PVs will also become more important where conventional grid supplies are unreliable (e.g. if the surge in demand on hot summer afternoons causes black-outs that shut down air-conditioning systems). In low-energy buildings cooling is easily achieved with PV-powered ceiling fans or passive heating or cooling system fans. (PV systems cannot run large air-conditioning systems, although great steps have been made in the field of solar cooling; see Figure 23.3)
7. PV systems are quiet, robust and require little maintenance or repair.
8. PV arrays are actually a building material and can be used as an external skin, so providing a prestigious alternative to traditional building envelope materials. They are considerably less expensive than many granite finishes, for example.

Figure 23.3 This polycrystalline PV façade of the Matra Library in Spain powers the desiccant air-conditioning system developed by Tony Llorett at Matao, Spain

9. PV arrays can perform a range of different functions – acting as rain screen cladding, roofing, sun shades, covered walkways, brise-soleil, roof tiling systems and motorway barriers.

10. Over 3 billion people today are not connected to conventional electricity supply systems, and PVs offer them the chance to have electricity.

Today, PVs provide power for a multitude of purposes:[13]

- atmospheric monitoring stations
- battery charging and maintainenance
- cathodic protection of pipelines and underground foundations
- ceiling fans for cooling buildings
- disaster power systems and civil defence
- disaster lighting systems
- electric fence charging
- electric gate openers on remote fences
- emergency lighting systems
- fans (small) in passive heating and cooling systems in buildings
- fire alarm systems (off grid)
- irrigation systems
- medical refrigeration
- microwave repeaters

- military target practice ranges
- novelty lighting systems
- pavilion lighting
- pond aeration systems
- portable electricity systems
- portable lighting systems
- power for remote buildings, including schools and health clinics
- radiation measuring equipment
- railroad switching and signal lights
- refrigeration for homes or villages
- security and parking lot lighting
- sign and billboard lighting
- street furniture and lighting
- telecommunications systems
- toys for children
- emergency power back-up systems
- water pumping from wells, tanks, rivers, and lakes
- water pumping systems for buildings
- weather stations.

PVs – an expanding market

The most commonly stated barrier to the greater up-take of PVs is cost. They are still relatively expensive in relation to the current low costs of gas and electricity. They are also most cost-effective when placed on very low-energy buildings, and at the moment there are not enough of these being built.

The cost of a solar system is directly proportional to how much energy is required, and the PV modules themselves are typically one-third to one-half of the total system cost. PV systems in the United States that generate 100 W or more generally cost between $5 and $30 per watt. Smaller systems are more expensive on a per-watt basis. In the USA today a small cabin system may cost a few thousand dollars while a typical household system could cost anywhere from $10,000 to $40,000.[14]

In the UK, the International Energy Agency (IEA) reports that average module prices during 2002 were typically in the range £3 to £3.70 per watt for reasonable volume orders.[15] For small orders retail prices range from approximately £3.8 up to £5.4, but lower minimum prices have been achieved. For example, the lowest price achieved during 2002 was for multi-crystalline modules at £2.69 per watt. Overall system prices range considerably because they take into account the significant differences in the projects, the level of integration and technology used.[16]

The other perceived barrier to the use of PVs is lack of availability: they can be difficult to get hold of, and it can be hard to find a local installer.

However, the targets set by the Kyoto Treaty are driving national governments and international organisations to seek new ways to stimulate the market – to boost demand and thereby reduce the unit price. There is now evidence that these initiatives are beginning to take effect.

The global market for PV power applications is expanding rapidly,[17] from 80 MW_p ($_p$ = peak system output) sold in 1995 to 200 MW_p sold in 2000.[18] This is a rise of 29 per cent per year, and over the next ten years this growth is predicted to continue at 15–30 per cent. Between 2001 and 2002 the "total installed capacity" in those countries monitored by the IEA grew by 34 per cent, reaching 1328 MW. Of the 338 MW installed during 2002, 79 per cent were installed in Japan and Germany; Japan now has over 310 MW installed, largely on homes.

As Table 23.1 shows, Germany dominates the European market for PVs. This is because government programmes promoted early investment. However, Figure 23.5 suggests that the picture is changing rapidly, with an exponential growth of the UK PV market since 1992.

The European Union has instigated the important process of benchmarking the performance of photovoltaics technologies in a rigorous programme under the

Table 23.1 Installed PV power and module production in the IEA reporting countries

YEAR	CUMULATIVE INSTALLED POWER AND PERCENTAGE INCREASE						POWER INSTALLED DURING YEAR	MODULE PRODUCTION IN YEAR
	OFF-GRID		GRID-CONNECTED		TOTAL			
	MW	%	MW	%	MW	%	MW	MW
1992	78	–	32	–	110	–	–	–
1993	95	21	42	32	136	24	26	52
1994	112	19	51	24	164	20	28	–
1995	132	18	66	29	199	21	35	56
1996	157	19	87	32	245	23	46	–
1997	187	19	127	45	314	28	69	100
1998	216	15	180	42	396	26	82	126
1999	244	13	276	54	520	31	124	169
2000	277	14	449	63	726	40	206	238
2001	319	15	671	49	990	36	264	319

Source: From the IEA Photovoltaic Power Systems Programme website, www.iea-pvps.org

Table 23.2 Size of PV market in European Countries

COUNTRY	SHARE OF TOTAL (APROX. 126 MW$_p$)
Germany	55%
Italy	15%
France	7%
Netherlands	7%
Spain	7%
Austria	2%
Finland	2%
Sweden	2%
Denmark	1%
United Kingdom	1%
Portugal	< 1%
Belgium	no data
Greece	no data
Ireland	no data
Luxembourg	no data

Source: www.mysolar.com

CORDIS project.[19]

Action in the UK

In the UK, lobby groups are working to encourage the implementation of a 70,000 solar roof market enablement programme by 2010, in line with similar programmes introduced by the Japanese, German, US, Italian, and Spanish governments. There are now several initiatives in the UK designed to promote the installation of PVs:

- The UK government launched a major PV demonstration programme in March 2002 in which systems up to 5 kW$_p$ qualify for a government grant of 50 per cent, and systems over 5 kW$_p$ qualify for grants of between 40 per cent and 65 per cent, depending upon the status of the applicant.[20]
- Under the Climate Change Levy, introduced in 2001, companies are exempt from paying the levy on any electricity used that is generated from clean, renewable sources.
- VAT on any solar installation now stands at 5 per cent (reduced from 17.5 per cent).[21]
- TXU (Eastern Electricity) was the first utility in the UK to introduce "Net

Figure 23.5 Trends in UK installed PV power 1992–2002

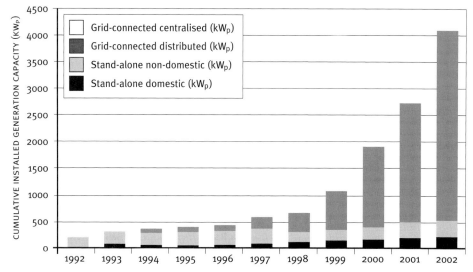

Source: *National Survey Report of PV Power Applications in the United Kingdom*, 2002, International Energy Agency (2003)
www.iea-pvpsuk.org.uk

Metering" in homes installing solar power);[22] and to pay the same rate for solar electricity as they charge for conventional electricity. Ecotricity, the first all-green electricity supplier in the UK has followed suit.[23]

There is one other driver that will encourage companies to invest in solar: public relations. There is growing evidence that companies who install PV gain kudos among increasingly eco-aware consumers, and that the "green" image can differentiate companies from their competitors.[24]

References

1   The full text of the Kyoto Treaty can be seen at *http://unfccc.int/resource/convkp.html*

2   A fuller exposition of the Kyoto Protocol can be read in Global Climate Change Treaty: The Kyoto Protocol (memorandum 98-2) by Susan R Fletcher, 6 March 2000 at: *www.ncseonline.org*

3   In 1995 Leichhardt Municipal Council in Sydney, Australia, was the first local authority to require that the solar potential of a site should be maximised as a precursor for the granting of planning permission to a new development. They have some excellent advice to offer on the basis of their experience in this field in "Putting it to the Panel – The Leichhardt Solar Experience 1995–99" – notes of a presentation prepared by David Eckstein, Leichhardt Council,

Strategic Environmental Planning. View the document at *www.leichhardt.nsw. gov.au*

4   See http://oxfordsolar.energyprojects.net

5   See report *Sustainable Development Guidelines* prepared by Cambridge City Council, 5 November 2002, available at *www.cambridge.gov.uk*. See also London Borough of Enfield in their Planning Policy Statement at: *www.enfield.gov.uk*

6   Source: *www.solarcentury.co.uk*

7   See "Further reading" for resources that offer a fuller description of how PV works and how to design a system

8   For an excellent description of the composition of the different types of solar cells see *www.pvpower.com/pvtechs.html*

9   Current and predicted future efficiencies of PV cells are discussed in the ESTIR Working Document (23/12/02) Scientific and Technological References; Energy Technology Indicators; Photovoltaics at *ftp://ftp.cordis.lu*

10   There are several PV array-sizing tools available on the Internet such as PVSYST, a program described in "Performance of grid-connected PV systems at different tilt angles", Baumgarten/JRC/040901, at: *www.solargenossen schaft.li*

11   RCEP (2000) Royal Commission on Environmental Pollution 22nd Report: *Energy – The Changing Climate*, chapter 7 at (*www.rcep.org.uk*)

12   Roaf S, Fuentes M and Gupta R (2002), *Feasibility Study for the Carbon Trust on Attitudes to Solar Energy in Oxford*. Available from the Author

13   Source *www.bpsolar.com*

14   The Clean Power Estimator (*www.bpsolar.com*) shows how much you can save on your energy bills by installing solar power in the US

15   Source *www.iea-pvpsuk.org.uk*

16   Various online tools for calculating the costs, including life cycle costs of PV systems, can be found at *www.eere.energy.gov*

17   The excellent IEA website has a full review of global PV markets and methods of reporting on them: *www.iea-pvps.org*

18   National PV capacity is usually measured in W_p i.e. the total installed peak load capacity, in watts, as defined by manufacturers' data (measured under standard test conditions of 25°C; above this temperature PVs generally become less efficient).

19   These performance benchmarks are discussed at *ftp://ftp.cordis.lu*

20   See: *www.est.org.uk/solar*

21   HM Customs and Excise: *www.hmce.gov.uk*

22 See Renew On Line, July-Aug 2000 Edition (no. 27) at *http://technology.open*
   .ac.uk/eeru
23 See *http://www.ecotricity.co.uk*
24 See *http://www.mysolar.com/mysolar/pv/country_uk.asp*

On-line resources

PV projects in any region of the UK: *www.pv-uk.org.uk*
Detailed glossaries of photovoltaic-related terms can be seen at
www.pvpower.com and *www.bpsolar.com*, the home page of BP Solar Division
(United States).
Full descriptions of how PVs work and how to design PV systems can be found at:

- National Renewable Energy Laboratory (United States), *www.nrel.gov*
- Center for Renewable Energy and Sustainable Technology (CREST) (United
  States), *http://solstice.crest.org*
- Solar power page of Wind and Sun Ltd, of Herefordshire, *www.windandsun*
  .demon.co.uk/solar.htm

Further reading

(Items marked * include full descriptions of how PVs work and how to design PV
systems.)

Chadwick H, Batley-White S and Fleming P (2002), "The UK planning process and
   the electricity supply industry – what role renewables?", *Proceedings of the
   Conference on Creating Sustainable Environments*, September 2002, Oxford
   Brookes University, Oxford

Krishan A et al (2001), *Climate Responsive Architecture*, Tata McGraw-Hill
   Publishing Company, New Dehli

* Roberts S (1992), *Solar Electricity: A practical guide to designing and installing
   small photovoltaic systems*, Prentice Hall, New Jersey

* Roaf S, Fuentes M and Thomas S (2003), *Ecohouse 2: A design guide*,
   Architectural Press, Oxford

Sick F and Erge T (1996), *Photovoltaics in Buildings: A design handbook for architects and engineers*, International Energy Agency, James and James, London

* Thomas R et al (1999), *Photovoltaics in Buildings: A design guide*
   (s/p2/00282/REP), DTI/ETSU, London

Planning policy guidance – related documents (see Appendix 1 for details)

1	2	3	4	5	6	7	8	9	10	11	12	13
X												

14	15	16	17	18	19	20	21	22	23	24	25	
								X				

Building Regulations – related Approved Documents (see Appendix 2 for details)

A	B	C	D	E	F	G	H	I	J	K	L1	L2	M	N
											X	X		

Sustainable products and materials

Related indicators
    Climate change; Energy; Biodiversity; Air pollution; Contaminated land; Water quality; Waste.

Related tools
    Environmental impact assessment; Life cycle assessment; Ecological foot-printing; Regeneration-based checklist; Monitoring waste.

About this chapter

This chapter is written with Julia Mackenzie Bennett, who is an architect working as a sustainability specialist with WS Atkins.

The subject of sustainable materials and products is vast – indeed there are a large number of books and websites dedicated to it – so we did not set out to cover everything here. Instead we have provided an overview of the very urgent reasons why we should all change our purchasing practices; have given a handful of case studies as a taster of the issues you will need to consider; and have provided an extended glossary and bibliography that lists some of the schemes and terms that you may encounter in your search for sustainable products.

Introduction

Each year we buy more products, use them in inefficient ways, throw more of them away. The only way to ensure that this does not cause an exponential increase in our environmental problems is to manage their performance in use and disposal. There are four main ecological impacts associated with this trend:

- the energy and water used in these products – to make, transport, run and dispose of them
- their toxicity in production, use and disposal

353

- the waste implications in relation to their disposal and landfill
- the use of finite reserves of raw materials.

Consumers wield considerable power. Households, businesses and the local authorities should promote sustainability by buying environmentally benign products. Focusing on product impacts also connects us to the working conditions of the people who produce them, touching on health issues, fair wages and contracts, and the avoidance of child labour.

Ethical and environmental purchasing does not harm jobs – it should generate business opportunities by making environmentally and socially sound goods more popular and profitable and thus more economically viable.

Green procurement practices are being developed around the world. The Swedish government, for instance, has a strong policy on green procurement, promoting and buying eco-labelled goods and services. A fair number of municipalities and cities throughout the European Union are developing and adopting policies on green procurement.

A number of local authorities in the UK are now developing ethical approaches to the use of materials, for instance on the specification of tropical hardwoods.[1] For example, Bristol City Council has adopted a policy for the buying of certified timber/wood products and fair-trade tea and coffee for the use of the elected council, and promoting fair trade together with partners in the city to the public. Furthermore, the UK government is promoting the Ethical Trading Initiative[2] with businesses as part of the commitment to sustainable development world-wide.

Building materials

Building materials account for 30–50 per cent by volume of all manufactured goods, excluding food production.[3] This reflects the enormous impact their extraction and production have on the global environment in terms of energy consumption and pollution. Therefore, the architects and building engineers who design and specify materials into buildings shoulder a considerable environmental responsibility when doing so, and for this reason the rest of this chapter focuses primarily on building materials.

Traditionally, vernacular buildings were constructed of local materials, the earth they rested on, the woods in which they lay, or the stones of the hills around them. Today, the world is our materials depot and we can, and do, exploit it, often without a second thought.

Real economies can be made at the design stage by using materials sparingly. It is surprising that many modern designers never consider rationalising their design to reduce the waste in construction. Why design a room so wide that every floorboard has to be cut to size? Not only does this cost more, it creates a huge amount of waste that then goes to landfill (see Chapter 20). Why not make the room a standard size? Why design a wall so long that for every course, corner and opening, bricks have to be cut, again wasting time, energy and materials? It used to be standard practice to design a brick wall according to brick sizes, but this is seldom done nowadays.

According to Bjørn Berge[4] a "minimalised" building (in terms of size rather than appearance) is far more resource-efficient than installing things like heat pumps, solar energy and superinsulation. This underscores what is probably the most important and obvious task for architects in the future: to create small buildings that appear to be as large as possible.

There is enormous scope for recycling non-construction waste for building purposes (see case studies, below). This helps to reduce pressure on ordinary waste deposits. Waste materials from one product can be used as the basic for new materials, for instance in the wood chip industry.

And we should not overlook the opportunity to recycle the buildings themselves. Using ADISA-constructions (Assembly for DISAssembly) high levels of recycling can be achieved.[5]

Of course, all the materials in building are recycled if a new use for that building is found. In Canada there is a move to promote large-scale renovations and "adaptive reuse conversions" (ARCs), which are proving to be the most cost-effective and practical means to preserve historical buildings and their materials. Examples of ARCs include a church converted to condominiums in Quebec City; a school to a regional building in Ottawa; the conversion of the Bank of Montreal to the Hockey Hall of Fame in Toronto; industrial buildings to sheltered housing in Winnipeg; the former Lieutenant Governor's mansion turned into a museum in Edmonton and downtown Vancouver offices refitted for use by the University of British Columbia.

What to choose

Choose healthy products

Building materials can affect our health in a number of ways,[6] as we have learned over recent years with scandals over products such as asbestos and internal finishing products with high levels of volatile organic compounds[7] (see Chapter 17).

Many products have an inherent toxicity[8] that can adversely affect building occupants, and the toxicity can be significantly magnified in buildings with fixed windows, where the toxins are mixed with outside air, already polluted, that may also have picked up more dirt from air-conditioning filters and ducts.

Choose durable products

How often have you walked past a building built in the past 40 years, and been horrified at how badly it has lasted? Look around and you will see stained concrete, once-shiny metals dirty and corroded and, as I saw recently, the mastic sealing the windows in a number of modern buildings in London dried up, cracked, and disintegrating, leaving actual holes from the outside to the inside of the building clearly visible! And how many designers who are about to specify a silicon mastic for the 50th floor of their new building check the manufacturer's warranty for ten years and realise there may be a real problem for the building in 30 years time when the mastic fails and, perhaps in high winds, the glass falls out?

A classic book on the subject was written by Stephen Brand. It details how just such problems should be appreciated and dealt with as a matter of day-to-day good housekeeping in design practices. (It is interesting to note that the book dared to point out that one of our top British architects designed buildings with astronomical maintenance costs. The publisher was made to destroy a whole publication run, and remove all references to the architect in the final edition, under threat of legal action.)

In the increasingly litigious construction industry we seldom hear details of how often buildings, materials or components fail, but that does not mean that such failures are not responsible for millions of pounds' worth of lawsuits every year. Unfortunately, due to this enforced silence, many young architects don't realise how important it is to take account of the durability of materials and products. They assume there is no problem, with often worrying consequences.

This is where we can begin to appreciate the true value of systematic post-occupancy evaluation (POE, see Chapter 39). POE can provide a process for learning and recording which building materials last well, with the least long-term maintenance and replacement.

Every client should ask his designers about how the building will look and perform in the climate of 2050, and we need a new approach whereby designers do not make their bread and butter from throw-away buildings, but one in which we all build as if those buildings will be inhabited in the climates of the future by our own grandchildren – as if it really matters.

Indeed, the impacts of climate change for buildings will be noticed indoors and out, as more extreme weather conditions – such as driving rain, wind, condensation patterns, frost damage, freeze–thaw cycles and drought – lead to accelerated weathering rates.

To make matters worse, the construction process itself will be affected by weather, and the building season may well change because work cannot continue in extreme weather, because the transportation of materials to site has been interrupted, because site working conditions become dangerous, or because the production of raw materials has been affected.[10]

Choose monomaterials

Bjørn Berge recommends that as a rule we use so-called monomaterials, and he makes a distinction between primary and secondary monomaterials. A primary monomaterial is pure, and consists only of itself as provided by nature, e.g. wood, straw and clay. In principle these materials can circulate time and time again, without losing their quality or value as a resource. A secondary monomaterial is defined as an industrialised but still homogeneous material, such as steel or glass. They are both materials that can be repeatedly recycled.

When monomaterials are combined in building, the following criteria should be satisfied:

- ease of dismantling
- ease of repair
- robust durability requiring low maintenance.

These three criteria are often closely related. If something is easy to dismantle, it is also easy to repair and keep. The same criteria may in fact be used for most products – from cars to computers.

There is, however, a trend to develop composite materials and products that solve several design requirements at once, such as roofing panels that combine waterproofing, insulation, and structural bracing. These complex products should be evaluated to assess whether they can be dismantled and repaired, or will have to be replaced if damage if they are linked in complex junction details will the whole roof have to be replaced if one panel fails?

Choose products with low embodied energy

Bjørn Berge[11] has drawn a useful model of the "cycle of materials" (see Figure 24.1). It illustrates the various points at which energy is used during the creation of a material or product. This is the "embodied energy"[12] – the energy used in the extraction, processing and transport of the raw material to site, and the energy used on site to install the product. Embodied energy is discussed in more detail in Chapter 30, but it is important for purchasers and specifiers to appreciate that care should be taken with how the term is used by some manufacturers. Some industries that develop products with high embodied energy products have their own definition of the term; they include the energy used in relation to the product over the whole life of the building.

Figure 24.1 Bjørn Berge's cycle of materials

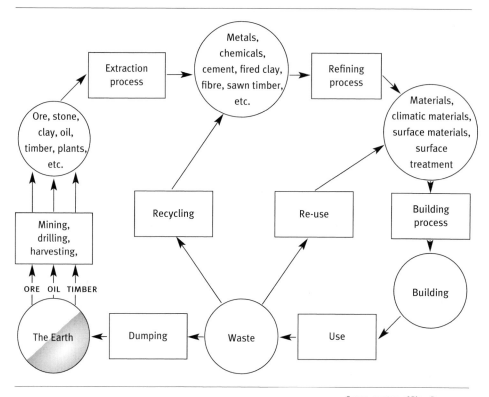

Source: courtesy of Bjørn Berge, 2001

Another issue is that a material from a local factory will look the same as a product that may have been imported from thousands of miles away. This dilemma is addressed in the new move towards "bio-regional" sourcing of materials: i.e. using local materials where possible to cut down on transport costs and stimulate local industries.

Finally, embodied energy does not cover the toxicity of a production process, the waste it creates, the environmental impacts of its mining and production. Waste minimisation in production and reuse of process waste can both significantly reduce the overall environmental cost of producing a material.

Choose products from renewable sources

It is sensible to use, where possible, building materials from renewable resources, such as timber rather than steel (except where it has been demonstrably recycled). However, even renewable sources of materials have to be checked, and many species of trees, particularly tropical hardwoods, are threatened.[13]

How to choose

Some designers will choose materials according to cost, despite the possibility that the cheapest material may not be the best for the job. Others will use the latest fashionable material, to test it, through experience, in the hope that it may provide a magic solution to a particular problem in a building, perhaps making it warmer, cooler, stronger or more attractive. A third approach is to go on using traditional materials that perform in a known fashion and can be safely specified in an understood context, in order to reduce the risk of failure in a building. But a fourth school of designers are re-educating themselves about the ecology of building materials and their impacts.

There are, however, few simple answers when specifying a building material. It is not possible to say that one particular material is the best solution in every similar situation, because building design is such a complex synthetic process. For every building, the context is different. What is the climate, the culture, the altitude, exposure, orientation, budget and function you are designing for?

The "international style" of design has resulted in buildings of the same form and components wherever they are located in the world, regardless of climate and environment. This is patently madness and results in buildings that are sub-optimal for every region, apart perhaps from the one they were originally designed for (but maybe not even there). Such generic solutions are favoured by the global players in the building markets, both designers and materials manufacturers, but are mindlessly mimicked by ordinary local developers who want to follow the fashion.

So the first question any designer should ask is: "Am I designing the right 'type' of building for the climate?" The issue of materials choice then becomes clearer.

Just as it is important to understand the invisible physics of the building – heat, coolth, light, sound, smell, pollutants and so on – so it is important to understand the multiplicity of characteristics that each material has. This requires work, time and tools, including good source books, methods for evaluating performance and impacts of materials, and a degree of care that ensures that buildings are revisited, their performance over time is evaluated, and the lessons learnt are reapplied in future designs.

The great problem with the drive to "innovate" is that designers do not have time to get to know the strengths and weaknesses of new materials, and by the time failures do become apparent the designers have moved on to using the next innovative material that may, or may not, work as required.

Using a palette of tried-and-tested materials makes good sense if the aims of the design include durability, robustness and the production of relatively risk-free buildings.

There is no excuse in the 21st Century for not understanding the environmental performance and impacts of the materials used in buildings.[14]

There is only one way to choose sustainable products and materials, and that is to answer these questions:[15]

- Raw materials. Are the raw materials either plentiful, or if not renewable? They should be durable products, easy to recycle, and suited to use in material-economising structures.
- Energy. Do production processes have low energy use and minimal transport distances?
- Pollution. Are the products based on fossil fuels and toxic industrial processes? If so the materials should be avoided. These should also be avoided in the stages of use, reuse and scrapping.
- International solidarity. Does this material take into account the north–south conflict and the physical, financial and health costs to the human beings of producing it?
- Human ecology. Are the processes based on face-to-face relationships? Technology ought to be suited to craftsmen and users, and production in smaller industries close to the consumer, if we are to achieve a really humane and sustainable society.

Case studies – opportunities for recycling

This selection of short case studies is intended to give you a taster of the very wide range of opportunities for reusing and recycling materials and products. There are many more out there – some are described elsewhere in this book. The underlying message is don't give up; new solutions are being created every day.

Timber

Norway is a heavily wooded country, with large pine forests in most districts. The local building traditions are based mostly on wood, a renewable resource, and the production of wood is usually simple and low in energy use. Timber is a durable material, and as long as it is kept as a monomaterial and not treated with fungicides and insecticides it will return to the natural cycles without causing problems. It can be used as a structural element, as weatherboard, panelling and, as wood shavings, as insulation. In Norway wood shavings from industrial activities are often looked upon as waste,[16] but pressed to a density of 150 kg/m^3 and with 3–5 per cent lime added to discourage rats and insects, they can be a very effective insulating material.

Newspapers

Cellulose fibre in the form of shredded newspapers is growing in popularity as insulation. With the application of relatively harmless additives, this material can be rendered fireproof and can be used in larger buildings. There are many manufacturers of this product, and it was used for instance on the Oxford Ecohouse.[17]

Straw

In Norway 600,000–800,000 tons of straw is burned on the fields every year. What a waste! Compressed bales of straw can be stacked up like bricks with a separate wooden construction to carry the roof. The surfaces are coated with a mixture of lime, cement and sand, and the material stabilises itself. In the USA, straw-bale construction is based on long-standing traditions. Between the two World Wars many houses, schools and military buildings were built in this material. Most of them are still standing. Recently a 75-year-old straw bale school in Nebraska was dismantled. The straw was fresh enough to be used as cow fodder.[18]

Earth

Earth, as a construction material (mixed with a certain amount of clay), has a low ecological impact.[19] Earth-building methods are highly refined and developed in un-industrialised countries, and interest is growing in Europe. There are several arguments in favour of earth constructions as a strategy for the future:

- They are based on resources available in practically unlimited quantities in most places.
- Only low energy inputs are required in the building process, approximately 1–3 per cent of that used in similar concrete buildings.[20]
- Earth houses are long-lasting if built correctly, and when the house is scrapped the earth returns to its original state without any degrading of quality.
- Earth houses are labour intensive rather than cost intensive.

Today approximately 30 per cent of the world's population live in earth houses. If these dwellings had been built in so-called modern materials like aluminium, plastic, or concrete we would have been far closer to a global ecological breakdown.[21]

Rubber tyres

There are over 121 million tyres on vehicles in Great Britain alone. The number of vehicles and distances travelled have more than doubled in 30 years, so more and more tyres are being used. It takes around 6 litres of oil to produce one car tyre, and fuel is consumed during their lifetime overcoming friction. To put this into perspective there has been talk in Europe of a 2010 benchmark for buildings of using 3/4 litres of oil to heat, cool and light a square metre of building every year as being an acceptable sustainable standard (44 kWh/m²/yr). As tyres are used, small particles are worn off, and these can pollute the environment. Pollutants from roads can be washed into the ground and rivers, and eventually to estuaries and the sea. Zinc, copper and cadmium from tyre wear all contribute to contamination of the environment by runoff from roads.

About 40 million car and lorry tyres reach the end of their lives each year in the UK. In 1999 the main disposal routes for about 427,000 tonnes of used tyres were:

- 29 per cent landfilled
- 27 per cent recycled
- 16 per cent retreaded for reuse
- 16 per cent underwent energy recovery.

The rest were marketed again as part-worn tyres, physically reused (for example weighting down plastic sheeting on farms), or exported.[22]

The European Landfill Directive bans the landfill of whole tyres by 2003 and shredded tyres by 2006. Without more recycling and recovery options the environment is at risk from illegally dumped tyres and potential tyre fires. There are

Figure 24.2 An 'earthship' building in Scotland built using recycled tyres

Source: www.earthship.org

more than 20 million tyres in semi-permanent dumps awaiting reuse, recovery or disposal, and there have been several major tyre fires in recent years. In Powys a tip containing 10 million buried tyres has been burning for over 10 years.[23]

In the face of such challenges great people come forward with great ideas. The Earthship organisation has pioneered the use of tyres as the primary building materials for their "earthship" buildings (see Figure 24.2). The only long-term problem is that tyres have some very toxic constituents and, just as the cosmetics industry has to face-up to the challenge of eliminating animal test, so the tyre industry will have to come up with a non-toxic tyre that can be used without compunction as a building component.

Recycling materials from demolition sites

In developing countries nothing is thrown away that can be used again, but in the richer countries there is a surprising growth in the market for demolition waste. In Canada, for example, there is a real market for "carefully planned deconstruction" and the reselling of used building materials, and this has resulted in the creation of specialist building supply outlets. Initially these retailers were operated on a not-for-profit basis and heavily subsidised by the government. Later, the private sector made significant inroads into the reused building materials market, demonstrating that recycling can be profitable, as well as good for the environment.

Happy Harry's Used Building Materials[24] is a good example of how the industry is dealing with waste more proactively. Happy Harry's was founded in Winnipeg by contractor/property manager Harry Bohna in 1989. The company now runs 20 stores across Canada, organised as an owner-operated association. As with any successful retail operation, Harry's has benefited from the buying power leveraged by a national chain. Working with its affiliate, the National Salvage Network, the company supplies a wide range of top-quality used building materials as well as a broad selection of liquidation goods.

The National Salvage Network often works with conventional demolition companies to help recycle and reduce the waste from their projects. The rapid growth of the Happy Harry's chain has dramatically increased demand for used building materials, and the company is now aggressively pursuing partnerships with other companies to source materials.

In addition to stock items such as windows, doors, cupboards and toilets, the Salvage Network also sources unique or architecturally significant artefacts from older buildings. Key projects include renovations to the Banff Springs Hotel, deconstruction of Via's century-old Winnipeg headquarters, decommissioning Harrod's at Toronto Airport's Terminal Three, and Woolco's Stores conversion to Walmart.

A recent project at Simcoe Place in Toronto broke new ground by teaming the Salvage Network with the Carpenters' Union, to remove the construction hoarding from around the completed building. In the past, much of this material would have been damaged and sent to the dump. With a little planning and skilled labour, over 350 sheets of 3/4-in plywood, 4,100 feet of lumber, dozens of steel ceiling supports and massive wooden support beams were saved for reuse.

Green power

In the United States, the Department of Energy supplies information on green power providers, products, consumer issues, and policies affecting green power markets.[25]

In the UK, green power has entered the mainstream, with several major energy suppliers now offering customers the option to purchase "green" electricity. One of the first schemes (Juice Power) was created by Greenpeace and npower, one of the UK's main electricity supply companies. Juice Power – enough for 500,000 homes – is generated at a windfarm off the coast of North Wales and supplied to the grid in the normal way. This scheme will displace 180,000 tonnes of carbon dioxide,[26] but consumers receive the usual quality of supply.

Sourcing sustainable products

There are many publications and web sites that discuss the multiplicity of issues in relation to the choice of a material. Many rate products in a user-friendly format to help inform the choices of busy professionals who do not have time to get to grips with the complexities of the labelling schemes.

The glossary and extended bibliography in Table 24.1 describes a selection of the labelling schemes and recycling initiatives around the world. See also Chapters 30–32.

References

1 Roaf S, Fuentes M and Thomas S (2003), *Ecohouse 2: A design guide*, *Architectural Press*, Oxford, pp 168–170
2 *www.ethicaltrade.org*
3 Altenpohl D (1980), *Materials in World Perspective*, Springer-Verlag, Berlin
4 Bjørn Berge, a Norwegian architect with the firm of Gaia Lista, is the author of the best book I know on materials: see Berge B (2001), *Ecology of Building Materials*, Architectural Press, Oxford
5 See Roaf et al (2003), op cit, pp 299–301, for an example of a Gaia Lista ADISA house; and Curwell S et al (2002), *Hazardous Building Materials*, Spon,

Table 24.1 A brief guide to labelling schemes and selecting sustainable products

SUBJECT/TITLE	DESCRIPTION	CONTACTS
Association for Environment-Conscious Building	The Association for Environment-Conscious Building (AECB) publishes a regular journal that includes much information on building materials and their proper use. The GreenPro website is produced in association with the Association for Environment-Conscious Building. The environmental criteria used in the GreenPro listings cover a broad spectrum of concerns for the environment and health of the building user, and each product is assessed by "attributes" – the more attributes a product obtains, the higher the position in the listings. Attributes: building friendly, fuel friendly, health friendly, nature friendly, ozone friendly, resources friendly.	*www.aecb.net* *www.newbuilder.co.uk/greenpro*
Construction materials	The Construction Information and Research Association (CIRIA) has published an extremely detailed assessment of individual materials, entitled *Environmental Impacts of Materials* (1995). Volumes A–F cover minerals, metals, plastics, timbers and paints.	*www.ciria.org.uk*
Eco-labels – Australia	The Australian government has adopted and developed the US Energy Star scheme (see below) and tailored it for domestic use. There is also an appliance energy rating scheme. See also the energy-related websites of individual Australian states.	*www.energystar.gov.au* *www.energyrating.gov.au*
Eco-labels – European	European eco-labels are awarded to products that prove to be environment-friendly at each stage of their life cycle: extraction of raw materials, manufacturing process, distribution (including packaging), use and final disposal. The EU Eco-labelling Board is working towards a comprehensive scheme to label all products with their "daisy" branding, but so far construction products have not featured significantly. The EU label is currently used for a wide range of products – from tissue paper to dishwashers. There are also national schemes, e.g. Blue Angel in Germany and Nordic Swan in the Nordic countries.	*http://europa.eu.int/ecolabel* Blue angel: *www.blauer-engel.de* Nordic Swan: *www.svanen.nu/eng/ecolabel.htm*
Eco-labels – UK	In the UK, many products carry the EU daisy logo, but there are other schemes in development (see energy-efficient products, below, for example). The *Green Claims Code* was introduced in 1998, to ensure that manufacturers present an accurate picture of the eco-benefits of their products. The Code was designed to as an interim measure, and has since been superseded by ISO 14021. However, the Code is still applicable to organisations that are not ready to implement the International Standard (copies are available from the Department for the Environment, Food and Rural Affairs). *Continued*	*www.defra.gov.uk* For a list of other schemes applicable in the UK see, for example: *www.brookes.ac.uk/eie/ecolabels.htm* and *www.envirolinkuk.org*

Table 24.1 A brief guide to labelling schemes and selecting sustainable products *continued*

SUBJECT/TITLE	DESCRIPTION	CONTACTS
Eco-labels – USA	The Environment Protection Agency of the US government has developed the Energy Star programme.	*www.energystar.gov*
Energy-efficient products	EU Directives 94/2/CE, 97/17/CE and 98/11/CE made energy-labelling compulsory for the following categories of products: refrigerators/freezers, washing machines, tumble-driers, dishwashers and domestic lightbulbs. The label has to be clearly visible on the product and must contain details of the technical features of the model and its energy consumption, a specific eco-label logo (if this has been devised) and a concise indicator of the product's energy efficiency (and of washing and drying efficiency in the case of washing machines and tumble-driers). There are seven energy classes, ranging from A (lowest consumption) to G (highest consumption). Products belonging to class A or class B are defined as "energy-efficient products".	*www.ukepic.com/ domestic.htm* is an excellent UK website that tells you how much energy products use, and also how much they cost, for a range of consumer electrical and white goods *www.sedbuk.com* gives full details on boiler efficiency and gives helpful advice on how to size the boiler correctly
Environmental profiles	The Building Research Establishment (BRE) has developed environmental profiles of construction materials, working in collaboration with manufacturers. BRE hold a database of the results of this ongoing research. This research data feeds into other BRE profiling products, such as Ecopoints (see Chapter 30) and the Green Guide to Specification (see below), but is perhaps too detailed for day-to-day reference, although it does provide the framework for comparative analysis.	*http://collaborate.bre.co. uk/envprofiles*
Ethical consumers	The Ethical Junction is a gateway to the ethical sector for people in the UK and Ireland. The Ethical Consumer website provides details of corporate ethics research consultancy services including a database for checking the ethical and environmental performance of companies (limited free access provided). *The Ethical Consumer Magazine* is a guide to a more environmental and socially aware lifestyle. It includes in-depth reports on everyday and one-off purchases – everything from banking to baked beans. Articles include profiles of the companies behind the brands plus tips on how to reduce environmental impacts.	*www.ethical-junction.org* *www.ethicalconsumer .org*
Fair trade products	"Fair trade products" are imported products certified by specific national labelling associations, such as Transfair, Max Havelar, Fairtrade, which are part of the Fairtrade Labelling Organizations (FLO).	*www.fairtrade.net*
Green Guide To Specification (The)	This publication rates construction elements against their environmental impacts. A simple A-B-C rating is used to indicate the summary of the environmental performance (see Chapter 30).	Anderson J, Shiers D and Sinclair M (2002) *The Green Guide to Specification (3rd Edition)*, Blackwells, Oxford.

Table 24.1 A brief guide to labelling schemes and selecting sustainable products *continued*

SUBJECT/TITLE	DESCRIPTION	CONTACTS
Green suppliers	This is a growing sector in the UK. Specifiers and consumers should ensure that products or materials sourced from such websites carry appropriate eco-labelling.	*www.greenshop.co.uk* *www.greenbuildingstore.co.uk* *www.greenconsumerguide.com*
Handbook of Sustainable Building (The)	This book uses the "environmental preference method" to compare materials and products currently on the market, and ranks them according to their environmental impact throughout the whole life cycle from extraction to decomposition. Each element of construction is then summarised in four boxes of varying colour from light to dark, representing light to heavy negative impact.	Anink D, Boonstra C and Mak J (1996), *Handbook of sustainable building: an environmental preference method for selection*, James and James, London
Organic products	Organic products are defined as products in which at least 95% of the ingredients are derived from agriculture using organic methods. They are controlled and certified by public and private certification bodies (each one has its own label). On 31 December 1997 a new organic product labelling system came into effect. From that date onwards it has been possible to find three categories of products on the market: organic products, products primarily made with organic ingredients, and products made with ingredients coming from agriculture in the process of adopting organic methods.	*www.ifoam.org*
Recycled products	In the UK The National Recycling Forum/Waste Watch produces the *Recycled Products Guide*, a searchable database of products and materials	*www.nrf.org.uk*
Timber products	Choose timber that comes from sources known to the designer, or from trusted sources such as the Forest Stewardship Council (FSC). The Forest Stewardship Council certification is an independently verified certificate for forest products which encompasses all stakeholders and interests in the social, economic and environmental spheres . It is the most sustainable label to have on timber and wood products (other labels and claims do not seem to offer an unbroken guarantee of the chain of custody from forest to retailer).	*www.fscoax.org*

367

London, pp 30–41

6 Excellent publications on the health issues related to materials include: Curwell S, Marsh C and Venable R (1990), *Buildings and Health*, RIBA Publications, London; Curwell et al (2002), op cit; Wooley T and Kimmins S (2000), *Green Building Handbook*, vol. 2, E & FN Spon, London; Pearson D (2000), *The Gaia Natural House Book* (first published 1989), Gaia Books, London; Borer P and Harris C (1998), *The Whole House Book*, Centre for Alternative Technology, Machynlleth; Roaf et al (2003), op cit

7 See Curwell et al (1990), op cit; Curwell et al (2002), op cit

8 Curwell et al (2002), op cit, and Wooley et al (2000), op cit, both include check-lists on the toxicity of materials

9 Brand S (1994), *How Buildings Learn*, Viking Press, New York

10 In the UK the most extensively used of all mineral products are sand, gravel and crushed rock, and some production of these may be interrupted by weather, flooding, sea-level rises and hot summers. See DOE (1996), *Review of the Potential Effect of Climate Change in the United Kingdom*, Department of the Environment, London

11 See Berge (2001), op cit

12 See Roaf et al (2003), op cit; Curwell et al (2002), op cit, chapter 3; and Wooley and Kimmins (2000), op cit

13 *www.panda.org/about_wwf*

14 See Lawson B (1996), *Building Materials and the Environment*, Royal Australian Institute of Architects, Canberra; Szokolay S (2003), *Introduction to Architectural Science: The basis for sustainable design*, Architectural Press Oxford; and Berge (2001), op cit

15 Berge B (2000), "Some ecological aspects of building materials", *Proceedings of the 3rd International TIA Conference*, Oxford Brookes University, Oxford, July 2000, section 4.01

16 Ibid

17 See Roaf et al (2003), op cit, pp 290–293; and Vale B and Vale R (2000), *The New Autonomous House*, Thames & Hudson, London, pp 147–171

18 See Lacinski P and Bergeron M (2000), *Serious Straw Bale: A home construction for all climates*, Real Goods Solar Living Books, Ukiah, CA; and Steen S et al (1994), *The Straw Bale House*, Chelsea Green Publishing Company, New York

19 See Minke G (1984), *Bauen mit Lehm*, Ökobuch Verlag Grebenstein; Norton J (1996), *Building With Earth: A handbook*, 2nd edn, Intermediate Technology, London; and Wojciechowska P (2001), *Building With Earth: A guide to flexible-form earthbag construction*, Chelsea Green Publishing Company, New York

20 Berge (2001), op cit
21 Minke, G (2001), *Earth Institution Handbook*, Cathederal Communications Ltd, Tisbury, UK
22 *www.tyredisposal.co.uk*
23 "How to set up a recycled/used building materials store" is at *www.happy-harrys.com*
24 *www.eren.doe.gov/greenpower*
25 See *www.greenpeace.org.uk* and Friends of the Earth *www.foe.co.uk*

UK legislation

There are numerous initiatives, strategies, programmes and laws on this topic, including:

- The Landfill (England and Wales) Regulations 2002
- Environmental Protection (Duty of Care) Regulations 1991
- The Packaging (Essential Requirements) Regulations 1998
- Producer Responsibility Obligations (Packaging Waste) (Amendment) (No. 2) Regulations 1999

For general guidance, see *www.environment-agency.gov.uk*

Further reading

Atkinson C (1993), *Ecolabelling of Building Materials and Building Products*, Information Paper 11/93, BRE, Watford
Berman A (2001), *The Healthy Home Design Handbook*, Frances Lincoln, London
Borer P (1993), *Energy Requirement for Manufacturing Selected Building Materials*, Centre for Alternative Technology, Wales
Chapman P (1974), "Energy costs, a review of methods", *Energy Policy*, 2 (2), 91–103
Connaughton J (1992), "Real low -energy buildings: the energy cost of materials", in Roaf S and Hancock M (eds), *Energy Efficient Building: A design guide*, Blackwell Scientific Publishing, Oxford
FOE (1990), *The Good Wood Guide*, Friends of the Earth, London
Hall K and Warm P (1995), *Greener Building: Products & Services Directory*, 3rd edn, The Green Building Press, Llandysul
Howard N (1991), "Energy in balance", *Building Services*, 13 (5), 36–8
Howard N and Sutcliffe H (1993), *Embodied Energy: The significance of fitting-out offices*, BRE 180/22/9, BRE, Watford
Marglef F (1963), "On certain unifying principles in ecology", *American Naturalist*,

97(897), 357–363

Pitts G (1998), *Energy Efficient Housing: A timber frame approach*, Timber Research and Development Association, High Wycombe

Ransom W (1987), *Building Failures: Diagnosis and avoidance*, E & FN Spon, London

Richardson B (2002), *Defects and Deterioration in Buildings*, E & FN Spon, London

Stevenson F and Ball J (1998), "Sustainability and Materiality: the bioregional and cultural challenges to evaluation", *Local Environment*, 3 (2), 191–209

Talbot J (1995), *Simply Build Green*, The Findhorn Press, Forres

Wells M (1981), *Gentle Architecture*, McGraw-Hill, New York

Wooley T et al (1997), *Green Building Handbook*, vol. 1, E & FN Spon, London

Mitigating transport impacts

> *Related indicators*
> Quality of life; Community; Health; Climate change; Energy; Transport; Land use; Noise; Air pollution; Waste.
>
> *Related solutions*
> Sustainable products and materials; Energy management schemes.
>
> *Related tools*
> Environmental impact assessment; Life cycle assessment; Ecological foot-printing; Regeneration-based checklist.

Introduction

In the developed world, the ability to move from place to place, and to ferry goods from one part of the world to another, is regarded as an inalienable right. Everyone thinks they have a right to drive up and down the motorways daily, from one side of town to the other to reach the supermarket, or round the corner to pick up a newspaper – with scant regard for the environmental damage they are causing or, perhaps more pertinent, the very real cost to the individual.

Getting goods from place to place has become big business. "Logistics" – the art of getting things to a place on time – has become a huge industry which, until recently, few had heard of. The UK foot-and-mouth crisis of 2001 provided an excellent example of the sheer madness of current behaviour. Then the public heard, probably for the first time, how livestock is transported – usually in small numbers, by road – up and down Britain to various markets and "holding centres", and at each stopping place the "value" (cost) of the stock rises as another intermediary adds on a fee. The movements apparently benefit no-one but the hauliers (and the retailers) – small farmers certainly don't gain from this system.

The surprising fact about transport is that people do not seem to be aware of the real cost of their actions. Well, they are aware that traffic jams are now a fact of life, and that roadworks are endemic; and thousands are happy to turn out in protest against a small increase in fuel tax. But how many people have stopped to consider the real price they pay for the privilege of driving a car? Most people only think of the cost of the vehicle, repairs, insurance, fuel and road tax (and they complain bitterly when these rise). But what about the invisible costs, which must surely run to many £100s per year per person in the UK? These include: road building and maintenance; installation and maintenance of signage, signals and "traffic calming" measures; policing and emergency services for accidents; policing costs for highway patrols; health-care costs for injuries and chronic illnesses (caused by traffic-related pollution); business costs in terms of lost time and absenteeism ... and many more.[1]

Sustainable transport does not mean no "transport". There are plenty of ways that we can move about in a less damaging – and less expensive – way. The key is to give people more options; to make public transport more accessible and convenient. Better still, to minimise the number of journeys people need to make.

This chapter discusses some ideas for minimising the impacts of transport. But travel – in all its forms – is an integral part of daily life, so readers are strongly advised to read Chapters 13 and 17, which discuss transport issues in more detail, and also to read Kevin Paulson's case study in Chapter 31, which describes a technique for analysing the transport impacts of an organisation or planned development.

Regional and city-level solutions

Once again local authorities are taking the lead in the sustainability challenge. Many are introducing sensible policies to reduce transport impacts. However, every region has different physical, social and economic characteristics, so each regional and local transport strategy will have different emphases. Nevertheless, their key concerns are similar and include reducing:

- damage to the physical and ecological environment, including landscapes and plant and animal populations
- air pollution, to which transport is a major contributor
- greenhouse gas emissions, for which transport in the UK accounts for around 23 per cent
- noise – a growing problem, even in rural areas, where the fastest-growing cause is an increase in visitor numbers (a result of the successful leisure industry)
- damage to health

- other impacts such as the high level of aggregates used for road building.

Clearly, local transport departments cannot act in isolation; they must work closely with other policy-making departments. This is usually achieved through a "local transport plan". In Oxfordshire, for example, the local authority's Local Transport Plan (2001–06) covers many cross-departmental issues:

- climate change
- air quality
- health
- social inclusion
- disability
- road safety
- work and school journey reduction
- modes of transport – walking and cycling, two-wheelers, buses and taxis, passenger rail transport
- highways
- rail freight
- waterways
- parking
- traffic management.

Each issue will require detailed assessments and policies for the areas, and a range of strategies to reduce transport impacts at every level.[2]

Published in 1999, the Ninth Report of the Select Committee on Environment, Transport and Regional Affairs[3] made the following recommendations to government:

- "*Forbid future out-of-town or edge-of-town shopping centres or other developments which generate large amounts of private car travel, regardless of whether or not they are in public transport corridors;*
- *Stress the importance of concentrating new hospitals, schools, office, leisure, and retail developments at major public transport interchanges; such developments should be safe and pleasant to reach by foot or on cycle-cycle tracks and segregated foot paths will normally be a requirement; and*
- *Insist on appropriate parking provision at new developments; more restrictive standards were proposed to be applied at most sites – both to encourage greater use of alternatives to the car and ensure a higher density of development; however, it was considered important that parking provision at new developments in city centres take into account the needs of urban regeneration so that customers are not attracted to out-of-town centres ...*

- "...Insist that the preferred locations for new housing are those where the need to travel in general, and travel by car in particular, is reduced, and where there are good alternatives to the car;
- Ensure that most new housing is built on brownfield sites in urban areas – in some regions with a plethora of brownfield sites, such as the North West, North and Yorkshire and Humberside there is no need to build homes on greenfield sites;
- Permit new housing to be built in rural locations, only to meet local needs;
- Insist that, where there has to be new housing development on greenfield sites, the great majority of it is at edge-of-town locations;
- Ensure that new housing is built to higher and more appropriate densities than at present; and
- Replace minimum standards for parking provision by maximum standards."

It also suggested that home delivery strategies be an element of local transport plans.[4]

The Select Committee also noted that a key publication in the planning process is *Design Bulletin 32*, and a companion Guide published by the Institution of Civil Engineers: *Places, Streets and Movement*.[5] These documents deal with the emerging priorities of mixed-use developments and residential layouts, and build on the experience of innovative developments such as Poundbury, on the edge of Dorchester (see Figure 25.1).

In March 2000 the government published revised guidance on housing (Planning Policy Guidance Note 3) and this was followed a year later by PPG13 on Transport. These PPGs incorporate many of the recommendations made by the Select Committee in 1999.

Strategies for buildings and businesses

Businesses that are planning to move to different premises, or commission a new building, should now be thinking about the transport impacts of their decisions.

Informal evidence from colleagues who conduct occupant evaluations suggests that there is a growing trend amongst workers in the UK to have their work located on good public transport routes rather than in isolated greenfield sites. And there is increasing emphasis, among businesses and their employees, on minimising journey lengths and times to buildings. There is a substantial amount of ongoing research into the optimal patterns to reduce transport impacts of buildings and settlements,[6] but clients can investigate potential impacts themselves in a fairly

Figure 25.1 Poundbury, Dorchester, is cited by the Select Committee on Environment, Transport and Rural Affairs as an exemplar of local transport management

rudimentary way, as discussed in Chapter 31 (Case study).

For established buildings there is much that can be done through good management. For example, the Environmental Forum at Oxford Brookes University undertook a major analysis of the transport impacts of its various campuses in the 1990s. Under the direction of Professor John Glasson the staff and students of the University were surveyed, and the results of this work were used to:

- complete an ecological footprint of the University's transport impacts (see Chapter 31 for methodology)
- inform the Green Commuter Plan for the University, completed in 1999.

Oxford Brookes University is a major land user and employer, generating over 2,000 jobs and annual income to Oxfordshire of approximately £100 million. The university quite clearly has impacts in many ways. An institution with over 1,800 staff and over 14,500 students generates many daily traffic movements, by a variety of modes.

The purpose of the Green Commuter Plan was to develop a strategy for a more sustainable approach to the transport activities of the university within the context of university, local authority, central government and other considerations.

It draws on the findings of a major staff and student survey, completed in 1998, which established baseline data on travel patterns. The research team also gathered information about people's views on future transport options, and provided an overview on options to reduce the use of the private car, and on attitudes to such options.

The plan sets out a proposed travel and transport strategy, emphasising that any such strategy must be capable of adaptation – building and developing over time in line with the interests of various parties, resources and management practicalities. The final section of the plan provides a framework for implementation, and for complementary measures and collaborative working with other key stakeholders involved including, in particular, the local authorities and the local hospital trusts.[7]

The plan demonstrates that there are a number of ways that larger businesses can influence transport behaviour among their clients and employees. Strategies in the plan include:

- Provide new bus routes.
- Negotiate discounted public transport fares.
- Improve support for cycling.
- Review staff parking permits.
- Consult and agree parking charge system.
- Develop a car share system.
- Explore scope for more flexitime and home working.

For businesses and organisations that are heavy users of transport – for goods or people – there are many ways to reduce the impact of their operations (see Chapter 26 and reference 8).

Personal strategies

At a time when our standard of living is going up so rapidly and travel is so closely associated with leisure as well as business, it is difficult to see how the impacts of our everyday travel will not increase unless people are willing to make the conscious decision to travel in lower-impact vehicles, not to travel, or to cycle, walk and sail more. Will it happen? Yes! We all want to survive – but have to be given the opportunity to do so by enlightened government and judicious personal choice.

There are many ways you can reduce your transport impacts. Most significantly, think twice about flying.

- Check how your own ecological footprint is affected by your life style and its

Table 25.1 Ecological footprints for different car types

	NUMBER OF PASSENGERS	LITRES/100 km	ANNUAL FOOTPRINT (m^2)*
Luxury cars	1	12	0.61
	2	13	0.33
Standard car	1	8	0.41
	2	9	0.23
	4	10	0.13
Economic car	4	5.5	0.07

*   See Chapter 31 for an explanation of footprint units

Source: Kevin Paulson, unpublished paper on transport ecological footprints

associated transport needs[9] (see Table 25.1, for example).

- Wean yourself off the car by walking, cycling, using public transport or getting a lift more often.
- If you have to drive, choose a low-impact – and that means low road-tax – car.
- If you think you can manage without it, sell the car.

Your choice of car could halve your annual transport footprint, with very little loss of amenity. Who in the UK could not resist a zero-tax model? I couldn't, and have an electric car powered off my PV solar electric roof. I also drive a second car (my "between-towns" car), a little 999-cc VW Lupo, the lowest emission conventional car in the UK.

I become very annoyed when I hear people say: "I wouldn't be without my people carrier" or "I would simply die without my ... (brand X) four-wheel-drive." What total nonsense! These cars are merely status symbols that consume huge amounts of fuel (see Table 25.2), and are particularly dangerous to pedestrians too. (Of course, it probably wouldn't harm me if I rode my bike to work every day – two miles each way ... but that's another story.)

Table 25.2 Comparison of emissions per km and tax costs for different car types

BRAND	MODEL	ENGINE CAPACITY (cc)	CO$_2$ EMISSIONS (g/km)	ROAD TAX PER YEAR (£)
Rolls Royce	Phantom	6,749	385	155
Porsche	Boxter S; Tiptronic S	3,179	268	155
Skoda	Fabia Hatch Comfort	1,390	180	140
VW	Lupo	999	139	100
Kewet	El Jet	electric	none*	000

* Powered by solar energy

Source: www.vcacarfueldata.org.uk

Figure 25.2 A Honda Insight at the Oxford Ecohouse. A dual-fuel petrol/electric car – and a very tasty ride! (Lent by Honda of Chiswick)

There are now some very tempting, high-performance cars with a bit of ecological edge to them. For example, for a while I drove the Honda Insight Dual Fuel (petrol/electric) – a lovely drive to it (see Figure 25.2)! There is also a very tasty Electric Lotus, and a number of large family electric cars are now on the road.[10] By driving an electric car over a year it is possible to save 62 per cent in energy use on transport in comparison to a normal car assuming the same weekly mileage over short distances.[11] However, electric cars are still in-town vehicles, say for the school or shopping run, as they are not yet suitable for long-distance travel.

References

1 Department for Transport (2003), *Transport Statistics for Great Britain (TSGB) 2002*, available at *www.dft.gov.uk*
2 See, for example, *www.oxfordshire.gov.uk/travel*
3 DETR (1999), "Integrated Transport White Paper" (Paragraphs 42–60), in *Ninth Report of the Select Committee on Environment, Transport and Regional Affairs*, The Stationery Office, Norwich
4 See *A Good Practice Guide for the Development of Local Transport Plans* at

www.dft.gov.uk

5   ICE (1998), *Places, Streets and Movement: A companion guide to Design Bulletin 32*, Institution of Civil Engineers, London

6   Recommended reading: Williams K, Burton E and Jenks M (eds) (2000), *Achieving Sustainable Urban Form*, E & FN Spon, London

7   View the details at *www.brookes.ac.uk/services/environment*

8   See, for example, government-funded publications such as *Transport and Environmental Management Systems*, *The Road to More Efficient Transport* and the *Sustainable Transport Fact sheet* – all available in .pdf format at *www.transportenergy.org.uk*

9   Calculate your ecological footprint at *www.ecologicalfootprint.com*

10 Choosing an electric car? See the website of the London electric car campaigner Simon Roberts, where you can also find out how to get an electric charging point installed in London: *http://website.lineone.net/~simon.h.roberts /ev/cccc.htm*

11 See BRE (1999), "Pioneering approach to housing design and use of an electric car; Case Study 11, Sue Roaf's Eco House", in *TRIP (Transport Related Environmental Impacts of Buildings Project)*, CRC Ltd, Watford (available from *www.bre.co.uk*)

On-line resources

Calculate car carbon dioxide emissions at *www.vcacarfueldata.org.uk*

Further reading

Black WR (1999), "An unpopular essay on transportation", *Journal of Transport Geography*, 9, 1–11

Curtis C and Coleman C (1996), *A guide to conducting a travel audit of employees*, School of Planning, Working Paper No. 166, Oxford Brookes University

Goodwin P (1996), "Road traffic growth and the dynamics of Sustainable Transport Policies", in: Cartledge B (ed), *Transport and the Environment, The Linacre Lectures 1994–5*, Oxford University Press, Oxford, pp 6–22

Sheller M and Urry J (2000), "The city and the car", *International Journal of Urban and Regional Research*, 24 (4), 737–757

Stead D, Williams J and Titheridge H (2000), "Land use, transport and people: identifying connections", in Williams K, Burton E and Jenks M (eds), *Achieving Sustainable Urban Form*, E & FN Spon, London, pp 174–186

Environmental management schemes

Related indicators
  Climate change; Energy; Biodiversity; Transport; Waste.

Related solutions
  Sustainable products and materials; Mitigating transport impacts.

Related tools
  Environmental impact assessment; Monitoring waste; Post-occupancy evaluation.

Introduction

Environmental management schemes (EMSs) are designed to enable businesses to put in place processes that will reduce their environmental impact over time, and they are part of the growing management phenomenon of process management – the best known example of which is ISO 9000, the de facto standard for "quality management". Whereas many international standards are about ensuring that products perform in a pre-defined way, the process management standards are about the way businesses behave. For example, ISO 9000 is an international "reference" for quality requirements in business-to-business dealings, and some 500,000 organisations in over 60 countries have adopted the standard.

The development of EMSs in the UK can be traced back to the "energy crisis" of the 1970s, when organisations began to search for ways to control their energy use. As other environmental issues rose up the agenda – chemical pollution being a particularly powerful driver – other management schemes began to emerge. For example, in 1991 British Standards introduced BS 7750, which contains the specification for environmental management policies and objectives.

By 1992, when the United Nations Conference on Environment and Development convened the "Earth Summit" in Rio de Janeiro, there were a large number of global environmental issues and recommended solutions to be addressed. Two important outcomes of this conference were Agenda 21 (see Chapter 4) and ISO 14000, a group of standards that focus on "environmental management".

The ISO 14000 family of standards are designed to be implemented in any type of organisation in either the public or private sectors (from companies to administrations to public utilities). Their aim is to minimise the harmful effects on the environment caused by business activities, and to enable the business to achieve continual improvement of its environmental performance.

Other standards relating to sustainability include the following:

- The Eco-Management and Audit Scheme (EMAS) was launched in the UK in March 1995. This provides a methodology for companies to establish and implement environmental policies, objectives, management systems and auditing procedures and also to effect a system of information disclosure to the public.
- SA8000, defined by the Council on Economic Priorities Accreditation Agency (CEPAA), is an international standard focused on workplace conditions in supply chains. It was inspired by the International Labour Organisation (ILO).
- AA1000, defined by the UK-based Accountability Foundation, is not currently positioned as a certifiable standard, but it could emerge as a possible common European standard for social, ethical and corporate governance activity.

Meanwhile, Sustainable Integrated Guidelines for Management (SIGMA) was initiated in 1999 by Forum for the Future, BSI-UK and several international business partners to try to integrate elements of ISO 14001, AA1000 and any other management tool/system that encompasses good environmental, social and ethical practices[1].

The business benefits

The introduction of standards can be a daunting process, particularly for new or small organisations, but there are very clear business benefits.

There are obvious environmental and financial benefits – efficient resource management will save money in the short term, and minimising environmental impact will reduce financial penalties such as the Climate Change Levy, Landfill Tax and so on. But additional advantages include differentiation in the marketplace and improved corporate image. The "green dollar" and corporate social responsibility (CSR – see Chapter 3) are becoming more important for:

- large corporations such as Shell or BP with a close eye on consumer attitudes
- smaller companies wishing to trade on their green credentials

- UK companies wishing to do business with organisations such as local authorities and public bodies such as health authorities, or other businesses who are keen to promote their own green credentials and practices by association.

The interesting thing is that companies which introduce EMSs gain in other ways too. There are recognised "virtuous circles", where lower waste and lower energy consumption can not only significantly reduce business running costs but also improve comfort and health conditions in buildings, and increased staff productivity and work satisfaction. This was well demonstrated when the ING Bank in Holland moved from its air-conditioned headquarters to a new low-energy, naturally ventilated and daylit building, which resulted in significant increases in staff productivity[2]. The new building uses 10 per cent of the energy consumed by the previous office. Most significantly, an adjacent bank constructed at the same time for a similar cost uses five times as much energy. The ING Bank's building has achieved:

- a 15 per cent cut in absenteeism, because working conditions are more comfortable
- a saving of over £500,000 in energy systems, and £1.5 million cut off the annual energy bill.

The total savings in absenteeism and energy are well over £2 million a year from this one office alone.

Introducing environmental management

Environmental management systems help organisations to define the key environmental impacts for a building, to agree acceptable benchmarks of performance for those issues, and to agree performance targets to reduce or manage those benchmarks. The system provides a framework for sustained effort to ensure that those targets are met and maintained over time.

The process of implementing an EMS depends on the standard you have chosen to adopt. Working towards ISO14001, for example, requires specialised management assessment tools. However, there are simple tasks that can be implemented quickly and can start the ball rolling. In the UK, government-sponsored energy and environmental efficiency programmes advocate a simple five-step approach:

- Gain commitment for the concept from a senior manager.
- Understand – investigate how environmental issues affect the organisation. This will involve collecting headline data on energy usage, materials

supplied, volumes of waste etc, plus investigating the needs and desires of the organisation's various stakeholders.

- Plan and organise a strategy for reducing or eliminating waste of resources. This step includes writing an environmental policy, if one does not exist.
- Implement the strategy.
- Control and monitor the processes you have introduced.

The final step "closes the loop" – feeding back into earlier levels to stimulate continuous improvement.[3]

"Understanding" is the key element in this process – you need to know where you are now, where you want to go, and how to reach the goal. Understanding the current position could be a relatively simple matter of looking at utility bills, or it could be a full-scale environmental impact assessment of the organisation, encompassing auditing, ecological footprinting, and post-occupancy evaluation (see Chapters 27, 31 and 39). Where the organisation wants to go is a question of benchmarking – comparing the organisation's performance with comparators, or with previous performance. The indicators described elsewhere in this book are an excellent starting point.

How to reach the goal is beyond the scope of this chapter, or even this book, but suffice to say that a workable management programme needs to be put in place, and annual audits of the action programme should be used to review the whole process. It is also essential that results are periodically reported back to employees, shareholders and customers as a demonstration of good financial management and environmental practice – and to encourage ongoing improvement.

References

1   For more information on the SIGMA project, visit *www.projectsigma.com*
2   Source: "Greening the building and the bottom line: increasing productivity through energy-efficient design" by JJ Romm and WD Browning, quoted at: *www.cityofseattle.net/light* See also *www.smartoffice.com/go2.htm*
3   For full details see "Going green – putting energy and environmental management at the heart of your organisation" (GPG 376) published by Action Energy (March 2004) at *www.actionenergy.co.uk*

On-line resources

www.envirowise.gov.uk

Further reading

Journal of the Institute of Environmental Management, Edinburgh, Scotland

Beggs C (2002), *Energy Management, Supply and Conservation,* Butterworth Heinemann, Oxford

BSRIA (1997), *Green Criteria for Buildings: A survey of reviews*, BSRIA, Bracknell

Capenhurst B, Turner W and Kennedy W (1997), *Guide to Energy Management*, The Fairmont Press, Georgia

CIBSE (1991), *Energy Audits and Surveys: Application manual*, CIBSE, London

Halliday S (1994), *Environmental Code of Practice for Buildings and Their Services*, BSRIA, Bracknell

Wever G (1996), *Strategic Environmental Management: using TQEM and ISO 14000 for competitive advantage*, John Wiley & Sons, London

DEGENERATION   SUSTAINABILITY   REGENE

-100 always
-75 usually
-50 sometimes
-25 a bit
0 balance
25 a bit
50 sometimes
75 usually
100 always

cleans air
cleans water
stores rai
produce
creates
consu
pro
rec
m

THE

pollutes air
pollutes water
wastes rainwater
consumes food
destroys rich soil
au   aste unused
detroys wild   abitat
requires fuel-powered transportatio
intensifies local weather
excludes natural light
uses mechanical heating
uses mechanaical cooling
needs cleaning and repair
produces human discomfort
uses fuel-powered circulation
pollutes indoor air
cannot be recycled
serves as an icon for the apocalypse
is a bad neighbour
is ugly

THE BUILDING

section 5
Tools and techniques

NEGATIVE SCORE
2000 POSSIBLE

DEGENERATION SUSTAINABILITY REGENER...

	-100 always	-75 usually	-50 sometimes	-25 a bit	0 balance	25 a bit	50 sometimes	75 usually	100 always	cleans ai...	cleans w...	stores...	prod...	crea...	co...	p...

THE SITE

- pollutes air
- pollutes water
- wastes rainwater
- consumes food
- destroys rich soil
- dumps waste unused
- detroys wildlife habitat
- requires fuel-powered transportation
- intensifies local weather

THE BUILDING

- excludes natural light
- uses mechanical heating
- uses mechanaical cooling
- needs cleaning and repair
- produces human discomfort
- uses fuel-powered circulation
- pollutes indoor air
- cannot be recycled
- serves as an icon for the apocalypse
- is a bad neighbour
- is ugly

NEGATIVE SCOR...
2000 POSSIB...

Environmental impact assessment

Definition

Environmental impact assessment (EIA) is the process of systematically evaluating the ways in which a project will affect the natural or man-made environment. It results in a report that can be used to inform planning decisions. EIA has been developed as a means of balancing the needs of development with the needs of the environment, and the process involves both consultation with, and the participation of, all stakeholders in the project.

In the UK, the local planning department will state whether an EIA is required for a particular site, based on the requirements of the relevant European Directives (see below) and under the requirements of the related UK Regulations. However, clients (usually developers) could also ask project teams or commission an independent third party to prepare an environmental impact statement (EIS) or to undertake an EIA, even if it is not required as part of the planning process.

Where a public enquiry is instigated for a major project, the EIA provides a source of information for the project and its contents are "material considerations" in the related deliberations (see Chapter 7).

Related tools

BREEAM; ENVEST; Post-occupancy evaluation.

Introduction

EIA was first developed in the USA as a result of the National Environment Policy Act (NEPA) of 1969. The NEPA requires an environmental impact statement (EIS) to be published before a development proposal is given permission to proceed. The EIS describes in detail the impacts that are likely to arise from the development, and decision-makers use this to weigh up the benefits and impacts of the scheme, with the theoretical aim of preventing environmentally unacceptable schemes from being built.

Many US states and other countries have followed the NEPA lead by adopting EIA processes through design advice procedures, regulations or legal enforcement.[1] By the end of the 1970s, Canada, New Zealand, Australia, Columbia, Thailand, France, Germany and the Netherlands had introduced some form of EIA-related legislation.[2]

In 1985, after 8 years of gestation, a European Directive (85/337/EC)[3] finally consolidated and unified the EIA processes for the various Member States.

Britain was relatively slow in its adoption of EIA, due to the belief that the environmental benefits and disadvantages of schemes were already assessed by the "effective" and "flexible" planning system in the UK, and it was not until the EC Directive of 1985 that UK legislation was introduced to require EIAs on major projects. Four local authorities – Cheshire, Kent, Manchester and Essex – prepared guides to EIA after the Directive was introduced, but only one remains. This one, the *Essex Guide to Environmental Impact Assessment*,[4] has been regularly updated since it was originally published in 1992 and is now a standard text on the subject, used by a number of local authorities.

EIAs and the planning system

An EIA is produced to quantify the likely environmental impacts of a project on any particular site and provide proposals on how these impacts may be mitigated within a planned development. The responsibility to produce an EIA lies with the developer, or a consultant acting on behalf of the developer. The rationale behind most EIAs has been to raise the profile of environmental concerns in the planning and operating phases of business. This is achieved via the EIS, which draws together the various environmental issues raised by the project.

Generally, an EIS describes:

- the "baseline environment" (the prevailing situation plus likely future trends if the project does not go ahead)
- the project itself
- the likely changes to the baseline environment caused by the project
- alternative designs for the project, where appropriate.

It will also propose mitigation measures for any significant negative impacts that the project might involve.

EC Directives 85/337, 97/11 and 2001/42/EC require that an EIA be completed for projects that are likely to have a significant environmental impact – projects with large areas, that use many natural resources, that produce much waste and pollution, that are located in environmentally sensitive areas, or those that have large, complex, long-term impacts. Such projects include major developments – airports, motorways, crude oil refineries, thermal power stations, iron and steel smelting works, timber pulp mills, electrical power lines, and even poultry and pig rearing installations.[5]

EC Directives 85/337 and 97/11 require that:

"The environmental impact assessment shall identify, describe and assess, in an appropriate manner . . . the direct and indirect effects of a project on:

- *human beings, fauna and flora*
- *soil , water, air, climate and landscape*
- *the interaction between the(se) factors*
- *material assets and the cultural heritage."*

This is the minimum requirement for an EIA, but there are many other issues that may be covered, particularly if the EIS is for "internal" use only, as shown in Table 27.1.

In the UK, local authorities are increasingly seeking EISs for smaller projects. To date, EIA has not been applied to individual buildings, but in future the EIS methodology may well provide a model for the "sustainability statements" that

Table 27.1 The issues that an EIA might include are described in more detail elsewhere in this book

PRIMARY ENVIRONMENTAL ISSUES (GLOBALLY AND REGIONALLY SIGNIFICANT)	SECONDARY ENVIRONMENTAL ISSUES (REGIONALLY AND LOCALLY SIGNIFICANT)	HEALTH ISSUES (SIGNIFICANT AT THE BUILDING AND LOCAL LEVEL)
• Energy (including transport, acid rain, greenhouse effect and resource depletion) • Ozone depletion (CFCs, refrigerants, air-conditioning) • Species diversity (endangered species and uses of some materials) • Sensitivity of site (rural and cultural heritage and SSIs) • Air and water pollution • Resource optimisation (employment, durability of design, material sourcing and reuse etc)	• Pollution impacts (soil, water and air) • Landscape • Communities • Planning (brownfield sites, transport implications of sites, town planning) • Local wildlife (not endangered species) • Materials (recycling, demolition, embodied energy) • Flexibility of fabric and plant (change of use of buildings) • Water conservation	• Internal and external air, soil and water quality • Lighting • Internal layout • Noise • Comfort • Odours • Healthy materials and building form • Quality of life

Source: Sue Roaf

are increasingly required within the planning system for a range of smaller developments, including those on environmentally sensitive sites (see Chapter 1). EIA is increasingly being applied to the strategic actions that precede, and set the context for, projects.

There is a strong argument for all potential development and redevelopment sites to be subject to EIA early in the design process, not only to inform the design and ensure that mitigation opportunities are optimised, but also to alert potential buyers, owners and users of the risks associated with the proposed developments. There are, however, concerns that in practice this may result in "planning blight" in some areas.

Ideally, all stakeholders in the building process, including the general public, should be privy to the EIA process for a site and retain access to the results of the analysis, possibly through the planning system. However, the developer is under no legal obligation to contact the general public and associated interest groups during the process of developing an EIA, although government guidance is clear about the benefits of doing so early on in the process.

Where an EIA is required, the developer must consult with a range of statutory consultees, including such bodies as English Heritage and the Environment Agency, from the outset of the project, and is under a legal obligation to supply them with relevant information, including a free copy of the EIS for their comments. These comments are duly considered by the planners before the planning authority makes its decision on the scheme.[6]

EIA in practice

It is particularly important to note that every site and building design is unique and will potentially generate a unique range of environmental impacts, but the underlying principles of the EIA are the same.

The process of EIA, which results in the production of an EIS, should be undertaken at the feasibility study stage, i.e. very early in the project's life, because the results can then be used to shape the project brief as well as to provide benchmarks that can be used for monitoring the impacts resulting from the project. In this way, the EIS can function as an environmental performance benchmarking tool; after project completion it can be used to assess the extent to which the mitigation aspirations of the project were met. In fact, the EIS can then be developed for use as the basis for regular monitoring of the project's impacts over its life within the framework of an environmental management scheme (see Chapter 26).

The production of the EIS is part of the four-stage EIA process:

Figure 27.1 This flow-chart summarises the EIA process for buildings

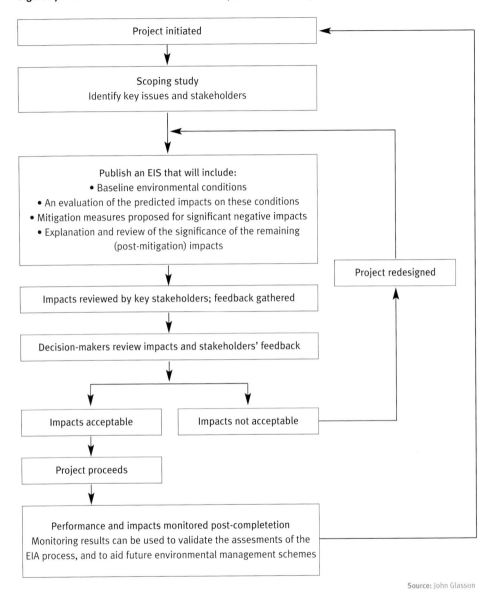

Source: John Glasson

1. The local planning authority, in conjunction with the developer, decides whether EIA is needed for a particular development project (sometimes known as "screening").
2. The developer or a contractor undertakes a study to identify the likely key environmental impacts resulting from the project. This involves consultation with the planning authority and possibly the wider public. (This process is called "scoping".)
3. An EIS is produced, and a free copy is given to the statutory consultees, and may be made available to other stakeholders in the project. The EIS includes a description of the baseline environment, the predicted environmental impacts of the proposed building and site, and the proposed mitigation measures for any significant negative environmental impacts.
4. Information in the EIS and feedback from stakeholders are taken into account by the developer when they decide on the final form of the proposed development, and by the planning authority when deciding whether or not to allow the development to go ahead.

If the planning authority rejects the proposed development, the developer is allowed to re-draft the mitigation strategies and re-submit a new design and associated EIS.

One of the frustrations with compulsory EIAs is the lack of a formal requirement for post-construction monitoring. If, for instance, the future occupier does complete a post-occupancy evaluation (POE) (see Chapter 39), the information gathered can be fed back to inform future projects, the purchase or rental of other buildings. And in an ideal world EIA should be integrated with other environmental management and assessment processes, so that it will be used to continually monitor and influence the environmental performance of the development from "cradle to grave".

References

1 In the USA around a third of all States have a "Little NEPA", and the term "NEPA" applies only to national government projects. California, for instance, has perhaps the best Little NEPA process. More can be learnt of these in: Glasson J, Therivel R and Chadwick A (1999), *Introduction to Environmental Impact Assessment*, 2nd edn, UCL Press, London, pp 28–31.
2 Wood C (1995), *Environmental Impact Assessment*, Longman Scientific and Technical, Harlow
3 Amended in 1997 (97/11/EC)

4 Essex County Council (2002), *The Essex Guide to Environmental Impact Assessment* is the fourth comprehensive rewrite of the original 1992 Report

5 A full copy of the legal text of European Directive (2001/42/EC) is available on *http://europa.eu.int/comm/environment/eia/full-legal-text/0142_en.pdf* For a detailed elaboration of projects that require EIAs see Glasson et al, op cit, pp 42–47

6 For a clear description of this process see Glasson et al, op cit, pp 73–75

Further reading

European Commission (1994), *Environmental Impact Assessment: Review checklist*

Environment Agency (1996), *Environmental Assessment: Scoping handbook for projects*, The Stationery Office, Norwich

Her Majesty's Government (1990), *This Common Inheritance: Britain's environmental strategy*, Cm 1200, HMSO, London.

Kent County Council (2000), *Kent Environmental Assessment Handbook*.

Lee N, Colley R, Bonde J and Simpson J (1999), *Reviewing the Quality of Environmental Statements and Environmental Appraisals*, Occasional Paper 55, Department of Planning and Landscape, University of Manchester.

Morris P and Therivel R (eds) (2001), *Methods of Environmental Impact Assessment*, 2nd edn, Spon Press, London.

RSPB (1997), *RSPB Good practice Guide for Prospective Developments: General Principles*, Royal Society for the Protection of Birds, Sandy

RTPI (1995), *Environmental Assessment: Practice Advice Note 13*, Royal Town Planning Institute

Planning policy guidance – related documents (see Appendix YY for details)

Planning policy guidance – related documents (see Appendix 1 for details)

1	2	3	4	5	6	7	8	9	10	11	12	13
x	x	x	x	x		x		x	x	x	x	x

14	15	16	17	18	19	20	21	22	23	24	25
x	x	x				x	x		x	x	x

Life cycle assessment

Definition

Life cycle assessment (LCA) is a way of analysing the impact of a product (or service) throughout its life cycle from an environmental perspective. LCA is often confused with life cycle costing (LCC), which examines only the financial parameters of products (see Chapter 29). The two methods can be used in conjunction, but are fundamentally different.

Related indicators

Energy, Biodiversity, Transport, Waste.

Related tools

Environmental impact assessment, Life cycle costing, Impact assessment in the UK – Ecopoints, BREEAM and Envest, Ecological footprinting, Energy toolkit.

LCA aims to examine the material and energy inputs and waste arising over the whole life of a product – from "cradle to grave". However, a full LCA study is potentially complex because it calls for a great deal of information about the component parts of the system or product, and their manufacturing and assembly processes. Given the time-consuming nature of such studies LCA is mainly used to support decisions on the scale of a single material or functional component, rather than a whole product, especially products as complex as buildings.

LCA would include an investigation into the environmental impacts of:

- extraction and processing of the raw materials and their geographical source
- location of, transport to, and techniques of, secondary processing and/or assembly
- transportation to site of use or assembly
- assembly process and waste arising
- product in use
- end of life, disassembly, recycling and disposal.

This means taking account of all the material and energy "inputs" into the system, plus wastes and emissions arising during manufacture, use and eventual disposal.

LCA is an activity that is particularly relevant to the construction industry, where the environmental impacts of decisions last for a considerable period of time, and where control of the buildings and associated resources passes through various hands.

Figure 28.1 summarises the life cycle of a single product; clearly an assessment of a whole building would be very complex.

Figure 28.1 From cradle to grave – a study of the life cycle of a single building component can be complex

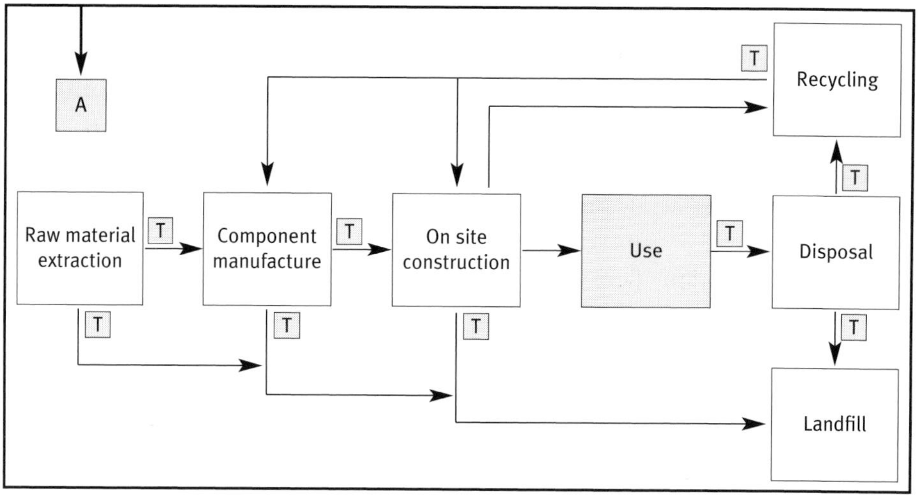

Key: A represents all the energy and material inputs into the system; T represents transport

Source: Andrew Horsley

To simplify the process, researchers using LCA tend to work with manageable qualities known as "functional units". This strategy is pivotal to the success of LCA, because it allows researchers to make accurate comparisons of the impact of various products. For example, paints from different manufacturers may have radically different coverage properties, so a sensible "functional unit" for paint might be 1 m² of finished surface. Similarly, when assessing the environmental performance of a building frame, it would not be appropriate to compare a tonne of structural steel with a tonne of pre-cast concrete, because a greatly different mass of each of these products is required to provide similar structural properties.

This approach is particularly important in construction, where literally thousands of components come together on site to deliver a product, but each component has a different life-span, and maintenance regime. The changing use of a building over its potentially long life is difficult, if not impossible, to predict, so LCA studies tend to focus only on the impacts that occur as a result of the manufacture and delivery of a product to site, plus any planned replacement of parts that may be needed over the component's typical life. Most LCA information is currently in this form, and care should be taken to ensure that the effects of material selection on operational performance are not overlooked.

A more detailed analysis of the predicted impact of the component during its operational life and beyond can only be achieved using a combination of other tools described elsewhere in this section. For example, the fenestration of a building – from the number of windows to the type of glass or frame material – can have a considerable direct impact on the total energy consumption of the building, and may even have an indirect impact on the useful life of the building.

Although LCA is more developed for some industries (e.g. car manufacture), it is still very much in a developmental phase for construction, where the baseline analyses are conducted by specialist researchers. However, publicly available data sources are growing. The UK-based Building Research Establishment (BRE) is one of a handful of organisations that maintain a central database of life cycle inventory information[1]. Some manufacturers are also beginning to publish this type of data for their products[2].

Clients and designers who wish to use LCA to inform their projects face two problems: the lack of a broad range of data, and the difficulty in making useful comparisons across ranges of products. Although there are international standards[3] for LCA, there are many ways that impact can be measured. BRE, for example, has adopted a system of "ecopoints" to underpin several of its impact assessment tools (see Chapter 30), where one ecopoint is equivalent to the environmental impact of the average UK citizen in a year. The *Green Guide to Specification*[4] takes this underlying numerical analysis to its logical conclusion, by giving products an "A, B, C" rating system (see Chapter 24) – a simplification that is reminiscent of the EC's A–E ratings for consumer products such as freezers and dishwashers. However, it is important to remember that the *Green Guide* ratings are relative, so an "A" rating means "best in class", not necessarily environmentally favourable.

References

1 Access to the BRE's data is by subscription. For more information, visit *http://collaborate.bre.co.uk/envprofiles*

2 See, for example, the window manufacturer Velfac, which publishes a detailed

Environmental Declaration about its products. Download the .pdf of this document from *www.velfac.co.uk* (choose "About Velfac", then "The Environment")

3   ISO 14040–14049 relate to life cycle assessment. These standards are published in the UK by BSI. Visit *http://bsonline.techindex.co.uk* for details

4   Anderson J, Shiers DE and Sinclair M (2003), *The Green Guide to Specification* 3rd edn, CRC, Garston

Life cycle costing

> **Definition**
>
> Life cycle costing (LCC) is a process that enables some or all of the long-term costs of operating and maintaining a building to be considered during its design stage.
>
> **Related tools**
>
> Life cycle assessment, Energy toolkit, Post-occupancy evaluation.

Introduction

Cost control is a key part of the building design process. In fact, building design revolves around cost: the cost of design and the cost of construction. Of course, buildings do not stop consuming money and resources once they are constructed. In commercial buildings, operational costs – incurred for heating, lighting, cooling and maintaining the building – can be very significant. The same is true of a building's environmental impacts. Some of the largest environmental impacts occur when the building is in operation.

Theories of LCC began to emerge in the 1930s, when people started to realised that the cost of operating buildings was often more significant than the construction cost. This led to the notion that the lowest-cost system of procurement was not always the cheapest solution over the operating life of the building: a fact that the UK clients are still coming to terms with.

The design process has a substantial influence on both capital costs (the up-front costs borne by clients for the design, construction, commissioning and hand-over of a building) and operating costs, but to date considerations of capital costs have been allowed to dominate. Given that lower operating costs are a key benefit of a sustainable building, designers should now turn their attention to the operating costs. LCC can be used to show clients how a small additional up-front cost can generate a significant saving in the long term.

More recent procurement routes such as PFI (Private Finance Initiative), in

which the building is designed, constructed and operated through a single contract, represent a significant opportunity to begin to consider capital and
operating costs as more unified financial parameters.

LCC is growing in importance because people have realised that there is a
strong link between the initial specification and the long-term impact (and therefore cost) of the building. Energy efficiency is a neat example of the principle.
Energy-efficient buildings may cost marginally more to build than their non-
efficient neighbours, but they usually cost less to operate.

LCC techniques and their applications

LCC can be used to underpin a wide range of studies:

- Life cycle cost planning (LCCP) is used to identify the total costs of the
  acquisition of a building or building element. It takes explicit account of
  initial capital costs and subsequent running costs, usually, but not always,
  using discounted cash flow techniques. (Discounted cash flow (DCF)
  techniques are methods of adjusting the magnitude of expenditure in the
  future to account for the effects of inflation and interest rates.) LCCP can be
  used to facilitate the choice between various methods of achieving a given
  objective. This technique is particularly useful at the outset of a new
  construction or refurbishment project.
- Full year effect costs (FYEC) is essentially similar to LCCP, but is usually
  client-driven in an attempt to get a very accurate short-term picture of the
  running costs of a building, usually over a period of one to three years.
  Because of the short-term nature of the analysis, future costs are not
  usually discounted. This data is used for internal budgeting purposes.
- Life cycle cost analysis (LCCA) is a research technique that involves
  establishing a database on the running costs and performance of occupied
  buildings. This information can then be fed back into the design process to
  assist decision making and to provide definitive benchmarks.
- Life cycle cost management (LCCM) is a derivative of LCCA. It identifies
  areas in which the running cost of a particular system may be reduced by
  changing either the characteristics of the system or the operating practices.

In fact, the term "life cycle costing" is a misnomer because it is rare for an LCC
assessment to take account of the actual life of the building. This is because
assessing the operating life of a building is inherently difficult, and a building will
usually end its prescribed definition of "life" before the end of its physical life. This
disparity is known as obsolescence, and occurs for a number of (mainly) function-

Table 29.1 Understanding the life-span of a building

TYPE OF OBSOLESENCE	DEFINITION	BASIS FOR ASSESSMENT OF BUILDING LIFE	EXAMPLES OF FACTORS LEADING TO OBSOLESCENCE
Economic	Life of the building until such time as occupation is no longer the least-cost alternative of meeting a particular objective	How long will the building be economic for the client to own and operate?	The value of the land on which the building stand is more than the capitalised full rental value that could be derived from letting the building
Physical	Life of the building until such time as physical collapse is possible	How long will the building stand up?	Deterioration of structural components affecting building stability
Functional	Life of the building until such time as the building ceases to function for the purpose for which it was built	How long will the building be used for the purpose for which it was initially built?	Cinemas converted to bingo halls Rural railway stations converted to private homes
Technological Social	Life of the building until its technological superiority over alternatives is undermined	How long will the design be technologically acceptable/superior to comparable alternatives?	Prestige office unable to accommodate introduction of high-level computing facilities Storage warehouse unable to accommodate the introduction of robotics for materials handling
	Life of the building until such time as the aesthetic acceptability of the design and/or decor is no longer favourable	How long will the design be aesthetically acceptable?	Demolition of multi-storey flats Frequency of facade changes for retail outlets

al and economic reasons, illustrated in Table 29.1. The definition of a building's lifespan can have a considerable impact on the outcome of the analysis, so it is important to establish the most suitable definition at the outset of a study.

LCC is not used often enough, and reasons given for this range from the fact that it is simply not asked for, to problems of data availability and some problems with the various techniques themselves.

Lack of appropriate data is often seen as a reason for delaying or failing to undertake an LCC analysis. While it is true that there are few independent detailed sources of such information, the belief that mountains of "accurate" data are required in order to engage with the concept is unfounded. Decisions taken without the benefit of even simple life cycle indices are often far more risky than those taken on simple life cycle cost data made with explicit and reasonable professional assumptions.

However, it is likely that the most significant barrier to its wider use is the current common building procurement route, in which parties involved in the design, construction and operation of a building are segregated in the delivery chain.

In reality LCC is a simple concept, and clients, practitioners, consultants and contractors should be able to make the first steps to more holistic life cycle decision making, and use LCC to support simple design and specification decisions without too much difficulty.

LCC in practice

There are a number of different ways to account for the life cycle cost of a building, or of any individual component. The easiest is to use the "simple payback period" (SPB), which assumes that any additional capital resource being invested in the building will reduce operating costs. The SPB is the time taken from the initial investment to when the additional capital expenditure is equal to the cumulative operational cost benefits. For example, the cost of installing additional insulation in the roof of a house can be "recovered" in, say, two years, because of lower energy bills. The SPB can be calculated using this equation:

$$SPB = \frac{C}{A - a}$$

where C is the capital cost of the item/option, A is the Annual saving, and a is the additional annual costs associated with the item/option.

Discounting

Discounting is central to LCC. Essentially, it recognises that there is a time value to money. For example, saving £ 1million in year 10 is not worth the same to a decision maker as saving £1 million in year 1 because of the effects of inflation and interest rates. It also takes account of the fact that estimates are cast into the future, so there is not only a greater uncertainty in terms of the business circumstances, but also a risk of making errors or inaccurate assumptions in the analysis.

Table 29.2 Life-cycle cost data for two electric heaters

ELECTRIC HEATER TYPE A (REPLACEABLE)										
COST AT YEAR: 0	1	2	3	4	5	6	7	8	9	10
1500 (capital)	100	100	100	100	500	100	100	100	100	500

ELECTRIC HEATER TYPE B (REPLACEABLE)										
COST AT YEAR: 0	1	2	3	4	5	6	7	8	9	10
1800 (capital)	50	50	50	50	400	50	50	50	50	400

Source: Andrew Horsley

Some researchers have questioned the ethics of the discount rate because it inevitably devalues future resource consumption, contrary to the notion of sustainable development.[1] In practice, however, provided that the rate of discount is kept at a reasonable level, its impact is not really felt on options with relatively short payback periods (less than 10 years).

Selecting a discount rate is one of the most contested areas of LCC study. The discount rate should reflect the client's perspective on the temporal nature of their investment, but should be realistic.[2]

Net present value

Perhaps the most widely accepted method for long-term analysis is the net present value (NPV) method. The NPV approach can be used to ascertain the relative financial merits of a number of design options over a specified period of time. The basic principle behind the method is discounting.

NPV calculations are based on a full set of cost information over the study period. The data is tabulated year by year (see example, below). This sort of information may be obtained from manufacturers, or from the independent sources highlighted at the end of this chapter.

Example – net present value of electric heaters

The NPV of either heater can be calculated using this equation:

$$NPV = \sum_{t=0}^{T} \frac{C_t}{(1 + r)^t}$$

Where C_t is the estimated cost at year t (from Table 29.2), r is the percentage discount rate, and T is the period of analysis in years.

To perform this calculation, you need to choose a discount rate. This can be calculated from a differential of interest and inflation rates (see equation below), or

Figure 29.1 This graph of the life cycle costs of options A and B, illustrated the benefit of an NVP Calculation: it appears that option B will be cheaper in the long term (at the chosen discount rate)

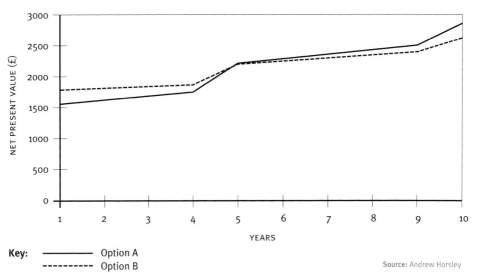

Key: ———— Option A
------- Option B

Source: Andrew Horsley

pre-set at, for instance, the HM Treasury rate of 6 per cent.

$$\text{Net discount rate (NDR)} = \frac{(1 + \text{interest}\%)}{(1+\text{inflation}\%) - 1}$$

Figure 29.1 shows what happens when the data presented in Table 29.2 are fed into the NPV equation, choosing a discounting rate of 4.7 per cent (6 per cent inflation and 11 per cent interest rate).

From Figure 29.1, it appears that after 5 years option B is financially more viable, despite the higher capital costs. However, as the discount rate is increased, the impact of high running costs in option A are diminished, hence making this option appear increasingly favourable.

References

1 The Building Research Establishment (BRE), for example, has recently criticised the whole concept of life cycle costing because of its approach to discounting, saying that an economic analysis tool in which favourable emphasis is placed on costs occurring early in the products life is incompatible with the long life of buildings. See: Clift M and Bourke K (1998), *Study of Whole Life Costing*, BRE Report 367, CRC, London

2   See the HM Treasury approach to this issue at *http://www.hm-treasury.gov.uk/economic_data_and_tools/greenbook/data_greenbook_index.cfm*

Further reading

Best R and DeValence G (1998), *Building in Value*, Arnold, London

Kirk SJ and Dell'Isola A (1995), *Life Cycle Costing for Design Professionals*, McGraw-Hill, New York

HM Treasury (2000), *Procurement Guidance Note No. 7: Whole Life Costing,* Treasury Taskforce, London

Horsley A (2002), *Better By Design: Integrating energy performance assessment into building design,* EngD. thesis, University of Surrey, School of Engineering

Other resources

Life cycle data can often be found from manufacturers' data, but the following may also be useful sources:

The Building Cost Information Service Ltd; see *www.bcis.co.uk*

Housing Association Property Mutual (HAPM) *Component Life Manual*; copies can be downloaded from *www.hapm.co.uk/publications.htm*

Department of the Environment: PSA Specialist Services (1991) *Costs in Use Tables*, HMSO, London

Impact assessment in the UK: Ecopoints, Envest and BREEAM

> **Definition**
>
> The environmental impact of a building depends on its context – where it is located and the prevailing economic and social climate. Impact assessment tools for buildings tend to be country-specific, although at least one international tool has been developed.[1] Currently, in the UK, the best known tools are those developed by the Building Research Establishment (BRE) with the support of the UK government. Their tools – Envest, BREEAM and the *Green Guide to Specification*[2] – are underpinned by "Ecopoints", a single-score environmental assessment technique developed as a way of normalising a range of environmental impacts so that dissimilar impacts (e.g. environmental pollution and depletion of resources) can be compared.
>
> **Related tools**
>
> Environmental impact assessment; Life cycle assessment; Energy toolkit.

Introduction

Any construction project will have a wide range of environmental impacts, each of which will be measured in a different way – for example, mineral extraction can be measured in tonnes, while energy use can be measured in terms of carbon dioxide emitted. This makes it difficult to compare the various impacts, or to calculate the total impact of a product or project.

This chapter describes two of the UK-specific performance analysis tools that have been developed by BRE – Envest and BREEAM – both of which use the Ecopoints system[3] as a basis for some of their impact calculations.

The Ecopoints system was developed by comparing each impact with a "norm", which BRE chose to be the annual environmental impact of a UK citizen (total impact of the population divided by the number of citizens). The normalised impacts were then further attenuated by an "impact weighting". This weighting is necessary because some impacts are perceived to be more damaging than others. BRE used a panel of UK industry experts to rank a range of environmental, social and economic issues in order of importance.

In this way, Ecopoints give a numerical value to the overall impact of a particular product or process, based on a range of environmental impacts:

- climate change
- fossil fuel depletion
- ozone depletion
- freight transport
- air and water toxicity to humans
- waste disposal
- water extraction
- acid deposition
- ecotoxicity
- eutrophication[4]
- summer smog
- minerals extraction.

Envest

Envest is a software tool that enables designers to analyse and compare the environmental impact of commercial buildings at the design stage. It was the first UK software product for estimating life cycle environmental impacts. It can:

- help designers to optimise the form of the building, for the least environmental impact over the building life cycle
- inform choice about the environmental impacts of the main elements of the building structure
- provide and maintain reference data acquired from materials manufacturers
- help designers to balance the environmental impact of the energy and water consumed during the operational life of the building, with the choice of building materials.

Now in its second version (Envest II), the tool has been successfully used on a number of projects, including the prestigious Wessex Water Operations Centre[5]

The tool is simple to use and requires the designer to enter details of the building's design – number of storeys, window area etc – plus choices for building elements such as external wall construction and roof covering. The program then identifies which element will have the most significant environmental impact. It can also be used to look at the effects of selecting different materials, or how various heating and cooling strategies will affect the overall impact. This process can be very useful to demonstrate the effect of various choices to clients.

The key to the success of this system is its simplicity (see Figure 30.1). Data input is via menu choices, so there is no need to look up U-values, Building Regulations requirements and the like.

BREEAM

Since its launch in 1990, BREEAM has become one of the best-known environmental impact assessment tools in the UK. Like Envest, this was developed by BRE,

Figure 30.1 Schematic diagram of the Envest environmental impact assessment tool for a building design

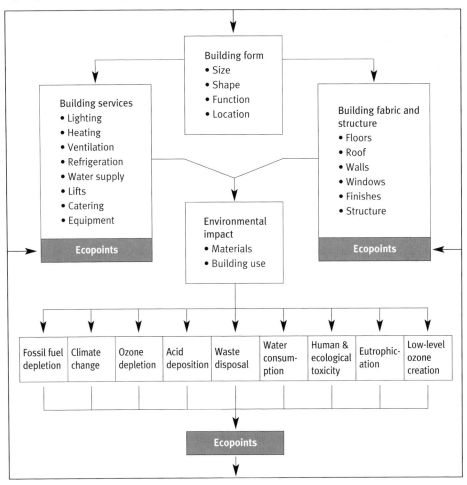

and some aspects of it use the Ecopoints scoring system. However, unlike Envest, BREEAM was not intended as a design tool, although it has become a *de facto* standard for clients wishing to commission environmentally sensitive buildings.

BREEAM assessments are generally conducted by third party (licensed) assessors[6] and are tailored to specific building types. To date, there are BREEAM-based schemes covering:

- offices
- industrial units
- supermarkets
- homes (branded as Ecohomes)
- schools (branded as SEAM, the Schools Environmental Assessment Method)
- health facilities (branded as NEAT, the NHS Environmental Assessment Tool).

BRE can also provide tailor-made BREEAM-based assessments for other building types.

In each case, the assessments cover energy, transport, pollution, water, materials, ecology and land use, health and well-being, and internal environment.

Assessment is via checklists, which detail a series of absolute requirements. This simple system gives clients or designers a quick result in the form of a simple score. The Wessex Water Operations Centre, for example, scored 10 in Environmental Performance Index within BREEAM – the highest possible score.[7]

The system is intended for use on completed buildings, but it is becoming a useful way for clients to gain a "green" label for their buildings, and some are using it to specify and target a building's performance. Indeed, BRE used the system during the development of its own Environment Building.[8] However, designers would do well to treat this type of usage with caution. Many clients will ask for an "excellent BREEAM rating" without understanding what it means. This usually leads to a relaxation of the standards during the later stages of design, especially when affordability issues are involved.

Nevertheless, BREEAM remains a useful tool for demonstrating the environmental performance of a building or a potential building to stakeholders who are not familiar with construction terminology and techniques. Given the slow turnover of the building stock (2–3 per cent per year), the performance and sustainability of existing buildings is just as important as that of new build, and BREEAM can be a valuable means of analysing and setting targets for these properties before and after refurbishment.

References

1 GBTool has been developed by Natural Resources Canada as a result of a world-wide dialogue called the "Green Building Challenge", which set out to achieve a consensus on what constitutes a green or sustainable building. The tool can be used for buildings from around the world, but results must be "normalised" by a national GBTool team to have local relevance. See *www.buildingsgroup.nrcan.gc.ca/software/gbtool_e.html*, or download the software from *http://greenbuilding.ca/iisbe/gbc2k2-start.htm*

2 Anderson J, Shiers DE and Sinclair M (2003), *The Green Guide to Specification,* 3rd edn, CRC, Garston

3 A full description of Ecopoints and how they can be applied can be found in Dickie I and Howard N (2000), *Assessing Environmental Impacts of Construction: Industry consensus, BREEAM and UK Ecopoints*, BRE Digest 446, CRC, London

4 Over-enrichment of water by natural or artificial nutrients.

5 For details, download a case study from the BRE website at *www.bre.co.uk/services/envest.html*

6 Details of licensed assessors, fee scales, and pre-assessment checklists are available from *www.breeam.com* See also the Ecohomes website *http://products.bre.co.uk/breeam/ecohomes.html*

7 See *www.wessexwater.co.uk/operationscentre/index.html*

8 Download details from *http://projects.bre.co.uk/envbuild/index.html*

Further information

Howard N and Kapoor P (2000), "Estimating the environmental impact of buildings", *Proceedings of the TIA 2000 Conference*, Oxford Brookes University, section 6–10

Ecological footprinting

> **Definition**
>
> The "ecological footprint" is the land and water area required to support a specified level of natural resource consumption. It is most often used to express the "load" imposed on nature by a given population (and its associated lifestyle), but the term is increasingly being used to also describe the impact of organisations, products and services.
>
> **Related tools**
>
> Environmental impact assessment, Life cycle analysis, Life cycle costing, Impact assessment in the UK – Ecopoints, BREEAM and ENVEST.

About this chapter

This chapter is based on text supplied by Craig Simmons, Co-founder and Director of the sustainability consultancy Best Foot Forward[1] and co-author of *Sharing Nature's Interest*,[2] and by Kevin Paulson, who is a physicist and mathematician, currently working in the Radio Communication Research Unit at the Rutherford Appleton Laboratory in Oxfordshire.

This chapter describes the ecological footprinting method, including the concept of "fair earth shares" – a simple way to compare the impact of the activities of nations or populations. It also includes an extended case study about one application of the method at Oxford Brookes University.

Introduction

The ecological footprint was first described by Wackernagel and Rees in their excellent book of 1996.[3] The technique has since been developed and used to measure the sustainability of products, services, organisations, communities, lifestyles and countries.

Though ecological footprinting, as a term, was only coined in the early 1990s, the concepts underpinning it can be traced back through more than 200 years of literature in the fields of economics, ecology and geography. Primarily, footprint-ing draws on the body of research pertaining to "carrying capacity" – the ability of the earth to support life.[4] The maximum carrying capacity of our planet has taxed many minds, from the work of Malthus in 1790[5] to the recent comprehen-sive review of the subject by Joel E. Cohen.[6]

Across Europe, footprinting is rapidly gaining acceptance among local authori-ties and other organisations responsible for housing provision, campaigning, and urban design, as a tool for comparing the ecological impact of planning decisions. In 1995 the International Institute for Environment and Development (IIED) pub-lished an influential report[7] on the ecological footprints of British citizens, and organisations such as Best Foot Forward in Oxford now specialise in environ-mental impact assessment using ecological footprinting.

A footprint can be calculated for any population, activity or consumer item. Footprinting converts the ecological impacts into "sustainable land units". The sustainable land unit is measured in "hectares of world average productive capac-ity", now commonly referred to as "global hectares" (gha), and is a measurement that is easy to comprehend. It resonates with a broad audience, and enables us to compare the ecological effects of disparate activities and to monitor our total impact on the Earth. (Global metres squared is represented by gm^2.)

When undertaking or presenting an ecological footprint analysis it is convenient to distinguish between the following general categories of land and water:

- energy land – used for growing fuel crops or the forested land necessary to sequester the carbon dioxide produced by burning fossil fuels (taking into account that some is also absorbed by the oceans)
- built land (also known as hardened land) – land that is built over and is therefore unavailable for ecologically productive purposes, e.g. land used for buildings and roads
- arable and pasture land – land used mainly for the production of animal- and plant-based foods but also harvested materials such as cotton
- forest land – land used to produce timber products such as paper
- sea space – productive sea space used mainly for catching seafood
- biodiversity land – defined as land used to ensure the welfare of the planet's 15 million or so non-human species (commonly estimated as a minimum 12 per cent of the Globe's productive area).

The development of ecological footprint analysis (EFA) has given us a much better understanding of the possibilities for living within the regenerative means of the planet. EFA recognises the finite capacity of the planet and gives a clear

---

Example – What is the footprint of a newspaper?

Assume a newspaper weighs 200 g and is made out of virgin paper (i.e. has no recycled content).

It takes approximately 1 hectare of (world average) forested area to produce 1 tonne of paper, or about 2 m² per newspaper. In addition, energy is needed to harvest the timber, to convert it into paper, to print the newspaper, and for all the transportation of materials from forest to your door. It has been estimated that this requires a similar area of forested land again to absorb the emissions arising from the use of fossil fuel derived energy. Therefore, the total footprint of a single newspaper is about 4 m².[8] This doesn't sound like much, but when you consider all the other products and services you consume in a year, it soon adds up!

---

indication of the amount of nature we have and what we are currently using. However, the footprint is necessarily a relatively simple model of the world's ecological systems. As such, it provides a conservative estimate of ecological impact. A more accurate policy tool is undoubtedly desirable, but there is barely the data available to support the current level of analyses. EFA, and similar analyses[9] that require accurate consumption data, will invariably become more sophisticated as data recording and monitoring systems improve.

Fair shares for all?

The ecological footprint embodies the concept of the "earth share". This allows us to compare an individual's footprint (the demand) with the average supply – the amount the earth can sustainably support. One earth share (*ES*) is the ecologically productive area (*A*) of the earth divided by the population (*P*). This can be expressed with the formula:

$$ES = A/P$$

The global population (*P*) in year 2000 was approximately 6 billion. Estimates of the planet's productive area (*A*) vary, but has been conservatively calculated as just under 11.5 billion hectares. This gives an *ES* of 1.91 hectares, excluding any allowance for the needs of animal species.[10]

A hectare equals 10,000 m² or 2.47 acres, about the size of a large football pitch. Therefore, to be sustainable, the average per capita footprint needs to be less than 19,100 m² or 4.94 acres. Latest estimates show that this is already being exceeded globally by 22 per cent although, as would be expected, the size of the

Table 31.1 Ecological footprints neatly illustrate which countries use more than their 'fair earth share'

	ECOLOGICAL FOOTPRINT (HA/PERSON)	FES PER PERSON (%)
Canada	4.3	287
USA	5.1	340
India	0.4	27
World	1.8	120

Source: Wackernagal and Rees, 1996

average footprint varies by country.[11] From Table T31.1, it is clear that the average North American uses about five times the average ES.

To think of it another way, we are demanding 445 days of the planet's regenerative capacity every 365 days. This is unsustainable, and only possible because we are able to draw on planetary capital (the Earth's "reserves") – depleting non-renewable resources and accumulating pollution in local and global ecosystems.

The Earth's ecological systems and resources, such as its fisheries and forests, can be thought of as "natural capital" that produces a return in the same way that capital invested in a bank account produces interest. When the total human footprint is larger than the Earth, we are living off the interest generated by natural capital and consuming some of the capital as well.

This type of analysis also shows that the people in European countries with similar lifestyles, such as the UK and the Netherlands, have broadly similar footprints. However, the footprint of an entire country can be larger (or smaller) than its geographical borders. For example, the footprint of the UK (expressed in world average hectares) is more than three times the actual productive capacity of the UK (when also expressed in world average hectares). The "excess" demand is met either by appropriating capacity from countries that live within their footprint (e.g. India), or because it forms part of the global ecological overdraft. Appropriation takes place through trade, such as the importation of edible oils and tropical hardwoods, or by reliance on the forested areas in under-developed countries as sinks for carbon dioxide produced by the burning of fossil fuels. In this way, industrialised nations are dependent on the rest of the world, and this appropriation could be described as ecologically parasitic.

Scarcity of resources is often blamed on the high population growth rates in many poorer countries – the more people there are, the less there is to go round. But this line of thinking ignores the resource-intensive lifestyles in most rich countries. The average American has an ecological footprint equivalent to six people from China or 12 from India. It is important to count not only the numbers of heads, but also the size of the feet!

In the future, the gap between global demand and supply is likely to widen. And as the human population increases, the average earth share decreases. By 2050, the ES is projected to reduce to 1.35 gha.[12] If per capita consumption also increases, as more of the world's population adopt Western lifestyles, then the situation could be even worse. We are already experiencing global problems such as falling fish stocks, deforestation, water shortages, climate change and soil degradation – all predictable consequences of drawing down the Earth's natural capital. The Earth is a forgiving bank manager, but a bank without funds is of no use to anyone.

None of this is inevitable. Improvements in efficiency, technology and more

---

EcoCal

One easy way to calculate the potential impacts of new developments, in relation to land, is to use the EcoCal tool, which is based on the methodology of ecological footprinting.[14]

The on-line eco-calculator enables a household to measure its "ecological garden" – the amount of bioproductive space required to support the lifestyles of the occupiers. For practical reasons, the EcoCal questionnaire comprised just 45 questions organised into categories:

- Household impact – mainly related to purchasing e.g. amount of food purchased, grown in EU, transported by air, transported by sea, percentages of meat products, percentage of organic products, number of newspapers, number and type of nappies purchased, nights spent in hotel and the rating of the hotel.
- Transport – distance travelled by car, by bus/train and by air, plus the number of air trips.
- Energy consumption – coal, gas, oil, LPG.
- Water – number of washing machine and dishwasher runs, hours of hosepipe use, number of baths and showers.
- Waste – categories of items recycled or composted, weight of bulk waste produced, volume of oil disposed of improperly.
- House and garden – size and type of property, size of plot occupied by property, volume of hardwoods purchased, volume of peat purchased.

All of these issues are crucial in the equation for calculating the carrying capacity of a particular site.

Table 31.2 Ecological footprints for the average daily commute (10 km) per year in Canada

MODE OF TRANSPORT	ECOLOGICAL FOOTPRINT (m^2)
Cycle	122*
Bus	303
Car	1,530

Source: Chambers et al, 2000

* Cycle commuting is not quite as benign as you might expect, and is responsible for a range of land-related impacts:
  - Energy is required to build the bicycle and the parts used to maintain it throughout its lifetime. Typically, this energy will be produced by burning fossil fuels. The "energy footprint" for these activities is the area of forest required to recycle the carbon liberated into the atmosphere by this combustion.
  - The "hardened land footprint" is the proportion of the land area dedicated to roads and cycle parking that can also be attributed to these cycle journeys.
  - While cycling, the cyclist converts energy from food eaten, so this "food land" must be accounted for.
  - Few timber products are used by the cyclist, and so the forest land footprint is negligible.

frugal lifestyles can still mitigate the worst effects. There are some encouraging examples of improvements – the increase uptake of renewable energy, eco-house developments, more recycling. But these first steps must be followed by larger strides if fundamental change is to occur.

"Despite having turned from hunter-gatherers to supermarket-browsers, it seems that humanity has not yet lost the instinct to survive." [13]

Case study – the transport footprint of Oxford Brookes University

This case study, contributed by Kevin Paulson, calculates the footprints of staff commuting by road and air and the university's use of of electricity, gas and paper.

Oxford Brookes University is a new university in Headington, Oxford. In 1994 it had approximately 1,500 staff and 13,000 students. The university's Environmental Forum, established in 1994, aimed to increase awareness of the impact of the activities and teaching of the university and to reduce the total environmental impact of these.

The work of Wackernagel and Rees[15] had already highlighted that transport, especially commuting, accounts for a significant proportion of the footprint of someone living and working in a developed country. The transport group of the university's Environmental Forum decided to quantify the impact of the transport demands of the university so that it could:

- compare the impact of different classes of transport demand
- compare the ecological impact of transport demands with that of other

university activities

- model the effect of a range of policy options to identify cost-effective ways of moving the university to sustainable operation
- monitor the university's ecological impact over time to determine the effectiveness of impact control policies.

This meant quantifying the impact of a diverse range of activities, and ecological footprinting was chosen as the tool for the study.

The transport group identified a range of transport demands generated by the university:

- staff and student commuting to the university
- staff and student travel between campuses
- business travel by staff visiting other institutions
- deliveries of resources and removal of waste.

Transport footprints were based on data published by Chambers et al (see Table 31.2).

Order of magnitude estimates of the footprints of these activities indicated that staff and student car commuting and staff business flights were the largest contributors to the total travel footprint.

Car commuting

In 1994/5 only 12 students had parking permits for the Headington Campus (for medical reasons) although parking for students is provided at halls of residence. However, the university has significant numbers of mature students: 50 per cent of students are over 21, and probably have similar travel patterns to staff. No data on student transport use was available, so their contribution to the transport footprint was not included.[16]

Staff commuting at Oxford Brookes was studied by Curtis and Coleman in 1995.[17] All the staff were asked to fill in a questionnaire about their transport to and from the university. Valid responses were obtained from 48 per cent of staff. Table 31.3 shows the proportion of staff who live in 11 different geographic areas around Oxford and the proportion of those who live in each area who drive to the university. The average return journey distance was estimated for each area, and these data were used to calculate the total distance commuted each week by staff. To take into account the flexibility of academic work, it was assumed that people who lived the furthest away from the university commuted less often: e.g. it was assumed that the 4 per cent of staff who lived outside the Midlands commuted twice a week.

Table 31.3 Distances driven by staff commuting to Oxford Brookes University

HOME LOCATION	PERCENT		ESTIMATED RETURN JOURNEY (km)	TOTAL (CAR km/WEEK)
	OF STAFF	CAR DRIVERS		
Headington	18	22	3	891
Rest of Oxford	26	37	5	3,608
Inner Oxon NE	9	74	40	19,980
Inner Oxon SE	11	68	20	11,220
Inner Oxon W	5	70	30	7875
Outer Oxon NE	4	84	70	14,112
Outer Oxon SE	6	94	40	13,536
Outer Oxon W	9	95	50	25,650
London	3	50	160	10,800
Rest of Midlands	5	92	120	24,840
Rest of South East	4	100	200	24,000
				Total 157,000

Source: Kevin Paulson

The total number of car kilometres driven per week by staff commuting to University was estimated to be 157,000 km/week, or 6.3 million km/year. This was then converted into a footprint, as follows:[18]

1. Energy land

Assuming that the UK average petrol consumption is 11 km per litre, then the energy footprint can be calculated using the formula:

$$\text{Energy land (per vehicle km)} = \left(\frac{\text{litres of petrol}}{\text{per kilometre}}\right) \times \left(\frac{CO_2 \text{ per}}{\text{litre petrol}}\right) \times \left(\frac{\text{forest area to}}{\text{absorb } CO_2}\right) \times \left(\frac{\text{forest equiv-}}{\text{alence factor}}\right) \times \left(\frac{\text{uplift}}{\text{factor}}\right)$$

Where:

- litres of petrol per kilometre = 1/11 or 0.091 (as per assumption)
- CO_2 per litre of petrol = 2.36 kg
- forest area required to absorb 1 kg of CO_2 = $1.92 m^2$
- forest equivalence factor (required to adjust forest land to world average productivity) = 1.17
- uplift factor (multiplier to account for the additional fuel use arising from vehicle construction and maintenance) = 1.45

Thus, energy land = 0.091 x 2.36 x 1.92 x 1.17 x 1.45 = 0.699 gm^2 per car-km.

If car-km per week is 157,000 (from Table 31.3), then the annual energy footprint attributable to car commuting is: 157,000 x 52 x 0.73 = 596 gha.

2. Consumed land

Motor vehicles also "consume" built land in the form of roads, garages and car parks. To arrive at an estimate of this, the following formula is used:

$$\text{Built land (gha per car-km)} = \left(\begin{array}{c}\text{road surface}\\ \text{area in UK}\end{array}\right) \times \left(\frac{\text{percentage used by cars}}{\text{total number of car km in UK}}\right) \times \left(\begin{array}{c}\text{built land}\\ \text{equivalence factor}\end{array}\right)$$

Where:

- road surface area (UK) = 2,581,747 hectares
- percentage used by cars = 86%
- total number of car-km (UK) = 362,400,000,000 km/year
- built land equivalence factor (required to adjust built land to world average productivity) = 2.8

Thus, built land (gm² per car-km) = 2,581,747 x 0.86/362,400,000,000 x 2.8 = 0.17 gm² per car-km.

If the car-km per week is 157,000 (from Table 31.3), then the annual built land footprint attributable to car commuting is: 157,000 x 52 x 0.17 = 139 gha.

3. Food and forest land

Negligible.

4. Total

Total annual staff car commuting footprint is 735 gha.

Staff business flights

The university has its own travel agency and encourages staff to use it to book their business travel arrangements. A record was maintained of the number of booked flights and destinations for the financial year 1995/96. This record does not include business trips booked at other agencies but does include pleasure flights booked by university staff. It was assumed that these two effects would cancel. A return flight distance and the number of take-offs and landings were estimated for each destination, and these data were used to estimate the total flight distance on staff business trips: see Table 31.4.

Wackernagel[19] calculates that the energy required by each passenger on a commercial flight is similar to an individual driving a car the same distance, with a correction for take-off and landing. As a rule of thumb he suggests that each take-off and landing requires the same energy as flying for 1 hour 15 minutes. For the purposes of this study, only general long-haul and short-haul factors have been used, reflecting data supplied by the UK Department of Transport. The footprint

Table 31.4 Distances travelled by plane

DESTINATION	NUMBER OF FLIGHTS	TOTAL DISTANCE TRAVELLED (,000 km)	TOTAL NUMBER OF TAKE-OFFS PER RETURN FLIGHT	
Asia	119	2,167	4	476
Europe	585	1,299	2	1170
North America	88	1,113	4	352
Australasia	8	296	6	48
South America	11	170	4	44
Africa	11	157	4	44
Total	822	5,211		2,134

Source: Kevin Paulson

is calculated as follows:

1. Energy land

The total distance flown on business flights was calculated to be 5.2 million km/year, equivalent to 100,000 km/week. To take into account more accurately the effect of take-offs and landings where substantial fuel is used, it is best to treat short-haul and long haul flights differently, using the data in Table 31.4 and conversion factors in Table 31.2. The footprint can then be calculated in a similar manner to the car energy footprint.

Where:

- short-haul factor = 0.9 gm²/pass-km
- long-haul factor = 0.6 gm²/pass-km
- short-haul passenger km = 1,299,000
- long-haul passenger km = 3,912,000

Energy footprint = (short-haul factor x short-haul pass-km) + (long-haul factor x long-haul pass-km)

Energy footprint = (0.9 x 1,299,000) + (0.6 x 3,912,000) = 352 gha

2. Consumed land, food land and forest land

Negligible.

3. Total

Total annual staff business flight footprint is 352 gha.

Other significant activities

Other significant activities of the university, in terms of its environmental impact, are its use of energy and its use of paper.

Energy

The energy supplied to the university's campuses as electricity and gas in the year 1996 was:

- gas: 7.7 GWh per year
- electricity: 4.4 GWh per year.

Thus the university used 12.1 GWh of energy directly or indirectly from the burning of fossil fuels. Using conversion factors of 110.6 gha/GWh and 45.3 gha/Gwh for electricity and gas respectively (from Chambers et al) gives a footprint of 836 gha per annum.

Paper

The amount of paper used is of major concern to many people at the University. The majority of paper is for printing and photocopying, and is purchased centrally by the university. In the year 1996/97 the university purchased 50,000 reams of paper each weighing 2.325 kg – a total of 116.25 tonnes! Chambers et al state that each tonne of paper has a footprint of 1.88 gha. Using these figures yields a footprint of:

$$50,000 \text{ reams} \quad \times \quad \frac{2.325 \text{ kg}}{1,000} \quad \times \quad 1.88 \text{ gha} \quad = \quad 219 \text{ gha per year}$$

Conclusions

A lower bound on the total transport footprint was calculated by summing the annual staff car commuting and business flights footprints, and was greater than 1,000 gha. This is larger than the footprint of direct energy use by the university's campuses, and at least five times larger than the footprint of the university's paper use.

Effective ways of reducing the university's footprint can be identified from the analysis.

- Business flights to Asia account for 14 per cent of staff flights but around 35 per cent of the flying footprint. The majority of these flights are to South East Asia, where the university has franchised courses to local institutions. It is possible that many of the staff visits to these institutions could be replaced by (considerably more cost-effective) telephone or mail interactions. The new video-conferencing facilities at the university could be used as an alternative to physical visits. Each flight to SE Asia that is avoided reduces the flying footprint by more than 1 gha.
- Although flights within Europe are inefficient because of the overhead of

take-off and landing, each flight covers a short distance and so does not significantly add to the total footprint. Five average European flights have about the same impact as one flight to East Asia.

- The university has 633 parking places for staff cars at its Headington Campus. These spaces are allocated to staff using a range of criteria such as disability and distance of journey to work. The land and maintenance costs associated with each parking place cost the university approximately £250 per year. The parking spaces are provided free to staff motorists. The introduction of parking charges to staff who choose to drive to university could reduce the number of journeys to the university made by private cars and hence reduce demand for parking and the transport footprint of the university. Initially, reduction in car journeys would be short-distance commuters, such as the 10.6 per cent of staff who commute by car from within Oxford. Eliminating car commuting from within Oxford would reduce the transport footprint by less than 3 per cent, as these people travel such a small distance, but would reduce the impact of car commuting on the people of Headington. It is the long-distance commuters who contribute most to the car commuting footprint: the 12 per cent of staff who live outside Oxfordshire contribute 38 per cent of the commuting footprint. Sustainable reductions in the commuting footprint can only be achieved by persuading people to live closer to their place of work. Progressive car parking charges, which increase with the distance of the commute combined with relocation loans in exchange for giving up parking places, would exert pressure on staff to reduce their commuting footprint.

The question arising from this research is: "Is the operation of the university sustainable?"

The question is difficult to answer. Although the footprint provides a useful and measurable definition of environmental sustainability, this is not readily applicable at the organisational level. A university, such as Oxford Brookes, forms only part of a person's daily life. In turn, the university is only one element in the economy. How much of your earthshare it is "worth" spending, or should be spent, on education is open to discussion. Clearly, it is desirable to keep the environmental impact of university life to a minimum, and it is useful to help put this impact in context.

Summing the key impacts associated with Oxford Brookes, commuting, business flights, energy use and paper consumption, the average impact is around 0.22 gha per student (full-time equivalent). This is just over 10 per cent of the average earthshare – it seems that a good education need not cost the earth.

It is worth noting that this figure is similar to that reported for other educational establishments (Chambers et al[20]) and consistent with the 0.08 gha per person UK average jointly attributed to the education and health sectors nationwide.[21]

References

1   See *www.bestfootforward.com*

2   Chambers N, Simmons C and Wackernagel M (2000), *Sharing Nature's Interest: Ecological footprints as an indicator of sustainability*, Earthscan Publications, London

3   Wackernagel M and Rees WE (1996), *Our Ecological Footprint: Reducing human impact on the earth*, New Society Publishers, Gabriola Island, BC

4   The ecological footprint is often wrongly confused with environmental space when the indicators are complementary. Environmental space is a set of individual indicators which measure resource consumption whereas the footprint provides a single aggregated index. See: McLaren D, Bullock S and Yousuf N (1998), *Tomorrow's World*, Earthscan, London; and Hille J (1998), *The Concept of Environmental Space: Implications for policies, environmental reporting and assessments*, European Environmental Agency.

5   Malthus' full essay *An Essay on the Principle of Population,* printed for J Johnson in St Paul's Church-Yard, 1798, can be viewed at *http://socserv2. socsci.mcmaster.ca/~econ/ugcm/3ll3/malthus/popu.txt* For a more detailed analysis of Malthus' arguments see Cohen JE (1995), *How Many People can the Earth Support?*, WW Norton, New York

6   Cohen (1995), op cit

7   IIED (1995), *Citizen Action to Lighten Britain's Ecological Footprints*, edited by Nick Robins, International Institute for Environment and Development, Edinburgh

8   This example slightly simplifies the calculations by ignoring the conversion of forested land to world average productive land. Although the difference in result is relatively small, and can be ignored for such an illustrative calculation, it is important to note the fact that the footprint is properly expressed in units of world average productive space.

9   Other methodologies include: Total Material Flows (TMF), Material Intensity per unit of Service (MIPS), Mass Balance Analysis and Resource Flow Analysis. The methods typically vary in the degree to which they account for the hidden flows and wastes which are "embodied" in the final products and the pollution arising from consumption. See: Spangenberg JH et al (1998), *Materials Flow-based Indicators in Environmental Reporting*, European Environment Agency;

WRI (1997), *Resource Flows: The material basis of industrial economies*, World Resources Institute, Washington; Schmidt-Bleek F (1994), *Wieviel Umwelt braucht der Mensch? MIPS Das Maß fürökologisches Wirtschaften (How much nature do people need? MIPS a measure for ecological management)*, Birkhäuser Verlag, Basel; *Fresenius Environmental Bulletin*, vol 2, no 8, Special edition on Material, Intensity per Unit Service (MIPS) project of the Wuppertal Institute für Klima, Umwelt, und Energie Wuppertal, Germany 1993.

10 Wackernagel M et al (2002), "Tracking the ecological overshoot of the human economy", *Proceedings of the National Acadamy of Sciences of the USA*, 99 (14), 9266–9271.

11 Op cit and Loh J et al (2002), *Living Planet Report 2002*, WWF, Gland, Switzerland

12 Best Foot Forward, Personal communication

13 Chambers et al (2000), op cit

14 Roaf S, Fuentes M and Thomas S (2003), *Ecohouse 2: A design guide*, Architectural Press, Oxford

15 Op cit

16 Student transport could have a significant footprint due to shear numbers. If the average student travel footprint was a tenth of that of a staff member, their contribution would almost double the total travel footprint. By attributing zero footprints to student transport and other transport activities we calculated a strict lower bound on the total travel footprint.

17 Curtis C and Coleman C (1996), *A Guide to Conducting a Travel Audit of Employees*, School of Planning, Working Paper No. 166, Oxford Brookes University.

18 Raw data for the calculations came from Chambers et al (2000), op cit

19 Wackernagel M (private correspondence)

20 Op cit

21 Barrett J and Simmons C (2003), *An Ecological Footprint of the UK: Providing a tool to measure the sustainability of local authorities*, Stockholm Environment Institute, York

On-line resources

www.naturalstep.org
www.ecologicalfootprint.com
www.redefiningprogress.org

Further reading

Haberl H (1997), "Human appropriation of net primary production as an environmental indicator: implications for sustainable development", *Ambio*, 26 (3), 143–146

Holmberg J, Robèrt K-H, and Eriksson K-E (1996), "Socio-ecological principles for a sustainable society: scientific background and swedish experience" in: Costanza R, Olman S and Martinez-Alier J (eds) *Getting Down to Earth*, Washington, Island Press, pp 17–48

Holmberg J et al (1999), "The ecological footprint from a systems perspective of sustainability", *The International Journal of Sustainable Development and World Ecology*, 6, 17–33

Krotscheck C and Narodoslawsky M (1996), "The sustainable process index – a new dimension in ecological evaluation", *Ecological Engineering,* 6 (4), 241–258

Krotscheck C (1997), "How to measure sustainability? Comparison of flow-based (mass and/or energy) highly aggregated indicators for eco-compatibility", *EnvironMetrics*, 8, 661–681

Krotscheck C (1998), "Quantifying the interaction of human and the ecosphere: the sustainable process index as measure for co-existence", in: Müller F and Leupelt M (eds), *Eco-Targets, Goal Functions, and Orientors*, Springer Verlag, Berlin

Meadows DH, Meadows DL, and Randers J (1992), Beyond the Limits, Earthscan Books, London

Vitousek PM et al (1986), "Human appropriation of the products of photosynthesis", *BioScience*, 34 (6), 368–373

The Energy Toolkit

Definition

The Energy Toolkit is a procedure that has been developed to study and thereby improve the energy efficiency of new buildings or refurbishments. The procedure combines the use of existing performance analysis tools with a bespoke spreadsheet-based tool for analysing the energy and cost performance of a design.

Related indicators

Climate change; Energy; Building form and daylighting; The building envelope.

Related tools

Environmental impact assessment; Life cycle analysis; Life cycle costing; Impact assessment in the UK – Ecopoints, BREEAM and Envest.

About this chapter

This chapter is based on text supplied by Andrew Horsley and Chris France. Andrew is a senior consultant with Ecofys UK, a consultancy company in the field of renewable energy, energy efficiency and climate change, and formerly of Carillion Building Special Projects; Chris is programme director of the University of Surrey's Engineering Doctorate programme, and Deputy Director of the Centre for Environmental Strategy.

This chapter describes the Energy Toolkit procedure and the underlying reasons for its development, and uses a case study to demonstrate one way that it can be applied to a large construction project. The Energy Toolkit has been developed by Andrew Horsley and Chris France as part of an EngD research project, with Carillion Building Special Projects and the Centre for Environmental Strategy, University of Surrey.

Introduction

We cannot underestimate the importance of buildings' energy consumption. Buildings have relatively long life-spans, and up to 90 per cent of the environmental impact of a building is directly related to the energy consumed during its operation (see Figure 32.1). In the UK, most of the existing building stock is substantially less efficient than current technology allows. Over the next 10 years, it is estimated that only 10 per cent of this inefficient building stock will be replaced, but during the same period the actual area of the built environment will increase by 3 per cent,[1] hence exerting a significant responsibility on both new build and refurbishment projects to make appropriate design decisions.

Figure 32.1 Whole-life environmental impact of a typical building

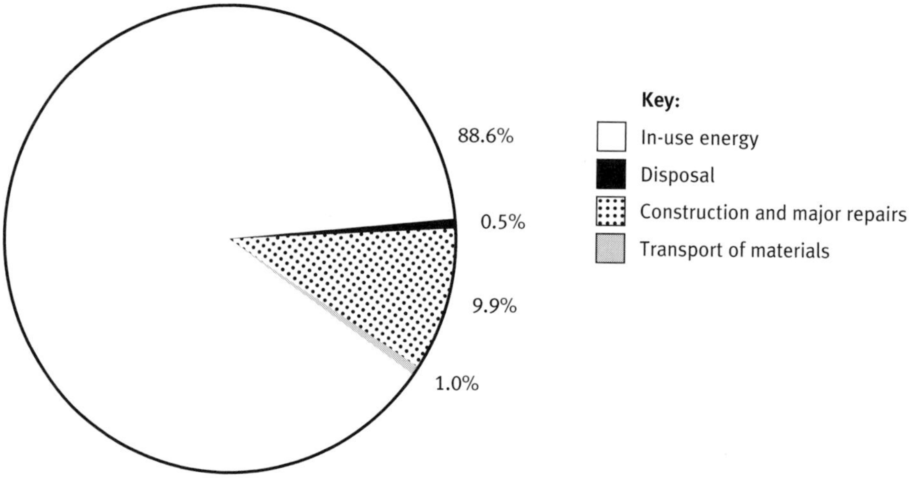

88.6%

0.5%

9.9%

1.0%

Key:
☐ In-use energy
■ Disposal
▦ Construction and major repairs
▨ Transport of materials

Source: Andrew Horsley

Delivering an energy-efficient building depends on a number of factors, but basically can be summarised as a combination of :

- the location and performance of the building envelope and structure
- the performance of the services
- the behaviour of its occupants.

These features are not mutually exclusive, and to achieve energy efficiency each must be evaluated and optimised. One of the key problems in delivering an efficient building is that "complication [is] added before the fundamentals have been made efficient".[2] Furthermore, attempts to estimate the energy performance of buildings, where they are made at all, are often done at the end of the design process when the opportunity to influence the finished product is severely curtailed.

Our research has identified very few processes and indices to guide fundamental design decisions. Of those that do exist, most are in-house tools that can only be accessed by commissioning a specific design team or specialist consultant.

We have designed the Energy Toolkit to help designers, developers, clients and others to make the fundamental decisions that will result in an energy-efficient building. The process we have developed recognises the fact that there is an inherent "window of opportunity" in the design process, the time when you can exert the maximum influence on a design. This window occurs during pre-design activities (i.e. before the process of architectural design).

Clearly, then, methods of procurement will have a significant impact on the resulting building, because traditional procurement routes do not allow for the necessary pre-design discussions. With this in mind, we developed the Energy Toolkit through PFI projects[3] where one party is responsible for design and build functions as well as having a long-term interest in the building's operation[4].

The Energy Toolkit procedure was developed through practical engagement with eight live construction projects. The procedure should be structured, but is intended to be a medium through which ideas can develop and can be tested rather than a rigid procedure that can never be appropriate for all types of project and team. The most important difference between the Energy Toolkit and other energy/design analysis tools is that the Toolkit also takes into account life cycle costing of the various options under consideration at an early stage of the design, encouraging the development of design options or fundamental design strategies.

The procedure

The procedure is divided into three stages, shown in Table 32.1. Basically, the procedure acts as a guide to inform the user what types of analysis should be used, and when.

Figure 32.2 illustrates how the central procedure is supported by two information streams:

- energy assessments, made using commercial software tools
- environment/cost assessments, developed using a bespoke spreadsheet.

The environment/cost spreadsheet is used to convert energy and cost data inputs into graphical and data outputs. The costing process is streamlined so that only those components affected by the energy efficiency strategy are modelled. The model compares a baseline and enhanced option for a specific energy

Figure 32.2 A 'map' of the Energy Toolkit process, and how this fits with the PFI Development process

PROCESS	SELECTION	OPTIMISATION	VALIDATION

Energy assessments

- Interpretation of design brief
- Develop preliminary design
- Identify energy efficiency opportunities
- Identify a low-energy and reference case

- Review energy profile
- Identify major consuming elements
- Develop specific strategies to address these demands
- Assess impact of energy efficiency packages on building performance

- Confirm selected scenarios work together
- Perform final energy analysis and present performance statement, and potential overall energy savings

Procedure

- Establish design brief
- Prioritise energy-efficient approaches and define purpose of assessment
- Perform 'Building Design' energy assessment
- Detail potential environmental benefits
- Perform outline cost assessments

- Identify major remaining opportunities
- Perform energy analysis
- Perform detailed cost assessments
- Provide feedback to design team

- Confirm performance goals have been met (internal and client)
- Conduct final validation analysis (external)
- Complete archive record

Costing assessments

- Generate inventory of additional basic facade components
- Undertake initial life cycle cost analysis of reference and low-energy options

- Consider life cycle cost of each efficiency option using defined methodology
- Evaluate environmental and economic benefits
- Ascertain whether option is viable by determining payback periods and the strength of differentiator in bid

- Incorporate energy efficiency options into overall cost plan
- Confirm savings are realistic
- Confirm total cost savings over initial reference solution
- Prepare cost figures for archive material

DESIGN	OUTLINE DESIGN	SCHEME DESIGN	DETAIL DESIGN
PFI DEVELOPMENT	BID		PREFERRED PROVIDER

ITN response (invitation to negotiate) — BAFO (best and final offer) — **Contract signed**

Source: Andrew Horsley

Table 32.1 The Energy Toolkit procedure is divided into three stages

	STAGE 1	STAGE 2	STAGE 3
For best results, use during:	Pre-design/outline design	Scheme design	Detail design
	to achieve optimal balance of basic building characteristics to seek synergy between architectural and engineering concepts	to apply and test various energy efficiency strategies	to confirm performance is acceptable, and that predictions are accurate

Source: Andrew Horsley

efficiency strategy. For example, in an enhanced insulation strategy mechanical and electrical specifications will be modelled in addition to the wall/roof constructions for both the baseline and enhanced option, thus ensuring that all additional and avoided costs are captured.

The final output of the procedure is a dataset that is meaningful to all members of the design delivery chain, and figures that make sense at the front end of the design, and in the boardroom. The assessment pays specific attention to life cycle cost predictions for energy efficiency measures. It is important that the costing predictions are an accurate reflection of the true costs of installing energy efficiency features, so the system captures both additional and avoided costs. Further financial analysis can be undertaken by examining the sensitivity of the discount rate selected (see Chapter 29), future energy prices, and the accuracy of the energy assessments themselves.

Case study

Carillion Building Special Projects used the Energy Toolkit process during the design of the residential buildings at the University of Hertfordshire's new residential de Havilland Campus. The procedure was introduced at design inception, where it helped to demonstrate the most appropriate way of orienting, insulating, glazing the building. The result is a building that is expected to consume up to 60 per cent less energy than those built to Building Regulations minimum standards at the time (Summer 2000).

These predicted savings are purely as a result of the enhancements made to the insulation and glazing properties of the building, which surpass even the recent amendments to the Building Regulations[5] The Energy Toolkit prediction, and more

Figure 32.3 This graph shows the payback period for proposed insulation enhancements calculated using three discount rates

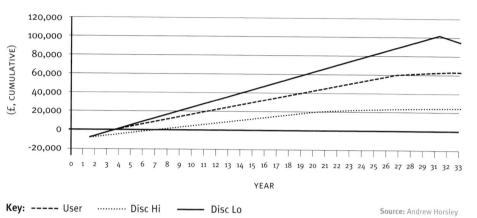

Key: ----- User ·········· Disc Hi —— Disc Lo

Source: Andrew Horsley

recent detailed assessments, suggest that the design target of slightly over 100 kWh/m²/yr will be achieved.

Figure 32.3 shows one of the financial outputs of the Energy Toolkit – the financial implications of the proposed insulation enhancements. The three lines illustrate the influence of the choice of a discount rate in the life cycle cost model (see Chapter 29), and in fact show that the rate does not affect the predicted payback period (indicated by the point where the lines cross the *x*-axis).

The results show that the payback period for the total package of enhancements is approximately 3 years. The procedure also predicted that up to £3 million energy savings could be achieved over the term of the PFI contract, to the benefit of the client. Moreover, the emissions savings calculated by the process are also substantial, at more than 40,000 tonnes of CO_2 over 25 years. This equates to each of the campus's 1,600 students driving nearly 10,000 miles a year for each of the 25 years.

References

1 Slavid R (1998), "What is sustainability?", *Architects Journal*, 5 February, 44
2 Bordass W et al (2001), "Assessing building performance in use: technical performance of the PROBE buildings", *Building Research and Information*, 29 (2), 103–128
3 The Private Finance Initiative (PFI) was introduced in the 1990s as the preferred procurement route for major UK government construction projects such as schools and hospitals.
4 Design-and-build contracts frequently offer a similar level of design control,

but additional constraints are added because the client may want to sell the building on, so will have a lesser interest in funding features that enhance whole life performance.

5   The latest revisions to Building Regulations Approved Documents Part L1 *Conservation of fuel and power in dwellings* and L2 *Conservation of fuel and power in buildings other than dwellings* were published in 2002. See *www.odpm.gov.uk*

On-line sources

www.ecofys.co.uk
www.surrey.ac.uk/engd

Further reading

Clarke J (2001), *Energy Simulation in Building Design*, Architectural Press, Oxford

Horsley A, France C, and Quatermass B (2003), "Delivering energy efficient buildings: a design procedure to demonstrate environmental and economic benefits", *Construction Management and Economics*, 21 (4), 345–356

Horsley A (2002), *Better By Design: Integrating Energy Performance Assessment into Building Design*, Thesis submitted for University of Surrey's Engineering Doctorate programme, and available in the University Library.

Energy use in dwellings

Definition

In the UK, all new dwellings must comply with the minimum standards laid down in Approved Document L1 of the Buildings Regulations, which is concerned with the conservation of fuel and power, i.e. the energy efficiency, of the dwelling. This document, commonly known as Part L1, gives designers three ways to calculate the energy use of the dwelling: the "elemental method", the "target U-value method", and the "carbon index method". For many years, consumers were unaware of the energy performance of their new homes. However, in 2000 the UK government introduced a requirement for developers to display the "energy rating" of their dwellings – calculated using the Government's Standard Assessment Procedure (SAP). The SAP can also be use to rate the performance of existing dwellings.

Related indicators

Energy, Health

Related tools

Environmental impact assessment, Ecological footprinting

About this chapter

This chapter is based on text supplied by Rajat Gupta, who works as a building performance consultant to local architectural practices and local authorities. He is also pursuing doctoral research at Oxford Brookes University on the subject of mitigating domestic carbon dioxide emissions, using a combination of energy-efficiency measures and renewable energy technologies.

It discusses the rationale behind home energy rating, and describes the various methods that designers and developers currently use to calculate the energy performance of dwellings.

Introduction

Dwellings account for 29 per cent of UK energy consumption, resulting in approximately 38 million tonnes of carbon emissions per year.[2] Over the next 20 years, the population of England is set to grow by around 3.5 million and, because of the rising trend towards smaller households, the total number of households in England is predicted to be 24 million by 2021. Thirty-five per cent of these will be one-person households – 2.7 million more one-person households than there were in 1996. Without a concerted effort by everyone involved in the housing sector, this will mean more households using more energy, causing more environmental damage.

Domestic energy use is a political issue with a long history (see Chapters 8 and 9), but it wasn't until the 1980s that workable energy models began to emerge. The best known model in the UK was introduced by the Building Research Establishment (BRE). Known as BREDEM (BRE Domestic Energy Model), this research tool has become the basis on which new and existing dwellings are compared, because it is the foundation for the UK government's Standard Assessment Procedure (SAP).

The SAP was incorporated in the Building Regulations in England and Wales in 1994, and developers are still required to report the SAP rating of dwellings to building control bodies.

In an attempt to raise the public's awareness of domestic energy use, the government introduced an additional requirement in 2000 which means that developers are now obliged to display the SAP rating on new dwellings, and in the literature used to sell them. The intention was to turn the SAP rating into a marketing tool for developers and to generate demand for homes that are more energy-efficient.

But energy rating is not confined to new dwellings. The Home Energy Conservation Act (HECA) 1995[3] requires all UK local authorities with housing responsibilities to assess the energy efficiency of all residential accommodation in their area and to take steps to implement measures that will improve the performance of the housing stock. The SAP is an important tool here, because it is equally applicable to existing dwellings, and can be used in assessments of fuel poverty and to demonstrate the benefits of refurbishment projects.

However, the SAP is not the only way to measure the energy efficiency of dwellings. Part L1 offers designers a choice of calculation methods for new buildings; and there are at least two other popular techniques unrelated to Part L that can also be applied to existing buildings.

Each method is based on well-documented research into building performance, but it is important to remember that the result of any assessment is a calculation based on a model, not an assessment of the dwelling's actual performance. The actions of residents, the care over detailing and, in particular, the airtightness of the dwelling can have a significant impact on the actual energy efficiency.

Part L1 calculations

Approved Document Part L1 lays down various requirements designed to ensure that dwellings meet minimum energy efficiency standards. Energy efficiency is to be achieved by:

- limiting the heat loss through the fabric of the building, from the space heating system and from hot water storage tanks
- providing space heating and hot water systems that are energy-efficient
- providing lighting systems that can use energy efficiently.

The "elemental method" and the "target U-value method" give an indication of how successful (or not) the building will be at resisting heat loss; the "carbon index method" assesses the likely carbon dioxide emissions that will be produced by the space and water heating under prescribed conditions.

The elemental method

The elemental method is the simplest way for a designer to demonstrate that a building complies with the requirements of the Part L1. Calculation is kept to a minimum, because the designer selects construction elements that comply with the U-values[4] listed in Part L1. The disadvantage of this method is that the result-ant building is likely to meet the minimum energy-efficiency standard – and no more. Also, there are restrictions on the type of heating system that can be used – another barrier to innovation.

The target U-value method

This method is intended to give designers a little more flexibility of choice when it comes to construction elements such as windows, doors and rooflights, and the insulation levels of individual elements in the building envelope. The idea behind this method is that the designer chooses a target U-value for the building as a whole, so some elements can be significantly better than the required minimum, while others might be a little outside the minimum requirements[5] This method can be applied to any heating system, and it also makes it easier to address issues such as solar gain.

The carbon index method

The CI was introduced in the latest version of Part L1 (2002), with the aim of giving designers more flexibility in the design of new dwellings while achieving similar overall performance to that obtained by following the elemental method. The CI rates dwellings on a scale from 0.0 to 10.0, based on the annual CO_2 emissions associated with space and water heating – the higher the value, the more efficient the dwelling. To meet the Building Regulations requirements, a dwelling (or each dwelling in a block of flats or converted building) must be designed to achieve at least 8.0.

The CI is calculated using particular sections of the SAP worksheet (see below).

The standard assessment procedure (SAP)

The SAP is the UK government's standard for home energy rating. Although it is still linked to the Building Regulations, the SAP has other uses because it can provide an indicator of the efficiency of energy use for space and water heating in new and existing dwellings, for instance, to assess a sample of the housing in an area. The original SAP rating was a scale of 1 (poor) to 100 (excellent). The scale was extended to an upper limit of 120 when the latest version of the system was introduced in 2001.[6]

Basically, the SAP is a lengthy calculation of the heat loss that can be attributed to the form of the building, the thermal properties of the fabric, and the level of ventilation. This information is equated with the cost of making good the heat loss by means of the heating system and the cost of fuel. It also takes into account the benefits of solar gain. In other words, it takes into account the fixed aspects of the building, such as the heating system, controls, insulation levels, and double glazing. The impact of the geographical location of the dwelling is incorporated into the calculations in the form of a "degree day" adjustment.

But like the other calculations methods described in Part L1, it does not take account of actual occupancy patterns or the behaviour of occupants (e.g. use of domestic appliances, individual heating patterns).

In summary:

- The SAP assumes a standard occupancy, a standard heating pattern and demand temperature.
- Using this standard heating regime as a target against which to test the dwelling, SAP uses the information described above to calculate the amount of energy required each year to achieve this space and water heating target.
- This total annual energy requirement, expressed in gigajoules (GJ), is converted to an annual cost using national average cost per GJ figures for each fuel as appropriate.

- Finally, this cost is divided by the total floor area, and this annual heating and hot water cost per square metre (described in SAP as the Energy Cost Factor or ECF) is converted into the SAP rating.

Thus the SAP rating can be described as a form of energy cost index: the more the annual space and water heating costs per square metre, the lower the rating.

Carbon dioxide emissions are calculated by converting the dwelling's annual energy requirement into tonnes of CO_2 using national average CO_2 per GJ figures for each fuel, as appropriate. The emission factors used in the calculation include all CO_2 emitted by the dwelling's space and water heating systems plus those emissions associated with the generation of fuel used by the dwelling, for example, at the power station generating electricity.

The SAP can be calculated by hand using the SAP worksheet,[6] or by using software developed for the purpose. The software is licensed to a number of developers who also offer additional services.[7]

The data needed to complete the worksheet includes:

- dimensions and U values for walls, floor, roof, windows and doors
- number of chimneys, flues etc
- local shelter and over shading
- draught stripping
- orientation
- main heating system (and secondary heating system if present)
- water heating system and hot water systems size and insulation
- fuel(s) used for space and water heating.

The results will include:

- an SAP rating (1–120)
- a carbon index (0.0–10.0)
- the annual space and heating requirements
- the annual cost per square metre of space and heating requirements
- the CO_2 emissions due to space and water heating in tonnes/year.

The National Home Energy Rating scale

The National Home Energy Rating (NHER) scale predates SAP by a few years.[8] It was developed in the 1980s from work done in Milton Keynes to develop the UK's first domestic energy rating, the Milton Keynes Energy Cost Index (MKECI).

The NHER assesses home energy efficiency on a scale of 0 (poor) to 10 (excellent). The rating reflects the total fuel costs per square metre of floor area needed to achieve an adequate overall temperature. The higher the NHER score, the more energy-efficient the dwelling.

NHER calculations take into consideration, among others:

- the method of space heating
- domestic hot water
- appliances and lighting.

The main difference between NHER ratings and SAP ratings is that NHER takes account of the total annual fuel running costs for the dwelling including cooking, lighting and appliances.[9] In addition, the NHER also takes into account the physical location of the dwelling, including site exposure.

Since NHERs can only be calculated using computer software, they can include more sophisticated analysis than is possible with a worksheet. For example, NHER calculations include the effect of solar gain from an unheated conservatory; in the SAP an unheated conservatory is considered merely as providing shelter to the external wall that is covered by it.[10]

Table 33.1 summarises the differences between NHER and SAP.

A dwelling built to 1990 Building Regulations would have a NHER of between 5 and 7, depending on where in the UK it was built. A dwelling built to the most recent Building Regulations minimum standard would have an NHER of between 7 and 9, depending on location.

Building Energy Performance Index

The Building Energy Performance Index (BEPI) assesses the thermal perform-

Table 33.1 NHER compared with the SAP

NHER	SAP
Ratings of 0–10	Ratings of 0–120
Variety of locations	Centre of UK
Height above sea level	Not assessed
Site exposure	Not assessed
Local weather conditions	Not assessed
Fuel costs of: • space and water heating • cooking • lighting • appliances	Fuel costs of: • space and water heating
Differences in room temperature between zones	Not assessed

Source: Rajat Gupta

The NHER scheme

The NHER scheme, administered by National Energy Services Ltd, is a membership scheme that examines, registers and monitors NHER assessors. NHER assessors are able to issue quality assured SAP ratings and NHER ratings, plus a range of other services.

NES Ltd has produced a number of software tools under the NHER branding:

- NHER Builder, for assessing new housing energy ratings and Building Regulations compliance from plans
- NHER Evaluator, which expands the capabilities of NHER Builder, covering existing housing, and evaluating the effect of energy efficiency improvements
- NHER Surveyor, for assessing the energy rating of existing homes based on site surveys
- NHER HECA Manager, and a property database used to issue energy advice to a large number of households
- NHER AutoEvaluator, which allows organisations to report on the energy efficiency of their housing stock
- NHER ProBase 2, a property database that allows organisations to manage and report on the energy efficiency of their housing stock.

---

ance of the fabric of the building taking into account its orientation,[11] and can be used to gain an indication of the degree to which the fabric complies with the Building Regulations.

The advantage of this measure is that it only assesses the building fabric. As such, it is a good representation of the insulating properties of a dwelling, because it leaves no opportunity for the developer to compensate for poor building fabric by installing efficient boilers or choosing a more efficient fuel. In addition, it acknowledges that installed appliances have a relatively short life, and there is no guarantee that replacements will measure up to the previous standard.

This index will give a relatively accurate picture of the housing stock but, as with the other calculation methods, the on-site execution of designs and improvements can affect energy usage.

There is a range of NHER software that can be used to calculate BEPI.

References

1   Building Regulations Approved Document L1 *Conservation of fuel and power*

in dwellings (2002 edition), published by Department of the Environment, Transport and the Regions,(DETR) can be downloaded from *www.odpm.gov.uk* These are the regulations covering England and Wales. The Scottish equivalent is *Technical Standards Part J*. For ease of reading, this chapter will only refer to Approved Document L1 (Part L1).

2 DTi (2003), *Our Energy Future: Creating a low carbon economy*, Government Energy White Paper, The Stationery Office, Chart 1.5, p 17.

3 Home Energy Conservation Act (HECA) 1995 can be viewed at *www.hmso. gov.uk*

4 The U-value is a measure of the "thermal transmittance "of a substance or, in the case of the construction industry, a building element: i.e. how much heat will pass through 1 m² of a structure when the air temperatures on either side differ by one degree. U-values are expressed in units of watts per square metre per degree of temperature difference (W/m²K).

5 The target U-value is based on the overall exposed form factor of the dwelling, and then modifies this value based on the efficiency of the boiler and relative area of exposed south-facing glazing. To comply, the overall average area-weighted U-value of the elements of the building must be no greater than the target U-value.

6 BRE (2001), *The Government's Standard Assessment Procedure for Energy Rating of Dwellings*, 2001 edition, BRE, Watford

7 The current list of approved SAP software developers is at *http://projects.bre .co.uk/sap2001*

8 For details of the NHER and the NHER Scheme, visit *www.nher.co.uk*

9 The NHER is based on BREDEM 121, which takes into account lighting, appliances and cooking when calculating typical annual energy consumption; SAP is based on BREDEM 9, a simplified version of BREDEM 12.

10 The calculations in SAP 2001 (see 6) suggest that the separation between a dwelling and a conservatory treats the walls, floors, doors and windows between the conservatory and dwelling as if they were comparable to the corresponding exposed elements of the dwelling.

11 Smith PF (2001), *Architecture in a Climate of Change: A guide to sustainable design*, Architectural Press, Oxford.

Further reading

DETR (1996), General Information Leaflet 31 (GIL31) *Building Research Establishment Domestic Energy Model (BREDEM)*, Energy Efficiency Best Practice Programme, The Stationery Office, Norwich

Shorrock LD and Anderson BR (1995), *A Guide to the Development of BREDEM*, BRE Information Paper, IP 4/95, BRE, Watford

Sociological survey techniques

> *Related indicators*
>   Quality of life, Health, Community.
>
> *Related tools*
>   Post-occupancy evaluation.

Introduction

Buildings will only be valued, liked, forgiven for their faults and made to last if they meet the needs of all stakeholders. Thus the quality of life (QOL) of occupants and the local community should be of paramount importance throughout the life of a building – from inception to demolition.

But what are the stakeholders' needs, and how can these be balanced with the various constraints that burden any project? These questions are rarely high on the client's brief, partly because we still live in an age where projects are profit-driven. However, as this book clearly demonstrates, any forward-thinking client should now be putting sustainability, and therefore social issues, at the top of their priorities list. For those enlightened clients who are willing to embrace sustainability and all that it entails, a problem still remains – how to understand (and, ultimately, predict) stakeholders' expectations and needs.

Pioneers in the field of building performance evaluation, such as Bill Bordass, Adrian Leaman and Jim Ure, have spent many years trying to improve the lot of the ordinary building occupant. Rather than measuring air velocity, ambient temperatures or lighting levels, their methods are based largely on asking "How do you feel about …?" Their techniques are a stark contract to the traditional building services approach – where calculations rule the day and occupants are merely "passive heat generators". Studies of modern buildings in the glossy magazines are full of images of uninhabited expanses of façades, walls or floors, and they rarely discuss how the building will make people "comfortable", "delighted" or even, significantly, "more productive".

Part of the problem is that social issues can't be measured with a thermometer. To make matters worse, needs and expectations are different for each project, and they change over time. The only solution is to go out and ask people what they think, feel or perceive. But this is not a one-off exercise. Questions must be asked at inception, during the project, and periodically once the building is occupied. If the data is gathered systematically, it can be analysed to show how the project is performing against expectations, similar projects can be compared, and lessons learnt can be passed on to future projects – part of the "virtuous circle" we discussed in Chapter 1.

Given the modern trend towards market-led, customer-focused business, it is surprising that many designers do not discuss social issues with their clients, even at the stage of completion when the "snagging" is done,[1] let alone when the occupants move into the completed building, or have settled in. Project team feedback conferences are rare, so there are few opportunities to discuss even the most basic and obvious lessons about the strengths and weaknesses of a completed design.

Understanding stakeholder needs is not "mission impossible". There are a number of sociological surveying techniques that can be used to assess expectations and outcomes. These range from simple like/dislike questionnaires to more sophisticated tailor-made surveys that look at a broad range of indicators. This chapter gives an overview of some successful methods, including the Overall Liking Score technique developed by Jim Ure and his colleagues at ABS Consulting.[2]

General principles of sociological surveying

It is important to ensure that surveys produce sensible results that can be compared across projects.

For national or international benchmarking projects, such as the European Sustainable Cities and Towns Campaign,[3] you will need to follow very clear rules about the size of the sample groups. You will also need to follow the project's guidelines on sampling techniques to maintain scientific credibility for the results, and use prescribed analytical methods to obtain the results. For this sort of work you will need either to employ a statistician to ensure the scientific validity of the work, or to adopt a standard methodology.

For smaller-scale research, for example of a single large building, there are already well-established post-occupancy evaluation methodologies (see Chapter 39). However, it is perfectly possible for smaller design practices to develop, and refine over time, an in-house method that will provide valuable feedback to improve the performance of future projects.

The key to a good survey is preparation. You must first develop a list of key issues, or indicators, for the scheme or project. The information in Section 2 and 3 of this book will help you decide on the indicators most appropriate to your project. You must also decide how to describe the positive or the negative attributes of each issue, and what sort of scale you will use to measure responses, and then compile a questionnaire.

A "pre-survey" exercise will be most beneficial. Ask a selection of subjects a few "open" questions such as: "What do you like about the building?" or "What are the three worst things about the building?" Give the subjects an opportunity to explore their feelings about the building by asking: "Is there anything else you would like to add on this subject?" The responses obtained at this stage will help to shape the main questionnaire.

For any survey, the questions must be devised so as to avoid bias in the answers. For example, you should avoid rating responses on a scale from "good" to "excellent", and be wary of making all the questions at towards a single conclusion. For example, questions like "Does the building smell?" or "How would you rank the odour of the building?", imply that it has an odour, and the responses you obtain will have been steered by the question. Also, the questions themselves should be unambiguous. If you ask "What do you think about the project?" then the respondent may be confused about whether you are talking about a building, or the people who live in or manage it.

Be aware that the measurement scale gives a dimension to an answer, whether you choose a simple yes/no scale or a more complex rating. If you have carried out the preparation carefully, you will be able to establish benchmarks once the survey has been repeated a number of times, although care must be taken to ensure that the survey form and technique used is identical, to give the comparison scientific validity.

A common mistake is to collect too much data – this makes the responses difficult to analyse. And it is always important to ensure that a representative sample of people are surveyed. Common mistakes include surveying the views of only men or only women on a housing development, or only the management or the workers on a project. The survey needs to provide a rounded view from all the stakeholders. You will also need to be careful to achieve an adequate response rate across the various stakeholder groups to ensure that your analysis does not unduly favour one group.

It is also very important to repeat the survey at various stages of the project (and remember to re-word questions, if necessary). Typically, survey at the brief stage to develop the design aspirations or themes, then again once the occupiers have settled into the scheme to check if the aspirations have been successfully achieved.

Survey techniques

There are a standard range of well-used survey methods one can choose from. These surveys are tools for learning and as such can be useful and thought pro-voking, even if fairly crude in their construction.

Simple better/worse/same scales

This is, in effect, a crude three-point scale: "Are conditions better, worse or the same as before". The UK government uses this type of scale to summarise per-formance on its "Quality of life barometer" (see, for example, Chapter 5, Table 5.2)

Point-scoring questionnaires

This is the typical questionnaire favoured by women's magazines, where a series of questions are asked with three to five possible answers, each with a designated score against it. A tally of the scores tells you how well or poorly suited you are to the topic of the questionnaire. The Hockerton Housing Project uses this technique to good effect in its survey sheet "Are you ready to live in a small community?"[4] which ask questions on trust, possessiveness, sociability etc. A score of more than 30 gains the response: "You must already be part of a successful community", while a score of 0 suggests that you might consider becoming a hermit!

Range-of-opinion scales

Surveys based on a scale of, say, 1–5, 1–7 or 1–9 give an opportunity for more detailed analysis.

A 1–5 scale, where (1) is "best", (3) is "neutral" and (5) is "worst", can be applied to virtually any indicator. For example:

Which of the following feelings best expresses how you regard this building?
(1) Like it a lot; (2) like it; (3) neither like nor dislike; (4) dislike; (5) dislike it a lot.

A 1–7 scale amplifies the distinctions, with (4) as the neutral point:
(1) Excellent; (2) good; (3) OK; (4) no strong feeling; (5) poor; (6) bad; (7) dire
This type of scale can be used successfully on communities before the design stage to determine their own particular priorities, and it is equally useful for post-occupancy evaluations, such as the PROBE surveys (see Chapter 39) to test whether the various design requirements and aspirations have been met.

A more foolproof way take on this technique is to present a strong statement and then ask the respondent how much they agree with the statement:

"When I come into this building I get a feeling of a very strong sense of place."
Do you:
(1) Strongly agree; (2) agree; (3) neither agree nor disagree; (4) disagree; (5)
strongly disagree."

In some fairly well-established questionnaire techniques the 1–7 or 1–9 scale is drawn up with increments of +10 per cent or −10 per cent, so the results can be turned into percentages in the final analyses. Thus the questions may be asked:

"Do you feel that the move to this office has resulted in an increase or decrease
in your productivity? Mark where appropriate:

Less	1	2	3	4	5	6	7	8	9	*More*
productive										*productive*

−40%−30%−20%−10% none +10%+20%+30%+40%

The results of such surveys give percentage figures that can lend a useful authority to the final analysis.

Overall liking score (OLS)

Written with the generous assistance of Jim Ure, ABS Consulting.

The "overall liking score" (OLS) was developed by ABS Consulting, in collaboration with the University of Manchester Institute of Science and Technology (UMIST) to measure the reaction of occupants to their surroundings. The technique rates the importance of particular issues, features and services for the building occupants, and discovers whether they like those features. It is also useful for identifying successful features of a building, or as a "key performance indicator" for maintenance and other facilities management services. The results provide information that can be used as a basis for making informed decisions about improvements, or to identify areas that deserve closer scrutiny before capital expenditure is incurred.

Other applications of the OLS include:

- gathering the views of a local community about various environmental issues as part of a study for a local authority's town planning department
- seeking feedback from engineers on the profession's ability and desire to deliver sustainable solutions and whether the incentives and encouragement provided by government, employers and the engineering institutions are adequate
- obtaining staff opinion on their employer's customer care performance

453

- determining the level of staff support for their employer's sustainability and environmental policies
- seeking customer feedback on service and products.

OLS has been used to assess some 30 buildings in the UK.
The OLS process involves a five-part questionnaire:

- Section A deals with personal information, work details, hours at work, PC use etc.
- Section B deals with summer and winter comfort using semantic differential rating questions.
- Section C is a "Double Likert" survey that assesses the importance of a number of factors relating to the indoor environment and the organisation.
- Section D is a sickness symptoms questionnaire for deriving a "building sickness score".
- Section E is on stress.[5]

The Likert scale

The psychologist Rensis Likert[6] devised a special technique to get at real attitudes of respondents – to measure not only whether they like a house but the way in which they like a house. Likert-type survey items on a questionnaire can be useful in assessing people's opinions, beliefs, or attitudes to specific topics. However, if the goal is to facilitate discussion, Likert-type items are not useful because they are designed to assess opinion rather than stimulate discussion.

When using the Likert scale the questioner makes a number of statements that are attempting to look at similar aspects of a subject.[7] The questioner makes different statements around the idea of, say, "this building is nice" or around a reverse statement, and the respondent is asked whether they agree or disagree. For example, the questioner could say: "This building looks nice", "This building is practical to live in" or "This building is conveniently located" or "This building is ugly", to which the response each time will be: "I agree/disagree". For each of the agree/disagree statements a number is attached to the response, and the scores from the positive and negative responses are totalled, respectively. Degrees of "agreement" are possible with this technique. For example, if "strongly agree" scores 5, "agree" scores 4, "neither/nor" scores 3, "disagree" scores 2 and "strongly disagree" 1, then if six people respond, and all strongly agree, then this statement scores 30 points.

Figure 34.1 Two examples of the seven-point like/dislike scale

DO YOU LIKE THE [INSERT ISSUE, E.G. NOISE LEVEL] IN THE OFFICE?						
. . . Dislike				Like . . .		
−3	−2	−1	0	1	2	3
Comments:						

HOW IMPORTANT IS THIS [INSERT ISSUE, E.G. NOISE LEVEL] IN THE DESIGN OF YOUR IDEAL OFFICE?						
. . . Unimportant				Important . . .		
−3	−2	−1	0	1	2	3
Comments:						

Source: Jim Ure

Sections B, D and E are optional but A and C are always included.

Section C uses a seven-point scale for like and dislike (see Figure 34.1).

A like/dislike scale rather than a scale of satisfaction and dissatisfaction is used to ease understanding, which is important for a self-administered questionnaire. Issues that can be discussed in this way include:

- noise level
- electric lighting
- amount of daylight
- glare level in the room
- glare level around your desk or VDU
- your distance away from the window
- office temperature
- ventilation
- amount of air movement
- freshness of your room
- humidity level in the room
- state of your health when in the room
- the control you have over the heating
- the control you have over the ventilation
- the control you have over the lighting
- amount of working space you have in the room/office in general

• the outward appearance of your building.

A score is derived by multiplying and normalising the liking and importance scores for each factor and for each respondent. This yields a score between +21 and −21. The overall liking score for an individual, ILS, is the average of all the question multiplications normalised by dividing by the maximum possible score

Figure 34.2 Typical 'fingerprint' obtained using the OLS system

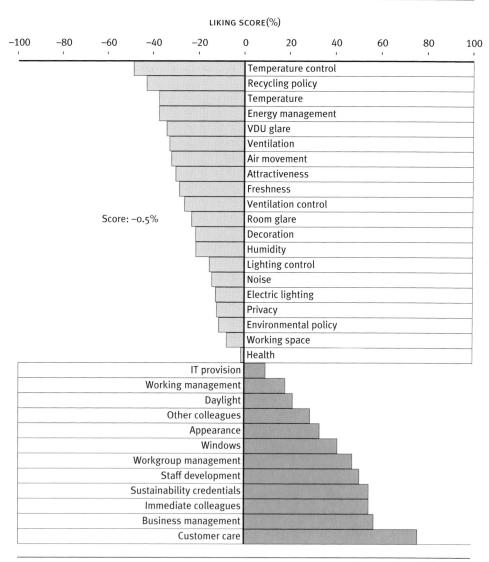

Source: Jim Ure

and expressing it as a percentage. The group overall liking score, OLS, is the average of the ILSs for the group. In this way, the importance assigned by the individual is, effectively, a weighting factor. For example, two factors may be equally liked but one may well be more important to the occupant than the other, so it scores slightly higher.

The responses to the questionnaires can also be drawn graphically to provide a "fingerprint" of the building, as shown in Figure 34.2. This fingerprint normalises each question to a score between +100 per cent and −100 per cent.

References

1 Snagging: the detailing of design faults to be made good before a building is handed over to the client.
2 ABS Consulting, 6–8 Marshalsea Road, London SE1 1HL *www.absconsulting.uk.com*
3 Further details can be found at *www.sustainable-cities.org/action.html*
4 See *www.hockerton.demon.co.uk*
5 Sections D and E are not discussed in this chapter.
6 Guidelines for writing questions suited to this technique can be found at: *http://usfweb.usf.edu/ugrads/mmc4420/Guidelines%20for%20Writing%20Likert%20Items.htm*
7 Likert R (1967), *The Human Organization: Its management and value*, McGraw-Hill, New York

On-line resources

Website of International Society for Quality of Life Studies at *www.cob.vt.edu/market/isqols*
Methodology sheets for the EU Sustainability indicators can be found at *www.sustainable-cities.org/indicators/index.htm*
UK government indicators can be viewed at *http://www.sustainable-development.gov.uk/uk_strategy/content.htm*

Further reading

Baird G et al (1996), *Building Evaluation Techniques*, McGraw-Hill, New York
Bordass, B. (1998), "Factors for success or how to compensate for things you take away", *Workplace Comfort Forum*, London, 3 December
Boudon P (1972), *Lived-In Architecture*, Lund Humphries, London
DEFRA (2002), *Achieving a Better Quality of Life: Review of progress towards sus-*

tainable development, Department for Environment, Food and Rural Affairs

Fowler F (2002), *Survey Research Methods*, 3rd edn, Applied Social Research Methods Series Volume 1, Sage, Thousand Oaks, CA

Hedge A and Wilson S (1987), *The Office Environment Survey*, Building Use Studies, London

Markus T et al (1972), *Building Performance*, Building Performance Research Unit, London

Newman O (1973), *Defensible Space: Crime prevention through urban design*, Colliers Books, New York

Preiser W et al (1988), *Post-Occupancy Evaluation*, Van Nostrand Reinhold, New York

Ravetz A (1970), *Model Estate: Planned housing at Quarry Hill, Leeds*, Croom Helm for Rowntree Trust, London

Robertson G (1992), "A case study of Atria", in: Roaf S and Hancock M (eds) *Energy Efficient Buildings*, Blackwell Scientific Publishers, Oxford

Vischer J (1989), *Environmental Quality of Offices*, Van Nostrand Reinhold, New York

Wates N and Knevitt C (1987), *Community Architecture*, Penguin Books, London

Wates N (2000), *The Community Planning Handbook*, Earthscan Books, London

Zeisel J (1984), *Inquiry by design: Tools for environment-behaviour research*, Cambridge University Press, Cambridge

Regeneration-based checklist

About this chapter

This chapter is based on text supplied by Bruce Haglund, who is a Professor of Architecture at the University of Idaho, USA. He teaches environmental technologies and architectural design with an emphasis on sustainable architecture. A charter member of the US-based Society of Building Science Educators (SBSE),[1] he serves as editor of the quarterly *SBSE News*.

Introduction

For many years, members of the SBSE had been using Malcolm Wells's "Wilderness-Based Checklist for Design and Construction"[2] to teach architecture students about green or sustainable architecture

When Wells devised his rating system in 1969, sustainable and green architecture had not been christened. His checklist consisted of 15 issues with stated positions at the polar extremes of the scale, e.g. "destroys pure air" versus "creates pure air". The way a building addressed each issue could be rated from bad

(−100, always destroys pure air) to good (+100, always creates pure air) with four levels of conformity in 25 point increments (−75, usually; −50 sometimes; and so on). Figure 35.1 shows how, in Wells's opinion, wilderness scores a perfect 1,500 while a typical 1960s research laboratory scores a dismal −750.

Figure 35.1 Wilderness-based checklist evaluations are subjective, but their graphical nature makes them simple to use and easy to analyse

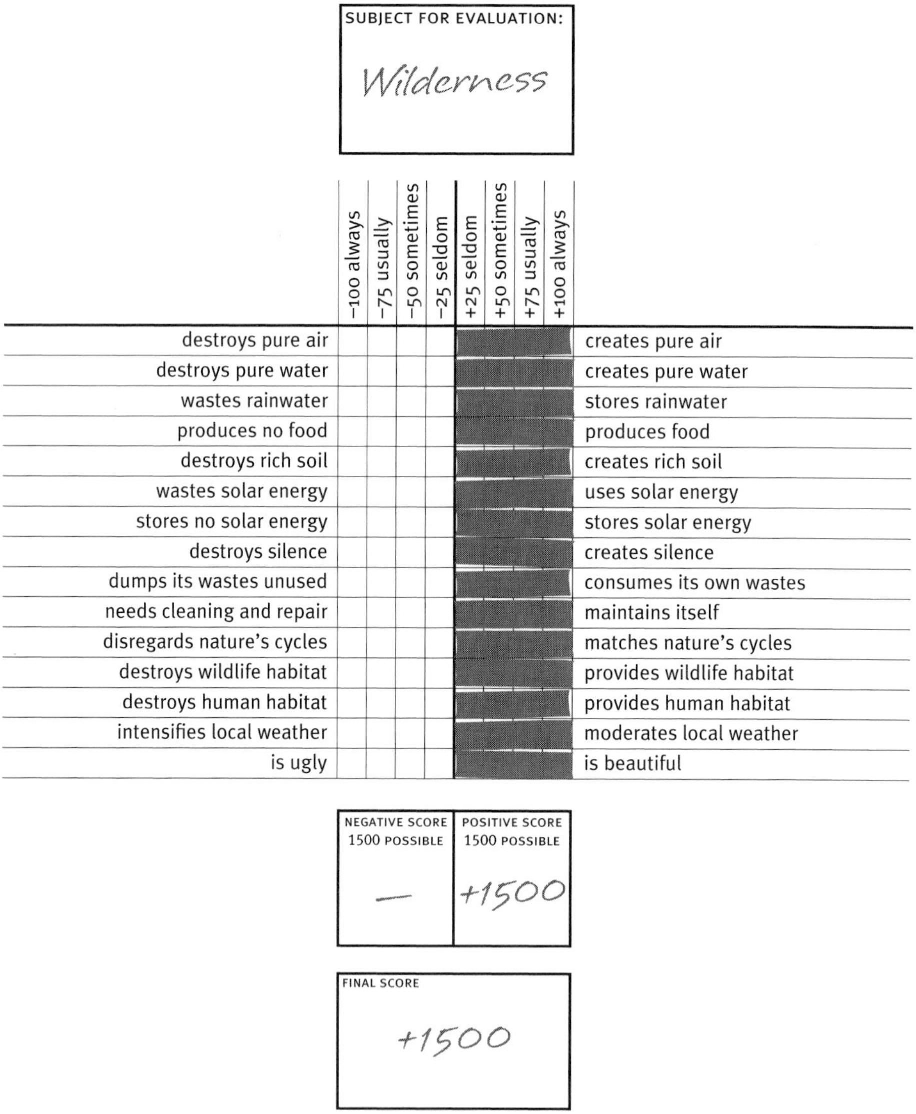

SUBJECT FOR EVALUATION:

Wilderness

	−100 always	−75 usually	−50 sometimes	−25 seldom	+25 seldom	+50 sometimes	+75 usually	+100 always	
destroys pure air					▨				creates pure air
destroys pure water					▨				creates pure water
wastes rainwater					▨				stores rainwater
produces no food					▨				produces food
destroys rich soil					▨				creates rich soil
wastes solar energy					▨				uses solar energy
stores no solar energy					▨				stores solar energy
destroys silence					▨				creates silence
dumps its wastes unused					▨				consumes its own wastes
needs cleaning and repair					▨				maintains itself
disregards nature's cycles					▨				matches nature's cycles
destroys wildlife habitat					▨				provides wildlife habitat
destroys human habitat					▨				provides human habitat
intensifies local weather					▨				moderates local weather
is ugly					▨				is beautiful

NEGATIVE SCORE 1500 POSSIBLE	POSITIVE SCORE 1500 POSSIBLE
—	*+1500*

FINAL SCORE
+1500

In 1999, a group of over 20 SBSE members met at their annual curriculum development retreat, and reviewed Wells's checklist with the intention of updating the list to incorporate the past 30 years' advances in thinking about sustainable architecture. These three decades had seen the revival of passive solar design techniques that included considerations for both heating and cool-

	SUBJECT FOR EVALUATION: *Suburban research lab*								
	-100 always	-75 usually	-50 sometimes	-25 seldom	+25 seldom	+50 sometimes	+75 usually	+100 always	
destroys pure air			▓						creates pure air
destroys pure water	▓								creates pure water
wastes rainwater	▓								stores rainwater
produces no food	▓								produces food
destroys rich soil	▓								creates rich soil
wastes solar energy			▓						uses solar energy
stores no solar energy			▓						stores solar energy
destroys silence				▓					creates silence
dumps its wastes unused	▓								consumes its own wastes
needs cleaning and repair		▓							maintains itself
disregards nature's cycles		▓							matches nature's cycles
destroys wildlife habitat						▓			provides wildlife habitat
destroys human habitat							▓		provides human habitat
intensifies local weather				▓					moderates local weather
is ugly					▓				is beautiful

NEGATIVE SCORE 1500 POSSIBLE	POSITIVE SCORE 1500 POSSIBLE
-850	*+100*

FINAL SCORE
-750

461

ing buildings, the rise of technologies for daylighting buildings and integrating the electric light and daylight systems, the birth of the nomenclature "green," "sustainable," and "ecological" architecture, and John Lyle's advocacy for "regenerative" architecture.[3]

Figure 35.2 The regeneration-based checklist for design and construction (right) has retained the look and feel of Well's original (below)

PROJECT:

	-100 always	-75 usually	-50 sometimes	-25 seldom	+25 seldom	+50 sometimes	+75 usually	+100 always	
destroys pure air									creates pure air
destroys pure water									creates pure water
wastes rainwater									stores rainwater
produces no food									produces food
destroys rich soil									creates rich soil
wastes solar energy									uses solar energy
stores no solar energy									stores solar energy
destroys silence									creates silence
dumps its wastes unused									consumes its own wastes
needs cleaning and repair									maintains itself
disregards nature's cycles									matches nature's cycles
destroys wildlife habitat									provides wildlife habitat
destroys human habitat									provides human habitat
intensifies local weather									moderates local weather
is ugly									is beautiful

NEGATIVE SCORE	POSITIVE SCORE
1500 POSSIBLE	1500 POSSIBLE

FINAL SCORE

462

The group made several recommendations about scoring, organisation, and inclusiveness that improve the clarity and timeliness of the checklist without reducing its ease of use, intent, or quality of analysis (see Figure 35.2).

Figure 35.2 (continued) Regeneration-based checklist for design and construction

Project:

	DEGENERATION				SUSTAINABILITY		REGENERATION			
	−100 always	−75 usually	−50 sometimes	−25 a bit	0 balance	25 a bit	50 sometimes	75 usually	100 always	
THE SITE										
pollutes air										cleans air
pollutes water										cleans water
wastes rainwater										stores rainwater
consumes food										produces food
destroys rich soil										creates rich soil
dumps waste unused										consumes wastes
detroys wildlife habitat										provides wildlife habitats
requires fuel-powered transportation										requires human-powered transporation
intensifies local weather										moderates local weather
THE BUILDING										
excludes natural light										uses natural light
uses mechanical heating										uses passive heating
uses mechanical cooling										uses passive cooling
needs cleaning and repair										maintains itself
produces human discomfort										provides human comfort
uses fuel-powered circulation										uses human-powered circulation
pollutes indoor air										creates pure indoor air
cannot be recycled										can be recycled
serves as an icon for the apocalypse										serves as an icon for regeneration
is a bad neighbour										is a good neighbour
is ugly										is beautiful

NEGATIVE SCORE 2000 POSSIBLE	POSITIVE SCORE 2000 POSSIBLE

FINAL SCORE

Source: © SBSE / Taloussac 1999

- **Scoring**. Following John Lyle's logic, sustainability is just good enough to guarantee survival of the planet. A greater goal is to improve the planet through design, planning, and building. To achieve this goal, regeneration is required. In order to acknowledge this distinction in the checklist, a column for balance (0 points) labelled "sustainability" was added. The extremes are now labelled "degeneration" for actions that diminish environmental quality and "regeneration" for those that improve the environment. A total score of zero indicates that a building is sustainable, meaning it does no further damage to the planet.
- **Organisation**. The issues were sorted into two divisions – the site and the building – to help users visualise the results of their scores. Issues of site design and building design are roughly equal in weight, emphasising that a building's influence extends beyond its walls, beyond its site.
- **Inclusiveness**. Several issues were revised, and their total number was increased from 15 to 22 to reflect changes in understanding and technology and to address regenerative architecture more comprehensively. Prominent among the changes is the addition of the issues of wastes, circulation, transportation, neighbourliness, recyclability, and materials. More subtly, the solar energy issue was divided into heating, cooling, and lighting. The issue of beauty was retained and supplemented by the new issue of symbolism, "Is the building an icon for regeneration or for the apocalypse?"

Using the tool

The Regeneration-Based Checklist for Design and Construction and detailed instructions for its use are maintained on the SBSE website.[4] Versions of the checklist are available in a variety of languages – French, Italian, Japanese. Korean, Russian, and Spanish at present – and the SBSE welcomes new translations.

To use the checklist you must first find out as much as you can about the building and its site, and then exercise your best judgement to score each issue. None of the issues has quantitative guidelines, so your opinion may differ from that of another scorer. However, when a large group of people rate a building, tendencies become apparent. Also, when an individual rates several buildings their relative strengths and weaknesses become evident. Therefore, the best way to use the checklist is to serially rate a number of buildings, or rate a single building in collaboration with a group. Discussing the ratings with or presenting them to a group exploits the strength of the tool to provoke thought about the meaning of ecologically responsible architecture.

Figure 35.3 Sixty architecture students completed the checklist for the 'Idaho solar house'. This scoring distribution scatter chart shows a wide degree of agreement

Project: *Title*

	DEGENERATION				SUSTAINABILITY			REGENERATION		
	−100 always	−75 usually	−50 sometimes	−25 a bit	0 balance	25 a bit	50 sometimes	75 usually	100 always	
THE SITE pollutes air			▦							cleans air
pollutes water										cleans water
wastes rainwater	▦									stores rainwater
consumes food	▦									produces food
destroys rich soil				▦						creates rich soil
dumps waste unused	▦									consumes wastes
detroys wildlife habitat										provides wildlife habitats
requires fuel-powered transportation	▦									requires human-powered transporation
intensifies local weather				▦					▦	moderates local weather
THE BUILDING excludes natural light								▦	▦	uses natural light
uses mechanical heating								▦	▦	uses passive heating
uses mechanical cooling								▦	▦	uses passive cooling
needs cleaning and repair			▦	▦	▦					maintains itself
produces human discomfort	▦		▦		▦					provides human comfort
uses fuel-powered circulation								▦	▦	uses human-powered circulation
pollutes indoor air								▦		creates pure indoor air
cannot be recycled								▦	▦	can be recycled
serves as an icon for the apocalypse				▦	▦					serves as an icon for regeneration
is a bad neighbour					▦					is a good neighbour
is ugly					▦				▦	is beautiful

NEGATIVE SCORE 2000 POSSIBLE	POSITIVE SCORE 2000 POSSIBLE
−500	*700*

FINAL SCORE
200

Case study

A University of Idaho architecture class was asked to use the checklist to rate a prize-winning solar home in Sun Valley, Idaho. The 800 m², $7 million (£4.5 million) actively and passively cooled and heated vacation home, built in 1982, was presented to the 60-strong group in a slide show that described its solar features and site and building design.[5]

Their individual scores were combined in a scatter plot showing consensus that the site design is not sustainable whereas the building design is sustainable (see Figure 35.3).

To demonstrate the checklist's value as a tool that provokes thought and discussion, the students were asked to defend their scoring of the issue: "Is it an icon for regeneration or the apocalypse?" Their responses ranged from appreciation of its cutting-edge solar features to outrage at its gross excess:

"I think the home is an affront to regenerative design."

"Overall, since this project only focuses on heating and cooling systems, I don't consider it a sustainable project despite its positive score."

"It is an icon for regeneration because of the amount of good publicity it has received and the fame that awards have given it ... they will associate good and beauty with sustainable architecture."

Figure 35.4 September snowfall on South façade of Sun Valley house

Figure 35.5 Owner and architect entertain a tour group in the Sun Valley house living room

Source: Bruce Hagland

References

1 SBSE members include architectural educators from around the world. Full details of the Society can be found at *www.sbse.org*

2 First published in 1969, Malcolm Wells's wilderness-based checklist was reissued in his book *Gentle Architecture* (1982), McGraw-Hill, New York

3 Lyle JT (1996), *Regenerative Design for Sustainable Development*, 1st edn, John

Wiley & Sons, New York

4   See *www.sbse.org/resources*

5   Details of the home were published in *Progressive Architecture* (1987), Vol 4 April, 85–95

Further reading

Orr DW (1992), *Ecological Literacy: Education and the transition to a postmodern world*. State University of New York Press

Ryn SVD (1995), *Ecological Design*, Island Press, Washington, DC

Climate data tools: Meteonorm and the Nicol Graph

Definition

Meteonorm is a simple software tool that provides climatic data – including temperature, solar radiation, wind speed and direction and relative humidity – for many locations around the world, so that the building can be designed to take full advantage of passive climatic design strategies. The Nicol Graph, devised by Professor Fergus Nicol, gives designers a simple way to determine the optimum internal temperature so that they can specify the correct passive or active heating or cooling systems.

Related indicators

Climate change; Energy; Thermal comfort; The building envelope; Insulation and infiltration; Building form and daylighting.

About this chapter

This chapter is based on text supplied by Rajat Gupta, who works as a building performance consultant to local architectural practices and local authorities. He is also pursuing doctoral research at Oxford Brookes University on the subject of mitigating domestic carbon dioxide emissions, using a combination of energy efficiency measures and renewable energy technologies.

Introduction

When designing a building the first step should always be to try to understand the overall climate of the site. This will enable you to make sensible choices about the amount of protection the building will need from the prevailing weather, but will also help you to choose appropriate passive heating and cooling systems and take full advantage of other location-related factors, such as solar gain.

Sustainable buildings are those that use the least energy and other resources but provide the most acceptable indoor conditions for the occupants. Ideally, the building will be "free running" – not mechanically heated or cooled. This will require a careful balance between the thermal mass of the building, solar access and other passive heat gains plus, possibly, the use of solar power for heating or electricity generation.

The two tools described in this chapter have been developed to aid building designers achieve these goals.

Meteonorm

Meteonorm is a software tool that will generate climate data for almost anywhere in the world. Building designers can use this information for determining the optimum inclination for a roof or façade of a building so that it will catch the maximum solar radiation for solar hot water or solar electric systems. The solar radiation data can also be used to determine the amount of daily, monthly or hourly solar radiation that passes through a window, which helps in calculating the direct solar gain within a space in a building for estimating the thermal performance.

Table 36.1 Meteonorm generates a wide range of climatic-related data

INPUT INFORMATION	DATA OUPUT
Year	Wind speed
Hour of the year	Wind direction
Day of the year	Air pressure
Local time	Air temperature
Hour	Mixed ratio
Day of the month	Dewpoint temperature
Month	Wet bulb temperature
	Relative humidity
	Cloud cover fraction
	Surface temperature
	Global radiation horizontal
	Direct radiation horizontal
	Diffuse radiation horizontal
	Height of sun
	Solar azimuth
	Beam
	Hemispherical radiation, tilted plane
	Diffuse radiation, tilted plane
	Hemispherical radiation, tracked
	Global illuminance
	Diffuse illuminance
	Extra-terrestrial radiation
	Longwave radiation, incoming
	Longwave radiation, vertical plane
	Radiation balance
	Emissivity, horizontal plane
	Emissivity, vertical plane

Meteonorm was developed by Meteotest, a company based in Bern, Switzerland.[1] Version 4.0 was released in 1999 and the latest, 5.0, in June 2003. It uses a combination of measured data plus models of solar geometry and climate types to produce a range of climate data that can then be used as input to a number of building models such as NewQUICK,™ Suncode,™ DOE,™ PV Syst™ and many more.

Table 36.1 shows the full range of data that the tool can calculate. The results can be displayed as hourly or monthly data, and in SI or Imperial units.

Using the tool

Meteonorm is simple to use. The user must specify the particular location (anywhere in the world) for which meteorological data is required, using either an interactive map, i.e. from a geographical information system (GIS), or other database, then make a series of choices before the data is delivered as hourly intervals (for dynamic simulation programs) or averaged over a month (monthly data), as shown in Figure 36.1. This data is delivered as an ASCII text file, which can be further manipulated by a spreadsheet package (e.g. Excel™), text editor (e.g. Notepad™) or word processing software (e.g. MS Word™). Version 4.0 operates in English, German, French, Italian and Spanish.

Figure 36.1 The main menu from Meteonorm v5, with status (input) data on the left and results displayed on the right

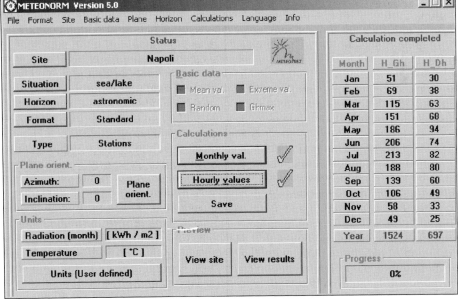

Source: © METEONORM/METEOTEST www.meteotest.com

A typical session will include entering the site data:

- Choose measured data by selecting the Stations button (this will give the most accurate results) or choose pre-calculated data by selecting the Cities button. Alternatively, choose visually by clicking on Map, then zoom and select the location on the map.
- Select user-defined options such as radiation data for a non-horizontal plane; units; and hourly/monthly data.

The radiation data in Meteonorm may be displayed as:

- H, the time-integrated radiation, measured in energy per unit area (e.g. kWh/m²)
- G, the average radiation intensity or irradiance (e.g. W/m²).

The type of radiation (i.e. global, diffuse etc) is a combination of the two. For example, H_G_h is the global solar radiation on a horizontal plane.

When used as a data source for other design programs, Meteonorm can therefore help in determining the optimum roof design for solar hot water or solar electric systems, or the direct solar gain within a space in a building.

The Nicol Graph

In buildings that incorporate climate controls – air-conditioning and central heating – the indoor temperature has effectively been decoupled from the outdoor temperature, so the comfort temperature is, to a large extent, determined either by building systems engineers or by occupants' preferences. As long as the rate of change is sufficiently slow, people can accept a range of indoor temperatures, and to a certain extent they will adjust their clothing, posture and activities with the weather. Thus the lowest temperature considered comfortable might be anywhere from 17°C or 23°C in buildings in the same climate, depending on their purpose, the attitudes and wealth of occupants or maybe the habits of the building manager.

The decision about which indoor temperature to specify in periods of heating or cooling will have a big effect on the energy used by the building. For instance, in the UK, approximately 10 per cent of heating energy is saved for every degree reduction in indoor temperature.[2] It is always worth making this clear to occupants and encouraging them to allow a building to be "free-running" for as long as possible into the traditional heating (and now, cooling) season, and to accept a variable indoor temperature to save energy. This also emphasises the importance of using passive heating and cooling wherever possible.

The Nicol Graph[3] starts from the finding, by Humphreys[4] and others, that the temperature which people find comfortable indoors varies with the mean outdoor temperature. This is especially true for people in buildings that are free running. Although – in theory – people are able to "wrap up warm", there is a limit to the amount of clothing they will find acceptable and therefore to how low the indoor temperatures can fall. However, to a large extent, people adapt to the typical temperatures in the buildings they occupy.

Using the Nicol Graph

The Nicol Graph shows the mean maximum and mean minimum outdoor temperatures (in degrees Celsius) for each month – a double curve for the year.

The thermal comfort line or the comfort temperature (T_c) for the year is calculated using the equation devised by Michael Humphreys:[5]

$$T_c = 0.534(T_{mean}) + 11.9$$

where T_{mean} is the monthly mean outdoor temperature:

$$T_{mean} = (T_{max} + T_{min}) / 2$$

and

T_{max} is the monthly mean of the daily outdoor maximum temperature, and T_{min} is the monthly mean of the daily outdoor minimum temperature. T_{max} and T_{min} are usually available from meteorological data (which could be derived from e.g. Meteonorm).

The T_c equation, strictly speaking, applies to summer conditions in freely running buildings (not air-conditioned ones) but gives a general idea of the comfort conditions required by the building occupants who have adapted to the local climate.[6]

The T_c line does not represent a single temperature but a running mean of the sort of temperatures that an indigenous person would feel comfortable in. The T_c line for summer comfort might show that people in Scotland would be happy at 18°C, while in Malaysia, Japan, Indonesia and the Caribbean, T_c is around 27°C.

A Nicol Graph for a climate in which buildings are generally free running throughout the year is shown in Figure 36.2.

The relationship between T_c and T_{mean} shows whether, for instance, night cooling is likely to be a viable way to keep the building comfortable in summer, or whether passive solar heating will be enough in winter. Basically, if the outdoor temperature, T_o, is below the T_c line, then the building will need to be heated to make the occupants warm. If T_o is above the T_c line, then the building will need to be cooled to make the occupants comfortable. This method has been extended by Roaf et al[7]

Figure 36.2 The Nicol Graph for free-running buildings in Islamabad, Pakistan, showing the seasonal changes in the mean comfort temperature (T_c) and its relationship to the mean daily indoor maximum, minimum and outdoor temperatures (T_o)

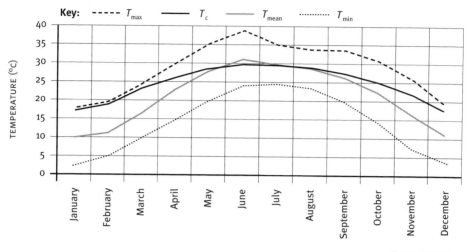

to include the mean solar intensity (G_G_h) to help identify passive heating options.

If this tool is to be applied to buildings that are heated or cooled, the free-running Nicol Graph (Figure 36.2) needs to be modified. For example, if the customary temperature in the heating season is 19°C (not unusual in a house), the indoor

Figure 36.3 Typical Nicol Graph for buildings in a climate where heating is needed in colder months. The customary indoor temperature has been taken as 19°C – typical for residential buildings, but probably lower than normal in offices

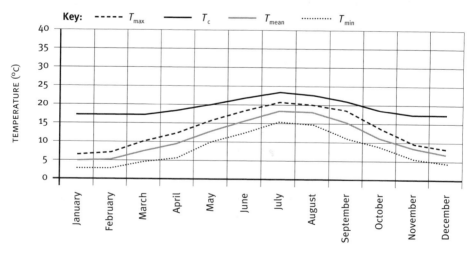

Worked example – how to make a Nicol Graph

1. From the nearest meteorological station (or library) find for each month of the year:

   - the mean daily maximum of the outdoor air temperature (Tom_{max})
   - the mean daily minimum of the outdoor air temperature (Tom_{min})
   - the mean daily solar irradiance (G_G_h in W/m²) on the horizontal (optional)

   Preferably this data should be expressed as averages for several years, but use the best you can find.

2. Determine from local people (either from experience or by conducting a survey) what are the customary temperature limits in the type of building you are designing.

3. Calculate the value of the outdoor temperature T_{mean} for each month:

$$T_{mean} = (T_{max} + T_{min}) / 2$$

4. Use Humphreys's formula to find the comfort temperature T_c.

$$T_c = 0.534 \, (T_{mean}) + 11.9$$

5. If T_c falls below customary comfort limits, for instance indicating that people will be comfortable at temperatures lower than we would intuitively expect, particularly in winter, then we often flatten off the winter comfort line at a point at which we know that people, well-clothed in a good passive building, would be comfortable. For example, we chose 17°C for the flat winter temperature, based on our experience of indoor winter comfort temperatures in the Oxford Ecohouse. In reality, we have measured considerably lower indoor comfort temperatures in places such as the city of Swat, in the North West Frontier Province of Pakistan, where we conducted annual thermal comfort field studies in homes and offices.

6. Plot T_{max}, T_{min}, T_{mean} and T_c for each month of the year

7. Where it is available, show the solar irradiation as a monthly bar as a guide to the possibilities for passive solar heating (the Roaf extension)

   If, for example, we load the monthly data for Naples (weather station) from Meteonorm such that you get monthly solar irradiance in W/m², and perform the routine outlined above, the result will probably look as shown in Figure 36.4.

Figure 36.4 Worked example of a Nicol Graph using climate data for Naples, Italy

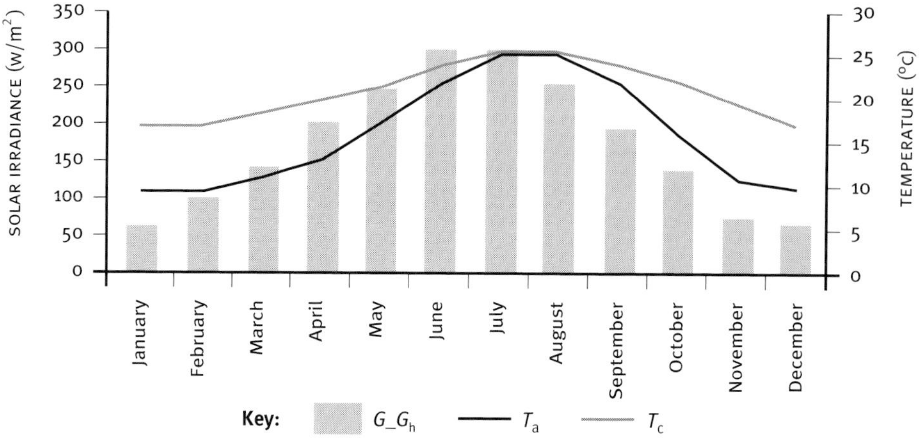

comfort temperature should not fall below this (Figure 36.3).

Other considerations

The Nicol Graph gives building designers a guide to the optimum temperature, but that is not the end of the story. Designers also need to know:

- How far can we range from the optimum without causing discomfort?
- Are there limits to the comfort temperature?
- How quickly does the comfort temperature change?

Achieving thermal comfort is related to the possibilities for change as well as to the actual temperature. If measured in purely physical terms, the width of the "comfort zone" depends on the balance between these two. Where there is no possibility of changing clothing or activity, and where air movement cannot be used, the comfort zone may be as narrow as ±2°C, but in situations where these adaptive opportunities are available the comfort zone may be considerably wider.

Clearly, there are limits to the range of temperatures that are acceptable. Indoor temperatures that require occupants to wear thick coats, for example, will be incompatible with many indoor activities such as office work. Conversely, temperatures that require high rates of sweating to maintain thermal balance may cause a physiological strain on the body, even if they are considered acceptable in terms of comfort.

Finally, it is important to remember that the Nicol Graph is based on the idea that people's comfort temperature changes from time to time. The assumption behind the way the graph is constructed (using monthly data) is that the comfort temperature only changes from month to month. In fact the rate of change can be much higher. Research has shown[8] that the characteristic rate of change is more like a week. This means that if the weather changes from week to week, the comfort temperature will also change. Thus the Nicol Graph does not say what the comfort temperature will actually be at any time, but merely suggests the average value in that particular climate.

References

1   Visit *www.meteotest.ch*
2   Rudge J and Nicol F (2000) *Cutting the Cost of Cold*, E & FN Spon, London
3   Nicol JF et al (1994), *A Survey of Thermal Comfort in Pakistan Toward New Indoor Temperature Standards*, Oxford Brookes University, Oxford
4   Humphreys MA (1976), "Field studies of thermal comfort compared and applied", *Journal of the Institute of Heating and Ventilating Engineers*, 44, 5–27
5   Humphreys MA and Nicol JF (2000), "Outdoor temperature and indoor thermal comfort: raising the precision of the relationship for the 1998 ASHRAE database of field studies", *ASHRAE Transactions*, 206 (2), 485–492
6   People can adapt to the most remarkable range for temperatures. For instance, one person can be very happy sitting in a pleasant breeze in the warm sunshine and then go inside and feel deliciously cool indoors at 7°C cooler climate.
7   Roaf SC, Fuentes M and Taylor S (2001), *The Eco-house Design Guide*, Architectural Press, Oxford
8   Humphreys and Nicol (1976), op cit

Vital Signs

Definition

Vital Signs (VS) was designed by universities in the United States to intro-duce architecture students to the environmental performance characteristics of real buildings. The VS project has produced resource packages, toolkits, and case studies that can be used to evaluate the performance of existing buildings. The project has also spawned two successors, the Agents of Change (AoC) project and Tool Days (described below), which perpetuate and update Vital Signs methods.

Related indicators

Health; Thermal comfort; Energy; Noise; Air pollution; Water quality.

Related tools

Post-occupancy evaluation.

About this chapter

This chapter is by Bruce Haglund, who is a Professor of Architecture at the University of Idaho, USA. He teaches environmental technologies and architec-tural design with an emphasis on sustainable architecture. A charter member of the Vital Signs project, he has written a resource package, participated in VS train-ing workshops, and produced web-based VS case studies. He is also an active participant in the Agents of Change project, serving as a training workshop facil-itator and advisory board member. Acting with Alison Kwok and Walter Grondzik, he has conceived and implemented Tool Day workshops to involve practitioners in the VS methodologies. While on sabbatical in the UK during 2002–03, he brought Tool Day to Ove Arup offices in Bristol and Manchester.

Introduction

The developers of the Vital Signs project[1] believe that, in order to design more environmentally responsible buildings, architecture students should gain first-hand knowledge of the successes and failures of actual buildings, much as medical interns are required to assess patients' health. They named their project after the medical procedure of measuring the physical state of a human body.

Funded by the Energy Foundation, Pacific Gas & Electric, and the National Science Foundation, the VS project began in 1993. The project was the collaborative work of educators and students at scores of universities in the US, coordinated by educators at the Center for Environmental Design Research at the University of California, Berkeley. Collaborators were recruited to write the ten resource packages, to conduct and participate in the annual training workshops, and to develop case studies of buildings using VS methods. As a result, educators at over 50 universities worldwide have adopted VS elements for their courses, including Oxford Brookes University, Portsmouth University, Dublin University and Manchester Metropolitan University.

Figure 37.1 Vital Signs has given students the incentive and means to perform hands-on investigations of building performance

Source: Alison Kwok

When the funding for VS ended, the Agents of Change (AoC) project[2] was conceived at the University of Oregon and funded by the US Department of Education Fund for the Improvement of Postsecondary Education (FIPSE). The philosophy of AoC is to train teams of faculty and their teaching assistants (TAs) in VS methods. By training TAs, the project aims at giving the teachers of the future experience and expertise that will enrich teaching and learning for years to come. AoC has also taken advantage of the progress in instrumentation technology that has made handheld measurement devices both more accurate and less expensive. Moreover, experience with the full VS toolkit has identified the instruments that are most suited for short-term, hands-on assessments of building performance. As a result, the basic VS toolkit, which cost about US$25,000, has been replaced by the AoC basic tool kit at US$1,600, which is suitable for AoC training and serves as a basis for a more extensive set of instruments. The project website gives details on the toolkit, examples of measurement exercises, and guidance for grant proposals to replicate and/or augment a toolkit.

The second VS offshoot is known as "Tool Days". These one-day sessions raise awareness of VS methods and provide AoC training for a wider audience of educators, students, and practitioners (architects and engineers).[3]

Using the toolkits

VS resource packages can be downloaded in PDF format from the VS website. There are ten packages:

- building balance point
- whole building energy use
- HVAC systems
- thermal mass
- air flow in buildings
- shading and solar heat gain
- indoor air quality
- thermal performance
- interior illuminance
- glazing performance.

Each package provides a basic description of its subject and protocols for its investigation at three levels (level 1 – brief visit, level 2 – several days, level 3 – long-term). The assessment methods described can be applied to practically any building.

Although the materials were written for university courses and workshops, they can be adapted for use by anyone interested in building performance, from homeowners to professional firms in the design and building industry. They are also suitable for those studying all aspects of buildings, environment, and energy.

The VS methods can be used in various combinations for examining diverse aspects of building performance – using the protocols in one or more of the resource packages, conducting a case study based on the guidelines and examples given on the web site, or using the toolkits for exercises described on the AoC web site.

Both the VS and AoC websites describe the operation of a wide array of instruments for building performance monitoring or assessment, including handheld

Figure 37.2 Students testing the air temperature for a vital signs case study

instruments and the data loggers, and also describe a variety of exercises for honing measurement and analysis techniques. These activities range from the simple "Hotseat," a 15-minute exercise for determining the use of a chair by using temperature as a proxy for occupancy, to "Your Secret Life," a one-week exercise to familiarise you with developing a hypothesis, collecting temperature and relative humidity data with a data logger, and analysing results in the form of a graph to reach a conclusion.

Conducting a case study

The VS and AoC websites offer guidance and examples of the case study method. The basic method is to research the building, visit it and interview the occupants, form a hypothesis or hunch about an aspect of its performance, use VS-inspired techniques to test the hypothesis, collect supporting data, analyse the test results, clearly make a conclusion, and present the findings.

Figure 37.4 (a) and (b) illustrate one such case study. The owner of the bookshop (Figure 37.4(a)) never observed his furnace running, but did notice significant heating bills. Three days of logger data solved the mystery. A logger placed near a ceiling heating vent detected furnace on–off cycling from midnight until opening time each day and no further heating activity until the next night (Figure 37.4(b)). When the shop was opened, the vast array of 100 w lamps provided sufficient heat to preclude furnace operation!

Figure 37.3 This bookshop had unusually high heating bills. Collecting temperature data showed that the furnace was on–off cycling from midnight until opening time.

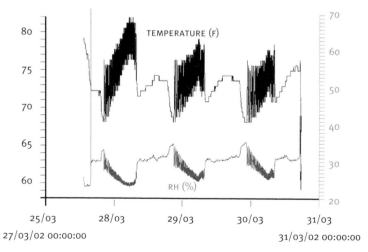

Source: Stephen Magham

CHAPTER 37

References

1 Visit *http://arch.ced.berkeley.edu/vitalsigns*

2 Visit *http://aoc.uoregon.edu*

3 Tool Day workshop descriptions are available on-line at *www.sbse.org/toolday*

Monitoring waste

Related indicators
  Air pollution; contaminated land; water pollution.

Related solutions
  Specifying for sustainability; environmental management schemes.

Related tools
  Environmental impact assessment; life cycle assessment.

Introduction

Waste management is a growing problem. As discussed in Chapter 20, when it comes to waste, there are three simple objectives:

- reduce
- reuse
- recycle.

However, this requires a degree of understanding of the various wastes being generated. Undertaking a "waste audit" of a business or a building will enable managers and producers of waste to understand where the best business opportunities lie, not only for reducing the impacts of the waste stream, but also for making money out of those economies.

This chapter describes the best available methodology we could find for waste auditing: the method used by the Southern Waste Strategy Authority of Australia in their excellent waste management programme,[1] which can be used to introduce effective waste management schemes to any business, project, school or community. This auditing technique focuses on the business-related wastes, although it could be applied to any situation. However, the issue of waste in construction is rising up the agenda, and a number of tools are being developed to simplify and streamline the data collection and analysis process.[2]

The audit process

The objective of a waste audit is to map out existing waste management practices to serve as a tool for planning future programmes. It will also enable you to assess your present system with regard to the number and location of rubbish bins within your business, major areas where waste is generated, and the number, size and location of skip bins. It is important to remember that a waste audit is only a snapshot of the waste generated in an average week. Some organisations will have periods when there is a significant additional flow of waste, so it is advisable to repeat the audit procedure several times to help identify unexpected peaks or a pattern of regular increases.

Preparation

In the run-up to the audit, inform staff that it is going to happen and encourage them to begin the waste-separation process by separating wet wastes from dry wastes to minimise contamination. This may simply mean that you will need to have two bins present at each location. Instruct employees and staff regarding which materials are to be placed in each bin:

- Wet waste – left-over lunch items, sandwiches, fruits, yoghurt, cheese, chips, breads, soups, milk, contaminated paper trays, pizza boxes and bags, used paper towels and tissues, contaminated paper and newsprint.
- Dry waste – all types of food wrappers, empty crisp packets, bakery containers, empty soft drink and water bottles, any type of uncontaminated paper, plastic wrap or packaging, catalogues, magazines, cardboard and paperboard.

Dealing with waste can be unpleasant and is a health hazard. Careful preparation is essential.

- Thick gloves must be worn by anyone handling waste.
- Safety glasses must be worn to ensure no foreign objects (i.e. glass) get into the eyes; and a face or breathing mask is essential if toxic waste is being handled.
- Suitable shoes and clothing must be worn to ensure participants don't get cut by broken glass, etc.
- Use fly spray to ward off flies and other pests attracted to the waste.
- Use long-handled tongs to collect and handle the waste.
- Washing facilities with soap and towels for washing and drying hands are essential.

You will also need:

- tarpaulins for tipping and sorting the waste
- a rake to spread out the waste
- scales for weighing the waste
- clearly labelled bins or collection bags to separate materials in the audit
- a supply of waste audit forms (see Table 38.1).

The audit

Collect and sort through the rubbish, weighing all the material, and recording the results on the waste audit forms. This process might be repeated each day for one week, say, to obtain a true picture of the volumes and types of materials involved.

The data can then be collated and results presented as graphs. The results obtained should be used to develop a waste management program for the business.

Waste management programme

Once you know the types and quantities of wastes generated, you can begin to develop a strategy to deal with them. The waste audit form is the starting point for developing a strategy, as this will give an indication of the various reduction

---

Opportunities for recycling

Recycling is discussed in more detail in Chapter 20, but it is worth noting here that there are still a number of barriers to the reprocessing of different types of waste:

- Paper is vulnerable to international commodity-based pricing and trading, and careful investment is required by both collectors and reprocessors to compete on international markets with the finished products of reprocessing.
- The metals industries may continue to accommodate imports of packaging waste. In the case of steel, total UK recycling capacity dwarfs the potential UK demand for packaging waste recycling; the influence of any waste packaging imports is minimal; collection needs to increase.
- Aluminium also has a current recycling over-capacity, which is being utilised by importing packaging waste to make the process economic; collection needs to increase.

CHAPTER 38

Table 38.1 Typical waste audit form

BIN LOCATION/NUMBER		USE THE BOXES BELOW TO INDICATE WHAT CAN BE DONE WITH THE MATERIALS FOUND IN YOUR WASTE AUDIT				
TYPE OF MATERIAL	WEIGHT OF MATERIAL (GRAMS, KG)	REDUCE	REUSE	RECYCLE	COMPOST	RESPONSIBLE DISPOSAL
White paper						
Mixed paper (coloured, glossy, etc)						
Newsprint						
Cardboard						
Plastic bottles						
#1 PET						
#2 HDPE						
#2 HDPE (coloured)						
#3 PVC						
Other plastic						
#4						
#5						
#6						
#7						
Glass bottles and jars						
Aluminium cans						
Steel cans						
Food wastes						
Green wastes						
Other waste (including contaminated paper, newsprint, cardboard and tissues)						

Source: Southern Waste Strategy Authority, *www.southernwaste.com.au*

strategies available (reuse, compost etc). But further research will be necessary. Talk to waste/recycling contractors to find out which materials can be collected, how they must be presented for efficient collection, and what costs are associated with different materials. Contractors may be able to supply colour-coded skips. Spend time researching possible solutions to your present and future waste needs by referring to existing models, websites etc.

Developing a waste management plan could be part of a wider environmental management scheme (see Chapter 26), and the same principles apply:

- Produce a written company policy on waste management that maps out a continuous improvement programme for waste reduction.
- Estimate the cost benefits that will accrue to the company/project from the scheme. This will gain the support from senior management and employees alike.
- Set realistic goals by starting small.

Once implemented, the waste management plan should not be filed away and forgotten – it will need to be continually monitored for costs and feedback about waste flows. All staff must know how it works, so a suitable budget for education and training must be included in your waste management plan.

References

1 See *www.southernwaste.com.au*
2 For example, the SMARTWaste system developed by the Building Research Establishment is a set of computer-based tools that can be used to monitor construction and demolition wastes, monitor segregation targets, and calculate environmental performance indicators. It also links with the SalvoMIE system to help identify opportunities for reuse and recycling, and the location of suitable facilities for this. See *www.smartwaste.co.uk* and *www.salvomie.co.uk*

Post-occupancy evaluation

Definition

Post-occupancy evaluation (POE) of buildings tries to answer two broad questions: "How is a building working?" and "Is this what was intended?" POE is about real-world outcomes and their consequences ("ends") rather than design prescriptions ("means"). It aids learning from experience to improve the next generation of buildings – a kind of quality control writ large.

Related indicators

Quality of life; Health; Thermal comfort; Energy; Noise.

Related tools

Sociological survey techniques; Regeneration-based checklist; The Vital Signs project.

About this chapter

The chapter gives an overview of POE and its many benefits, as well as describing eight case studies, four of which were conducted during the UK-based Probe project. It is written by Adrian Leaman, who runs Building Use Studies Ltd, which carries out studies of building performance, primarily from the users' point of view. The text was first prepared for Gaia Research Sustainable Construction Professional Development Seminars 2002, Edinburgh.

Adrian Leaman would like to thank George Baird and staff of the Victoria University School of Architecture, Wellington, New Zealand for help with the preparation of this chapter.

Introduction

The phrase "post-occupancy evaluation" (POE) was probably first coined in the 1970s in the USA to describe the process of assessing buildings in use, initially from the occupants' point of view. There is some debate about who first used the phrase:[1] Wolfgang Preiser and Gerald Davis both say they did not, despite many thinking that one of them did; while Bob Bechtel says that some used the term "post-occupancy assessment" because they thought "evaluation" would be too threatening to architects. Interestingly, when Joanna Eley interviewed facilities managers in the UK in 2002 the response was: "POE is what happens after we've gone".

The more informative phrase "building performance appraisal" was introduced by the Building Performance Research Unit (BPRU) in the UK in the early 1970s.[2] This tells us more of what POE is about, including early decisions, the design and production processes, and the building in use.

Baird and colleagues[3] say that the performance approach is:

"...the practice of thinking and working in terms of ends rather than means ...concerned with what the building (or building product) is required to do, rather than prescribing how it is to be constructed."[4]

Generally there are three types of feedback about buildings:

- Review of project performance. This covers the brief, design, project management, programming and co-ordination, cost control, build quality, etc.
- Feedback during the first year or so after completion. This can help to fine-tune, inform the client and the design and building team, and ease transition into full and effective operation.
- Assessment of the complete product and its performance in use.

POE is normally understood to fall in the third of these, although it can sometimes be included in any or all three.

Feedback has recently come to prominence:

"Those of us who study buildings in use regard...feedback as essential. Not only can a recently completed building be better understood and improved in operation, but all those involved in procuring and making it can learn from their experience and do better next time. Forty years ago the Royal Institute of British Architects put a feedback stage into their Plan of Work for Design Team Operation. In spite of this, such feedback is by no means routine. Indeed, after briefly blossoming in the late 1960s, POE in the UK has struggled to maintain its existence, at least until recently."[5]

However, the gathering of feedback in the UK is still relatively rare, and funding especially difficult to obtain. There are many reasons for this, some of them embedded historically in the way knowledge about buildings is organised and applied.

- A sustained programme of POE is harder to carry out than most realise at the outset. The most difficult and under-estimated aspect is data management, i.e. the maintenance of the benchmarks and methods over a series of buildings. Organisations rarely have the foresight to see this.
- The industry is not organised to collect POE and feedback information or to deal with it. It also sees it as a threat, despite the tendency for most POEs to accentuate the positive in reporting their findings.
- Clients do not see why they should be doing something they hope to take for granted. Nor does government – in spite of the major public interest aspects. Nobody wants to "own" POE.
- Academic disciplines do not regard building performance as an area of legitimate interest. It seems both too trivial – even anecdotal – and at the same time too difficult.
- POE is interdisciplinary, so it does not fit well into career paths and funding stereotypes. In addition, POE has a real-world bias, so it is not very fashionable because it does not theorise overly or draw on trendy computer models and simulations.
- Professions tend to be territorial, defending their perceived areas of expertise, and are often ill-equipped to include the client's and user's perspectives. Partly this goes with the job – they know too much about buildings to step back far enough.
- Most designers and builders go straight on to the next job without learning from the one they have just done; this is also related to time/cost pressures.
- There is a tendency of those concerned with running buildings (e.g. facilities managers and surveyors) not to talk to those who provide them. Learning curves are quite steep and ill-defined. You need to know a lot in order to do POE. It is basically a real-world, not a laboratory problem; and systemic, not single-issue. Only a handful of schools of architecture (e.g. the Victoria University of Wellington, New Zealand) have courses on building performance.
- There is a lack of a quality-control tradition at the level of the building itself (although products and components within the building do have this tradition). Integration between systems is often the sticking point.
- Finally, there is the "not invented here" tendency, endemic in the UK, for research organisations not to recognise the work of competitors.

POE techniques

Because we live in buildings and use them every day, they seem to be simpler than they actually are. In fact, buildings have many physical sub-systems (e.g. site, fabric, shape, services, fit-out etc.), and relationships with the external environment (e.g. lighting and ventilation), and many of their governing processes are intangible (e.g. the normally invisible time dimension is just as important as visible spatial form but gets less attention). Buildings are also a mixture of physical ('hard') and behavioural ('soft') systems. It is often difficult to resolve this complexity.

If this were not enough, the most problematic complicating factor is often a building's context, which includes not just its physical location but also e.g. procurement, design, operation, management and use patterns. Contextual factors often explain a lot (e.g. why one building's performance may differ substantially from another although they seem to be superficially similar). Management factors often turn out to be more important than designers envisage.

Given these problems, it is often better to approach buildings with a real-world research framework.[6] This involves examining things that are likely to happen in a given real situation, rather than looking at cause and effect, which may require contrived situations like laboratory experiments (see Table 39.1).

Table 39.1 Real-world research looks less for causes and effects and more for risk factors and consequences

"REAL WORLD" RESEARCH		TRADITIONAL (ACADEMIC) RESEARCH
Solving problems		Just gaining knowledge
Predicting effects		Finding causes
Looking for robust results and concern for actionable factors		Looking for statistical relationships between variables
Developing and testing services		Developing and testing theories
Field		Laboratory
Outside organisation (e.g. business)	*RATHER THAN . . .*	Research institution
Strict time and cost constraints		R&D environment
Researchers with wide-ranging skills		Highly specific skills
Multiple methods		Single method
Oriented to client		Oriented to academic peers
Viewed as dubious by some academics		High academic prestige

Source: adapted from *Real-World Research*, C Robinson, Blackwell, Oxford, 1993, pp12

A real-world approach also helps:

- to create improvement strategies which involve occupants and management rather than just solely being technically or physically based
- to deal with system-wide complexity (taking in not just the building and its occupants but other related factors like company culture or journeys to work)
- with the practicalities of an occupied building (managers may not allow you to do all the improvements you want or they may not have enough time or money).

Capturing how an occupied building really works can be a mesmerising task. For example, the Centre for Building Performance Research (CPBR) Checklist of Techniques[7] has over 150 possible POE analysis methods. A list recently prepared for a UK project "Feedback"[8] has 50 potential POE methods.

With this embarrassment of riches the dangers are that you will choose the wrong method, waste time reinventing an approach that has already been tried elsewhere, generate far more data than you can manage to analyse, subsequently discover that you have focused on the wrong area, or used a technique for which no robust benchmarks are available, making it difficult to interpret your findings. For example, your building may score 2 out of 5 on your study but is the average building 1.5 or 3?

POE has taken 30 or more years to get off the ground, partly because it has not been obvious which techniques are best. Weakly developed inter-disciplinary research, lack of support by the professions and lack of funding continuity are also to blame. However, there have been thousands of studies which can potentially be called POEs. Unfortunately, many of them are hard to get hold of, or are not published at all; and they cannot be effectively compared with each other (they often do not use performance benchmarks, and are effectively "one-off" projects). Some do not report their analysis procedures clearly enough, so it is often difficult to assess findings to find out whether they are believable (this is especially so with research studies carried out by design firms for their own purposes, the results of which may be used in their publicity); while others are hard to follow because they include jargon and do not report conclusions in formats which designers, managers or building owners can easily follow and from which they can easily learn. Most reports seldom take sufficient account of context.

The problem for anyone embarking on a POE is deciding which techniques:

- work well and can be applied quickly and efficiently
- are reliable (i.e. they give roughly the same results when used by different people in similar circumstances)

- do not intrude too much on occupants' and managers' time and patience
- are most relevant in a given situation
- give results which are easiest to compare with other studies
- give good value in terms of the quality, content and range of information derived
- rely too much on measured data from e.g. physical monitoring equipment, which can be time-consuming to set up and collect, and sometimes still be incomplete and thus hard to interpret
- do not suffer from incomprehensible "normalisation" (that is, results have been adjusted, but the assumptions for the adjustments are not made clear).

This chapter includes four short descriptions of POE studies conducted as part of the Probe project.[9] One of the reasons why the Probe project has been relatively successful is that it used just three existing methods, which were known already to be practical and robust:

- The Energy Assessment and Reporting Methodology (EARM),[10] which comprehensively covers building energy performance from both a supply and a demand perspective. This helps researchers to gain a thorough understanding of technical performance, and is helpful with diagnostics. For example, it tells you not just how well the building is doing overall compared with benchmarks, but precisely where it succeeds and fails.
- Building Use Studies' (BUS) occupant questionnaire,[11] which covers occupant issues like comfort, health and productivity in a format which gives useful information across a range of disciplines (e.g. architecture, building services, facilities management) and is also helpful to non-specialists. Altogether, 65 variables are covered to give a comprehensive coverage, but not too much or too little.
- An air pressure test to CIBSE TM23[12] specifications, which examines the air-tightness of the fabric.

Each of these three assessment methods incorporates benchmarks based on per-formance evaluations of the building in use rather than on models, simulations or design prescriptions, all of which tend to introduce un-testable, and often unre-alistic, assumptions.

As well as these three methods, the more recent Probe investigations also have added:

- A pre-visit questionnaire (PVQ)[13] to collect basic data about hours of use, technical systems, plans and other background information in advance of the actual survey. This is valuable because it improves consistency and is a useful test of the seriousness of the client. If they cannot give you the information, it will usually be best not to attempt the POE.

- A water consumption method, but this is not yet fully benchmarked.
- A supplementary questionnaire to the occupant survey for journey to work and transport mode.

The limit on the scope of Probe investigations was a practical decision based on what was achievable within onerous time and cost constraints. The Probe results were to be published, which added an extra dimension.[14] This approach gave an energy and services perspective, with an emphasis on sustainability through assessing the robustness of the building, the satisfaction of the occupants and management, and the avoidance of waste.

Results of the Probe project were published in the *Building Services Journal*, so it has been perceived as having a services bias. In fact, services is just one of the windows through which the material may be viewed. The Probe data can also be looked at with an architectural or facilities management perspective, for example. Probe also yields "strategic" conclusions at one level up from the individual building studies.

Probe deliberately did not attempt to cover directly:

- first costs
- costs in use
- aesthetics
- space efficiency, density or utilisation
- design and procurement history.

However, in the course of their work, the Probe team developed insights on each of these aspects. All may find their legitimate place in POEs. However some, like costs, are notoriously difficult to pin down.

Other topics which are of interest in POEs include:

- aesthetics, which has specialist methodologies that cannot be readily applied and compared in all situations
- space use – relatively easy to carry out, and can be included as an option, but is rarely asked for
- design and procurement history, which is often quite hard and expensive to study, especially as the design team will usually have dispersed, and can rake up old disputes which may be best left undisturbed.

Choice of content and approach often depends on:

- what you actually want to find out (for example, a relatively modest exercise based on walkthroughs and interviews may be all that is necessary)
- whether it is important that conclusions stand up to peer-group scrutiny (many building assessments do not report their assumptions, sampling procedures and methods clearly enough) but can nevertheless be useful for those involved
- whether the results are likely to be published (probably less than 10 per cent of POEs ever are)
- whether or not the work is to be carried out by investigators who are independent of the building project itself (which ultimately will carry more weight)
- the resources and time available.

In practice, Probe found that most of the salient points about performance can be arrived at either directly or indirectly without needing to cover everything in painstaking detail, and showed that it is possible to get perhaps 80 per cent of the performance story by collecting less than (say) 20 per cent of available data. Experience has shown that successful POEs have most of the following:[15]

- a sponsoring organisation with the initiative to collect the POE information, time to make sense of it, and the will to share it
- management support and long-term commitment to signal the importance of the exercise at senior levels
- broader opportunities and incentives for participation and reflection, especially with respect to the goals of the organisation and its business strategy
- opportunities to identify critical stages where lessons from feedback can be built in
- some kind of involvement in the POE in contracts and pre-qualification for suppliers
- information which is understandable for different audiences: e.g. policy and planning documents for senior management
- backed by simple databases, both for individual buildings studies (to extend the number of questions that may be asked of the data) and for the management of benchmarks over many buildings (to keep this process manageable)
- ideally include design hypothesis, photos, data summaries, some cost, size and technical data, lessons learned, connections to other studies and recommendations

- cover projects where there are complaints or controversy (not just on buildings which are perceived to perform well)
- cover innovative buildings to decide whether to continue with the innovations but give the designers due credit for innovations if outcomes do not work properly (otherwise the POEs may be criticised for nipping innovation in the bud)
- start modestly to demonstrate potential and usefulness, then build up the cases into a bigger sample so that benchmark comparisons can be made.[16]

Where do you start?

One of the main purposes of POE is feedback, so it is sensible to begin by organising the material so that it may be used first in a strategic brief, then later in the POE itself. In this way, the targets set in the brief may be followed through and eventually evaluated. This also provides a way of keeping the brief on track, and managing it throughout the course of the project. However, this also depends on access to a project with the foresight to do this! Unfortunately, most projects are not like this: the POE team only rarely has input at the briefing stage, so opportunities for management of the feedback loop are less.

If the opportunity arises, the following approach may be useful:

1. Organise the strategic brief using three main headings – context, qualities and implications.
2. Develop the detailed brief or briefs within the framework of the headings.
3. Use the headings for the main categories of assessment in the POE.
4. Then examine overall feedback in a more generic way, again within the overall discipline of the topics in the headings.

The headings may also be used as a means of managing the brief as it evolves, so that assumptions of various participants can be addressed, and the needs and expectations of the client and potential users set out. If circumstances permit, there is potential for POE to be extended into a fully fledged briefing and evaluation tool by management of the design brief to embrace it. This process can be as simple or detailed as you wish to make it – from a simple diagram to a detailed spreadsheet.

Context

Context covers:

- the "business case" – why was the building needed and for what main purposes?

- locational, site and planning considerations – the main "physical" constraints
- investment potential, including value
- adaptability options for future changes of user or use
- user requirements and human impacts for first and subsequent occupiers
- environmental considerations and impacts, especially energy, water, waste and demolition strategies
- transportation impacts created by users' journeys to work
- likely technological, social and economic impacts that may affect the project in the short and medium terms (here, the project should be "future-proofed" against premature obsolescence)
- organisation culture[17] and changing lifestyle considerations.

Usually, contextual factors turn out to be the most important in the final performance analysis. For example, the Centre for Mathematical Sciences at the University of Cambridge[18] was subject to planning constraints on building height to satisfy local residents' concerns about the visibility of artificial lighting after dark. This then affected factors such as ventilation strategy, which in turn had unexpected knock-on effects on performance.

Investment and planning criteria often dominate, with user and environmental requirements being left on one side. Investor caution is often the reason why environmental strategies are left out. Investors are notoriously risk-averse and tend to avoid anything which does not fit the market's perception of the norm. One role of POE is to provide factual information to help overcome scepticism, especially with newer ideas. For example, property investors have yet to appreciate the advantages of mixed-mode ventilation strategies, which can give good results in POEs on both energy performance and human comfort and can have flexibility/adaptability benefits.[19]

Human performance is also under-represented. After all, one of the purposes of a building is to help create added wealth through better human performance. Because human factors are not costed or given due value in the project itself, they often get much less attention than they deserve. This applies especially to fundamentals like thermal comfort, personal control, usability and responsiveness, which have been shown in many POE studies to be associated with health, satisfaction and productivity.[20]

The interpretation of the POE results will, to some extent, depend on taking regard of ruling circumstances and making due allowance for them, especially when constraints are more onerous and the level of difficulty of the project is higher. However, it will usually be impossible to quantify these factors, so judgement will be needed.

Qualities

"Qualities" are the essential and desirable features summing up the building as a whole. The central task of the POE is to assess the main performance attributes of a building given the context. These attributes (called "qualities" here, but they could equally be called "values" – there seems to be no English word which works properly!) depend on what the client who is paying for the POE actually wants to find out. In many POEs only two or three qualities will be emphasised, with the others given less or no consideration.

Almost every POE will use a slightly different list of qualities and give different weights to the attributes. Note that cost is treated here (below) as a quality in the sense of perceived qualities like "expensive", "typical" and "good value". As with other performance attributes, perceptions of cost attributes are usually context-sensitive.

Space

The physical attributes of the enclosed spaces, plus their ability to meet performance requirements, is an obvious area for POE analysis. Probe does not treat space as a primary object of enquiry (it could easily do so if funds were not restricted). For example, it is possible to measure occupant density, room utilisation and space efficiency if required. In Probe, information about spatial performance is derived mainly from observation, interviews and the occupant questionnaire. Information about space can cover:

- size and capacity, and the ability to cope with use bottlenecks
- adaptability and flexibility strategies, especially with respect to the management of change and churn
- density of occupation, especially in open-plan workspaces
- basic layout, workgroup and floor plate use
- disposition of circulation and support space uses
- evacuation strategies.

Operations

Operations covers most of the areas relevant to facilities management including maintenance. It reflects how well the building in use responds to needs over time, a neglected area of study in buildings. It is becoming clearer that a building's performance over time, especially user response times, is a vital element in good performance. The time dimension is given much less emphasis than space because it is harder to "see" and because time-series monitoring data are usually ignored (e.g. Building Management System (BMS) demand monitoring data) or non-existent. Operations performance in Probe is derived from the pre-visit questionnaire, interviews with key facility management staff, observations of systems in use and inference from occupant questionnaire data. Areas to cover include:

- operations, especially effectiveness out of core hours
- security
- maintenance
- usability, especially for personal controls for users, of heating, cooling, ventilation, lighting etc., and usability of main building management system control interfaces for facilities managers
- manageability, which is obviously connected to usability, but also includes, for instance, how well the building's operations manuals are understood and key areas implemented (including help-desk response times and the management of occupant complaints)
- flexibility in response to everyday needs, and adaptability in the longer term, in relation to the medium- and long-term requirements (including, for example, performance bottlenecks not just in the use of physical space – excess demand for meeting rooms, lengthy dwell time of lifts, car parking bottlenecks – but also other performance problems such as excessive IT network log-in times, slow speed of network access problems to remote network)
- cleaning, a vital area for human health but rarely given the importance it deserves
- health and safety requirements and their implementation.

Environment

Environment as a sub-heading covers both indoor environment requirements and environmental impacts. The Probe studies examine environmental performance as one of its primary areas, although Probe does not have a full coverage (e.g. embodied energy and demolition are excluded). Transport modes were included in Probe 22 for the first time because however well a particular building may perform for energy consumption, this always begs the question of how people travel to the building.[21] From a user point of view, thermal comfort is one of the main factors that is perceived to affect human performance and productivity. Also covered are other vital areas like lighting, noise and ventilation. Possible sub-headings here are:

- indoor environmental performance
- energy efficiency, and provision for effective waste management and avoidance
- embodied energy

- demolition strategies (for efficient disposal both for the base building and fit-out changes)
- transport modes and journey times (especially with respect to excessive car use).

Users

Gary Raw, who ran the Healthy Building Centre at the Building Research Establishment (BRE), has said: "People are the most valid measuring instruments: they are just harder to calibrate". With careful sampling even seemingly contradictory responses from wide ranges of people can yield useful information. Probe found that a short occupant questionnaire covering the main topics is by far the most effective means of eliciting useful data from a building in use. This type of survey can be carried out in a day or less, and managers and staff do not usually regard it as an intrusion.

Many people still think that "measured" data (e.g. temperature or lighting levels) is somehow more valid than the ratings of occupants, but as one occupant in a Probe questionnaire so succinctly put it: "The building management system may know about the temperature, but it does not sit in the draught it causes."

As well as questionnaires, structured interviews, walk-through surveys and focus groups are also valid means of gathering useful user data, but they may be less able to stand up to scrutiny for objectivity.

User surveys can successfully include comfort, health and satisfaction, demographic characteristics such as age, sex, time in building, time at VDU, and other building-related factors (see reference 17).

Image

The image of a building is one of its most potent characteristics. Organisations often place great emphasis on image; others, like military establishments, may deliberately want their buildings to look inconspicuous: either way, image is a factor.

During the emergence of environmental psychology in the 1970s, many techniques were developed to examine how people perceived buildings. Most of these do not now find their way into POEs because they are often costly to set up and ultimately do not yield sufficiently interesting results, but possible topics include:

- aesthetics, styling, branding
- wayfinding and signage
- mental mapping
- townscape imagery.

Cost

Cost is the biggest begged question in POEs. Probe specifically excludes it, for example, because it proved expensive and unwieldy to get credible cost data, and can be a hostage to fortune. Surprisingly, most organisations do not collect useful information about costs-in-use on a building-by-building basis. They can be reluctant to give researchers access to what they perceive as confidential information. This is one of the reasons why building economists tend to use cost models of theoretical buildings based on tender price indices for analysis of first costs, rather than continuously monitoring real examples.

This approach to cost, realistic as it is in the circumstances, begs the whole point of POEs, which are trying to piece together an empirical snapshot of a building in use, not just a hypothetical model of it. One of the most important questions POE needs to answer is not just first cost or cost-in-use but "perceived value for money". We have found cases of buildings that perform reasonably or very well on many of our POE criteria, but are still perceived as "poor value for money" even though their outturn costs per square metre are still close to industry norms!

If costs are to be included they should cover:

- first costs
- costs-in-use
- value for money.

Implications

Quality improvement is the main aim of POE, but the relevant qualities of a building depend on what is rated as important by the different parties involved. It is useful to think of four broad groups of users:

- "Corporate" users – executives and leading decision-makers in organisations of all types. They are often pre-occupied with the organisation's image (and thus the way the building reinforces or changes the image, sometimes trying to use a new building as an opportunity for culture change). They examine industry-wide benchmarks on, for instance, productivity and financial performance, and will usually want to see their organisation amongst the highest-rated. They often want evidence of "value for money" in their buildings, and will pay more attention to cost norms than to other performance features like user comfort or energy efficiency. Some POEs include interviews with corporate decision-makers, but this is not always found.
- "Normal or everyday" users – this includes the many sub-types of building occupants: individual users (e.g. visitors to libraries or museums,

permanent staff, contract staff), users in their workgroups or departmental groups, tenants as users, owner occupiers and also "user" organisations and interest groups like trade unions. Users' objectives are usually focused on the task in hand, either at an individual or group level. They want conditions in the building that help them carry out their tasks as well and as easily as possible. They are far more concerned with everyday practicalities than with the way the building looks, and will usually be satisfied if things work reasonably well. They often tolerate faults, and will be prepared to give designers and managers the benefit of any doubt that arises, but only if they like the building and/or the management well enough. Most POEs include detailed examination of users' attitudes and preferences.

- Facilities managers – although primarily concerned with support services for users, facilities managers have different priorities from ordinary users. In the best-performing buildings, they try to be as responsive and helpful in providing what users need, and making sure that the building is comfortable, healthy and safe. They may also be a source of performance data (e.g. energy data, maintenance logbooks or complaints registers). Ideally, occupants should be able to have enough control over their indoor environment so that there is no need for constant intervention by facilities managers. However, many modern buildings have reduced user control and replaced it with a facility management service, often operated via a help desk. This makes the FM service more critical in certain larger buildings. If this is under-resourced, then there will be performance penalties. Usually, a POE will involve detailed interviews with facilities managers as a first step in the analysis.

- The design team (perhaps also including other suppliers of services in the construction team) – tends to see the building from yet another perspective. Often (and for good reason), the time/cost/quality aspects of the project preoccupy this group, sometimes at the expense of the attention to detail required by users and facilities managers. They may caricature users' requirements, or fail to appreciate some of the goals in the brief. If the design team stresses corporate priorities (e.g. image) at the expense of user and/or FM requirements this may be a formula for disaster. Here the architect may be perceived as arrogant, obsessed with imagery and out of touch with reality. Best-performing buildings have been given due and equal emphasis to corporate, user and FM requirements, and have recognised that there may be conflicts between them that need to be resolved either at design stage or in the building management if they cannot be reconciled in the physical building.

Not only do user types have different goals, each of them may also have conflicting assumptions about behaviour, requirements and provision. For example, a corporate client may assume that the design team will provide an energy-efficient building, although it has not been explicitly mentioned in the brief. The design team, on the other hand, may work closely to the written brief and may not pay enough attention to energy efficiency if it has not been explicitly itemised.

Ordinary building users almost always assume that usability and comfort will be a "given" in the project, and can become disenchanted if it they do not find them in the finished product. If corporate managers have raised occupant expectations too much, and the finished building does not live up to the hype, then this can also be a recipe for disaster. The management of assumptions and expectations is a vital part of this process, especially so in buildings that have cost a lot of money or have been designed by a well-known architect. Users often give designers the benefit of the doubt in cases where they have been genuinely consulted, but will be much less forgiving if they have been treated peremptorily.

POE – what we have learned so far

Post-occupancy evaluation currently has many advocates but few practitioners. Although it may be obvious that feedback from buildings in use should be an integral part of the design and construction process – just as it is in most other industries as part of taken-for-granted quality control regimes – this rarely turns out to be so. Even the most technically advanced design practices and construction companies struggle to embrace it, even though they may wish to. These are some of the reasons:

- Occupied buildings are complex systems which are a challenge to study. There are hundreds of topics which might potentially be embraced. It is hard to distinguish between topics which are "nice-to-have" or "need-to-know", especially for the inexperienced or those working under the guidance of e.g. research project steering groups (who are myopic and usually ask for much more than can realistically be delivered).
- Whereas studies of single buildings are relatively easy, it is much harder to maintain them over larger samples of (say) ten or more. Managing the "meta-data" (the full multi-building data set that provides the benchmarks) defeats all but the most stoic. Research funds usually do not support meta-data activities, but equally, research organisations normally do not take the skills required seriously enough – including computer programming, statistics, web management, continuity between projects, in-house

learning, and continuous professional development.

- POE projects are often enthusiastically supported at lower levels in organisations, but vetoed higher up. Corporate decision makers tend to perceive POEs as risky and hostages to fortune, especially when they have never seen or understood what value POEs provide. Those who use POE understand this value and embrace it thereafter. This is self-fulfilling. The better managers are prepared to deal with consequences, which in turn helps to improve their skills and awareness. This puts POE at the "top" of the market because it embraces the very skills that got organisations to the top in the first place! This, also, means that POEs tend to report on the better-performing buildings.

- Designers and managers from their different perspectives find it hard to extract useful information from POEs. Reports are too verbose. They tend to deal too much with academic, research and professional sub-agendas (like design quality) rather than immediately useful results. Although this is easily said in fact, it is formidably difficult for the POE author (especially those doing it for the first time) to meet all needs and requirements, especially when a wide spectrum of topics are involved.

- POEs by their nature are multi-disciplinary. They have to deal with topics from the supply industry's perspective (e.g. the designers and construction team) and from the user side (e.g. clients, building occupants, developers and managers). All these want different things from POEs and can get impatient if they don't immediately see their special topic in the findings.

- POEs work best in multiple. One or two may tell you about individual buildings' quirks and features, but they do not tell you about the bigger picture. It became obvious in Probe that, as more buildings were done, the story emerging from them became consistent and the strategy clearer. But funding almost always sacrifices strategy in favour of short-termism or even tokenism.

POEs have confirmed that the best buildings operate as "virtuous" systems with a well-defined context helping to foster pre-conditions for good qualities to emerge from both the eventual design and serendipitous outcomes from the building in use.

Once established in the building, the qualities themselves (e.g. airtight fabric, the character of the spaces, ease of maintenance, thermal comfort) will normally make the building easier to look after, which again helps with their performance in use. This is why POEs often find clusters of variables, with good features occurring together (e.g. comfortable, energy-efficient buildings which are relatively easy to manage and a pleasure to work in). This inter-dependence between performance qualities and context is essential. Usually, POEs give too much emphasis to the performance aspects and not enough to the contextual.

The converse applies as well; in fact, it is more common. Where the context has not been properly described (for instance, an important constraint may have been absent from the design brief or the designers may have failed to act on it), or where context has been ignored altogether because the design used a standardised, "one size fits all" approach, the consequence will emerge later in the form of an acute or chronic problem with which the building users will eventually have to cope. This phenomenon has been termed the "revenge effect".[22]

Acute failures (e.g. structural collapse) are relatively rare because building and

Table 39.2 Summary of lessons learned from Probe POE studies

OBJECTIVE	GETTING THERE
Ends	Strategy first: don't confuse means and ends. Be clear about objectives. Be prepared to test objectives in a POE.
	Establish the essentials: concentrate on good quality baseline requirements, then decide what you want to forget about. Don't procure what you can't manage later on.
	Targets are always moving: constantly review objectives and don't become complacent about "solutions". Don't commit to a design too early in a project . Give the time dimension as much emphasis as space. Be aware that cures may be worse than diseases.
Feedback	Keep hold of reality: manage the brief. Don't let prescription trump performance. Identify risks and possible downsides. Don't be myopic about risk.
	Share your experiences: be brave, go public. Learn on the job. Be honest. Feed back internally and more widely. Use different mechanisms for attributable and unattributable items.
	Adopt open source data: use the same definitions, formulae and protocols as everyone else. Avoid "not invented here". Use licences. Acknowledge useful work of others.
Means to ends	Get real about context: identify constraints (site, budget, money, time, people, culture ...) then manage them realistically. Look at risk/relevance trade offs. Work to the occupiers' true capacities.
	Own problems, (don't hide them: don't export problems onto somebody else. Sort out which professional tasks should be owned by whom. Give occupiers or management more ownership of key areas (like noise) that can't be solved by design alone. Give more leeway to individual occupants and what can reasonably be left to them (e.g. personal control).
	Less can be more: now a design cliché but still true notwithstanding. Make essential features of intrinsically efficient options. Seek simplicity. Avoid unnecessary complication. Do not create more problems than you can solve!

Source: Probe Team

health regulations guard against them, but chronic defects (i.e. more frequent but less life-threatening) such as poor energy efficiency or poor thermal comfort conditions are endemic. Once established they are difficult to eradicate because of the self-fulfilling nature of the vicious circles of which they form a part. An example of this is "sick building syndrome,"[23] where a combination of chronic failures with e.g. cleanliness, discomfort, inadequate ventilation and poor air quality create a potentially unmanageable self-reinforcing cycle of deterioration. With "sick" buildings, correcting the management deficiencies is often more challenging than physical problems with the design.

Lastly, what has knowledge gained from POEs told us about strategy? Table 39.2 lists some of the overview points from Probe.

Case studies

Further details from these and other case studies can be found on the publications page of *www.usablebuildings.co.uk*

Case 1: BT Brentwood – a model for the future?

British Telecom (BT) Brentwood[24] is a particularly good example to begin with because the building has many of the features which earlier POEs have shown to be beneficial to users, such as stable thermal performance and higher provision of occupant controls than are usually found in open-plan workspaces. The "Workstyle" building comprises 15,000 m² of office space on three floors, with restaurant and "winter garden" conservatories.

First results from occupant surveys show that the approach has probably been vindicated. For example, independently audited perceived productivity gains of 8 per cent are reported. At the time of writing, energy efficiency measures and physical monitoring of the indoor environment were ongoing.

Noteworthy features at BT Brentwood include:

- Mixed-mode ventilation (with ventilation provided either naturally through openable sash windows or via air supplied mechanically through floor plenums and outlets). The ventilation strategy is both seasonal and zonal (with deep-plan space treated differently from peripheral areas). A red-green system of lights on interior columns tells occupants which operating mode is current. Red means "Don't open the windows." The system seems robust enough for occupants to ignore this if they like, although this is frowned on by facilities management.
- Relatively generous floor-to-ceiling heights (2.7–3.1 m is the norm in speculative offices) which allows cross-ventilation across a greater depth

than normal (18 m in this case; 15–16 m is normal). Better daylighting and views out are also achieved.

- Double-skin façade with single outer glazing, which creates a thermal flue and provides protection from high winds. The inner wall has double-glazed sash windows and manually controlled solar blinds.
- Programmable individual lighting, controlled by users from their desks via telephone handsets (which seemingly works well and fits the BT telecoms culture, although it may transfer less well elsewhere).

Case 2: Historic building under transformation – National Trust for Scotland headquarters building

The headquarters of the National Trust for Scotland is at 26–31 Charlotte Square, Edinburgh (with the 2–6 Hope Street Lane extension at the rear). NTS (and other bodies) wanted the restoration of the building to be an exemplar of sensitive restoration with conversion to modern uses. In keeping with the Trust's aims and philosophy, the terrace of (originally) large houses (with a Robert Adam façade) has been refurbished to accommodate the current functions of the Trust, while retaining as many of the original features as possible. The resultant building has 2,940 m² of net usable area, and the Hope Street Lane extension has 627 m²; a total of 4,200 m² gross. About 180 staff work in the offices, with 10 in support and 30 (including shift workers) in the gallery, shop and restaurant.

The strategy for conversion was to meet NTS's requirements while retaining and restoring the original domestic qualities. For example, vertical divisions between the six houses have been kept and sometimes reinstated, and all six front doors have been brought back into use. A main circulation spine in the basement connects all six houses, and a new basement link connects with the extension in Hope Street Lane.

An internal POE using Probe methods was commissioned to examine how well the aims of the project had been met, and to make recommendation for the future. As might be expected with an 18th Century terrace, the severe constraints of conservation had meant that many compromises had to be made to accommodate the modern activities. Nevertheless, the predominately cellular nature of the layout plus its city centre location and natural ventilation meant that staff, although critical of layout and the resulting effects on communication between departments, for example, found the building comfortable to work in. Energy consumption fell between good practice and typical benchmarks.

Case 3: Exception that proves the rule 1 – The Elizabeth Fry Building, University of East Anglia (UEA)

The Probe POE made the Elizabeth Fry building famous beyond its modest attributes.[25] The comfort ratings given by the occupants of the offices in the Elizabeth Fry building (EF) are the second highest ever recorded by Building Use Studies Ltd in the UK. At the time of the survey they were the highest. On occupant satisfaction, the building has one important physical property on its side – the cellular office. The next task is to achieve the similar excellence in energy and comfort in the open-plan offices that many organisations now require. As Case 1 shows, this may now be possible.

These results didn't just happen by chance, or by the selection of a particular technical system. They came from committed people and attention to detail, which is rare in an industry that puts too much emphasis on time and particularly cost, often to the detriment of quality. EF's energy performance, although excellent, still leaves room for engineering systems improvement. Services engineers Fulcrum think that with refinements – particularly attention to specific fan power – they might halve the fan energy consumption in a future building. Lighting efficiency and control could also be better.

Factors for success included:

- A good client. For the past decade at least, the UEA has been seriously trying to obtain better buildings.
- A good brief. UEA takes care in brief preparation, and since the late 1980s has been particularly interested in obtaining buildings with ground-breakingly low energy and maintenance costs.
- A good team. You seldom get the best out of a team on its first job: people are still getting to know each other! But clients often wish to shuffle the pack every time, in the hope that the organisation you don't know will be better, or cheaper. On EF, UEA used a team which had worked with them and with each other before.
- A good design. The response to the brief led the design team to seek to avoid air-conditioning in the lecture rooms; and they found that Termodeck™ (with modifications) was appropriate. Initially the offices were to be naturally ventilated, but Termodeck™ proved affordable here provided that the fabric insulation and airtightness performance was good enough to eliminate the costs of perimeter heating. Less is more!
- An appropriate specification. The team took advice on aspects of the design with which they were unfamiliar, in particular the Termodeck™ system and on obtaining the well-insulated and airtight shell which was so important to

achieving their objectives.

- A good contractor. For an innovative solution, a traditional JCT contract worked well, with a main contractor who entered into the spirit of the design; together with that seemingly vanishing species – the client's Clerk of Works.
- Well built, with attention to detail. Often the things that cause the most technical difficulties occur at the interfaces: an issue which subcontract packages, co-ordinated by management, too often ignore. At EF, designer, contractor and client all paid particular attention to the unusual insulation, airtightness and Termodeck™ details
- Well controlled. Here there was a false start. The client wanted "fit and forget" stand-alone controls. Although the building is a stable thermal flywheel, its slow response makes it like the proverbial supertanker: difficult to "steer" until you become familiar with its handling characteristics – and this needs good control and feedback! Fortunately, UEA was able to retrofit a building energy management system, and to use it effectively, improving comfort and performance and halving gas consumption.
- Post-handover monitoring and support. Probe advocated a "sea trials" period during the first year of occupation (Termodeck™ UK Ltd now suggest two years). At EF, as in most other buildings, this did not happen initially. However, following initial problems with controls, and feedback from monitoring, the attention devoted to understanding and fine-tuning has allowed the building to deliver such high levels of comfort and energy performance.
- Management vigilance. Universities tend to have limited resources for looking after their buildings. Recognising this, and having some maintenance nightmares from the past, UEA has clear requirements for simplicity and manageability. Having contained the problem, they then endeavour to keep on top of things, and have recently reorganised themselves to respond locally, effectively and rapidly. However, now EF is running sweetly, UEA will be turning its attention to other buildings.

Case 4: Exception that proves the rule 2 – One Bridewell Street, Bristol

If it is possible to call a building enigmatic then this is the one. Surveyed first in 1990, then subsequently in 1994 and 1996, but never the subject of a formal POE, One Bridewell Street has turned out, like the Elizabeth Fry Building, to be another exception that proves the rule.[26] For an air-conditioned, open-plan office, its energy and occupant performance has been exceptional, especially during the period in the 1990s when the building was operated under a diligent facilities management department.

Case 5: Modest project assessment – National Centre for Early Music

In 1975, the York Civic Trust assumed responsibility for five redundant churches. One of these, St Margaret's, Walmgate, was offered by the Civic Trust as a possible base for the activities of the York Early Music Foundation.

This post-project appraisal is a model example of a warts-and-all assessment of the lessons learned.[27] It includes:

- the original business plan
- initial organisation and project development
- strategic brief and appointment of professional team
- validation and briefing
- submissions and final plan
- detailed design
- negotiations with the Arts Council
- construction
- revisiting business plan during construction and restatement of need
- evaluation of project process
- budget out-turns
- building evaluation, including acoustics etc.
- evaluation of performance
- lessons for the future.

In essence, the performance space for musical recitals and events uses the restored church, and the ancillary and support services, including offices, reception and toilets, are accommodated in a new single-storey building immediately adjacent.

This project's scale is not really appropriate for a fully fledged POE. However, this review gives valuable insight into the processes involved, especially into the Lottery funding process, with particularly valuable information about the briefing stages.

Case 6: Small-scale "green" building – Woodhouse Medical Centre

Woodhouse Medical Centre (WMC), at just 640 m² gross, is the smallest building studied in Probe.[28] The single-storey medical centre on the outskirts of Sheffield is domestic in scale and construction. It is divided into three individual units occupied by two separate general practice surgeries and a dental practice. Opened in 1989, it was built to very high standards of insulation (wall U-value 0.2 W/m²K; roof U-value 0.1 W/m²K), and includes several other low-energy features such as mechanical ventilation and heat recovery (MVHR), gas condensing boilers and low-energy lighting. It was also completed within the strict financial and spatial constraints of the local Health Commission, with no additional funding for the low energy features.

WMC has the lowest carbon dioxide emissions per square metre of any of the Probe buildings. It is well liked by occupants despite several gaps in their understanding of the design intent – which appeared to stem from little contact between the designers and the building's end users during and after handover. For example, the heat recovery room ventilation units were generally assumed by users to provide a form of year-round air-conditioning, and hence to provide improve summer comfort. In fact, they had no bypass, so would actually tend to increase air temperatures. These units were largely unused at the time of the Probe survey. Similarly, the natural ventilation strategy was to use casement windows (sometimes now with their movement restricted by added external security bars) and if necessary to cross-ventilate with outlets through openable roof windows near the ridge in corridors and public areas. However, the roof windows were not used because they are high up and impossible to reach. Although operating poles or motors could quite easily have been added, they were not, and consequently summertime temperatures could be high. In addition, the intended cross-ventilation of doctor's surgeries via high-level windows to the corridors proved impossible owing to the need for acoustic privacy. One practice decided to retrofit split DX air-conditioning room units in a number of spaces: since these are only used in times of need, their contribution to annual energy consumption is low.

Case 7: Well-known "green" building – Queen's Building, De Montfort University

The Queen's Building has academic facilities for about 100 staff and 1,500 students in the School of Engineering and Manufacture at de Montfort University, Leicester.[29] Occupied in 1993, it is of particular interest for its daylighting strategy and its innovative use of natural ventilation, with its distinctive ventilation stacks. The 9,850 m² (gross) building has three distinct areas: the central building, the mechanical laboratories and the electrical laboratories. A full-height concourse in the central building acts as lightwell and thermal buffer zone for adjoining spaces, including ground floor main auditoria and classrooms ventilated by the stacks. The mechanical laboratories are mainly a naturally ventilated machine hall, flanked by small specialised mechanically ventilated labs, which also form an acoustic buffer. The electrical laboratories are housed in two shallow-plan, four-storey wings either side of a narrow courtyard which facilitates simple cross-ventilation and well-distributed daylighting, though with somewhat unusually placed windows.

The design team's concept was a highly insulated (e.g. wall U-value is 0.3 W/m²K), thermally massive envelope with generous ceiling heights (3 to 3.3 m) to facilitate natural ventilation and daylighting; and greater heights in main circulation and the mechanical laboratories.

Control of internal conditions relies extensively upon a BMS to control roof vents and motorised dampers.

It is also a good example of a building whose "green" credentials have been over-hyped, notwithstanding its innovative features. Probe found it to be not particularly energy-efficient for its type, and rather uncomfortable for the occupants.

Case 8: Transport counts too – Centre for Mathematical Sciences, University of Cambridge

The project came about from Cambridge University's need to rehouse the increasingly congested Faculty of Mathematics, together with a generous endowment. The resulting Centre for Mathematical Sciences pulls together several departments on a greenfield site less than 1 mile from the centre of Cambridge.[30]

With the site surrounded by houses, there were understandable restrictions on the development's height and its visibility at night. The complete development includes a gatehouse, a library, and central building (Pavilion A), surrounded by six pavilions (C–H) and a further double pavilion (B) at the west end. The design process incorporated a strong low-energy agenda, informed by the first series of Probe reports, with which the design team were familiar. The client was also averse to sealed, air-conditioned work spaces, preferring instead den-like spaces with openable windows for their cerebral occupants.

Key design lessons:

- The advanced natural ventilation strategy with solar shading, exposed thermal mass, single-sided buoyancy-assisted natural ventilation with secure night-time automatic ventilation works reasonably well.
- Occupants' ratings for summertime comfort are good for a building of this type.
- Energy management, however, was not so good, with split management responsibilities.

One of the noteworthy features was the low mean journey to work time (20 minutes compared with a UK average of about 45) and 77 per cent of staff either walking or cycling to work. Cambridge is one of the most cycle-friendly cities in the UK, but these are still exceptionally low journey times.

References

1   This information was kindly provided in an e-mail exchange by members of the Environmental Design Research Association (EDRA) in August 2002.

2   Building Performance Research Unit (1972), *Building Performance*, Applied Science Publishers, London

3   Baird G et al (1984), *Energy Performance of Buildings*, CRC Press Lyd, Boca Raton, FL, p 7

4   Note that, in the USA, the term "building" tends to be used to mean just the physical artefact and its enclosed spaces, whereas "facilities" is used to cover the whole building in use over time. This terminology has not caught on elsewhere. Outside the USA "facilities" is usually taken to mean the services that are provided in buildings (e.g. restaurant, cleaning, lifts, toilets), and "building" can mean either just the physical artefact or the building in use.

5   Bordass W (2002), "Learning more from our buildings – or just forgetting less?" Review for *Building Research & Information Journal* of Federal Facilities Council, Technical Report 145, *Learning from our buildings: a state-of-the-practice summary of post-occupancy evaluation*, National Academy Press, Washington, USA

6   Robson C (1993), *Real World Research*, Blackwell, Oxford

7   CPBR List of Techniques complied by Harry Bruhns. Chapter 8 of Baird G et al (eds) (1996), *Building Evaluation Techniques*, McGraw-Hill, New York. This book also has a review of cases and techniques.

8   *Feedback. A Partners in Innovation project to encourage clients and the industry to undertake feedback*, William Bordass Associates, London, 2003

9   Probe studies were published in *Building Services*, the CIBSE journal, from 1997–2002. A special issue of *Building Research and Information* (vol 29, number 2, March/April 2001) is also devoted to Probe. Probe information may also be downloaded from *www.usablebuildings.co.uk*

10 CIBSE (1999), *Energy Assessment and Reporting Methodology: The Office Assessment Method*, Technical Memorandum 22, CIBSE, London

11 BUS questionnaires may be obtained via licence from *www.usablebuilings .co.uk*

12 CIBSE (2000), *Testing Buildings for Air Leakage*, Technical Memorandum 23, CIBSE, London

13 The pre-visit questionnaire was first used in-house by William Bordass Associates and then by Probe. It is now available for a modest licence fee. Apply via *www.usablebuildings.co.uk*

14 Cohen R et al (2001), "Assessing building performance in use 1: the probe

process", *Building Research and Information*, 29 (2), 85–102.

15 Bordass (2002), op cit

16 BUS has a sample of UK buildings that is large enough for comprehensive occupant benchmarks. Samples of buildings in Australia and New Zealand are approaching the size required for robust benchmarks.

17 Organisational factors like changing staff morale or management quality may affect POE outcomes. People may use criticism of the building as an indirect way of getting at management they dislike. These factors may be detected, but are often hard to study directly. It may be wiser to avoid subjects like job stress or staff morale in a POE questionnaire, for example, because they give management an excuse for denying you access to the study building. It is best to stick to topics in POEs which are directly building-related.

18 The Probe Team (2002), "Probe 22: Centre for Mathematical Sciences", *Building Services Journal*, July, 57–62 (see *www.bsjonline.co.uk*) (also available from *www.usablebuildings.co.uk*)

19 See Case study 1, BT Brentwood, for example.

20 For a range of downloadable papers on this topic visit *www.usablebuildings .co.uk*

21 Probe 22 Centre for Mathematical Sciences included a journey to work survey which is now a standard part of the BUS occupant survey method.

22 By Edward Tenner, author of *Why Things Bite Back*, Fourth Estate, London, 1996

23 The term "sick-building syndrome" is another that does not work properly. "Building-related illness" is better. People get ill, not the building.

24 Hughes A, O'Carroll D and Uys E (2002), "BT 'Workstyle' Brentwood, Essex", *Arup Journal*, 13–18

25 M Standeven et al (1998), "Probe 14: Elizabeth Fry Building", *Building Services Journal*, April, 37–41 (see *www.bsjonline.co.uk*)

26 Published material on One Bridewell Street includes *Energy Efficiency in Offices*, Good Practice Guide Case study no 21, *One Bridewell Street*, Energy Efficiency Best Practice Programme (May 1991); J Eley (1996), "Proving an FM Point", *Facilities Management World*, 1, 11–13

27 Full details are available in pdf format from *www.usablebuildings.co.uk*

28 Standeven M, Cohen R and Leaman A (1996), "Probe 6: Woodhouse Medical Centre", *Building Services Journal*, August, 35–39 (see *www.bsjonline.co.uk*)

29 Asbridge R and Cohen R (1996), "Probe 4: Queens Building, de Montfort University", *Building Services Journal*, 1996, 35–44

30 Probe Team (2002), op cit

Further information

Landmark studies in POE are listed in Table 39.3.

Table 39.3 Summary of POE references

SEMINAL WORKS IN POE	DATE	TOPICS	BUILDING TYPES	PLACE	REFERENCE
Tom Markus, Tom Maver and others	1972	Appraisal techniques	Mainly schools	UK	Building Performance Research Unit (1972), *Building Performance* (Applied Science Publishers, London)
Philippe Boudon	1972	Architecture	Housing at Pessac	France	Boudon P (1972), *Lived-in Architecture* (Lund Humphries, London)
Oscar Newman	1973	Crime prevention	Urban housing	US	Newman O (1973), *Defensible Spaces: Crime prevention through urban design* (Colliers Books, New York)
Alison Ravetz	1970s	High-rise housing	Urban housing	UK	Ravetz A (1970), *Model Estate: Planned housing at Quarry Hill, Leeds* Croom Helm for Rowntree Trust
John Zeisel	1984	Methods	Various	US	Zeisel J (1984), *Inquiry by Design: Tools for environment-behaviour research* (Cambridge University Press, Cambridge)
Wolfgang Preiser	1988	POE methods	Mainly offices	US	Preiser W, Rabinovitz H and White E (1988), *Post-Occupancy Evaluation* (Van Nostrand Rheinhold, New York)
Alan Hedge, Sheena Wilson	1987	Health in buildings	Offices	UK	Hedge A and Wilson S (1987), *The Office Environment Survey* (Building Use Studies, London)
Jaqueline Vischer	1989	Environmental quality	Mainly offices	US	Vischer J (1989), *Environmental Quality in Offices* (Van Nostrand Rheinhold, New York)
George Baird, John Gray and others	1996	Methods and cases	Various	NZ	Baird G, Gray J, Isaacs N, Kernohan D and McIndoe G (eds) (1996), *Building Evaluation Techniques* (McGraw-Hill, New York)
The Probe Team	1997– 2002	Series of 20 buildings	Various	UK	*Building Services Journal* 1997–2002, *Building Research and Information* Special Issue March 2002

Planning Policy Guidance (PPG) Notes

Full details of these documents can be found at *www.odpm.gov.uk*

1   General policy and principles
2   Green belts
3   Housing
4   Industrial, commercial development and small firms
5   Simplified planning zones
6   Town centres and retail development
7   Countryside
8   Telecommunications
9   Nature conservation
10   Planning and waste management
11   Regional planning
12   Development plans
13   Transport
14   Development on unstable land
15   Planning and the historic environment
16   Archaeology and planning
17   Planning for open space, sport and recreation
18   Enforcing planning control
19   Outdoor advertisement control
20   Coastal planning
21   Tourism
22   Renewable energy
23   Planning and pollution control
24   Planning and noise
25   Development and flood risk

Building Regulations

Full details of these documents can be found at *www.odpm.gov.uk*

A   Structure
B   Fire safety
C   Site preparation and resistance to moisture
D   Toxic substances
E   Resistance to the passage of sound
F   Ventilation
G   Hygiene
H   Drainage and waste disposal
J   Combustion appliances and fuel storage systems
K   Protection from falling, collision and impact
L1   Conservation of fuel and power in dwellings
L2   Conservation of fuel & power in buildings other than dwellings
M   Access and facilities for disabled people
N   Glazing

Index